Private Letter
Gibbon (1753-17

Edward Gibbon

Alpha Editions

This edition published in 2024

ISBN 9789362515148

Design and Setting By
Alpha Editions
www.alphaedis.com
Email - info@alphaedis.com

Contents

GIBBON'S CORRESPONDENCE.

418.

To his Stepmother.

Bentinck Street, July 3rd, 1781.

DEAR MADAM,

Though your kind impatience might make the time appear tedious, there has been no other delay in my business, than the necessary forms of Election. My new constituents of Lymington obligingly chose me in my absence. I took my seat last Wednesday, and am now so old a member that I begin to complain of the heat and length of the Session. So much for Parliament. With regard to the board of trade, I am ignorant of your friend's meaning, and possibly she may be so herself. There has not been (to my knowledge) the most distant idea of my leaving it, and indeed there are few places within the compass of any rational ambition that I should like so well.

In a few days, as soon as we are relieved from public business, I shall go down to my Country house for the summer. Do not stare. I say my Country house. Notwithstanding Caplin's very diligent enquiries, I have not been able to please myself with anything in the neighbourhood of London, and have therefore hired for three months a small pleasant house at Brighthelmstone. I flatter myself that in that admirable sea-air, with the vicinity of Sheffield place, and a proper mixture of light study in the morning and good company in the evening, the summer may roll away not disagreably.—As I know your tender apprehensions, I promise you not to bathe in the sea without due preparation and advice.

Mrs. Porten has chosen, not for health but pleasure, a different sea-shore: she has been some weeks at Margate, and will scarcely return to town before my departure. I sincerely sympathize in all the melancholy scenes which have afflicted your sensibility, and am more particularly concerned about poor Miss Gould, to whom I wish to express the thoughts and hopes of friendship on this melancholy occasion. Lady Miller's sudden death has excited some attention even in this busy World, her foibles are mentioned with general regard. Adieu, Dear Madam, and do not let Mrs. Ravaud tempt you into Elysium: we are tolerably well here.

I am
Ever yours,
E. GIBBON.

419.

Bentinck Street, July 9th, 1781.

Dear Madam,

Nothing but my absence (on a visit to Mr. Jenkinson in Surrey) should have prevented me from writing by the *first* post to remove those fears which could be suggested only by too exquisite a sensibility. I am well and happy; the modest expression of *tolerably* was intended to express a very high degree of content, and I most sincerely assure you that my journey to Brighthelmstone is in search not of health but of amusement and society.

I am, Dear Madam,
Ever yours,
E. GIBBON.

420.

To his Stepmother.

Brighthelmstone, July 26th, 1781.

DEAR MADAM,

HIS HOUSE AT BRIGHTON.

After a short visit to Sheffield I came to this place last Sunday evening, and think it will answer my expectations. My house, which is not much bigger than yours, has a full prospect of the sea and enjoys a temperate climate in the most sultry days. The air gives health, spirits and a ravenous appetite. I walk sufficiently morning and evening, lounge in the middle of the day on the Steyne, booksellers' shops, &c., and by the help of a pair of horses can make more distant excursions. The society is good and easy, and though I have a large provision of books for my amusement, I shall not undertake any deep studies or laborious compositions this summer. You will rejoyce, I am sure, in hearing so favourable an account of my situation, and I wish I could propose to you to share it with me.

I am, Dear Madam,
Most truly yours,
E. GIBBON.

421.

To his Stepmother.

Brighthelmstone, August 24th, 1781.

DEAR MADAM,

Of all mortals I have the least right to complain of a friend's silence, but yours has been so *long* and so *unnatural* that I am seriously alarmed. If you can assure me by a line that it does not proceed from want of health or spirits, I shall be perfectly at ease. Notwithstanding our princely visitors (the Cumberlands) who are troublesome, I like the air and society so well that I shall certainly stay here at least till the end of September. Adieu.

I am, Dear Madam,
Ever yours,
E. G.

422.

To Lord Sheffield.

Brooke's, Thursday Evening, 1781.

What I *hear* would fill volumes, what I *know* does not amount to half a line.—All is expectation: but I fear that our enemies are more active than our friend. *He* is still at Bushy; a meeting is held next Saturday morn at eleven o'clock, but I think you need not hurry yourself. According to Louisa's phrase, I will be your grandfather. The black Patriot is now walking and declaiming in this room with a train at his heels. Adieu. No news.

E. G.

If there is another meeting Sunday evening you shall find a note. I have not seen Lord Loughborough, but understand he has preached war and any coalition against the Minister.

423.

To Lord Sheffield.

1781.

Mrs. Williams, No. 8, Downing Street, will embrace Lord S., Mr. Purden and Co. for two Guineas and a half per week. The stables and *Coach houses* will be empty, and Mr. Collier will provide the needful refreshments.—Sir R[ichard] W[orsley] has opened the trenches in Doctors Commons, and cryed down his wife's credit with tradesmen, &c. I supped last night at Lord L[oughborough]'s with Mrs. Abingdon,—a judge and an actress; what would Sir Roger Hill say? Dinner will be on table at five o'clock next Monday in Bentinck Street.

Saturday night. Brookes's absolutely alone. The town even yet very empty.

424.

To Lord Sheffield.

Friday, two o'clock, 7th Sept., 1781.

FRENCH AND SPANISH FLEETS IN THE CHANNEL.

Lord Hillsborough tells me that himself and Co. believe that the combined fleets are gone into Brest. Expresses that left Bristol yesterday, and Plymouth, Wednesday, cannot give the least account of them, and a Portuguese ship from Lisbon the 23rd last month, beat several days between Scilly and the Land's end without seeing or hearing of them. However, at all events more than twenty-five swift sailing vessels had been sent out to meet and warn the West India fleets. Adieu.

We shall meet at Brighton on Monday.

E. G.

425.

To Lady Sheffield.

Bentinck Street, Friday evening, ten o'clock, 1781.

*Oh, ho! I have given you the slip; saved thirty miles, by proceeding directly this day from Eartham to town, and am now *comfortably* seated in my library, in *my own* easy chair, and before *my own* fire; a style which you understand, though it is unintelligible to your Lord. The town is empty; but I am surrounded with a thousand old acquaintance of all ages and characters, who are ready to answer a thousand questions which I am impatient to ask. I shall not easily be tired of their Company; yet I still remember, and will honourably execute, my promise of visiting you at Brighton about the middle of next month. I have seen nobody, nor learned anything, in four hours of a town life; but I can inform you, that Lady * * * [erased] is now the declared mistress of Prince Henry of Prussia, whom she encountered at Spa; and that the Emperor has invited this amiable Couple to pass the winter at Vienna; fine encouragement for married women who behave themselves properly! I spent a very pleasant day in the little paradise of Eartham, and the hermit expressed a desire (no vulgar compliment) to see and to know Lord S. Adieu. I cordially embrace, &c.*

426.

To his Stepmother.

Bentinck Street, October 6th, 1781.

DEAR MADAM,

I have meditated a letter many posts, and the bell of Saturday evening now admonishes or rather reproaches. Allow me only to say that I am perfectly well, and expect very soon some more lines. The season no longer invites me to Brighthelmston, but the Sheffields, &c., insist on my passing another fortnight there, which will carry me (as I shall not go till Sunday seven-night) to the end of the month.

I am, Dear Madam,
Ever yours,
E. GIBBON.

427.

To Lord Sheffield.

Bentinck Street, Oct. 21st, 1781.

The last ten years by your advice I ensured my farm buildings at Buriton and no accident happened. This year after your example I have ceased my insurance, and—read Hugonin's two letters, which I have just received and answered. I thank him for undertaking the necessary work, press for Harris's immediate resignation, and propose to weigh during the Winter the choice of tenants and the scale of repairs. The present rent is only £50.—If any ideas occur to you, communicate your instructions, and *he* will receave them with deference, but the subject makes *me heavy.* The time is ill chosen. If you go to Coventry you must pass through town—when? But I have *almost* done with Hampton Court. I may see Lord Beauchamp, but do not understand that I have anything to say to him from you. His brother may be a tolerable accession to the Party, and let me tell you it is no contemptible one. I mean the party of the H. of C. If we ever meet at S. P. you will introduce me to the Lady of whom I hear a very amiable character. Adieu. I arrived this morn from Eden's. Lord Loughborough does not arrive this week. From Cambridge I understand that you have suffered by the fatigues of the Camp.

Inform me of your health.

E. G.

428.

To his Stepmother.

Brighthelmstone, Nov. 2nd, 1781.

DEAR MADAM,

If I had not been fortified by the friendly assurances which you sent me, I should indeed have been alarmed by the melancholy account that I heard of your health as soon as I arrived in Sussex. Since that time (an interval somewhat too long) I have been gradually better satisfied with the frequent and favourable dispatches from Bath, and I have now the satisfaction to find (however I might suspect your own friendly dissimulation) that even in Mr. H.'s apprehensive fancy you have in a great measure recovered that situation which I wish you long to preserve.

BRIGHTON IN NOVEMBER.

*I returned to this place with Lord and Lady Sheffield, with the design of passing two or three weeks in a situation which had so highly delighted me. But how vain are all sublunary hopes! I had forgot that there is some difference between the sunshine of August and the cold fogs (though we have uncommon good weather) of November. Instead of my beautiful sea-shore, I am confined to a dark lodging in the middle of the town; for the place is still full, and our time is now spent in the dull imitation of a London life. To compleat my misfortunes, Lord S. was hastily ordered to Canterbury, to suppress smuggling, and I was left almost alone with My Lady, in the servile state of a married man. But he returns to-day, and I hope to be seated in my own library by the middle of next week. However, you will not be sorry to hear that I have refreshed myself by a very *idle* summer, and indeed a much idler and more pleasant winter than the house of Commons will ever allow me to enjoy again.*

I hear of no public changes of administration, but you are perhaps already informed that a grand officer of my household (Mrs. Ford) at length retires on a pension, her wages for her life, with which she seems well contented, though I am ignorant of her plans. Mrs. Porten opened the business to her, but I have not yet sustained the last tender interview which I really dislike very much. Caplin assumes with pleasure the office of prime minister, and we hope that some lessons at White's will turn the housemaid (Edward's sister) into a good Cook for private ordinary days.

I had almost forgot Mr. Hayley; ungratefully enough, since I really past a very simple, but entertaining day with him. His place, though small, is elegant as his mind, which I value much more highly. And Adam might be happy if Eve had never been admitted into the paradise of Eartham. She is resolved (the air of Eartham after fifteen years' residence is found to be too cold) to eat another Bath apple, which as you properly apprehend will not be very wholesome either for her fame or his fortune. *Mrs. H. wrote a melancholy story of an American mother, a friend of her friend, who in a short time had lost three sons: one killed by the savages, one run mad from the fright at that accident, and the third taken at sea, now in England a prisoner in Forton hospital. For *him* something might perhaps be done. Your humanity will prompt you to obtain from Mrs. H. a more accurate account of names, dates, and circumstances; but you will prudently suppress my request, lest I should raise hopes which it may not be in my power to gratify. Lady S. begs to send her kindest Compliments to you.* The persons of Bath by whom and to whom I wish to be remembered are Mrs. Ravaud and the Goulds. What is become of poor Sir John Miller? I foresee very little prospect of visiting Bath at Christmas, but I depend, perhaps with too much confidence, on next Easter.

I am, dear Madam,
Ever yours.

429.

To Lord Sheffield.

Bentinck Street, ¼ before five, 1781.

I have seen the General. You are both wrong; he first in lending your papers without *special* leave, and then in the real or apparent slight of your messages; you in the serious anger which you expressed on so trifling a business. Unless you wish that this slight scratch should inflame into an incurable sore, embrace the lucky opportunity of his illness and confinement, which will excuse your dignity and should assuage your resentment. Call on him this evening, give and receive, between jest and earnest, a volley of *damns*, and then let the whole affair be no more remembered than it deserves. *Dixi et liberavi animam meam.*

430.

To Lord Sheffield.

Bentinck Street, November 20th, 1781.

I came yesterday from Jenkinson's (near Croydon), where I had spent two very agreeable days. We all tremble on the edge of a precipice, and whatever may be the event, the American war seems now to be reduced to very narrow compass both of time and place.

This morning Caplin was sent to reconnoitre: he reports that the *stables* are empty, but as the *coach-house* is full, the close alliance between carriage and horses will render the former circumstance of little avail. Nothing can be had in Parliament Street or the large streets adjoining except one whole house at four Guineas per week. In Fludyer and Downing-streets several indifferent and gloomy lodgings are at your service, but as I should prefer a Pall Mall, &c. situation, Caplin has paused till you send him more peremptory commands.—Your Monday dinner will be ready at five, and Adam, perhaps Batt, will be of the party.

Your Greeks were not carried from Brighton through carelessness, but as you are *seriously* absurd about lending books, I have directed Caplin to send them to S. P. per coach. By way of revenge I may inform you that I have now purchased a copy of Stephen's Greek Poets compared to which yours is very little more than waste paper. Adieu.

I embrace my Lady. I do not approve of her being called *Cat*.

E. G.

431.

To his Stepmother.

H. of Commons, December 6th, 1781.

DEAR MADAM,

I wish most sincerely that it were in my power to give you or myself any comfort on the present state of public affairs, which is indeed deplorable and I fear *hopeless*. But at last I can send you a favourable account of myself: the late, hot, melancholy hours of the house of Commons, which seem to oppress every body round me, have no effect on my health or spirits, and I feel myself heartily tired (*ennuyé*) without being in the least fatigued. Of Mrs. P. I shall say nothing, as by this time you will have seen her brother and his wife, who set out this morning for Bath. A month without business will be a new and wholesome scene for Sir Stanier. I hear nothing, and want to hear something of Mrs. Hayley. You have heard of Lady Worsley; your old acquaintance Sir Richard labours with copious materials for a divorce.

I am, Dear Madam,
Ever yours,
E. G.

Thanks for the Carpet.

432.

To his Stepmother.

Bentinck Street, December 26th, 1781.

DEAR MADAM,

Will you excuse my only transmitting the *needful*, with the necessary assurance that I am well and happy, and the unnecessary addition, that I wish you long to remain so? I envy Sir Stanier and Lady Porten the pleasure which I shall not enjoy till Easter: pray give my love to them. I pity poor Delacour and his friends, above all his Christian wife or daughter. Give my compliments to Mrs. Hayley, and tell her that both song and music have been much applauded. Will she accept this notice as a letter? Adieu, Dear Madam. Believe me,

Most truly yours,
E. GIBBON.

433.

To Lady Sheffield.

Bentinck Street, Dec. 29, 1781.

NOISE AND NONSENSE OF PARLIAMENT.

As Sheffelina has modernized herself by securing an unknown Cicisbeo, I have a great mind to propose a partie quarrée which might be easily furnished from Ickworth. If that project is rejected and I must make a solitary visit, I shall still obey the gracious mandate, but instead of the third day of the year (may it be more auspicious) 1782, I must delay my attendance till about the 8th or even the tenth, which will still allow me eight or ten days of fresh air and friendly converse, before I again descend into the noise and nonsense of the Pandemonium. At present we are as quiet in London as you can be in Sussex. Mrs. Stuart's shocking adventure is the only event that enlivens conversation; the family whisper insanity (a terrible resource), and strive without success to persuade that the whole scene passed only in her imagination—yet she certainly passed the whole night abroad. I did suppose that the Baron would be tired of his home in a week, but as this visit to the Regiment will abridge the remaining interval he may possibly support it. I hear nothing more of the house in D. S., but still believe that the minister will retire before your superior majesty; the last time I saw him he expressed great apprehension of your displeasure. I too am in pursuit of a house, in Harley Street, somewhat further in the country than my own: it has but one fault, a steep narrow staircase, but where must we seek (except at ——) either a house or a wife without *one* fault? I embrace the Angels, Princesses, &c. I believe the elder had rather be a Princess than an Angel. Adieu.

LE GRAND GIBBON.

434.

To his Stepmother.

Jan. 23rd, 1782.

DEAR MADAM,

I am not sorry that the indiscretion of certain female correspondents should give the opportunity of sending you a very fair but not flattering picture of myself.—It is very true that I have had a fit of the Gout; but if the name of agreable can ever be applied to the ugly monster, my Gout has deserved it on this occasion. It lasted on the whole no more than ten days, attacked only one foot, was attended with scarcely any fever, loss of appetite, or lowness of spirits, and has left me in perfect health both of mind and body.—Our busy scene commences to-morrow; and I am now entering into the hurry of the winter: but I will write again soon.

I am
Most truly yours,
E. G.

435.

To his Stepmother.

March 2nd, 1782.

DEAR MADAM,

I am much afraid that I have lost all credit by repeated promises and repeated neglects, yet I still persuade myself that you are glad to hear, though in two lines, of my health and good spirits, and that you will postpone more ample conversations to the Easter Holydays, when I can talk more in an hour than I could write in a month. Perhaps I should even have delayed this scrap of an Epistle, were I not apprehensive that the parliamentary events of this week would have given you some uneasiness both on a private and public account. Though I am not in the secret, especially of the adverse party, yet I know more than it is proper to trust to paper.

The situation of the administration, though dangerous, is not *absolutely* desperate, and with some concessions I still think that Lord N. may survive the impending storm of the next fortnight. At all events, if we fall (for, inconsiderable as I am, I am sure of being one of the first victims) I shall meet my fate with resolution.—I remember you asked me an age ago about a report of my having got a house in Harley Street and a wreck of wine on the Coast of Sussex: the former was a fruitless negociation, the latter related to my aunt's manor of Newhaven, but the wine is contested by the King's officers, and the litigation, if pursued, may cost her more than the object is worth. Adieu. My Dear Madam, on every account I am impatient for the Easter holydays.

I am
Ever yours,
E. G.

436.

To his Stepmother.

March 20th, 1782.

MY DEAR MADAM,

FALL OF LORD NORTH'S MINISTRY.

All is now over, and Lord North is no more. This day when the armies in the H. of C. were ready to engage, he gave solemn notice that the whole administration was dissolved, and the House has adjourned till Monday next to allow time for the new arrangements. Complaints are vain and useless for the past, and futurity is dark and dismal. It is my intention, unless I should be detained either by *serious* business, or by some threatening symptoms of the Gout, to visit Bath about Sunday sennight, when we may discuss freely and fully the strange events of the times. Till then Adieu. Remember me to Mrs. Hayley. The Eliots whom I see *sometimes* are well, and as you may suppose triumphant.

I am, Dear Madam,
Ever yours,
E. G.

437.

To his Stepmother.

Bentinck Street, March 28th, 1782.

DEAR MADAM,

In our common disappointment you will be pleased to hear that the Gout has totally left me, and that it is only the extreme shortness of our adjournment and the busy uncertainty of the times that have prevented my Easter visit to Bath. I am satisfied that Bath is very pleasant in the months of May and June, and you may be assured that I will come down, as soon as our fate is determined and the busyness of parliament has begun to subside. Pray give my compliments to Mrs. Hayley. I fear she will be gone before my arrival.

I am, Dear Madam,
Ever yours,
E. G.

438.

To his Stepmother.

May 4th, 1782.

DEAR MADAM,

HIS LOSS OF OFFICE.

The thunder-bolt has fallen, and I have received one of the circular letters from Lord Shelburne to inform me that the board of trade will be suppressed and that his Majesty has no further occasion for my services. I have been prepared for this event and can support it with firmness. I enjoy health, friends, reputation, and a perpetual fund of domestic amusement: I am not without resources, and my best resource, which shall never desert me, is in the chearfullness and tranquillity of a mind which in any place and in any situation can always secure its own independent happyness. The business of the House of Commons still continues, and indeed encreases, and though I am heartily tired of the scene, some serious reasons prevent me from retiring at the present season. Yet I still cast a longing eye towards Bath, and though I find it difficult, or rather impossible, to fix the moment of my summer visit, I can most sincerely promise that it will be the first use which I shall make of my freedom. As I have only *one* object, it will be perfectly indifferent to me whether the place be full or empty, dully or lively. Mrs. Holroyd, I suppose, has found, and Mrs. Hayley has left, you. Are you acquainted with Lady Eliza Foster, a bewitching animal? You have heard of my Gouts, they are vanished, and I feel myself five and twenty years old. Can you say as much? I hope you can. Adieu. Recommend me to the Goulds.

I am
Most truly yours,
E. G.

Next Wednesday I conclude my forty-fifth year, and in spite of the changes of Kings and Ministers, I am very glad that I was born.

439.

To his Stepmother.

Bentinck Street, May 29th, 1782.

DEAR MADAM,

From the very strong expressions of *anxious expectation*and frequent disappointments, I must think that I am much more guilty than I conceived myself to be on account of my silence. Your apparent indulgence had taught me to believe that you were accustomed to my faults, that you kindly forgave them, and that without the aid of the pen or the post your own heart would inform you of the sentiments of mine. Since my last letter nothing has happened, indeed nothing can happen to affect my situation: in the midst of a plague (such is the present influenza) my health and spirits are perfectly good, and in that tranquil state Saturdays and *Mondays* pass away without waking me from my gentle slumber. Even my curiosity is not excited, as I have frequent opportunities of hearing circumstantial and impartial accounts of the only object that interests me at Bath.

You ask with some anxiety when you may hope to see me. I know not what to say. Though I always foresee and recollect with heartfelt satisfaction the time which I spend at the Belvidere, yet the convenient season of my visit seems to retire before me. Public events have immoderately protracted the present session of Parliament; it will certainly continue the whole of June and a considerable part of July, and as it was my intention to attend it to the last, I began to think that you would excuse me if I delayed my journey (which would suit me far better) till the beginning of Autumn. But if you have any particular reasons that make you wish to see me sooner, say it in ten lines, and I will set off in ten days. I rejoyce in every subject of your joy both private and public, and I am better pleased to hear that you are free from pain than that Rodney has destroyed a French fleet. Alas! had he done it two months sooner our poor administration would have stood. Every person of every party is provoked with our new Governors for taking the truncheon from the hand of a victorious Admiral, in whose place they have sent a Commander without experience or abilities. To-morrow they will be exposed to a small fire in the H. of C. on that popular topic. Adieu, Dear Madam, in this sickly season all my acquaintance (masters, mistresses and servants) are laid up except *young* Mrs. Porten and myself.

I am
Most truly yours,
E. G.

440.

To his Stepmother.

July 3rd, 1782.

Dear Madam,

DEATH OF LORD ROCKINGHAM.
---

*I hope you have not had a moment's uneasiness about the delay of my Midsummer letter. Whatever may happen, you may rest fully secure, that the materials of it shall always be *found*. But on this occasion I have missed four or five posts; postponing, as usual, from morning to the evening bell, which now rings, till it has occurred to me, that it might not be amiss to inclose the two essential lines, if I only added that the Influenza has been known to me only by the report of others. Lord Rockingham is at last dead; a good man, though a feeble minister: his successor is not yet named, and divisions in the Cabinet are suspected. If Lord Shelburne should be the Man, as I think he will, the friends of his predecessor will quarrel with him before Christmas. At all events, I foresee much tumult and strong opposition, from which I should be very glad to extricate myself, by quitting the H. of C. with honour and without loss. Whatever you may hear, I believe there is not the least intention of dissolving Parliament, which would indeed be a rash and dangerous measure.

I hope you like Mr. Hayley's poem; he rises with his subject, and since Pope's death, I am satisfied that England has not seen so happy a mixture of strong sense and flowing numbers. Are you not delighted with his address to his mother? I understand that She was, in plain prose, every thing that he speaks her in verse. This summer I shall stay in town, and work at my trade, till I make some Holydays for my Bath excursion. Lady S. is at Brighton, and he lives under tents, like the wild Arabs; so that my Country house is shut up. Kitty Porten is gone on a fortnight's frolick to lodge at Windsor.

I am, Dear Madam,
Ever yours.

441.

To Lord Sheffield, at Coxheath Camp.

Saturday night, Bentinck Street, 1782.

I sympathise with your fatigues; yet Alexander, Hannibal, &c. have suffered hardships almost equal to yours. At such a moment it is disagreeable (besides laziness) to write, because every hour teems with a new lye. As yet, however, only Charles has formally resigned; but Lord John, Burke, Keppel, Lord Althorpe, &c. certainly follow; your Commander-in-chief stays, and they are furious against the Duke of Richmond. Why will he not go out with Fox? said somebody; because, replies a friend, he does not like to *go out* with any man. *In short, three months of prosperity has dissolved a Phalanx, which had stood ten years' adversity. Next Tuesday, Fox will give his reasons, and possibly be encountered by Pitt, the new Secretary, or Chancellor, at three and twenty. The day will be rare and curious, and, if I were a light Dragoon, I would take a gallop on purpose to Westminster. Adieu. I hear the bell. How could I write before I knew where you dwelt?*

E. G.

442.

To Lord Sheffield.

July 10th, 1782.

LORD SHELBURNE'S MINISTRY.

Authentic List.

{ Lord S[helburne].

{ W. Pitt, Chancellor [of the Exchequer].

Treasury { James Grenville.

{ Richard Jackson.

{ Ed. Eliot, Junior, of Port Eliot.

{ Aubrey Duncannon   } Lord Keppel has

Admiralty {   vice   } not yet resign'd

{ Pratt Jack Townshend   }

Secretaries of { Lord Grantham.

State { T. Townshend.

——of War. Sir George Young.

Treasurer of Navy.	Barré remain.
Paymaster.	Perhaps Advocate.
Ireland.	Lord Temple.

Yesterday *was* a rare day.

Vera Cop,
E. G.

———————————

443.

To Lord Sheffield.

July 23rd, 1782.

The papers say you are at Coxheath. Write. Bad news from India; I am afraid that we have lost a ship and that Hyder has won a battle. None, therefore good, from Lord Howe since every day fortifies him. Within this last fortnight prodigious exertions by the Admiralty, till then they were fast asleep. The Advocate arrived last night, but has not *yet* accepted. To-morrow I visit Eden at his farm near Bromley. If you and my Lady could give me a meeting in a *house*, I would run down even for three or four days: but I do not admire canvass. Adieu.

E. G.

Aunt Hester seems to want some intelligence.

444.

To his Stepmother.

August 10th, 1782.

DEAR MADAM,

A person whom you would scarcely suspect, General Conway as commander in Chief, is the real author of my silence, which as usual has insensibly lasted far beyond my first intentions. Lord Sheffield is a slave, his master's resolutions are obscure and fluctuating, and I have waited from post to post till he could mark some week for our meeting in Sussex, which might leave the rest of my time at liberty for my Bath expedition. Though I can obtain no satisfaction from him, I must not suffer another *Monday* to slide away without saying that I am alive, well, and unless the Arab should seize (*he* has no choice) that particular moment, in full expectation of gratifying my wishes by a visit to Bath about the 20th of next month. I flatter myself that I shall find you not affected by the long winter which we still feel, though a friend of mine, an Astronomer, assured me that yesterday was the last of the dog days.

It is impossible to know what to say of our public affairs, and the most knowing are only such by the knowledge of their ignorance. The next session of Parliament will be the warmest and most irregular battle that has ever been fought in that place, and each man (except some leaders) is at the moment uncertain of the party which inclination, opinion, or connection will prompt him to embrace. You see that Mr. Eliot, or at least his family, are become courtiers; his son (a very unmeaning youth) is a Lord of the Treasury, an office which was formerly the reward of twenty years' able and faithful service. The Minister has not lost, for he never possessed, the public confidence, and Lord N[orth], if he chuses to act, has the balance of the country in his hands. A propos of the Eliots they are still in town. We meet seldom, but with the utmost propriety and equal regard.

IMMERSED IN THE ROMAN EMPIRE.

My private life is a gentle and not unpleasing continuation of my old labours, and I am again involved, as I shall be for some years, in the decline and fall of the Roman Empire. Some fame, some profit, and the assurance of daily amusement encourage me to persist. I am glad you are pleased with Mr. Hayley's poem; perhaps he might have been less diffuse, but his sense is fine and his verse is harmonious.—Mrs. Porten is just returned from a six weeks' excursion in lodgings at Windsor, which she enjoyed (the Terrace, the Air, and the Royal family) with all the spirit of youth. Her elder brother is quiet in his new employment and apartments in Kensington palace. I envy him the latter, and had there been no Revolution I might have obtained a similar advantage. At present I am on the ground, but the weather may change, and compared with recent darkness, the clouds are beginning to break away.

I am, Dear Madam,
Ever yours,
E. G.

445.

To his Stepmother.

Bentinck Street, Sept. 14, 1782.

DEAR MADAM,

As you suffered by the long winter, I may reasonably, as I warmly, hope that your health and spirits have been permanently restored by the milder Spring or Autumn which this month has introduced:—For many reasons you will be surprised, though I think pleased, to hear that I have fixed myself for this season in a country villa of Hampton court. My friend Mr. Hamilton (I must distinguish him by the impertinent epithet of 'single speech') has very obligingly lent me a ready furnished house close to the Palace, and opening by a private door into the Royal garden, which is maintained for my use but not at my expence. The air and exercise, good roads and neighbourhood, the opportunity of being in London at any time in two hours, and the temperate mixture of society and study, adapt this new scene very much to my wishes, and must entirely remove your kind apprehensions of my injuring my health (which I have never done) by excessive labour. I find or make many acquaintance, and among others I have visited your old friend Mrs. Manhood (Ashby) at Isleworth in her pleasant summer-house on the Thames. She overwhelms me with civility, but you need not indulge either hopes or fears: as I hear she is going to accept Sir William Draper for her third husband.

You will naturally suppose, and will not I think be displeased that I should enjoy this new and unexpected situation as long as the fine weather continues, and our past hardships encourage us to depend on the favour, at least the first favours of the month of October. Beyond that period the prospect in every sense of the word is cloudy, and my future motions will be partly regulated by parliament, and the intanglement of some private pursuits with public affairs. I still flatter myself with the hope of securing two or three weeks for Bath; but if I should *again* delay that visit till Christmas, I shall prove my perfect confidence in your indulgent friendship, and in your firm belief of my tender attachment, which can alone justify such freedom of conduct. Of the Sheffields I know little, seldom hear from, and am totally ignorant when I shall see them. The Eliots are gone into Cornwall. They *say* that the son is going to marry Lady Sarah Pitt, sister to his intimate friend the Chancellor of the Exchequer.

From the little I have read I agree with you about Gilbert Stuart's book, but I cannot forgive your indifference and almost aversion to one of the most amiable men, and masterly compositions in the world.

I am, Dear Madam,
Most truly yours,
E. G.

I lay in town last night, and am just setting out for Hampton Court.

N.B.—I never travel after dark, but our dangers are almost over.

446.

To Lord Sheffield.

September 29th, 1782.

I should like sometimes to hear whether you survive the scenes of action and danger in which a Dragoon is continually involved. What a difference between the life of a Dragoon and that of a Philosopher! and I will freely own that I (the Philosopher) am much better satisfied with my own independent and tranquil situation, in which I have always something to do, without ever being obliged to do any thing. The Hampton Court Villa has answered my expectation, and proved no small addition to my comforts; so that I am resolved next summer to hire, borrow, or steal, either the same, or something of the same kind. Every morning I walk a mile or more before breakfast, read and write *quantum sufficit*, mount my chaise and visit in the neighbourhood, accept some invitations, and escape others, use the Lucans as my daily bread, dine pleasantly at home or sociably abroad, reserve for study an hour or two in the evening, lye in town regularly once a week, &c. &c. &c. I have anounced to Mrs. G. my new Arrangements; the certainty that October will be fine, and my encreasing doubts whether I shall be able to reach Bath before Christmas. Do you intend (but how can you *intend* any thing?) to pass the winter under Canvas? Perhaps under the veil of Hampton Court I may lurk ten days or a fortnight at Sheffield, if the enraged Lady or cat does not shut the doors against me.

The Warden passed through in his way to Dover. He is not so fat, and more chearful than ever. I had not any private conversation with him; but he clearly holds the balance; unless he falls asleep and lets it fall from his hand. The Pandæmonium (as I understand) does not meet till the 26th of November. I feel with you that a nich is grown of higher value, but think *that* only an additional argument for disposing of it. And so by this time Lord L. is actually turned off. Do you know his partner (Miss Courtenay, the Lord's sister), about thirty, only £4000, not handsome, but very pleasant. I am at a loss where to address my condoleance, I would say congratulation. Town is more a desert than I ever knew it. I arrived yesterday, dined at Sir Joshua's with a tolerable party; the chaise is now at the door; I dine at Richmond, lye at Hampton, &c. Adieu.

E. G.

447.

To his Stepmother.

Hampton Court, October 1st, 1782.

MY DEAR MADAM,

I feel your anxiety, and am impatient to assure you that the report of your officious visitor is absolutely without foundation. I had not any complaints when I came down to this place; but the air, exercise and dissipation have given me fresh spirits; and I should be apt to fix on the last month as the part of my life in which I have enjoyed the most perfect health. You may depend on my word of honour, that in case of any real alarm, you shall hear from myself or from Caplen.—Excuse brevity, as I save a day, perhaps more, by sending Caplen with Duplicates to London, one copy for the post, the other to take the chance of greater dispatch by the coach. I wish to know what you think of me and my schemes; if you are not perfectly satisfied with my confidence, you may be somewhat displeased with my seeming neglect. I fear we shall not meet till Christmas.

I am
Ever yours,
E. GIBBON.

448.

To Lord Sheffield at Coxheath Camp.

Bentinck Street, October 14th, 1782.

RELIEF OF GIBRALTAR.

---

*On the approach of winter, my paper house of Hampton becomes less comfortable; my visits to Bentinck Street grow longer and more frequent, and the end of next week will restore me to the town, with a lively wish, however, to repeat the same, or a similar experiment, next Summer. I admire the assurance with which you propose a month's residence at Sheffield, when you are not sure of being allowed three days. Here it is currently reported, that Camps will not separate till Lord Howe's *return* from Gibraltar, and as yet we have no news of his arrival. Perhaps, indeed, you have more intimate correspondence with your old school-fellow, Lord Shelburne, and already know the hour of your deliverance. I should like to be informed. As Lady S. has entirely forgot me, I shall have the pleasure of forming a new acquaintance. I have often thought of writing, but it is now too late to repent.

I am at a loss what to say or think about our Parliamentary state. A certain late Secretary of Ireland, the husband of Polly Jones, reckons the House of Commons thus: Minister 140, Reynard 90, Boreas 120, the rest unknown, or uncertain. The last of the three, by self or agents, talks too much of absence, neutrality, moderation. I still think he will discard the game.

I am not in such a fury with the letter of American independence; but it seems ill-timed and useless; and I am much entertained with the Metaphysical disputes between Government and secession about the meaning of it. Lord Lough[borough] will be in town Sunday sen-night. I long to see him and Co. I think he will take a very decided part. If he could throw aside his Gown, he would make a noble Leader. The East India news are excellent; the French gone to the Mauritius, Heyder desirous of peace, the Nizam and Mahrattas our friends, and 70 Lack of Rupees in the Bengal treasury, while we were voting the recall of Hastings. Adieu. Write soon.

E. G.

449.

To Lady Sheffield.

Bentinck Street, October 31st, 1782.

Although I am provoked (it is always right to begin first) with your long and unaccountable silence, yet I cannot help wishing (a foolish weakness) to learn whether you and the two infants are still alive, and what have been the summer amusements of your widowed and their orphan state. Some indirect intelligence inclines me to suspect that the Baron himself has quitted before this time a house of Canvas for one of brick, and that he enjoys a short interval between the fatigues of War and those of Government. Should he happen to find himself in your neighbourhood you may inform him that Hugonin (good creature) came to town purposely on my business and passed three hours with me this morning. Harris has resigned his Case of the conflagration, and either by a sale to Lord Stawell or by a new Tenant we shall make it rather a profitable affair.

ENTHUSIASM FOR SIR GEORGE ELIOTT.

You have doubtless received very accurate accounts of my proceedings from the Cambridges by which channel I have likewise obtained very frequent narratives of your life and conversation, and this mutual Gazette has contributed not a little to stifle the reproaches of my conscience. In my excursions round the Hampton neighbourhood, I have often visited and dined with them, and found him properly sensible of his happyness in the absence of his wife: indeed I never saw a man more improved by any fortunate event. My campaign, and it has been a pleasant one, is now closed, but in the time which remains before the opening of our Pandemonium, I should not dislike to breathe for a week or ten days the air of Sheffield Place, and as the Lord will be accessible in town before Christmas, my attack (according to modern rules) will be chiefly designed for the Lady. About Wednesday or Thursday next would be the day that I should think of moving, but I wish to be informed how far such a plan may consist (as the Scotch say) with other arrangements. Adieu. Is not Elliot a glorious old fellow? We suspend our judgment of Lord Howe, yet I like the prospect.

I embrace, &c.,
E. G.

450.

To his Stepmother.

November 7th, 1782.

DEAR MADAM,

Last week I finished my Hampton Court expedition, and think myself obliged to the person and to the accident which have thrown that unexpected but not unpleasing variety into my Summer life. I am now fixed in town till Christmas, or if Lord Sheffield who has quitted his camp should drag me into Sussex, it can be only for three or four days.

The Parliamentary campaign is approaching very fast, and a very singular one it must be from the conflict of *three* parties, each of which will be exposed in its turn to the direct or oblique attacks of the other two. As a matter of curiosity I shall derive some gratification from my silent seat, but at present I do not perceive its use in any other light. From honour, gratitude and principle I am and shall be attached to Lord N., who will lead a very respectable force into the field, but I much doubt whether matters are ripe for either conquest or coalition, and the havock which Burke's bill has made of places, &c., encreases the difficulties of a new arrangement. However a month or two may change the face of things, and the faces of men.

WILLIAM PITT AND MRS. SIDDONS.

Among those men surely Will Pitt the second is the most extraordinary. I know you never liked the father, and I have no connection public or private with the son. Yet we cannot refuse to admire a youth of four and twenty whom eloquence and real merit have already made Chancellor of the Exchequer without his promotion occasioning either surprize or censure.

We are much indebted to your Bath Theatre for Mrs. Siddons: two years ago, and in the part of Lady Townley, she did not strike me: but I saw her last night with the most exquisite pleasure. She gave sense and spirit to a wretched play (the Fatal Marriage), and displayed every power of voice, action, and countenance to a degree which left me nothing to wish. To-morrow I promise myself still more satisfaction from Jane Shore, as the character is more worthy of her talents. Adieu, Dear Madam. Inform me that the beginning of the winter has not affected your health. Whatever may be the state of my namesake, I hope at Christmas to bring you a sound body, and a mind not dissatisfied with external things, because it is not dissatisfied with itself.

I am
Ever yours,
E. G.

451.

To his Stepmother.

December 21st, 1782.

DEAR MADAM,

I write a little letter on little paper because I shall soon have the pleasure of conversing with you in a less laborious manner. Next Thursday I propose to begin my journey for Bath, but as the times (in a public and private light) are very *hard*, I shall travel with my own horses, lye two nights on the road, and reach the Belvidere for a late dinner Saturday. You will be so good as to secure me a lodging; the nearness to your house will be its best recommendation, as you are my sole inducement. If any business should detain me two or three days longer in town, you may depend on the earliest notice.

I am, Dear Madam,
Ever yours,
E. G.

452.

To his Stepmother.

Bentinck Street, December 26th, 1782.

DEAR MADAM,

It was not in my power to set out this morning (Thursday), and therefore I cannot hope to reach Bath Saturday. I am not perfectly sure whether Sunday or Monday will be the day of my arrival: for which reason I shall eat a mutton chop at the Devizes, and beg you would not wait dinner for me.

I am
Most truly yours,
E. G.

453.

To Lord Sheffield.

Tuesday evening, 1782.

THE DEARTH OF NEWS.

I have designed writing every post.—The air of London is admirable; my complaints have vanished, and the Gout still respects me. Lord L., with whom I passed an entire day, is very well satisfied with his Irish expedition, and found the barbarous people very kind to him: the castle is strong, but the volunteers are formidable. London is dead, and all intelligence so totally extinct, that the loss of an army would be a favourable incident. We have not even the advantage of Shipwrecks, which must soon, with the society of Ham[ilton] and Lady Shelley, become the only pleasures of Brighton. My lady is precious, and deserves to shine in London, when she regains her palace. The workmen are slow, but I hear that the Minister talks of hiring another house after Christmas. Adieu, till Monday seven-night. Shall Caplin get you a lodging?

———

454.

To his Stepmother.

DEAR MADAM,

I reached London after an easy and pleasant journey, and am now seated in my library before a good fire, and among three or four thousand of my old acquaintance. The prospect of my future life is not *gloomy*: yet I should esteem myself a very happy man indeed, if every fortnight could be of as pure a white as the last which I have spent at Bath in the society of the most sincere as well as amiable of my friends.

I am, Dear Madam,
Ever yours,
E. G.

455.

To Lord Sheffield.

January 17th, 1783.

As I arrived about five o'Clock on Wednesday last, we were some time in town in mutual ignorance. Unlucky enough: yet our loss will be speedily repaired. Your reason for not writing is worthy of an Irish Baron. You thought Sarah might be at Bath, because you directed letters to her at Clifton, near Bristol; where indeed I saw her in a delightful situation, swept by the winter winds, and scorched by the summer sun. A nobler reason for your silence would be the care of the public papers, to record Your steps, words, and actions. I was pleased with your Coventry oration: a panegyric on the Hertford family is a subject entirely new, and which no orator before yourself would have dared to undertake. You have acted with prudence and dignity in casting away the military yoke, yet even if I *had* a right I should try to moderate my indignation. *This next summer you will sit down (if you can sit) in the long-lost character of a country Gentleman.

For my own part, my late journey has only confirmed me in the opinion, that No. 7 Bentinck-street is the best house in the World. I find that peace and war alternately, and daily, take their turns of conversation, and this (Friday) is the pacific day. Next week we shall probably hear some questions on that head very strongly asked, and very foolishly answered. I embrace, &c. Give me a line by return of post, and possibly I may visit Downing-street on Monday evening; late, however, as I am engaged to dinner and cards. Adieu.*

E. G.

456.

To his Stepmother.

Feb. 19th, 1783.

DEAR MADAM,

On Monday or rather Tuesday last we gave the first blow to Lord S.'s Government by a majority of sixteen in the House of C. on the Peace, which will be followed by new and decisive attacks. The victory was obtained by the union of Lord North with Fox and the Rockingham party.—You would have blamed me for going, or rather being carried, down with flannels and crutches, and sitting all night till past eight in the morning: but I have the pleasure of assuring you that the heat and fatigue have done me no harm, that I have already changed my two crutches into a single stick, which I hope to throw away in three or four days. This fit of the Gout, though severe, has been short, regular, and I think beneficial. Adieu.

I am
Ever yours,
E. GIBBON.

457.

To his Stepmother.

March 29th, 1783.

DEAR MADAM,

RESIGNATION OF LORD SHELBURNE.

Will you credit and excuse the cause of my delay? I came home late and found your letter on my table: meaning to read it the next morning, I slipt it into my drawer, and till this moment it escaped my memory and my eye.—I would not bribe you to prefer my silence, yet you may always take it as an assured proof that the body Gibbon is in a perfect state of health and spirits, as it is most truly at the present moment, and since the entire retreat of my Gout. The state of public affairs is Anarchy without example and without end, and if the King does not decide before Monday, the consequences to the House of Commons will be fatal indeed. Every day produces its own lye, and nothing that is probable is true. Yet I believe that Pitt will not accept, and that the Coalition must succeed.

I am, Dear Madam,
Ever yours,
E. GIBBON.

458.

To his Stepmother.

March 31st, 1783.

DEAR MADAM,

THE COALITION MINISTRY.

In my last, written like this in a very great hurry, I used (if I am not mistaken) an expression which at a distance might alarm you too much. The *fatal* Monday is past without any *fatal* consequences, yet no Administration is appointed; but as Pitt has formally resigned, the K. will probably yield without expecting a second and more serious address on Thursday.—I rejoyce to hear that you have surmounted your complaint, and hope you will feel every day the genial influence of the spring.

I am
Ever yours,
E. G.

459.

To his Stepmother.

May 5th, 1783.

DEAR MADAM,

My cousin Robert Darrel gave me great pleasure by the information that he thought you perfectly recovered from your late indisposition. I depend on his testimony, which removed all my doubts and suspicions of your giving too favourable an account of yourself. For my own part, after paying my annual tribute to the gout, I find myself in the same even course of health and spirits which I have enjoyed for many years. The business of the house of Commons has been postponed by waiting first for peace and afterwards for Government; the long hot days will be crowded, and we shall wrangle with a strong June sun shining through the windows to reproach our folly. I have already made one short visit to my Cottage at Hampton Court; I propose every week to steal away like a Citizen from Saturday till Monday, and persuade myself that I shall be revived by such excursions. You express a kind indignation against the persons for whose sake I acted the devil upon two sticks. Notwithstanding their apparent neglect I have reason to think them well inclined towards me, and have even received some assurances, but as every thing that depends on ministers is precarious and uncertain, I would not raise too much either your hopes or my own. If any situation permanent and proper could be obtained, incompatible with a seat in parliament, I should retire from that Assembly without the least reluctance.

I am, Dear Madam,
Ever yours,
E. G.

460.

A Londres, ce 20 Mai, 1783.

*Que j'admire la douce et parfaite confiance de nos sentimens réciproques! Nous nous aimons dans l'éloignement et le silence, et il nous suffit à l'un et à l'autre, de savoir de tems en tems des nouvelles de la santé et du bonheur de son ami. Aujourd'hui j'ai besoin de vous écrire; je commence sans excuses et sans reproches, comme si nous allions reprendre la conversation familière du jour précédent. Si je proposois de faire un *compte rendu* de mes études, de mes occupations, de mes plaisirs, de mes nouvelles liaisons, de ma politique toujours muette, mais un peu plus rapprochée des grands événemens, je multiplierois mes *in quarto*, et je ne sais pas encore votre avis sur ceux que je vous ai déjà envoyés. Dans cette histoire moderne, il seroit toujours question de la décadence des empires; et autant que j'en puis juger sur mes réminiscences et sur le rapport de l'ami Bugnon, vous aimez aussi peu la puissance de l'Angleterre que celle des Romains. Notre chute, cependant, a été plus douce. Après une guerre sans succès, et une paix assez peu glorieuse, il nous reste de quoi vivre contens et heureux; et lorsque je me suis dépouillé du rôle de Membre du Parlement, pour redevenir homme, philosophe, et historien, nous pourrions bien nous trouver d'accord sur la plupart des scènes étonnantes qui viennent de se passer devant nos yeux, et qui fourniront une riche matière aux plus habiles de mes successeurs.

Bornons nous à cette heure à un objet moins illustre sans doute, mais plus intéressant pour tous les deux, et c'est beaucoup que le même objet puisse intéresser deux mortels qui ne se sont pas vûs, qui à peine se sont écrit depuis—oui, ma foi—depuis huit ans. Ma plume, très paresseuse au commencement, ou plutôt avant le commencement, marche assez vîte, lorsqu'elle s'est une fois mise en train; mais une raison qui m'empêcheroit de lui donner carrière, c'est l'espérance de pouvoir bientôt me servir avec vous d'un instrument encore plus commode, la langue. Que l'homme, l'homme anglois, l'homme Gibbon, est un sot animal! Je l'espère, je le désire, je le puis, mais je ne sais pas si [je] le veux, encore moins si j'exécuterai cette volonté.

Voici mon histoire, autant qu'elle pourra vous éclairer, qu'elle pourra m'éclairer moi-même, sur mes véritables intentions, qui me paroissent très obscures, et très équivoques; et vous aurez la bonté de m'apprendre quelle sera ma conduite future. Il vous souvient, Seigneur, que mon grandpère a fait sa fortune, que mon père l'a mangée avec un peu trop d'appétit, et que je jouis actuellement du fruit, ou plutôt du reste, de leurs travaux. Vous n'avez pas oublié que je suis entré au Parlement sans patriotisme, sans ambition, et que toutes mes vues se bornoient à la place commode et honnête d'un *Lord of Trade*. Cette place, je l'ai obtenue enfin; je l'ai possédée trois ans, depuis 1779 jusqu' à 1782, et le produit net, qui se montoit à sept cens cinquante livres sterling, augmentoit mon revenu au niveau de mes besoins et de mes désirs. Mais au printems de l'année précédente, l'orage a grondé sur nos têtes: Milord North a été renversé, votre serviteur chassé, et le *Board* même, dont j'étois membre, aboli et cassé pour toujours par la réformation de M. Burke, avec beaucoup d'autres places de l'Etat, et de la maison du Roi.

HIS VIEW OF ENGLISH POLITICS.

Pour mon malheur, je suis toujours resté Membre de la Chambre basse: à la fin du dernier Parlement (en 1780) M. Eliot a retiré sa nomination; mais la faveur de Milord North a facilité ma rentrée, et la reconnoissance m'imposoit le devoir de faire valoir, pour son service, les droits que je tenois en partie de lui. Cet hyver nous avons combattu sous les étendards réunis (vous savez notre histoire) de Milord North et de M. Fox; nous avons triomphé de Milord Shelburne et de la paix,* et mon ami (je n'aime pas à profaner ce nom) a remonté sur sa bête en qualité de secretaire d'Etat. C'est à présent qu'il peut bien me dire ç'etoit beaucoup pour moi, ce n'etoit rien pour nous, et malgré les assurances les plus fortes, j'ai trop de raison pour avoir de la foi. *Avec beaucoup d'esprit, et des qualités très respectables, notre homme* a la demarche lente et le cœur froid. Il *n'a plus ni le titre, ni le crédit de premier ministre; des collègues plus actifs lui enlèvent les morceaux les plus friands, qui sont aussitôt dévorés par la voracité de leurs créatures; nos malheurs et nos réformes ont diminué le nombre des graces; par orgueil ou par paresse, je solicite assez mal, et si je parviens enfin, ce sera peut-être à la veille d'une nouvelle révolution, qui me fera perdre dans un instant, ce qui m'aura coûté tant de soins et de recherches.

Si je ne consultois que mon cœur et ma raison, je romprois sur le champ cette indigne chaine de la dépendance; je quitterois le Parlement, Londres, l'Angleterre; je chercherois sous un ciel plus doux, dans un pays plus tranquille, le repos, la liberté, l'aisance, et une société éclairée, et aimable. En attendant la mort de ma belle-mere et de ma tante je coulerois quelques années de ma vie sans espérance, et sans crainte, j'acheverais mon histoire, et je ne rentrerois dans ma patrie qu'en homme libre, riche, et respectable par sa position, aussi bien que par son caractère. Mes amis, et surtout

Milord Sheffield, (M. Holroyd) ne veulent pas me permettre d'être heureux suivant mon goût et mes lumières. Leur prudence exige que je fasse tous mes efforts, pour obtenir un emploi très sûr à la vérité, qui me donneroit mille guinées de rente, mais qui m'enleveroit cinq jours par semaine. Je me prête à leur zèle, et je leur ai promis de ne partir qu'en automne, après avoir consacré l'été à cette dernière tentative. Le succès, cependant, est très incertain, et je ne sais si je le désire de bonne foi.

Si je parviens à me voir exilé, mon choix ne sera pas douteux. Lausanne a eu mes prémices; elle me sera toujours chère par le doux souvenir de ma jeunesse. Au bout de trente ans, je me rappelle les polissons qui sont aujourd'hui juges, les petites filles de la société du Printems, qui sont devenues grand-mères. Votre pays est charmant, et, malgré le dégoût de Jean Jacques, les mœurs, et l'esprit de ses habitans, me paroissent très assortis aux bords du lac Léman. Mais un trésor que je ne trouverois qu'à Lausanne, c'est un ami qui me convient également par les sentimens et les idées, avec qui je n'ai jamais connu un instant d'ennui, de sécheresse, ou de réserve. Autrefois dans nos libres épanchemens, nous avons cent fois fait le projet de vivre ensemble, et cent fois nous avons épluché tous les détails du Roman, avec une chaleur qui nous étonnoit nous mêmes. A présent il demeure, ou plutôt vous demeurez, (car je me lasse de ce ton étudié,) dans une maison charmante et commode; je vois d'ici mon appartement, nos salles communes, notre table, et nos promenades; mais ce marriage ne vaut rien, s'il ne convient pas également aux deux époux, et je sens combien des circonstances locales, des goûts nouveaux, de nouvelles liaisons, peuvent s'opposer aux desseins, qui nous ont paru les plus agréables dans le lointain. Pour fixer mes idées, et pour nous épargner des regrets, il faut me dévoiler avec la franchise dont je vous ai donné l'exemple, le tableau extérieur et intérieur de George Deyverdun. Mon amour est trop délicat, pour supporter l'indifférence et les égards, et je rougirois d'un bonheur dont je serois redevable, non à l'inclination, mais à la fidélité de mon ami.

PROPOSES TO SETTLE ABROAD.

Pour m'armer contre les malheurs possibles, hélas! peut-être trop vraisemblables, j'ai essayé de me détacher de la pensée de ce projet favori, et de me représenter à Lausanne votre bon voisin, sans être précisément votre commensal. Si j'y étois réduit, je ne voudrois pas tenir maison, autant par raison d'économie, que pour éviter l'ennui de manger seul. D'un autre côté, une pension ouverte, fut-elle montée sur l'ancien pied de celle de Mesery, ne conviendroit plus à mon age, ni à mon caractère. Passerois-je ma vie au milieu d'une foule de jeunes Anglois échappés du collège, moi qui aimerois Lausanne cent fois davantage, si j'y pouvois être le seul de ma nation? Il me faudroit donc une maison commode et riante, un état au dessus de la bourgeoisie, un mari instruit, une femme qui ne ressembleroit pas à Madame Pavilliard, et l'assurance d'y être reçu comme le fils unique, ou plutôt comme le frère de la famille. Pour nous arranger sans gêne, je meublerai très volontiers un joli appartement sous le même toit, ou dans le voisinage, et puisque le ménage le plus foible laisse encore de l'étoffe pour une forte pension, je ne serois pas obligé de chicaner sur les conditions pécuniaires. Si je me vois déchu de cette dernière espérance, je renoncerois en soupirant à ma seconde patrie, pour chercher un nouvel asyle, non pas à Genève, triste séjour du travail et de la discorde, mais aux bords du lac de Neufchatel, parmi les bons Savoyards de Chamberry, ou sous le beau climat des Provinces Méridionales de la France. Je finis brusquement, parceque j'ai mille choses à vous dire. Je pense que nous nous ressemblons pour la correspondance. Pour le bavardage savant ou même amical, je suis de tous les hommes le plus paresseux, mais dès qu'il s'agit d'un objet réel, d'un service essentiel, le premier courier emporte toujours ma réponse. A la fin d'un mois, je commencerai à compter les semaines, les jours, les heures. Ne me les faites pas compter trop long tems. Vale.*

461.

M. Deyverdun à M. Gibbon.

Strasbourg, le 10 Juin, 1783.

*Je ne saurois vous exprimer, Monsieur et cher ami, la variété, et la vivacité, des sensations que m'a fait éprouver votre lettre. Tout cela a fini par un fond de plaisir et d'espérance qui resteront dans mon cœur, jusqu'à ce que vous les en chassiez.

Un rapport singulier de circonstances contribue à me faire espérer que nous sommes destinés à vivre quelque tems agréablement ensemble. Je ne suis pas dégoûté d'une ambition que je ne connus jamais; mais par d'autres circonstances, je me trouve dans la même situation d'embarras et d'incertitude où vous êtes aussi à cette époque. Il y a un an que votre lettre, mon cher ami, m'auroit fait plaisir sans doute, mais en ce moment, elle m'en fait bien davantage; elle vient en quelque façon à mon secours.

Depuis mon retour d'Italie, ne pouvant me déterminer à vendre ma maison, m'ennuyant d'y être seul (car je suis comme vous, Monsieur, et je déteste de manger sans compagnie) ne voulant pas louer à des étrangers, j'ai pris le parti de m'arranger assez joliment au premier étage, et de donner le second à une famille de mes amis, qui me nourrit, et que je loge. Cet arrangement a paru pendant longtems contribuer au bonheur des deux parties. Mais tout est transitoire sur cette terre. Ma maison sera vuide, selon toute apparence, sur la fin de l'été, et je me vois d'avance tout aussi embarrassé et incertain, que je l'étois il y a quelques années, ne sachant quelle nouvelle société choisir, et assez disposé à vendre enfin cette possession qui m'a causé bien des plaisirs et bien des peines. Ma maison est donc à votre disposition pour cet automne, et vous y arriveriez comme un Dieu dans une machine qui finit l'embroglio. Voilà, quant à moi; parlons de vous maintenant avec la même sincérité.

Un mot de préambule. Quelque intéressé que je sois à votre résolution, convaincu qu'il faut aimer ses amis pour eux-mêmes, sentant d'ailleurs combien il seroit affreux pour moi de vous voir des regrets, je vous donne ici ma parole d'honneur, que mon intérêt n'influe en rien sur ce que je vais écrire, et que je ne dirai pas un mot que je ne vous disse, si l'hermite de la grotte étoit un autre que moi. Vos amis anglais vous aiment pour eux-mêmes; je ne veux moi que votre bonheur. Rappellez-vous, mon cher ami, que je vis avec peine votre entrée dans le Parlement, et je crois n'avoir été que trop bon prophète; je suis sûr que cette carrière vous a fait éprouver plus de privations que de jouissances, beaucoup plus de peines que de plaisirs; j'ai cru toujours, depuis que je vous ai connu, que vous étiez destiné à vivre heureux par les plaisirs du cabinet et de la société, que tout autre marché étoit un écart de la route du bonheur, et que ce n'étoit que les qualités réunies d'homme de lettres, et d'homme aimable de société, qui pouvoient vous procurer gloire, honneur, plaisirs, et une suite continuelle de jouissances. Au bout de quelques tours dans votre salle, vous sentirez parfaitement que j'avois bien vu, et que l'événement a justifié mes idées.

DEYVERDUN'S OFFER OF HIS HOUSE.

Lorsque j'ai appris que vous étiez *Lord of Trade*, j'en ai été faché; quand j'ai su que vous aviez perdu cette place, je m'en suis réjoui pour vous; quand on m'a annoncé que Milord North étoit remonté sur sa bête, j'ai cru vous voir très mal à votre aise, en croupe derrière lui, et je m'en suis affligé pour vous. Je suis donc charmé, mon cher ami, de vous savoir à pied, et je vous conseille très sincèrement de rester dans cette position, et bien loin de solliciter la place en question, de la refuser, si elle vous étoit offerte. Mille guinées vous dédommageront-elles de cinq jours pris de la semaine? Je suppose, ce que cependant j'ai peine à croire, que vous me disiez que oui: et la variété et l'inconstance continuelle de votre ministère, vous promettent-elles d'en jouir long tems constamment, et n'est-il pas plus désagréable, mon cher Monsieur, de n'avoir plus 1000 livres sterl. de rente, qu'il n'a été agréable d'en jouir? D'ailleurs ne pourrez-vous pas toujours rentrer dans la carrière, si l'ambition, ou l'envie de servir la patrie, vous reprennent; ne rentrerez-vous pas avec plus d'honneur, lorsque vos rentes étant augmentées naturellement, vous serez libre et indépendant?

En faisant cette retraite en Suisse, outre la beauté du pays, et les agrémens de la société, vous acquererez deux biens que vous avez perdus, la liberté et la richesse. Vous ne serez d'ailleurs point inutile; vos ouvrages continueront à nous éclairer, et indépendamment de vos talens, l'honnête homme, le galant homme, n'est jamais inutile.

Il me reste à vous présenter le tableau que vous trouveriez. Vous aimiez ma maison et mon jardin; c'est bien autre chose à présent. Au premier étage qui donne sur la descente d'Ouchy, je me suis arrangé un appartement qui me suffit, j'ai une chambre de domestique, deux sallons, et deux cabinets. J'ai au plein pied de la terrasse, deux autres sallons dont l'un sert en été de salle à manger, et l'autre de sallon de compagnie. J'ai fait un nouvel appartement de trois pièces dans le vuide entre la maison et la remise, en sorte que j'ai à vous offrir tout le grand appartement, qui consiste actuellement en onze pièces, tant grandes que petites, tournées au Levant et au Midi, meublées sans magnificence déplacée, mais avec une sorte d'élégance dont j'espère que vous seriez satisfait. La terrasse a peu changé; mais elle est terminée par un grand cabinet mieux proportionné que le précédent, garnie tout du long, de caisses d'orangers, &c. La treille, qui ne vous est pas indifférente, a embelli, prospéré, et règne presqu'entièrement jusqu'au bout; parvenu à ce bout, vous trouverez un petit chemin qui vous conduira à une chaumière placée dans un coin; et de ce coin, en suivant le long d'une autre route à l'anglaise, le mur d'un manège. Vous trouverez au bout, un châlet avec écurie, vacherie, petite porte, petit cabinet, petite bibliothèque, et une galerie de bois doré, d'où l'on voit tout ce qui sort et entre en ville par la porte du Chêne, et tout ce qui se passe dans ce Faubourg. J'ai acquis la vigne au-dessous du jardin; j'en ai arraché tout ce qui étoit devant la maison; j'en ai fait un tapis vert arrosé par l'eau du jet d'eau; et j'ai fait tout autour de ce petit parc, une promenade très variée par les différens points de vue et les objets même intérieurs, tantôt jardin potager, tantôt parterre, tantôt vigne, tantôt prés, puis châlet, chaumière, petite montagne; bref, les étrangers viennent le voir et l'admirent, et malgré la description pompeuse que je vous en fais, vous en serez content.

N. B. J'ai planté une quantité d'excellens arbres fruitiers.

Venons à moi; vous comprenez bien que j'ai vieilli, excepté pour la sensibilité; je suis à la mode, mes nerfs sont attaqués; je suis plus mélancolique, mais je n'ai pas plus d'humeur; vous ne souffrirez de mes maux que tout au plus négativement. Ensemble, et séparés par nos logemens, nous jouirons, vis-à-vis l'un de l'autre, de la plus grande liberté. Nous prendrons une gouvernante douce et entendue, plutôt par commodité que par nécessité; car je me chargerois sans crainte de la surintendance. J'ai fait un ménage de quatre, pendant quelque tems; j'ai fait le mien, et j'ai remarqué que cela marchoit tout seul, quand c'étoit une fois en train. Les petites gens qui n'ont que ce mérite, font grand bruit pour rien. Mon jardin nous fournira avec abondance de bons fruits et d'excellens légumes. Pour le reste de la table et de la dépense domestique, je ne demanderois pas mieux que de vous recevoir chez moi, comme vous m'avez reçu chez vous; mais nos situations sont différentes à cet égard; cependant si vous étiez plus ruiné, je vous l'offrirois sans doute, et je devrois le faire; mais avec les rentes que vous aviez, quand j'étois chez vous, en les supposant même diminuées, vous vivrez très agréablement à Lausanne. Enfin à cet égard nous nous arrangerons, comme il vous sera le plus agréable, et en proportion de nos revenus. Toujours serez vous ainsi, à ce que j'espère, plus décemment et plus comfortablement, que vous ne seriez par tout ailleurs au même prix.

Quant à la société, quoique infiniment agréable, je commence ce chapitre par vous dire que j'éviterois de vous y inviter, si vous étiez entièrement désœuvré; les jours sont longs alors, et laissent bien du vuide; mais homme de lettres, comme vous êtes, je ne connois point de société qui vous convienne mieux. Nous aurons autour de nous un cercle, comme il seroit impossible d'en trouver ailleurs dans un aussi petit espace. Madame de Corcelles, Mademoiselle Sulens, et M. de Montolieu, (Madame est morte,) Messrs. Polier et leurs femmes, Madame de Severy, et M. et Madame de Nassau, Mademoiselle de Chandieu, Madame de St. Cierge, et M. avec leurs deux filles jolies et aimables, Mesdames de Crousaz, Polier, de Charrières, &c. font un fonds de bonne compagnie dont on ne se lasse point, et dont M. de Servan est si content qu'il regrette toujours d'être obligé de retourner dans ses terres, et ne respire que pour s'établir tout à fait à Lausanne. Il passa tout l'hyver de 1782 avec nous, et il fut, on ne peut plus, agréable. Vous trouverez les mœurs changées en bien, et plus conformes à nos ages, et à nos caractères; peu de grandes assemblées, de grands repas, mais beaucoup de petits soupers, de petites assemblées, où l'on fait ce qu'on veut, où l'on cause, lit, &c. et dont on écarte avec soin les facheux de toute espèce. Il y a le Dimanche une société, où tout ce qu'il y a d'un peu distingué en étrangères et étrangers, est invité. Cela fait des assemblées de 40 à 50 personnes, où l'on voit ce qu'on ne voit guères le reste de la semaine, et ces espèces de *rout* font quelquefois plaisir. Nous sommes fort dégoûtés des étrangers, surtout des jeunes gens, et nous les écartons avec soin de nos petits comités, à moins qu'ils n'ayent du mérite, ou quelques talens. A cet égard un de nos petits travers, c'est l'engouement; mais vous en profiterez, mon cher Monsieur, comme Edward Gibbon, et comme mon ami; vous serez d'abord l'homme à la mode, et je vois d'ici que vous soutiendrez fort bien ce rôle, sans vous en fâcher, dût on un peu vous surfaire. *Je sens que tu me flattes, mais tu me fais plaisir,* est peut-être le meilleur vers de Destouches.

Voilà donc l'hyver; l'étude le matin, quelques conversations, quand vous serez fatigué, avec quelque homme de lettres, ou amateur, ou du moins qui aura vu quelque chose; à l'heure qu'il vous plaira un dîner, point de fermier général, mais l'honnête épicurien, avec un ou deux amis quand vous voudrez: puis quelques visites, une soirée, souvent un souper. Quant à l'été, vu votre manière d'aimer la campagne, on diroit que ma remise a été faite pour vous; pendant que vous vous y promènerez en sénateur, je serai souvent en bon paysan Suisse, devant mon châlet, ou dans ma chaumière; puis nous nous rencontrerons tout à coup, et tâcherons de nous remettre au niveau l'un de l'autre. Nous fermerons nos portes à l'ordinaire, excepté aux étrangers qui passent leur chemin; mais quand nous voudrons, nous y aurons tous ceux que nous aimerons à y voir; car on ne demande pas mieux que d'y venir se réjouir. J'ai eu, un beau jour d'Avril ce printems, un déjeûner, qui m'a coûté quelques Louis, où il y avoit plus de 40 personnes, je ne sais combien de petites tables, une bonne musique au milieu du verger, et une quantité de jeunes et jolies personnes dansant des branles, et formant des chiffres en cadence; j'ai vu bien des fêtes, j'en ai peu vu de plus jolies. Quand mon parc vous ennuyera, nous aurons, ou nous louerons ensemble (et ce sera ainsi un plaisir peu cher) un cabriolet léger, avec deux chevaux gentils, et nous irons visiter nos amis dispersés dans les campagnes, qui nous recevront à bras ouverts. Vous en serez content de nos campagnes; toujours en proportion vous comprenez, et vous trouverez en général un heureux changement pour les agrémens de la société, et une sorte de recherche simple, mais élégante. Les bergères du *Printems*, excepté Madame de Vanberg, ne sont sans doute plus présentables, mais il y en a d'autres assez gentilles, et quoiqu'elles ne soyent pas en bien grand nombre, il y en aura toujours assez pour vous, mon cher Monsieur. Peu à peu mon imagination m'a emporte, et mon style s'égaye, comme cela nous arrivoit quelquefois dans nos châteaux en Espagne. Il est bien tems de finir cet article, résumons nous plus sérieusement.

Si vous exécutez le plan que vous avez imaginé, j'aimerois même à dire que vous embrassez, surtout d'après ce que vous marquez vous même, *Si je ne consultois que mon cœur et ma raison, je romperois sur le champ cette indigne chaine*, &c. Eh! que voulez-vous consulter, si ce n'est votre cœur et votre raison? Si, dis-je, vous exécutez ce plan, vous retrouverez une liberté et une indépendance, que vous n'auriez jamais dû perdre, et dont vous méritez de jouir, une aisance qui ne vous coûtera qu'un voyage de quelques jours, une tranquillité que vous ne pouvez avoir à Londres, et enfin un ami qui n'a peut-être pas été un jour sans penser à vous, et qui malgré ses défauts, ses foiblesses et son infériorité, est encore un des compagnons qui vous convient le mieux.

Il me reste à vous apprendre pourquoi je vous réponds si tard: vous savez déjà actuellement que ce n'est pas manque d'amitié et de zèle pour la chose; mais votre lettre m'a été renvoyée de Lausanne ici, à Strasbourg, et je n'ai passé qu'une poste sans y répondre, ce qui n'est pas trop, vous l'avouerez, pour un pareil bavardage. Je suis parti de Lausanne la veille de Pâques pour venir voir un M. Bourcard de Basle, fort de mes amis; il est ici auprès du Comte de Cagliostro, pour profiter de ses remèdes. Vous aurez entendu parler peut-être de cet homme extraordinaire à tous égards. Comme j'ai été assez malade tout l'hyver, je profite aussi de ses remèdes; mais comme le tems du séjour du Comte ici n'est rien moins que sûr, le mieux sera que vous m'écriviez *à M. D. chez M. Bourcard du Kirshgarten, à Basle.*

Vous comprenez combien à tous égards, il est nécessaire m'écrire sans perte de tems, dès que vous aurez pris une résolution. Adieu, mon cher ami.*

462.

A M. Deyverdun.

HIS GRATITUDE TO DEYVERDUN.

*Je reçois votre lettre du 10 Juin, le 21 de ce mois. Aujourd'hui Mardi le 24, je mets la main à la plume (comme dit M. Fréron) pour y répondre, quoique ma missive ne puisse partir par arrangement des postes, que Vendredi prochain, 27 du courant. O merveille de la grace efficace! Elle n'agit pas moins puissamment sur vous, et moyennant le secours toujours prêt, et toujours prompt de nos couriers, un mois nous suffit pour la demande et la réponse. Je remercie mille fois le génie de l'amitié, qui m'a poussé, après mille efforts inutiles, à vous écrire enfin au moment le plus critique et le plus favorable. Jamais démarche n'a répondu si parfaitement à tous mes vœux et à toutes mes espérances. Je comptois sans doute sur la durée et la vérité de vos sentimens; mais j'ignorois (telle est la foiblesse humaine) jusqu'à quel point ils avoient pu être attiédis par le tems et l'éloignement; et je savois encore moins l'état actuel de votre santé, de votre fortune et de vos liaisons, qui auroient pu opposer tant d'obstacles à notre réunion.

Vous m'écrivez, vous m'aimez toujours; vous désirez avec zèle, avec ardeur, de réaliser nos anciens projets; vous le pouvez, vous le voulez; vous m'offrez dès l'automne votre maison, et quelle terrasse! votre société, et quelle société! L'arrangement nous convient à tous les deux; je retrouve à la fois le compagnon de ma jeunesse, un sage conseiller, et un peintre qui fait représenter et exagérer même les objets les plus rians. Ces exagérations me font pour le moins autant de plaisir que la simple vérité. Si votre portrait étoit tout à fait ressemblant, ces agrémens n'existeroient que hors de nous mêmes, et j'aime encore mieux les retrouver dans la vivacité de votre cœur et de votre imagination. Ce n'est pas que je ne reconnoisse un grand fond de vérité dans le tableau de Lausanne; je connois le lieu de la scène, je me transporte en idée sur *notre* terrasse, je vois ces côteaux, ce lac, ces montagnes, ouvrage favoris de la nature, et je conçois sans peine les embellissemens que votre goût s'est plu y ajouter. Je me rappelle depuis vingt ou trente ans les mœurs, l'esprit, l'aisance de la société, et je comprends que ce véritable ton de la bonne compagnie se perpétue, et s'épure de père en fils, ou plutôt de mère en fille; car il m'a toujours paru qu'à Lausanne, aussi bien qu'en France, les femmes sont très supérieures aux hommes. Dans un pareil séjour, je craindrois la dissipation bien plus que l'ennui, et le tourbillon de Lausanne étonneroit un philosophe accoutumé depuis tant d'années à la tranquillité de Londres. Vous êtes trop instruit pour regarder ce propos, comme une mauvaise plaisanterie; c'est dans les détroits qu'on est entrainé par la rapidité des courans: il n'y en a point en pleine mer. Dès qu'on ne recherche plus les plaisirs bruyans, et qu'on s'affranchit volontiers des devoirs pénibles, la liberté d'un simple particulier se fortifie par l'immensité de la ville. Quant à moi, l'application à mon grand ouvrage, l'habitude, et la récompense du travail, m'ont rendu plus studieux, plus sédentaire, plus ami de la retraite. La Chambre des Communes et les grands dîners exigent beaucoup de tems; et la tempérance d'un repas anglois vous permet de goûter de cinq ou six vins différens, et vous ordonne de boire une bouteille de claret après le dessert. Mais enfin je ne soupe jamais, je me couche de fort bonne heure, je reçois peu de visites, les matinées sont longues, les étés sont libres, et dès que je ferme ma porte, je suis oublié du monde entier. Dans une société plus bornée et plus amicale, les démarches sont publiques, les droits sont réciproques, l'on dîne de bonne heure, on se goûte trop pour ne pas passer l'après-midi ensemble; on soupe, on veille, et les plaisirs de la soirée ne laissent pas de déranger le repos de la nuit, et le travail du lendemain.

HIS HESITATION TO ACCEPT.

Quel est cependant le résultat de ces plaintes? c'est seulement que la mariée est trop belle, et que j'ose me servir de l'excuse honnête de la santé et du privilège d'un homme de lettres; il ne tiendra qu'à moi de modérer un peu l'excès de mes jouissances. Pour cet engouement que vous m'annoncez, et qui a toujours été le défaut des peuples les plus spirituels, je l'ai déjà éprouvé sur un plus grand théâtre. Il y a six ans que l'ami de Madame Necker fut reçu à Paris, comme celui de George Deyverdun pourroit l'être à Lausanne. Je ne connois rien de plus flatteur que cet accueil favorable d'un public poli et éclairé. Mais cette faveur, si douce pour l'étranger, n'est-elle pas un peu dangereuse pour l'habitant exposé à voir flétrir ses lauriers, par la faute ou par l'inconstance de ses juges? Non; on se soutient toujours, peut être pas précisément au même point d'élévation. A l'abri de trois gros volumes in-quarto en langue étrangère, encore ce qui n'est pas un petit avantage, je conserverai toujours la réputation littéraire, et cette réputation donnera du relief aux qualités sociales, si l'on trouve l'historien sans travers, sans affectation et sans prétentions.

Je serai donc charmé et content de votre société, et j'aurois pu dire en deux mots, ce qui j'ai bavardé en deux pages; mais il y a tant de plaisir à bavarder avec un ami! car enfin je possède à Lausanne un véritable ami; et les simples connoissances remplaceront sans beaucoup de peine, tout ce qui s'appelle liaison, et même amitié, dans ce vaste désert de Londres. Mais au moment où j'écris, je vois de tous côtés une foule d'objets dont la perte sera bien plus difficile à réparer. Vous connoissiez ma bibliothèque; mais je suis en état de vous rendre le propos de votre maison *c'est bien autre chose à cette heure*; formée peu à peu, mais avec beaucoup de soin et de dépense, elle peut se nommer aujourd'hui un beau cabinet de particulier. Non content de remplir à rangs redoublés la meilleure pièce qui lui étoit destinée, elle s'est débordée dans la chambre sur la rue, dans votre ancienne chambre à coucher, dans la mienne, dans tous les recoins de la maison de *Bentinck-street*, et jusques dans une chaumière que je me suis donnée à *Hampton Court*.

J'ai mille courtisans rangés autour de moi:

Ma retraite est mon Louvre, et j'y commande en roi.

Le fonds est de la meilleure compagnie Grecque, Latine, Italienne, Françoise, et Angloise, et les auteurs les moins chers à l'homme de goût, des ecclésiastiques, des Byzantins, des Orientaux, sont les plus nécessaires à l'historien de la Décadence et de la Chute, &c. Vous ne sentez que trop bien le désagrément de laisser, et l'impossibilité de transporter cinq ou six milles volumes, d'autant plus que le ciel n'a pas voulu faire de la Suisse un pays maritime. Cependant mon zèle pour la réussite de nos projets communs, me fait imaginer que ces obstacles pourront s'applanir, et que je puis adoucir ou supporter ces privations douloureuses. Les bons auteurs classiques, la bibliothèque des nations, se retrouvent dans tous les pays. Lausanne n'est pas dépourvu de livres, ni de politesse, et j'ai dans l'esprit qu'on pourroit acquérir pour un certain tems, quelque bibliothèque d'un vieillard ou d'un mineur, dont la famille ne voudroit pas se défaire entièrement. Quant aux outils de mon travail, nous commencerons par examiner l'état de nos richesses; après quoi il faudroit faire un petit calcul du prix, du poids et de la rareté de chaque ouvrage, pour juger de ce qu'il seroit nécessaire de transporter de Londres, et de ce qu'on acheteroit plus commodément en Suisse; à l'égard de ces frais, on devroit les envisager comme les avances d'une manufacture transplantée en pays étranger, et dont on espère retirer dans la suite un profit raisonnable. Malheureusement votre bibliothèque publique, en y ajoutant même celle de M. de Bochat, est assez piteuse; mais celles de Berne et de Basle sont très nombreuses, et je compterois assez sur la bonhommie Helvétique, pour espérer que, moyennant des recommandations et des cautions, il me seroit permis d'en tirer les livres dont j'aurois essentiellement besoin. Vous êtes très bien placé pour prendre les informations, et pour faire les démarches convenables; mais vous voyez du moins combien je me retourne de tous les côtés, pour esquiver la difficulté la plus formidable.

HIS FRIEND AND VALET.

Venons à présent à des objets moins relevés, mais très importans à l'existence et au bien-être de l'animal, le logement, les domestiques, et la table. Pour mon appartement particulier, une chambre à coucher, avec un grand cabinet et une antichambre, auroient suffi à tous mes besoins; mais si vous pouvez vous en passer, je me promenerai avec plaisir dans l'immensité de vos onze pièces, qui s'accommoderont sans doute aux heures et aux saisons différentes. L'article des domestiques renferme une assez forte difficulté, sur laquelle je dois vous consulter. Vous connoissez, et vous estimez Caplen mon valet de chambre, maître d'hotel, &c. qui a été nourri dans notre maison, et qui comptoit d'y finir ses jours. Depuis votre départ, ses talens et ses vertus se sont dévelloppés de plus en plus, et je le considère bien moins sur le pied d'un domestique, que sur celui d'un ami. Malheureusement il ne sait que l'Anglois, et jamais il n'apprendra de langue étrangère. Il m'accompagna, il y a six ans, dans mon voyage à Paris, mais il rapporta fidèlement à Londres toute l'ignorance, et tous les préjugés d'un bon patriote. A Lausanne il me coûteroit beaucoup, et à l'exception du service personnel, il ne nous seroit que d'une très petite utilité. Cependant je supporterois volontiers cette dépense, mais je suis très persuadé que, si son attachement le portoit à me suivre, il s'ennuyeroit à mourir dans un pays où tout lui seroit étranger et désagréable. Il faudroit donc me détacher d'un homme dont je connois le zèle, la fidélité, rompre tout d'un coup de petites habitudes qui sont liées avec le bien-être journalier et momentané, et se résoudre à lui substituer un visage nouveau, peut-être un mauvais sujet, toujours quelque aventurier Suisse pris sur le pavé de Londres. Vous rappellez-vous un certain George Suess qui a fait autrefois avec moi le voyage de France et d'Italie? Je le crois marié et établi à Lausanne; s'il vit encore, si vous pouvez l'engager à se rendre ici, pour me ramener en Suisse, la compagnie d'un bon et ancien serviteur ne laisseroit pas d'adoucir la chute, et il resteroit peut-être auprès de moi, jusqu'à ce que nous eussions choisi un jeune homme du pays, adroit, modeste et bien élevé, à qui je ferois un parti avantageux.

Les autres domestiques, gouvernantes, laquais, cuisinière, &c. se prennent et se renvoyent sans difficulté. Un article bien plus important, c'est notre table, car enfin nous ne sommes pas assez hermites, pour nous contenter des légumes et des fruits de votre jardin, tout excellens qu'ils sont; mais je n'ai presque rien à ajouter à l'honnêteté de vos propos, qui me donnent beaucoup plus de plaisir que de surprise. Si je me trouvois sans fortune, au lieu de rougir des bienfaits de l'amitié, j'accepterois vos offres aussi simplement que vous les faites. Mais nous ne sommes pas réduits à ce point, et vous comprenez assez qu'une déconfiture angloise laisse encore une fortune fort décente au Pays de Vaud, et pour vous dire quelque chose de plus précis, je dépenserois sans peine et sans inconvénient cinq ou six cens Louis. Vous connoissez le résultat aussi bien que les détails d'un ménage; en supposant une petite table de deux philosophes Epicuriens, quatre, cinq, ou six domestiques, des amis assez souvent, des repas assez rarement, beaucoup de sensualité, et peu de luxe, à combien estimez-vous en gros la dépense d'un mois et d'une année? Le partage que vous avez déjà fait, me paroît des plus raisonnables; vous me logez, et je vous nourris. A votre calcul, j'ajouterois mon entretien personnel, habits, plaisirs, gages de domestiques, &c. et je verrois d'une manière assez nette, l'ensemble de mon petit établissement.

HIS HOPES OF A POLITICAL PLACE.

Après avoir essuyé tant de détails minutieux, le cher lecteur s'imagine sans doute que la résolution de me fixer pendant quelque tems aux bords du Lac Léman, est parfaitement décidée. Hélas! rien n'est moins vrai; mais je me suis livré au charme délicieux de contempler, de sonder, de palper ce bonheur, dont je sens tout le prix, qui est à ma portée, et auquel j'aurai peut-être la bêtise de renoncer. Vous avez raison de croire, mais vous ignorez jusqu'à quel point vous l'avez, que ma carrière politique a été plus semée d'épines que de roses. Eh! quel objet, quel motif, pourroit me consoler de l'ennui des affaires, et de la honte de la dépendance? *La gloire?* Comme homme de lettres, j'en jouis, comme orateur je ne l'aurai jamais, et le nom des simples soldats est oublié dans les victoires aussi bien que dans les défaites. *Le devoir?* Dans ces combats à l'aveugle, où les chefs ne cherchent que leur avantage particulier, il y a toujours à parier que les subalternes feront plus de mal que de bien. *L'attachement personnel?* Les ministres sont rarement dignes de l'inspirer; jusqu'à présent Lord North n'a pas eu à se plaindre de moi, et si je me retire du Parlement, il lui sera très aisé d'y substituer un autre muet, tout aussi affidé que son ancien serviteur. Je suis intimément convaincu, et par la raison, et par le sentiment, qu'il n'y a point de parti, qui me convienne aussi bien que de vivre avec vous, et auprès de vous à Lausanne; et si je parviens à la place (*Commissioner of the Excise or Customs*) où je vise, il y aura toutes les semaines cinq longues matinées, qui m'avertiront de la folie de mon choix. Vous vous trompez à la vérité à l'égard de l'instabilité de ces emplois; ils sont presque les seuls qui ne ressentent jamais des révolutions du ministère.

Cependant si cette place s'offroit bientôt, je n'aurois pas le bon sens et le courage de la refuser. Quels autres conseillers veux-je prendre, sinon mon cœur et ma raison? Il en est de puissans et toujours écoutés: les égards, la mauvaise honte, tous mes amis, ou soi-disant tels, s'écrieront que je suis un homme perdu, ruiné, un fou qui se dérobe à ses protecteurs, un misanthrope qui s'exile au bout du monde, et puis les exagérations sur tout ce qui seroit fait en ma faveur, si surement, si promptement, si libéralement.

Mylord Sheffield opinera à me faire interdire et enfermer; mes deux tantes et ma belle mère se plaindront que je les quitte pour jamais, &c. Et l'embarras de prendre mon bonnet de nuit, comme disoit le sage Fontenelle, lorsqu'il n'etoit question que de decoucher, combien de bonnets de nuit ne me faudra-t-il pas prendre, et les prendre tout seul? car tout le monde, amis, parens, domestiques, s'opposera à ma fuite. Voilà à la vérité des obstacles assez peu redoutables, et en les décrivant, je sens qu'ils s'affoiblissent dans mon esprit. Grace à ce long bavardage vous connoissez mon intérieur, comme moi même, c'est à dire assez mal; mais cette incertitude, très amicale pour moi, seroit très facheuse pour vous. Votre réponse me parviendra vers la fin de Juillet, et huit jours après, je vous promets une réplique nette et décisive: *je pars* ou *je reste*. Si je pars, ce sera au milieu de Septembre; je mangerai les raisins de votre treille les premiers jours d'Octobre, et vous aurez encore le tems de me charger de vos commissions. Ne me dites plus, *Monsieur, et très cher ami*; le premier est froid, le second est superflu.*

463.

M. Deyverdun à M. Gibbon.

*Me voilà un peu embarrassé actuellement; je ne dois vous appeller ni Monsieur, ni ami. Eh bien! vous saurez qu'étant parti Samedi de Strasbourg, pendant que je venois ici, votre seconde lettre alloit là, et qu'ainsi je reçus votre troisième, Dimanche, et votre seconde, hier. La mention que vous y faisiez du Suisse George, dont je n'ai pu rien trouver dans la première, m'a fait comprendre qu'il y en avoit une seconde, et j'ai cru devoir attendre un courier, la troisième n'exigeant pas de réponse.

Pour votre parole, permettez que je vous en dispense encore, et même jusqu'au dernier jour, je sens bien qu'un procédé contraire vous conviendroit; mais certes il ne me convient pas du tout. Ceci, comme vous le dites, est une espèce de mariage, et pensez vous que malgré les engagemens les plus solemnels, je n'eusse pas reconduit chez elle, du pied des autels, la femme la plus aimable qui m'eut temoigné des regrets? Jamais je ne me consolerois, si je vous voyois mécontent dans la suite, et dans le cas de me faire des reproches. C'est à vous à faire, si vous croyez nécessaire, des démarches de votre côté, qui fortifient votre résolution; pour moi, je n'en ferai point d'essentielles, jusqu'à ce que j'aye reçu encore une lettre de vous. Après ce petit préambule, parlons toujours comme si l'affaire étoit décidée, et repassons votre lettre. Tout ce que vous dites des grandes et petites villes, est très vrai, et votre comparaison des détroits et de la pleine mer, est on ne peut pas plus juste et agréable; mais enfin, *comme on fait son lit, on se couche*, disoit Sancho Pancha d'agréable mémoire, et qui peut mieux faire son lit à sa guise qu'un étranger, qui, n'ayant ni devoirs d'état ni de sang à remplir, peut vivre entièrement isolé, sans que personne y puisse trouver à redire? Moi même, bourgeois et citoyen de la ville, je suis presqu'entièrement libre. L'été, par exemple, je déteste de m'enfermer le soir dans des chambres chaudes, pour faire une partie. Eh bien! on m'a persécuté un peu la première année; à présent on me laisse en repos. Il y aura sans doute quelque changement dans votre manière de vivre: mais il me semble qu'on se fait aisément à cela. Les dîners, surtout en femmes, sont très rares; les soupers peu grands; on reste plutôt pour être ensemble, que pour manger, et plusieurs personnes ne s'asseyent point. Je crois, tout compté et rabattu, que vouz aurez encore plus de tems pour le cabinet qu'à Londres; on sort peu le matin, et quand nos amis communs viendront chez moi, et vous demanderont, je leur dirai; "ce n'est pas un oisif comme vous autres, il travaille dans son cabinet," et ils se tairont respectueusement.

Pour les bibliothèques publiques, votre idée ne pourroit, je pense, se réaliser pour un lecteur ou même un écrivain ordinaire, mais un homme qui joue un rôle dans la république des lettres, un homme aimé et considéré, trouvera, je m'imagine, bien des facilités; d'ailleurs, j'ai de bons amis à Berne, et je prendrai ici des informations.

Passons à la table. Si j'étois à Lausanne, cet article seroit plus sûr, je pourrois revoir mes papiers, consulter; j'ai une chienne de mémoire. A vue de pays cela pourra aller de 20 à 30 Louis par mois, plus ou moins, vous sentez, suivant la friandise, et le plus ou moins de convives. Marquez moi dans votre première combien vous coûte le vôtre.

SOCIAL HABITS AT LAUSANNE.

Je sens fort bien tous les bonnets de nuit: point de grands changemens sans embarras, même sans regrets; vous en aurez quelquefois sans doute: par exemple, si votre salle à manger, votre salle de compagnie, sont plus riantes, vous perdrez pour le vase de la bibliothèque. Pour ce qui est des représentations, des discours au moins inutiles, il me semble que le mieux seroit de masquer vos grandes opérations, de ne parler que d'une course, d'une visite chez moi, de six mois ou plus ou moins. Vous feriez bien, je pense, d'aller chez mon ami Louis Teissier; c'est un brave et honnête homme, qui m'est attaché, qui aime notre pays; il vous donnera tout plein de bons conseils avec zèle, et vous gardera le secret.

Vous aurez quelquefois à votre table un poëte;—oui, Monsieur, un poëte:—nous en avons un enfin. Procurez vous un volume 8vo. *Poësies Helvétiennes, imprimées l'année passée chez Mouser, à Lausanne.* Vouz trouverez entr'autres dans l'épitre au jardinier de la grotte, votre ami et votre parc. Toute la prose est de votre très humble serviteur, qui désire qu'elle trouve grace devant vous.

Le Comte de Cagliostro a fait un séjour à Londres. On ne sait qui il est, d'où il est, d'où il tire son argent; il exerce *gratis* ses talens pour la médecine; il a fait des cures admirables; mais c'est d'ailleurs le composé le plus étrange. J'ai cessé de prendre ses remèdes qui m'échauffoient—l'homme d'ailleurs me gâtoit le médecin. Je suis revenu à Basle avec mon ami. Adieu; récrivez moi le plutôt possible.*

464.

A. M. Deyverdun.

Hampton Court, ce 1 Juillet, 1783.

HIS DECISION TO LEAVE ENGLAND.

Après avoir pris ma résolution, l'honneur, et ce qui vaut encore mieux l'amitié, me défendent de vous laisser un moment dans l'incertitude. JE PARS. Je vous en donne ma parole, et comme je suis bien aise de me fortifier d'un nouveau lien, je vous prie très sérieusement de ne pas m'en dispenser. Ma possession, sans doute, ne vaut pas celle de Julie; mais vous serez plus inexorable que St. Preux. Je ne sens plus qu'une vive impatience pour notre réunion. Mais le mois d'Octobre est encore loin; 92 jours, et nous aurons tout le tems de prendre, et de nous donner des éclaircissemens dont nous avons besoin. Après un mûr examen, je renonce au voyage de George Suess, qui me paroît incertain, cher et difficile. Après tout mon valet de chambre et ma bibliothèque sont les deux articles les plus embarrassans. Si je ne retenois pas ma plume, je remplirois sans peine la feuille; mais il ne faut pas passer du silence à un babil intarissable. Seulement si je connois le Comte de Cagliostro, cet homme extraordinaire, &c. Savez vous le Latin? oui, sans doute; mais faites, comme si je ne le savois point. Quand retournez vous à Lausanne vous même? Je pense que vous y trouverez une petite bête, bien aimable mais tant soit peu mechante, qui se nomme My lady Elizabeth Foster, parlez lui de moi, mais parlez en avec discretion, elle a des correspondences partout. *Vale.*

- 68 -

465.

To Lord Sheffield.

July 10th, 1783.

*You will read the following lines with more patience and attention than you would probably give to a hasty conference, perpetually interrupted by the opening of the door, and perhaps by the quickness of our own tempers. I neither expect nor desire an answer on a subject of extreme importance to myself, but which friendship alone can render interesting to you. We shall soon meet at Sheffield.

It is needless to repeat the reflections which we have sometimes debated together, and which I have often seriously weighed in my silent solitary walks. Notwithstanding your active and ardent spirit, you must allow that there is some perplexity in my present situation, and that my future prospects are distant and cloudy. I have lived too long in the world to entertain a very sanguine idea of the friendship or zeal of Ministerial patrons; and we are all sensible how much the powers of patronage are reduced.*

The source of pensions is absolutely stopped, and a double list of candidates is impatient and clamourous for half the number of desirable places. A seat at the board of customs or excise was certainly the most practicable attempt, but how far are we advanced in the pursuit? Could we obtain (it was indeed unprecedented) an extraordinary commission? Have we received any promise of the *first* vacancy? how often is the execution of such a promise delayed to a second or third opportunity? When will those vacancies happen? Incumbents are sometimes very tough. Of the Excise I know less, but I am sure that the door of the Customs (except when it was opened for Sir Stanier by a pension of *equal* value) has been shut, at least during the last three years. In the meanwhile I should be living in a state of anxiety and dependence, working in the illiberal service of the House of Commons, my seat in Parliament sinking in value every day and my expenses very much exceeding my annual income. *At the end of that time, or rather long before that time (for their lives are not worth a year's purchase), our ministers are kicked down stairs, and I am left their disinterested friend to fight through another opposition, and to expect the fruits of another revolution.

But I will take a more favourable supposition, and conceive myself, in six months, firmly seated at the board of Customs; before the end of the next six months, I should infallibly hang myself. Instead of regretting my disappointment, I rejoyce in my escape; as I am satisfied that no salary could pay me for the irksomeness of attendance, and the drudgery of business so repugnant to my taste, (and I will dare to say) so unworthy of my character. Without looking forwards to the possibility, still more remote, of exchanging that laborious office for a smaller annuity, there is surely another plan, more reasonable, more simple, and more pleasant; a temporary retreat to a quiet and less expensive scene. In a four years' residence at Lausanne, I should live within my income, save, and even accumulate, my ready money; finish my history, an object of profit as well as fame, expect the contingencies of elderly lives, and return to England at the age of fifty, to form a lasting independent establishment, without courting the smiles of a minister, or apprehending the downfall of a party. Such have been my serious sober reflections.

PLAN OF JOINING DEYVERDUN.

Yet I much question whether I should have found courage to follow my reason and my inclination, if a friend had not stretched his hand to draw me out of the dirt. The twentieth of last May I wrote to my friend Deyverdun, after a long interval of silence, to expose my situation, and to consult in what manner I might best arrange myself at Lausanne. From his answer, which I received about a fortnight ago, I have the pleasure to learn, that his heart and his house are both open for my reception; that a family which he had lodged for some years is about to leave him, and that at no other time my company would have been so acceptable and convenient. I shall step, at my arrival, into an excellent apartment and a delightful situation; the fair division of our expences will render them very moderate, and I shall pass my time with the companion of my youth, whose temper and studies have always been congenial to my own. I have given him my word of honour to be at Lausanne in the beginning of October, and no power or persuasion can divert me from this IRREVOCABLE resolution, which I am every day proceeding to execute.

I wish, but I scarcely hope, to convince you of the propriety of my scheme; but at least you will allow, that when we are not able to prevent the *follies* of our friends, we should strive to render them as easy and harmless as possible. The arrangement of my house, furniture and books will be left to meaner hands, but it is to your zeal and judgment alone that I can trust the more important disposal of Lenborough and Lymington. On these subjects we may go into a Committee at Sheffield-place, but you know it is the rule of a Committee not to hear any arguments against the *principle* of the bill. At present I shall only observe, that neither of these negociations ought to detain me here; the former may be dispatched as well, the latter much better, in my absence. *Vale.**

466.

To his Stepmother.

Bentinck Street, July 26th, 1783.

MY DEAR MADAM,

You have so long been acquainted with my indifference or rather dislike to the house of Commons, that you will not be much surprized, that I should entertain a thought or indeed a resolution of vacating my seat. Your vain hope (a kind and a friendly vanity) of my making a distinguished figure in that assembly has long since been extinct, and you are now convinced by repeated experience that my reputation must be derived solely from my pen. A seat in parliament I can only value as it is connected with some official situation of emolument: that connection which has fortunately subsisted about three years is now dissolved, and I do not see any probability of its being *speedily* restored. Whatever may be the wishes or sentiments of my political friends, their patronage has been extremely circumscribed by the double list of candidates, the reduction of places and the suppression of pensions. The most solid and attainable things (at the boards of Customs or Excise) are incompatible with a seat in parliament, and my prævious retreat (by taking from them a motive of delay) will promote rather than obstruct the accomplishment of my hopes and their promises. Thus restored for some time to the enjoyment of freedom, I propose to spend it in the society of my friend Deyverdun at Lausanne, who presses me in the kindest manner to visit him in the house and garden which he possesses in the most beautiful situation in the World.

I intend going about the middle of September, and though it is not possible to define precisely the time of my absence, it is not likely that I shall pass less than a year in Switzerland. I shall exchange the most unwholesome air (that of the house of Commons) for the purest and most salubrious, the heat and hurry of party for a cool litterary repose; and I have little doubt that this excursion, which will amuse me by the change of objects, will have a lasting and beneficial effect on my health. The lease of my house expires next Christmas, and I shall take the opportunity of disengaging myself from an useless expence, and of removing to a hired room my books, and such part of my furniture as may be worth keeping. You will be pleased to hear that the faithful Caplen accompanies me abroad.

HIS DEPARTURE A NECESSITY.

Such is the light in which my journey should be represented to those friends to whom it may be advisable to say any thing of my motives. Every circumstance which I have already stated is strictly true, but you will too easily conceive that it is not the *whole truth*: that this step is dictated by the hard law of æconomy or rather of necessity, and that the moment of my return will not entirely depend on my own choice. You have not forgot how a similar intention some years ago was superseded by my appointment to the board of trade. Perhaps it would have been wiser if I had left England immediately after the loss of my place, and the sense of this imprudent delay urges me more strongly every day to avoid the difficulties of a still longer procrastination. By this resolution I shall deliver myself at once from the heavy expence of a London life, my friend Deyverdun and myself shall join in a moderate though elegant establishment at Lausanne; and I can wait without inconvenience for one of the events, which may enable me to revisit with pleasure and credit my country, and the person, whom in that country, I most value, I mean yourself. Allow me to add (though I know such thoughts will be absorbed in your mind by higher and more tender sentiments), yet allow me to add that at the stated days of Midsummer and Christmas, you may regularly draw for your half year's annuity on Messieurs Gosling in Fleet Street, and that effectual steps shall be taken to secure you from a possibility of disappointment. It would not be my absence, but my stay in England that could create any delay or difficulty on that subject.

And now, my dear madam, let me submit to your consideration and final decision, a question which for my own part I am unable to determine, whether I shall visit Bath before I leave England. If I consulted only my wishes, the mere expence and trouble of the journey would be obstacles of small account, but I much fear, that on this occasion, prudence will dissuade what inclination would prompt, and that a meeting of three or four days (for it could be no more) would tend rather to embitter than to alleviate our unavoidable separation. If you decide for my coming down, it will probably take place between the 20th and 30th of next month, and I must beg that little, or nothing, may be said on the subject of my approaching journey, and that we may (silently) turn our thoughts to the happiness of seeing each other, after an interval of time, less considerable perhaps than those which commonly elapse between my Bath expeditions.

I am, my Dear Madam,
Ever most truly yours,
E. G.

467.

To Lord Sheffield.

Thursday night, 1783.

Elmsley and self have been hard at work this afternoon, and about ten quintals are preparing for foreign service. Can you save me ten pounds per annum, such is the rent of a good and safe room in the Strand? You offered me a room in Downing Street (did you mean an entire room?) for plate, china, &c. Is it the apartment on the ground floor from whence you was expelled by odours? If you can lodge my books you must give me a line per Saturday's coach, with a mandate to the maid that she may not scruple to shew and receive. Time presses and Elmsley is on the wing. Pelham is appointed Irish Secretary in the room of Wyndham who pleads bad health, but who had written very indiscreet letters at the general election. Adieu. I want to hear of My Lady, her tender frame has been too much agitated.

468.

To his Stepmother.

Sheffield-place, August 8th, 1783.

DEAR MADAM,

HIS REASONS FOR LEAVING LONDON.

Your truly *maternal* letters (which I have repeatedly perused) have agitated my mind with a variety of pleasing and painful sensations. I am grieved that you should contemplate my departure in so melancholy a light, but I shall always revere the affection which prompts your anxiety, and magnifies the evil. I receive with more gratitude than surprise your generous offer of devoting yourself and so large a portion of your income to my relief, and I am concerned to find on calmer reflection that such a project is attended with insuperable difficulties. After the mutual and unpleasant sacrifice of our habits and inclinations, I could not, even with your assistance, reduce the expence of a London life to the level of my present income, and the two hundred a year which you so nobly propose would be exhausted by the single article of a Coach.

With regard to the delays which you suggest, you may be assured that I shall take no material step without consideration and advice. Had I staid in London, I should have removed from Bentinck Street. On my return another house may at any time be procured, and I shall carefully preserve the most valuable part of my furniture, plate, linnen, china, beds, &c. My seat in Parliament cannot be vacated till the next Session, and I shall leave the disposal of it to our friend Lord Sheffield, in whose zeal and discretion we may safely confide. On his own account he regrets my departure, but he has been forced to give a full though reluctant approbation to my design. I wish it were in my power to remove all your kind apprehensions which relate to the length of my absence and the choice of my residence. I certainly do not entertain a very sanguine idea of political friendship, but I am convinced that such persons as really wish to serve me will not be discouraged by my temporary retreat to Switzerland. In the leisure and quiet which I shall enjoy at Lausanne, I shall prosecute the continuation of my history, and the care of publishing a work, from whence I may expect both honour and advantage, will secure, within a reasonable space, my return to England. Your idea of the climate of Switzerland is by many degrees too formidable; the air though sometimes keen, is pure and wholesome, the

Gout is much less frequent on the Continent than in our Island, and the provoking luxury of London dinners is much more likely to feed that distemper, than the temperance and tranquillety of Lausanne. In the society of my friend Deyverdun, I hope to spend some time with comfort and propriety, but my affections are still fixed in England, and it will be my wish and endeavour to shorten the term of this necessary separation, and in the meanwhile you may depend on the most regular communication of every circumstance that affects my health and happiness.

I am, my Dear Madam,
Ever yours,
E. G.

I have some questions to ask you about the disposal of certain pieces of furniture, such as the Clock and Carpet, but I would not mix those trifles with the more serious purpose of this letter.

469.

To Lord Sheffield.

Monday, August 18th, 1783.

*In the preparations of my journey I have not felt any circumstance more deeply than the kind concern of Lady S[heffield], and the silent grief of Mrs. Porten. Yet the age of my friends makes a very essential difference. I can scarcely hope ever to see my aunt again; but I flatter myself, that in less than two years, my *sister* will make me a visit, and that in less than four, I shall return it with a chearful heart at Sheffield-place. Business advances; this morning my books were shipped for Rouen, and will reach Lausanne almost as soon as myself. On Thursday morning the bulk of the library moves from Bentinck-street to Downing-street. I shall escape from the noise to Hampton Court, and spend three or four days in taking leave. I want to know your precise motions, what day you arrive in town, whether you visit Lord Beauchamp before the races, &c. I am now impatient to be gone, and shall only wait for a last interview with you. Your medley of Judges, Advocates, politicians, &c., is rather *useful* than pleasant. Town is a vast solitude. Adieu.*

470.

To Lord Sheffield.

Bentinck-street, Wednesday night, August 20th, 1783.

*I am now concluding one of the most unpleasant days of my life. Will the day of our meeting again be accompanied with proportionable satisfaction? The business of preparation will serve to agitate and divert *my* thoughts; but I do not like your brooding over melancholy ideas in your solitude, and I heartily wish that both you and my dear Lady S. would immediately go over and pass a week at Brighton. Such is our imperfect nature, that dissipation is a far more efficacious remedy than reflection. At all events, let me hear from you soon. I have passed the evening at home, without gaining any intelligence.*

471.

To Lord Sheffield.

Friday, August 22nd, 1783.

*I am astonished with your apparition and flight, and am at a loss to conjecture the mighty and sudden business of *Coventry,* which could not be delayed till next week. *Timeo* *Conways,* their selfish cunning, and your sanguine unsuspecting spirit. Not dreaming of your arrival, I thought it unnecessary to apprize you, that I delayed Hampton to this day; on Monday I shall return, and will expect you Tuesday evening, either in Bentinck or Downing-street, as you like best. Yon have seen the piles of learning accumulated in your parlour; the transportation will be atchieved to-day, and Bentinck Street is already reduced to a light, ignorant habitation, which I shall inhabit till about the 1st of September; four days must be allowed for clearing and packing; these I shall spend in Downing-street, and after seeing you a moment on your return, I shall start about Saturday the 6th. London is a desert, and life, without books, business, or society, will be somewhat tedious. From this state, you will judge that your plan coincides very well, only I think you should give me the whole of Wednesday in Bentinck-street. With regard to Bushy, perhaps as a compliment to Lord L. you had better defer it till your return.*

You have not forgot the model of a letter for Sainsbury, Way, Hearne, &c., with the 200 Guineas reward for the proper sale of Lenborough. I return your three letters with a fourth not less curious, which I have not yet answered. Mrs. G.'s pride is not inferior to her tenderness. *I admire Gregory Way, and should envy him, if I did not possess a disposition somewhat similar to his own. My lady will be reposed and restored at Brighton; the torrent of Lords, Judges, &c. a proper remedy for you, was a medicine ill-suited to her constitution. I *tenderly* embrace her.*

472.

To his Stepmother.

MY DEAREST MADAM,

I can easily attribute your silence to the true motive, the difficulty (of which I am likewise conscious) of our present situation. The subject which occupies our minds has been reciprocally exhausted: it is unpleasant to resume a melancholy train of ideas, and it is impossible to write with ease and chearfullness on indifferent subjects. Yet I almost flatter myself that if you are not satisfied with my reasons, you are at least disposed to acquiesce in a resolution which is the offspring of necessity, and will I trust be the parent of happiness. I repeat my promise that distance shall only render me a more punctual correspondent, and I must again intreat that you would turn your thoughts from the moment of our separation to that of our reunion.

After sending two boxes of books to Lausanne I have deposited the remainder of my library in Lord Sheffield's capacious mansion in Downing Street, whither I shall send next week my plate, linnen, beds, &c. I expect your commands with regard to the Clock and Carpet: if you have not room or occasion for them at Bath, I should probably dispose of the first, as it might be damaged by neglect, but the latter I shall carefully preserve both as your workmanship and as your gift. If among the China, &c. there should be any things you would desire to select, Lord S., their Guardian and mine, is instructed to obey your commands. As far as I can calculate I shall be ready to set out about the 6th of September, the end of next week, but I propose writing to you again before my departure.

I am, my Dear Madam,
Ever yours,
E. G.

473.

To Lady Sheffield.

Bentinck Street, August 30th, 1783.

MY DEAR FRIEND,

FAREWELL TO SHEFFIELD PLACE.

---

*For the names of Sheffelina, &c. are too playful for the serious temper of my mind. In the whole period of my life I do not recollect a day in which I felt more unpleasant sensations, than that on which I took my leave of Sheffield-place. I forgot my friend Deyverdun, and the fair prospect of quiet and happiness which awaits me at Lausanne. I lost sight of our almost certain meeting at the end of a term, which, at our age, cannot appear very distant; nor could I amuse my uneasiness with the hopes, the more doubtful prospect, of your visit to Switzerland. The agitation of preparing every thing for my departure has, in some degree, diverted these melancholy thoughts; yet I still look forwards to the decisive day (to-morrow Se'nnight) with an anxiety of which yourself and Lord S. have the principal share.

Surely never any thing was so unlucky as the unseasonable death of Sir John Russell, which so strongly reminded us of the instability of human life and human expectations. The inundation of the Assize must have distressed and overpowered you; but I hope and I wish to hear from yourself, that the air of your favourite Brighton, the bathing, and the quiet society of two or three friends, have composed and revived your spirits. Present my love to Sarah, and compliments to Miss Carter, &c. Adieu. Give me a speedy and satisfactory line.*

I am
Most truly yours,
E. GIBBON.

P.S.—You will find in Downing Street the *Histoire des Voyages* and the musical clock. During my absence I entrust them both to your care, but I desire that neither of them may be removed to Sheffield Place. You must direct to Downing Street, which I shall occupy next Monday.

474.

To his Stepmother.

Downing Street, Monday, Sept. 8th, 1783.

DEAR MADAM,

I am confined to this place (a better place than Dover) by the winds, and they likewise detain two Flanders mails by which I expect a letter from Deyverdun. I thought this advertisement necessary for fear you should suppose me tossing on the seas. I hope to get away by Friday, but you may rest assured that both for your sake and my own I will take very good care of my person.

I am, Dear Madam,
Ever yours,
E. GIBBON.

475.

To Lord Sheffield.

Downing Street, September 8th, 1783.

THE PEACE OF VERSAILLES.

*As we are not unconscious of each other's feelings, I shall only say, that I am glad you did not go alone into Sussex. An American rebel to dispute with, gives a diversion to uneasy spirits, and I heartily wished for such a friend or adversary during the remainder of the day. No letter from Deyverdun; the post is arrived, but two Flanders mails are due. Æolus does not seem to approve of my designs, and there is little merit in waiting till Friday. I should wait with more reluctance, did I think there was much chance of success. I dine with Craufurd, and if anything is decided will send an extraordinary Gazette. You have obliged me beyond expression, by your kindness to Aunt Kitty; she will drink her afternoon tea at Sheffield next Friday. For my sake, Lady S. will be kind to the old Lady, who will not be troublesome, and will vanish at the first idea of Brighton; has not that salubrious air already produced some effects? Peace will be proclaimed to-morrow; odd! as War was never declared. The buyers of stock seem as indifferent as yourself about the definitive Treaty. Tell Maria, that though you had forgotten the *Annales de la Vertu*, I have directed them to be sent, but know nothing of their plan or merit. Adieu. When you see Mylady, say everything tender and friendly to her. I did not know how much I loved her. She may depend upon my keeping a separate, though not, perhaps, a very frequent account with her. *Apropos*, I think aunt Kitty has a secret wish to lye in my room; if it is not occupied, she might be indulged. Once more, adieu.*

E. G.

476.

To Lord Sheffield.

Tuesday Night [September 9], 1783.

It is singular, or rather it is natural that we should both entertain the same idea, for I give you my word that I was very near running down to Sheffield and staying there till Wednesday. Another day, and no letter from Deyverdun; indeed the two Flanders mails are still due. I have written to him this post. To-morrow Crauford dines again with the Secretary, and the business is to be decided. I find Storer is now likely to succeed not so much from the zeal and activity of Lord's N.'s friendship, as because he could resign a place which Fox wants for Colonel Stanhope, to whom however he has given Thomas's company in the Guards. I will write another line to-morrow. Adieu.

E. G.

Newton, I think with reasons postpones any special power of Attorney till we are farther advanced, either with Cromwell's Client or some other purchaser: he says there will be sufficient time to send and return one while the title is under examination.

477.

To Lord Sheffield.

Thursday, September 11th, 1783.

*The scheme (which you may impart to My lady) is compleatly vanished, and I support the disappointment with Heroic patience. Crauford goes down to Chatsworth to-morrow, and Fox does not recommend my waiting for the event; yet the appointment is not yet declared, and I am ignorant of the name and merits of my successful competitor. Is it not wonderful that I am still in suspense, without a letter from Deyverdun? No, it is not wonderful, since no Flanders mail is arrived: to-morrow three will be due. I am therefore in a miserable state of doubt and anxiety; in a much better house indeed than my own, but without books, or business, or society. I send or call two or three times each day to Elmsley's, and can only say that I shall fly the next day, Saturday, Sunday, &c. after I have got my *quietus.**

Aunt Kitty was delighted with Mylady's letter; at her age, and in her situation, every kind attention is pleasant. I took my leave this morning; and as I did not wish to repeat the scene, and thought she would be better at Sheffield, I suffer her to go to-morrow. Your discretion will communicate or withhold any tidings of my departure or delay as you judge most expedient. Christie writes to you this post; he talks, in his rhetorical way, of many purchasers. Do you approve of his fixing a day for the Auction? To us he talked of an indefinite advertisement.

*No news, except that we keep Negapatnam. The other day the French Ambassador mentioned that the Empress of Russia, a precious B——, had proposed to ratify the principles of the armed neutrality, by a definitive treaty, but that the French, obliging creatures! had declared that they would neither propose nor accept an article so disagreable to England. Grey Elliot was pleased with your attention, and says you are a perfect master of the subject. Adieu. If I could be sure that no mail would arrive to-morrow, I would run down with my aunt. My heart is not light. I embrace My lady with true affection, but I need not repeat it.

E. G.

478.

To Lord Sheffield.

Downing Street, Friday, September 12th, 1783.

DEPARTURE DELAYED.

*Since my departure is near, and inevitable, you and Lady S. will be rather sorry than glad to hear that I am detained, day after day, by the caprice of the winds. *Three* Flanders mails are now due. I know not how to move without the final letter from Deyverdun, which I expected a fortnight ago, and my fancy (perfectly unreasonable) begins to create strange fantoms. A state of suspense is painful, but it will be alleviated by the short notes which I mean to write, and hope to receive, every post. A separation has some advantages, though they are purchased with bitter pangs; among them is the pleasure of knowing how dear we are to our friends, and how dear they are to us. It will be a kind office to soothe Aunt Kitty's sorrows, and to "rock the cradle of declining age." She will be vexed to hear that I am not yet gone; but she is reasonable and chearful.* I am grateful for Maria's attention to me or my corpse. Adieu.

Most truly yours,
E. G.

479.

To Lord Sheffield.

Downing Street, Saturday, September 13th, 1783.

Enfin la Bombe a crevé.—The three Flanders mails are arrived this day, but without any letters from Deyverdun. Most incomprehensible! After many adverse reflections, I have finally resolved to begin my journey on Monday; a heavy journey, with much apprehension, and much regret. Yet I consider, 1st, That if he is alive and well, (an unpleasant *if,*) scarcely any event can have happened to disappoint our mutual wishes; and, 2dly, That, supposing the very worst, even that worst would not overthrow my general plan of living abroad, though it would derange my hopes of a quiet and delightful establishment with my friend.* Upon the whole, without giving way to melancholy fears, my reason conjectures that his indolence thought it superfluous to write any more, that it was my business to act and move, and his duty to sit still and receive me with open arms. At least he is well informed of my operations, as I wrote to him (since his last) July 31st, from Sheffield-place; August 19th; and this week, September 9th. The two first have already reached him.

As I shall not arrive at, or depart from, Dover till Tuesday night, (alas! I may be confined there a week,) you will have an opportunity, by dispatching a parcel *per* post to Elmsly's, to catch the Monday's post. Let us improve these last short moments: I want to hear how poor Kitty behaves. I am really impatient to be gone. It is provoking to be so near, yet so far from, certain persons. *London is a desert.* I dine to-morrow with the Paynes, who pass through. Lord Loughborough was not returned from Buxton yesterday.* Sir H[enry] C[linton] found me out this morning; with very little trouble My Lady might rival Betsy; he talks with rapture of visits to be made at Sheffield, and returned at Brighton. I envy him those visits more than the red ribbon* or the glory of his American campaigns.

Adieu.

480.

To his Stepmother.

Downing Street, Saturday, Sept. 13th, 1783.

MY DEAR MADAM,

You will be surprized to receive another letter from this place, but I have been detained this whole week unpleasantly enough by the daily expectation of a Flanders mail, though considering the state of the winds and weather it is better to be detained in a good house in Downing Street, than at the Ship at Dover. My departure is now finally determined for Monday morning, and I travel with my own horses. I shall lye at Sittingbourne, and not reach Dover till the afternoon of the next day; my farther progress must depend on the caprice of Neptune and Æolus, but the moment I have escaped from their power I will send a line by the return of the packet.

Lord Sheffield spent two or three days with me in his way from Coventry races into Sussex.

KINDNESS OF THE SHEFFIELDS.

Nothing could exceed, both in word and deed, his kindness and that of his consort on the present occasion, which has indeed shewn me how dear I am to my real friends. They have taken poor Mrs. Porten down to Sheffield, and I am sure will contrive every thing that can support and dissipate her spirits. They both expressed to me in the most obliging terms how glad they should have been of a visit from you; but your mind is firmer, and your prospects are far more chearful than those of my poor Aunt. Adieu, my Dear Madam; though I go with pleasure from party and dependence to a Philosophical retreat, I cannot measure without a sigh the difference (in some degree imaginary) between one, and six, hundred miles.

Ever yours,
E. G.

481.

To Lord Sheffield.

Dover, Wednesday, September 17th, 1783,
Ten o'clock in the morning.

*The best laws are useless without proper guardians. Your letter *per* Sunday's post is not arrived, (as its fate is uncertain, and irrevocable, you must repeat any material article,) but that *per* Monday's post reached me last night. Oliver is more insolent than his grandfather; but you will cope with one, and would not have been much afraid of the other. Last night the wind was so high, that the vessel could not stir from the harbour; this day it is brisk and fair. We start about one o'clock, are flattered with the hope of making Calais harbour by the same tide, in three hours and a half; but any delay will leave the disagreable option of a tottering boat or a tossing night. What a cursed thing to live in an island! this step is more awkward than the whole journey. The Triumvirate of this memorable embarkation will consist of the grand Gibbon, Henry Laurens, Esquire, President of Congress, and Mr. Secretary, Colonel, Admiral, Philosopher Thompson, attended by three horses, who are not the most agreeable fellow-passengers. If we survive, I will finish and seal my letter at Calais. Our salvation shall be ascribed to the prayers of My lady and Aunt; for I do believe they both pray.

Boulogne, Thursday morning, ten o'clock.

Instead of Calais, the wind has driven us to Boulogne, where we landed in the evening, with much noise and difficulty. The night is passed, the Customhouse is dispatched, the post-horses are ordered, and I shall start about eleven o'clock. I had not the least symptom of sea sickness, while my companions were spewing round me. Laurens has read the pamphlet, and thinks it has done much mischief—a good sign! Adieu, the Captain is impatient. I shall reach Lausanne by the end of next week, but may probably write on the road.*

482.

To Lord Sheffield.

Langres, September 23rd, 1783.

*Let the Geographical Maria place before you the map of France, and trace my progress as far as this place, through the following towns: Boulogne, (where I was forced to land,) St. Omer, (where I recovered my road,) Aire, Bethune, Douay, Cambray, St. Quentin, La Fère, Laon, Rheims, Chalons, St. Dizier, and Langres, where I have just finished my supper. The Inns, in general, more agreable to the palate, than to the sight or smell. But, with some short exceptions of time and place, I have enjoyed good weather and good roads, and at the end of the ninth day, I feel so little fatigued, that the journey appears no more than a pleasant airing. I have generally conversed with Homer and Lord Clarendon, often with Caplin and Muff; sometimes with the French postillions—of the above-mentioned animals the least rational. To-morrow I lye at Besançon, and, according to the arrangement of post or hired horses, shall either sup at Lausanne on Friday, or dine there Saturday. I feel some suspense and uneasiness with regard to Deyverdun; but in the scale both of reason and constitution, my hopes preponderate very much above my fears. From Lausanne I will immediately write. I embrace my lady. If Aunt Kitty's gratitude and good breeding have not driven her away upon the first whisper of Brighton, she will share this intelligence; if she is gone, a line from you would be humane and attentive. "*Monsieur, les Chevaux seront prêts à cinq heures.*"—Adieu. I am going into an excellent bed, about six feet high from the ground.*

483.

To Lord Sheffield.

Lausanne, September 30th, 1783.

*I arrived safe in harbour last Saturday, the 27th instant, about ten o'Clock in the morning; but as the post only goes out twice a week, it was not in my power to write before this day. Except one day, between Langres and Besançon, which was laborious enough, I finished my easy and gentle airing without any fatigue, either of mind or body. I found Deyverdun well and happy, but much more happy at the sight of a friend, and the accomplishment of a scheme which he had so long and impatiently desired. His garden, terrace, and *park*, have even exceeded the most sanguine of my expectations and remembrances; and you yourself cannot have forgotten the charming prospect of the Lake, the mountains, and the declivity of the Pays de Vaud. But as human life is perpetually checquered with good and evil, I have found some disappointments on my arrival. The easy nature of Deyverdun, his indolence, and his impatience, had prompted him to reckon too positively that his house would be vacant at Michaelmas; some unforeseen difficulties have arisen, or have been discovered when it was already too late, and the consummation of our hopes is (I am much afraid) postponed to next spring. At first I was knocked down by the unexpected thunderbolt, but I have gradually been reconciled to my fate, and have granted a free and gracious pardon to my friend. As his own apartment, which afforded me a temporary shelter, is much too narrow for a settled residence, we hired for the winter a convenient ready furnished apartment in the nearest part of the Rue de Bourg, whose back door leads in three steps to the terrace and garden, as often as a tolerable day shall tempt us to enjoy their beauties; and this arrangement has even its advantage, of giving us time to deliberate and provide, before we enter on a larger and more regular establishment.

THE ABBÉ RAYNAL.

But this is not the sum of my misfortunes; hear, and pity! The day after my arrival (Sunday) we had just finished a very temperate dinner, and intended to begin a round of visits on foot, *chapeau sous le bras*, when, most unfortunately, Deyverdun proposed to show me something in the Court; we boldly and successfully ascended a flight of stone steps, but in the descent I missed my footing, and strained, or sprained, my ancle in a painful manner. My old latent Enemy, (I do not mean the Devil,) who is always on the watch, has made an ungenerous use of his advantage, and I much fear that my arrival at Lausanne will be marked with a fit of the Gout, though it is quite unnecessary that the intelligence or suspicion should find its way to Bath. Yesterday afternoon I lay, or at least sat, in state to receive visits, and at the same moment my room was filled with four different nations. The loudest of these nations was the single voice of the Abbé Raynal, who, like your friend, has chosen this place for the azylum of freedom and history. His conversation, which might be very agreable, is intolerably loud, peremptory, and insolent; and you would imagine that he alone was the Monarch and legislator of the World.

Adieu. I embrace My lady, and the infants.* Inform Maria that my accident has prevented me from looking out for a proper spot for my interment. *With regard to the important transactions for which you are constituted Plenipotentiary, I expect with some impatience, but with perfect confidence, the result of your labours. You may remember what I mentioned of my conversation with Charles Fox about the place of Minister at Bern: I have talked it over with Deyverdun, who does not dislike the idea, provided this place was allowed to be my Villa, during at least two-thirds of the Year; but for my part, I am sure that* a thousand guineas *is worth more than Ministerial friendship and gratitude; so I am inclined to think, that they are preferable to an office which would be procured with difficulty, enjoyed with constraint and expence, and lost, perhaps, next April, in the annual Revolutions of our domestic Government. Again Adieu.*

484.

To his Stepmother.

Lausanne, September 30th, 1783.

DEAR MADAM,

As I know you prefer a speedy to a long letter, I write by the first post to inform you that after an easy and pleasant journey of thirteen days, I arrived here on Saturday the 27th instant in perfect health both of mind and body. You will not expect that I should inform you how far my expectations are answered in any or in every respect. The very novelty and beauty of the scene would give a pleasing colour to every object, and the satisfaction of meeting and conversing with an old friend like Deyverdun is alone worth a journey of six hundred miles. He has not forgot his obligations to you, and begs me in his name to say everything that is kind and grateful. We have been so compleatly taken up and satisfied with each other that as yet I have scarcely stirred from home, and as this is the season of the vintage the town is remarkably empty. But the weather is good, and our terrace now affords such a prospect of the lake and mountains, as cannot perhaps be equalled in the World. I most sincerely wish that you were walking there, and you would soon forget the more humble beauties of your Belvidere. But I must content myself with the hope, and not a distant hope, of seeing you again on the hills, not of Switzerland but of Bath.

I am, Dear Madam,
Ever yours,
E. G.

That we may never resume the indelicate subject, I shall say once for all that every Christmas and Midsummer Day, without expecting any draught from me, you need only send your commands to Messrs. Gosling, Bankers in Fleet Street, as thus, Pay to Mr. —— the sum of one hundred and fifty pounds, and place to the account of E. G., Esq., for D. G. They are properly instructed.

485.

To Lady Sheffield.

Lausanne, October 28th, 1783.

*The progress of my Gout is in general so regular, and there is so much uniformity in the history of its decline and fall, that I have hitherto indulged my laziness, without much shame or remorse, without supposing that you would be very anxious for my safety, which has been sufficiently provided for by the triple care of my friend Deyverdun, my humbler friend Caplin, and a very conversable Physician (not the famous Tissot), whose ordinary fee is ten Batz, about fifteen pence English. After the usual encrease and decrease of my member (for it has been confined to the injured foot), the Gout has retired in good order, and the remains of weakness, which obliged me to move on the rugged pavement of Lausanne with a stick, or rather small crutch, are to be ascribed to the sprain, which might have been a much more serious business.

THE CHARMS OF LAUSANNE.

As I have now spent a month at Lausanne, you will inquire with much curiosity, more kindness, and some mixture of spite and malignity, how far the place has answered my expectations, and whether I do not repent of a resolution which has appeared so rash and ridiculous to my ambitious friends? To this question, however natural and reasonable, I shall not return an immediate answer, for two reasons: 1. *I have not yet made a fair tryal.* The disappointment and delay with regard to Deyverdun's house, will confine us this winter to lodgings, rather convenient than spacious or pleasant. I am only beginning to recover my strength and liberty, and to look about on persons and things; the greatest part of those persons are in the Country taken up with their Vintage: my books are not yet arrived, and, in short, I cannot look upon myself as settled in that comfortable way which you and I understand and relish. Yet the weather has been heavenly, and till this time, the end of October, we enjoy the brightness of the sun, and somewhat gently complain of its immoderate heat. 2. If I should be too sanguine in expressing my satisfaction in what I have done, you would ascribe that satisfaction to the novelty of the scene, and the inconstancy of man; and I deem it far more safe and prudent to postpone any positive declaration, till I am placed by experience beyond the danger of repentance and recantation.

Yet of one thing I am sure, that I possess in this Country, as well as in England, the best cordial of life, a sincere, tender, and sensible friend, adorned with the most valuable and pleasant qualities both of the heart and head. The inferior enjoyments of leisure and society are likewise in my power; and in the short excursions which I have hitherto made, I have commenced or renewed my acquaintance with a certain number of persons, more especially women, (who, at least in France and this country, are undoubtedly superior to our prouder sex,) of rational minds and elegant manners. I breakfast alone, and have declared that I receive no visits in the morning, which you will easily suppose is devoted to study. I find it impossible, without inconvenience, to defer my dinner beyond two o'Clock. We have got a very good Woman Cook. Deyverdun, who is somewhat of an Epicurean Philosopher, understands the management of a table, and we frequently invite a guest or two to share our luxurious, but not extravagant repasts. The afternoons are (and will be much more so hereafter) devoted to society, and I shall find it necessary to play at cards much oftener than in London: but I do not dislike that way of passing a couple of hours, and I shall not be ruined at Shilling whist. As yet I have not supped, but in the Course of the winter I must sometimes sacrifice an evening abroad, and in exchange I hope sometimes to steal a day at home, without going into Company.*

A *PENSION* FOR MISS HOLROYD.

As every idea which relates to you and yours is always uppermost in my mind, I have not forgot our schemes to finish in this School of freedom and equality the education of the future Baroness of Roscommon, and Deyverdun agrees with me in thinking that a couple of years spent at Lausanne would be of infinite service to her. But as I am convinced that she has attained the age in which it would be the most beneficial and the least dangerous, I would recommend speedy and decisive measures. If you could be satisfied with an ordinary plan (I hate the name and idea of a boarding school) Maria might be entrusted to a Madame Ostervald (Lord S. knew and liked her under the name of Mademoiselle Bourgeois), who educates with reputation and success several young ladies of fashion. But as your daughter deserves a special and superior guide, we have cast our eyes (without knowing whether she would accept it) on a lady, who, by her birth, station, connections, understanding, knowledge, and temper, appears, in the judgment of Deyverdun, her particular friend, to be not unworthy to supply your place. She lives next door to us, and *our* eyes and ears (two pair) would be continually open. If you found an opportunity of sending Maria in the spring with any proper travellers, We would meet her at Geneva, Lyons, &c. With such a hostage, I should be sure of seeing Lord S. and yourself, and a year's trial would determine you to leave or remove her. If you listen seriously to this idea, I will send you more particular accounts, and take every proper step. If you cannot resolve, accept this *bavardage* as a proof of love and solicitude.

*I have all this time been talking to Lord S.; I hope that he has dispatched my affairs, and it would give me pleasure to hear that I am no longer member for Lymington, nor Lord of *Lenborough*. Adieu. I feel every day that the distance serves only to make me think with more tenderness of the persons whom I love.*

On reading what I have written, I must laugh at my sudden and peremptory recommendations about Maria, yet I coolly think it the best scheme. You oblige me beyond expression by your kindness to Aunt Kitty. N.B. I always desire double letters.—I find I shall have some commissions for you (Sheffelina), but I do not suppose you in town till after Christmas.

486.

To Lord Sheffield.

Lausanne, November 14th, 1783.

*Last Tuesday, November 11th, after plaguing and vexing yourself all the morning about some business of your fertile creation, you went to the House of Commons, and passed the afternoon, the evening, and perhaps the night, without sleep or food, stifled in a close room by the heated respiration of six hundred politicians, inflamed by party and passion, and tired of the repetition of dull nonsense, which, in that illustrious assembly, so far outweighs the proportion of reason and eloquence. On the same day, after a studious morning, a friendly dinner, and a chearful assembly of both sexes, I retired to rest at eleven o'Clock, satisfied with the past day, and certain that the next would afford me the return of the same quiet and rational enjoyments. *Which has the better bargain?*

Seriously, I am every hour more grateful to my own judgment and resolution, and only regret that I so long delayed the execution of a favourite plan, which I am convinced is the best adapted to my character and inclinations. Your conjecture of the revolutions of my face, when I heard that the house was for this winter inaccessible, is probable, but false. I bore my disappointment with the temper of a Sage, and only use it to render the prospect of next year still more pleasing to my imagination. You are likewise mistaken, in imputing my fall to the awkwardness of my limbs. The same accident might have happened to Slingsby himself, or to any *Hero* of the age, the most distinguished for his *bodily activity*. I have now resumed my entire strength, and walk with caution, yet with speed and safety, through the streets of this mountainous city. After a month of the finest autumn I ever saw, the *Bise* made me feel my old acquaintance; the weather is now milder, and this present day is dark and rainy, not much better than what you probably enjoy in England. The town is comparatively empty, but the Noblesse are returning every day from their Chateaux, and I already perceive that I shall have more reason to complain of dissipation than of dulness.

OLD ACQUAINTANCES AT LAUSANNE.

As I told Lady S., I am afraid of being too rash and hasty in expressing my satisfaction; but I must again repeat, that appearances are extremely favourable. I am sensible that general praise conveys no distinct ideas, but it is very difficult to enter into particulars where the individuals are unknown, or indifferent to our correspondent. You have forgotten the *old* Generation, and in twenty years a new one is grown up. Death has swept many from the World, and chance or choice has brought many to this place. If you enquire after your old acquaintance Catherine Crousaz, you must be told, that she is solitary, uggly, blind, and universally forgotten. Your later flame, and our common Goddess, the Eliza, passed a month at the Inn. The greatest part of the time either in fit or taking the air on horseback. She came to consult Tissot, and was acquainted with Cerjat, but she appears to have made no conquests, and no fountain has been dedicated to her memory.*

And now to business. By this time those who would give me nothing else have nobly rewarded my merit with the Chiltern Hundreds. I retire without a sigh from the Senate, and am only impatient to hear that you have received the sum, which your *modesty* was content to take for my seat. Sir Andrew is an honourable man, yet I am satisfied that you have not neglected any of the necessary precautions. It will be advisable to have the odd hundred in Gosling's shop and to pay the thousand to Messrs. Darrel, Winchester Street, who will vest it for me in the three per cent. We must take advantage of this stupendous fall of the Stocks, which amazes and frightens many poor souls here who apprehend that poor old England is on the brink of ruin. But this same circumstance is equally hostile to the sale of Lenborough, and though £200 or 300 a year and some part of my tranquillity depend on being released from the claws of my Mortgagee, yet I am much afraid that in the present state of things an *equal* purchaser will not easily be found. But your native vigour excited by friendship will remove mountains and perform impossibilities. My salvation would be more assured if I had half as much faith in any body else.

*With regard to meaner cares, these are two, which you can and will undertake. 1. As I have not renounced my Country, I should be glad to hear of your Parliamentary squabbles, which may be done with small trouble and expence. After an interesting debate, Miss Firth or My lady in due time may cut the speeches from Woodfall. You will write or dictate any curious anecdote, and the whole, inclosed in a letter, may be dispatched to Lausanne. 2. A set of Wedgewood China, which we talked of in London, and which would be most acceptable here. As you have a *sort* of a taste, I leave to your own choice the colour and the pattern; but as I have the inclination and means to live very handsomely *here*, I desire that the size and number of things may be adequate to a plentiful table.

If you see Lord North, assure him of my gratitude; had he been a more successful friend, I should now be drudging at the board of Customs, or vexed with business in the amiable society of *the Duke of M[anchester].* To Lord Loughborough present a more affectionate sentiment; I am satisfied with his intention to serve me, if I had not been in such a fidget. I am sure you will not fail, while you are in town, to visit and comfort poor Aunt Kitty. I wrote to her on my first arrival, and she may be assured that I will not neglect her.* Any occasional hints from Bath will be wellcome, but nothing from hence must ever transpire. *To My lady I say nothing; we have now our private Correspondence, into which the eye of an husband should not be permitted to intrude. I am really satisfied with the success of the Pamphlet; not only because I have a sneaking kindness for the author, but as it shows me that plain sense, full information, and warm spirit, are still acceptable to the World. You talk of Lausanne as a place of retirement; yet from the situation and freedom of the Pays de Vaud, all nations, and all extraordinary characters, are astonished to meet each other. The Abbé Raynal, the grand Gibbon, and Mercier, author of the Tableau de Paris, have been in the same room. The other day, the Prince and Princess de Ligne, the Duke and Dutchess d'Ursel, &c. came from Brussels on purpose (literally true) to act a comedy at d'Hermanches's, in the Country. He was dying, and could not appear; but we had Comedy, ball, and supper. The event seems to have revived him; for that great man is fallen from his ancient glory, and his nearest relations refuse to see him. I told you of poor Catherine's deplorable state; but Madame de Mesery, at the age of sixty-nine, is still handsome. Adieu.*

487.

To Lord Sheffield.

Lausanne, December 20th, 1783.

I have received both your Epistles; and as any excuse will serve a man who is at the same time very busy and very idle, I patiently expected the second, before I entertained any thoughts of answering the first.

SALE OF LENBOROUGH.

And so poor Lenborough is at length sold; poor indeed I may call, for I must confess that I am most woefully disappointed in the price. Without going back to the Golden Age in which we looked down with disdain on the round twenty, you may remember that even this summer we scarcely allowed our most timid expectations to sink below seventeen, and this sum for which it is now sold falls £1400 short of that amount, without deducting the promised gratuity to Christie.

You might indeed reckon on my impatience to be delivered from a heavy burden both of fortune and of mind which I have often deplored with so much energy, but that burthen was much alleviated by my *rational* retreat from a scene of tumult and expence, and I always understood that we should take the chance of the winter and of the rise of stocks before we tryed the decisive and almost irrevocable measure of an auction. However the blow is struck, and I have already reconciled my mind to this new loss. I should have been afraid of writing thus much to Hugonin, but your nerves are more firmly strung, and through these expressions of disappointment, you discern, that instead of being displeased with your conduct, however inadequate to my hopes, I feel myself inexpressibly obliged to your pure fervent and persevering friendship. You will watch over the conclusion of this business, and whatever steps on my side may be necessary shall be diligently executed as soon as you send me the proper papers and instruction. When the money is paid (in February) you will leave the residue, a wretched fragment, in the hands of the Goslings on my account. I have not absolutely determined how I shall employ it. Something must be done in the way of annuity, and the French funds which are very fashionable in this country are wonderfully tempting to a poor man by the high interest, but I am aware of their slippery foundation, and you may be assured that I shall do nothing of that kind without full and mature and even cautious investigation. For the same reason, instead of paying the money to Darrel, I could wish that the £1100 or £1000 for Lymington (for we must not haggle about trifles) may likewise slumber for a little while in the shop in Fleet Street. Yet I should not be sorry to hear that the direction comes too late and that they are already more actively employed.

Sure I have been particularly unfortunate in my connections of business, for in good truth, Winton, Lovegrove, and Sir H. Burrard are more than should fall to the share of one man.

PRIDE IN FOX'S FAME.

Yet the last mentioned beast is no fool, and when that affectionate kinsman has squeezed the Minister to the utmost, he will be satisfied with *all* that he can get, and will not suffer his farm to lye fallow without being of any value either to landlord or tenant. *I therefore conclude, on every principle of common sense, that, before this moment, his own interest and that of the Government, stimulated by your active zeal, have already expelled me from the House, to which, without regret, I bid an everlasting farewell. The agreeable hour of five o'Clock in the morning, at which you commonly retire, does not tend to revive my attachment; but if you add the soft hours of your morning committee, in the discussion of taxes, customs, frauds, smugglers, &c., I think I should beg to be released and quietly sent to the Gallies, as a place of leisure and freedom. Yet I do not depart from my general principles of toleration; some animals are made to live in the water, others on the Earth, many in the air, and some, as it is now believed, even in fire. Your present hurry of Parliament I perfectly understand; when opposition make the attack—

——Horæ

Momento cita mors venit, aut victoria læta.

But when the Minister brings forward strong and decisive measure, he at length prevails; but his progress is retarded at every step, and in every stage of the bill, by a pertinacious, though unsuccessful, minority. I am not sorry to hear of the splendour of Fox; I am proud, in a foreign Country, of his fame and abilities, and our little animosities are extinguished by my retreat from the English Stage. With regard to the substance of the business, I scarcely know what to think: the vices of the Company, both in their persons and their constitution, were manifold and manifest; the danger was imminent, and such an Empire, with thirty millions of subjects, was not to be lost for trifles. Yet, on the other hand, the faith of Charters, the rights of property! I hesitate and tremble. Such an innovation would at least require that the remedy should be as certain as the evil, and the proprietors may perhaps insinuate, that *they* were as competent Guardians of their own affairs, as either *George North or L. Lewisham.* Their acting without a salary seems childish, and their not being removable by the Crown is a strange and dangerous precedent.

But enough of politics, which I now begin to view through a thin, cold, distant cloud, yet not without a reasonable degree of curiosity and patriotism. From the papers (especially when you add an occasional slice of the Chronicle) I shall be amply informed of facts and debates; from you I expect the causes rather than the events, the true springs of action, and those interesting anecdotes which seldom ascend the garret of a Fleet-Street editor.

LORD NORTH'S INSIGNIFICANCE.

You say that many friends (alias acquaintance) have expressed curiosity and concern; I should not wish to be immediately forgot. That others (you once mentioned Gerard Hamilton) condemn Government for suffering the departure of a man who might have done them some credit and some service, perhaps as much as Antony Storer himself. To you, in the confidence of friendship, and without either pride or resentment, I will fairly own that I am somewhat of Gerard's opinion; and if I did not compare it with the rest of his character, I should be astonished that Lord N[orth] suffered me to depart, without even a civil answer to my letter. Were I capable of hating a man, whom it is not easy to hate, I should find myself most amply revenged by the insignificance of the creature in this mighty revolution of India, his own peculiar department. But the happy Souls in paradise are susceptible only of love and pity, and though Lausanne is not a paradise, more especially in Winter, I do assure you, in sober prose, that it has hitherto fulfilled, and even surpassed, my warmest expectation. Yet I often cast a look toward Sheffield-place, where you now repose, if you can repose, during the Christmas recess.

Embrace My Lady, the young Baroness, and the gentle Louisa, and insinuate to your silent Consort, that separate letters require separate answers. Had I an air balloon, the great topic of modern Conversation, I would call upon you till the meeting of parliament. *Vale.**

488.

To his Stepmother.

Lausanne, December 27th, 1783.

DEAR MADAM,

Were we strangers to each other, I might amuse myself with deducing the causes of my silence; the long expectation of your answer and the propriety of taking a clear view of the ground on which I stood before I could transmit a just and satisfactory account of my situation. But it will be better to acknowledge that the old man, my ancient and habitual enemy, touched me with his wand, and that I am just awakening from the enchanted slumber. My silence however may be fairly interpreted as an evidence of content. Indeed, my Dear Madam, I *am* happy, with as few exceptions as the condition of human Nature will allow, and among the first of these exceptions I reckon the interval of time and space which separates me from Bath.

Since I formed and executed this plan of retiring into Switzerland I have not once repented, I have not felt a single moment of disappointment, and my only regret is the having so long neglected to obey the dictates of my reason; a more early obedience would have saved me some years of dependance, of anxiety, and of indiscretion. I have always valued far above the external gifts of rank and fortune two qualities for which I stand indebted to the indulgence of Nature, a strong and constant passion for letters, and a propensity to view and to enjoy every object in the most favourable light. The first has composed the daily happiness of my life and ensured the perpetual enjoyment of the most pleasing labours; the success of my works has given me a pure and extensive, perhaps a permanent reputation, and if the more substantial rewards have too easily slipped through my hands, I must ascribe their loss to the obstinacy with which I struggled to support a style of life to which the remains of my fortune were no longer adequate.

My propensity to be happy has been exercised on the most unfavourable materials; you have commonly seen a smile on my conversation and my letters, and as you never distrusted the sincerity of my professions you must have been surprized at the success of my endeavours. Yet what could be more adverse to my character than the life which for some years past I have led in London. With the warmest love of independence I have stooped the slave of Ministers. Without talents, or at least without resolution for a public life, I have consumed days and nights a silent spectator of noisy and factious debates. Conscious that true happiness is founded on œconomy, the disorderly state of my affairs has never allowed me to measure my income and my expence, and I have never dared to cast my eyes on the disbursment of the past or the supplies of the future year. How different is the prospect which I now enjoy. I find myself in a state of perfect independence and real affluence, and if I continue to enjoy a tolerable state of health, I cannot easily discover what event is capable of disturbing my tranquillity.

Among the ingredients of happiness you will agree with me in giving the preference to a sincere and sensible friend; and though you are not acquainted with half his merit, you will believe that Deyverdun answers that description. Perhaps two persons so perfectly fitted for each other were never created by Nature and education. Our studies, occupations, and reflexions have been sufficiently various to ensure a constant fund of entertainment; the lights and shades of our respective characters are happily blended; freedom and confidence are the basis of our union, and a friendship of thirty years has taught us to enjoy and to support each other. You have often read and heard the descriptions of this delightful Country, the banks of the lake of Geneva, and indeed it surpasses all description. A stranger is struck with surprize and admiration, and it is endeared to me by the remembrance of my youth and the lively attachment which I have always retained for the place and the people. Our autumn has been beautiful, and the winter has not hitherto been severe, but the season of rural enjoyments is for some time suspended and our comforts are confined to the fireside. M. Deyverdun's house is spacious and convenient, and his garden, which spreads over a various and extensive spot, unites every beauty and advantage both of town and country. But into this paradise we are not yet introduced; the family to whom he had lent or let the larger part of the house have started some difficulties about the time of their removal, and till the month of March or April we are obliged to content ourselves with a convenient ready furnished lodging. When to this disappointment I add that my boxes of books which were sent through France still loiter on the road, you will confess that my felicity in the approaching year is more likely to encrease than to diminish.

DAILY LIFE AT LAUSANNE.

With regard to the daily enjoyments of life, which rolls away in a quiet uniform tenor, they are made to be felt rather than to be related. I rise before eight, and our mornings are commonly invisible to each other. At two (an hour somewhat too early) we dine, one, two, or three agreably very often enliven our board, which is served with decent elegance. From four to between six and seven we read some amusing book, play at chess, retire to our rooms, look into the Coffee house, or make visits. The assemblies are numerous, and I play my three rubbers at shilling or half-crown whist with tolerable pleasure. They end between nine and ten, and a bit of bread and cheese, with some friendly converse, sends us to bed about eleven. This sober plan is indeed interrupted by too frequent suppers, which I want resolution to refuse, though I behave with exemplary temperance. Instead of lolling in a coach I walk the streets at all hours wrapped in a fur Cloak— the exercise is wholesome, and in my life I never enjoyed more perfect health and spirits. May you be able to say as much! If vanity and Deyverdun do not deceive me, I am already a general favourite, and as likings or dislikes are commonly mutual, I am pleased with the manners of the place, and the worthy and amiable characters of many individuals of both sexes.

Believe me, My dear Madam, I never cast a look on the politics or the amusements of London. The mob of political connections or casual acquaintance are unworthy of the regret of a rational mind. But in the midst of a very pleasant life and society I am not insensible of my separation from yourself, the Sheffields, and two or three real friends. If their zeal should succeed in procuring me any adequate office which I could accept with propriety and exercise without disgust, if Government should find any situation in which I could do them service and myself credit, I would quit (perhaps with a sigh) this agreable retreat, and obey without hesitation the calls of friendship, of honour, and of my Country.

489.

To Lord Sheffield.

Lausanne, January 24th, 1784.

*Within two or three days after your last *gracious* Epistle, your Complaints were silenced, and your enquiries were satisfied, by an ample dispatch of four pages, which overflowed the inside of the cover, and in which I exposed my opinions of things in general, public as well as private, as they existed in my mind, in my state of ignorance and error, about the eighteenth or twentieth of last month. Within a week after that date I epistolised, in the same rich and copious strain, the two venerable females of Newman-street and the Belvidere, whose murmur must now be changed into songs of gratitude and applause. My correspondence with the holy Matron of Northamptonshire has been less lively and loquacious. You have not forgotten the Atheist's vindication of himself from the foul calumnies of pretended Christians; within a fortnight after his arrival at Lausanne, he communicated the joyful event to Mrs. G. She answered *per* return of post, both letters at the same time, and in very dutiful language, almost excusing her advice, which was intended for my spiritual, as well as temporal, good, and assuring me that *nobody should be able to injure me with her.* Unless the Saint is an hypocrite, possible enough, such an expression must convey a favourable and important meaning: at all events, it is worth giving *ourselves* some trouble about her, without indulging any sanguine expectations of inheritance.

DELIGHT IN LORD SHEFFIELD'S LETTERS.

So much for my females. With regard to my male Correspondents, you are the only one to whom I have given any signs of my existence, though I have formed many a generous resolution. Yet I am not insensible of the kind and friendly manner in which Lord Loughborough has distinguished me: he could have no inducements of interest, and now that I view the distant picture with an impartial eye, I am convinced that (for a Statesman) he was sincere though not earnest in his wishes to serve me. When you see *him*, the Paynes, Eden, Crauford, &c., tell them that I am well, happy, and ashamed. On your side, the zeal and diligence of your pen has surprized and delighted me, and your letters, at this interesting moment, are exactly such as I wished them to be—authentic anecdotes, and rational speculations, worthy of a man who acts a part in the great theatre, and who fills a seat, not only in the general Pandæmonium, but in the private council of the princes of the infernal Regions. With regard to the detail of Parliamentary operations, I must repeat my request to you, or rather to Miss Firth, who will now be on the spot, that she will write, not with her pen, but her Scissars, and that, after every debate which deserves to pass the Sea and the Mountains, she will dissect the faithful narrative of Woodfall, and send it off by the next post, as an agreeable supplement to the meagre accounts of our weekly papers.

The wonderful revolutions of last month have sounded to my ear more like the shifting scenes of a Comedy or Comic Opera, than like the sober events of real and modern history; and the irregularity of our winter posts, which sometimes retarded, and sometimes hastened, the arrival of the dispatches, has encreased the confusion of our ideas. Surely the Lord has blinded the eyes of Pharaoh and of his servants; the obstinacy of the last spring was nothing compared to the headstrong and headlong madness of this Winter. I expect with much impatience the first days of your meeting: the purity and integrity of the Coalition will suffer a fiery tryal; but if they are true to themselves and to each other, a Majority of the House of Commons must prevail; the rebellion of the young Gentlemen will be crushed, and the Masters will resume the Government of the School. After the address and answer, I have no conception that Parliament can be dissolved during the Session; but if the present Ministry can outlive the storm, I think the death Warrant will infallibly be signed in the summer. *Here* I blush for my Country, without confessing her shame. Fox acted like a man of Honour, yet surely his union with Pitt affords the only hope of salvation. How miserably are we wasting the season of peace!

THE SALE OF HIS SEAT.

I have written three pages before I come to my own busyness and feelings. In the first place, I most sincerely rejoyce that I left the ship, and swam ashore on a plank; the daily and hourly agitation in which I must have lived would have made me truly miserable, if I had obtained a place during pleasure, Storer's for instance. On the first news of the dissolution, I considered my seat as so totally and irrecoverably gone, that I have been less affected with Sir Harry's obstinacy.* Yet his absolute refusal to treat throws us at least for the present into a very uncomfortable situation, and besides the danger of shipwreck, every day's voyage diminishes the value of the ship and cargo. You say you are schemeless. I can think only of two expedients.

1. You know or can know Sir Andrew Hammond, who is a fair and honourable character. Talk over the business and kinsman fairly with him,

and tempt him to exert himself by the lowness of the price. I should consider even five or six hundred pounds as so much saved out of the fire, and a part of that sum would be most deliciously employed in the embellishment of my new habitation.

2. The other scheme is somewhat more delicate, yet I cannot esteem myself as bound to sacrifice my essential interest to that motley crew surnamed a Coalition, nor does this superiority in Parliament depend on the loss of *half-a-vote*. Perhaps the new Minister would give Sir Harry for his relations those scandalous jobs which our late friends more conscientiously refused, and many a Candidate would purchase their effectual recommendation by giving me the £1000 or £1200. On this occasion remember you are acting for a *poor* friend; dismiss a little of the spirit of faction and patriotism, and stoop to a prudential line of conduct, which in your own case you might possibly disdain. If you attempt the negociation you will easily find the proper instruments, but I should think James Grenville, the Lord of the Treasury, a safe and convenient channel, and I am persuaded that he would embrace the opportunity of serving his party and obliging *me* at the same time. In the business of Lenborough you may be active, but I can only be passive to convey a fair Estate, and to receive a miserable pittance of three thousand and some pounds. I hope nothing will happen to perplex the title or to delay the payment, and that the sum will be safely lodged for my account and in Gosling's hands before the end of February.

Perhaps you will abuse my prudence and patriotism, when I inform you, that I have already vested a part (30,000 Livres, about £1300) in the new loan of the King of France. I get eight per Cent. on the joint lives of Deyverdun and myself, besides thirty tickets in a very advantageous Lottery, of which the highest prize is an annuity of 40,000 Livres (£1700) a year. At this moment, the beginning of a peace, and probably a long peace, I think (and the World seems to think) the French funds at least as solid as our own. I have empowered my Agent, M. de Lessart, a capital banker at Paris, to draw upon Gosling for the money two months hence; and to avoid all accidents that may result from untoward delays, and mercantile churlishness, I expect that you will support my credit in Fleet-street with your own more respectable name. Moreover when Lenborough purchase money is paid, I wish it were possible to withhold £1000 or 1500 of their mortgage on our joint bond; I could employ it to my satisfaction at present, and should certainly repay it in three or four years on the conclusion of my History. Perhaps you will be better reconciled to my pecuniary arrangements by the proposal which I seriously make of purchasing Lee's farm at Buriton, if it can be obtained for 25 years' purchase after deducting the Land Tax. My interest without principal will be compensated by principal without interest (you remember Soame Jenyns's definition), and whatever becomes of my French Creditor, my Hampshire acres will be safe, compact, and in due time clear of all incumbrances. You may consult with Hugonin, propose and conclude.

What say you now? Am I not a wise Man? My letter is enormous, and the post on the wing. In a few days I will write to my Lady herself, and enter something more into the details of domestic life. Suffice it to say, that the scene becomes each day more pleasant and comfortable, and that I complain only of the dissipation of Lausanne. In the course of March or April we shall take possession of Deyverdun's house. My books, which by some strange neglect, did not leave Paris till the 3rd of this Month, will arrive in a few weeks; and I shall soon resume the continuation of my history, which I shall prosecute with the more vigour, as the completion affords me a distant prospect of a visit to England. A-propos, if the box which I left in Downing Street for the Swiss Carrier be not already departed, I hope Elmsley and yourself will give it a speedy and vigorous shove; when you see Elmsley ask him whether he has answered my letters: he is almost as lazy as myself. To my Lady's taste I shall entrust the Wedgewood's ware, which in the course of the spring or summer may accompany some other boxes of plate, linnen, books which I shall probably invoke. Adieu. I embrace my Lady and Infants.

Ever yours,
E. G.

490.

To Lord Sheffield.

Lausanne, February 2nd, 1784.

BARON!—

*After my last enormous dispatch, nothing can remain, except some small gleanings, or occasional hints; and thus in order: I am not conscious that any of your valuable MSS. have miscarried, or that I have omitted to answer any essential particulars. They stand in my Bureau carefully arranged, and docketed under the following dates; September 23, October 23, November 18, December 2, December 15, December 19, December 23, December 29, January 16, which last I have received this day, Febr. 2nd. For greater perspicuity, it will not be amiss (on either side) to number our future Epistles, by a conspicuous Roman character inscribed in the front, to which we may at any time refer. But instead of writing by Ostend, the shorter and surer way, especially on all occasions that deserve celerity, will be to direct them to my Banker, M. de Lessert, at Paris, who will forward them to me. Through Germany the passage by Sea is more uncertain, the roads worse, and the distance greater: we often complain of delay and irregularity at this interesting moment.

A FACTIOUS OPPOSITION.

By your last I find that you have boldly and generously opened a treaty with the Enemy, which I proposed with fear and hesitation. I impatiently expect the result; and again repeat, that *whatever* you can obtain* for the seat, *I shall consider it as so much saved out of the fire, &c. &c.* I shall then have completely secured a tranquil though humble station, and my personal happiness will no longer hang in suspense upon every change of Ministry, and every vote of Parliament. I am not surprized that you grow sulky: your free and liberal spirit must disdain a set of Men, whose aim is their own restoration to power, and whose means may affect the principles of the Constitution. *Do you remember Dunning's motion (in the year 80) to address the Crown against a dissolution of Parliament? a simple address we rejected, as an infringement on the prerogative; yet how far short of these strong Democratical measures, for which you have probably voted, as I should probably have done: such is the contagion of party. Fox drives most furiously, yet I should not be surprised if Pitt's moderation and character should insensibly win the Nation, and even the house, to espouse his cause.*

Lenborough is a melancholy and unpleasant subject. I am grateful for your endeavours, and lament that your reflexions on the value of land and money are but too true and sensible. Greatly as I have been disappointed in the price, I should now be sorry that anything should happen to break the bargain or to delay the payment. The surmise of such a possible event obliged me to repeat my commands that you would instruct Gosling (in your own name) to accept M. de Lessert's draught on the 20th of March for 30,000 French Livres (about £1300). Whatever you may think of my economical measures, the deed is done, and my honour is now pledged for the performance. The other sum, £1000 or 1500 of the Lenborough price which I wished to deduct from the mortgage, is a more indifferent speculation, which should only take place as far as it is agreable to all parties.

ARRIVAL OF HIS LIBRARY.

*Unless when I look back on England with a selfish or a tender regard, my hours roll away very pleasantly, and I can again repeat with truth, that I have not regretted a single moment the step which I have taken. We are now at the height of the Winter dissipation, and I am peculiarly happy when I can steal away from great assemblies, and suppers of twenty or thirty people, to a more private party, of some of those persons whom I begin to call my friends. Till we are settled in our house little can be expected on our side; yet I have already given two or three handsome dinners; and though everything is grown dearer, I am not alarmed at the general view of my expence. Deyverdun salutes you; and we are agreed that few married Couples are better entitled to the flitch of bacon than we shall be at the end of the year. When I had written about half this Epistle my books arrived; at our first meeting all was rapture and confusion, and two or three posts, from the 2nd to this day, the fourteenth, have been suffered to depart unnoticed. Your letter of the 27th of January, which was not received till yesterday, has again awakened me, and I thought the surest way would be to send off this single sheet without any farther delay.

I sincerely rejoice in the stability of Parliament; and the first faint dawn of reconciliation, which must however be effected by the equal balance of parties, rather than by the wisdom of the Country Gentlemen.*

MISS FIRTH,

After due salutations I trouble you with three or four Commissions, which I should not presume to offer to the greatness of the Baron or the delicacy of My Lady, but which I am persuaded you will chearfully undertake to oblige an old and sincere friend. 1. The employment which I have already hinted of your scissars in carving and despatching occasional debates from Woodfall's paper. 2. You are desired to call on Elmsley to ask him from time to time when he wrote to me last, and to urge him about taking and sending a Catalogue of my library with all convenient or inconvenient speed. 3. As many things will be deficient and as carriage will be less expensive than purchase, I propose sending for my plate, linnen, and China which now lye in Downing Street. My Agent Prendergast, an honest Cabinet maker, has received his instructions from Caplen, and I only desire that when he calls for that purpose he may have free permission to examine, pack, export, &c. A list was entrusted to Lord Sheffield which might be compared, copied, signed by him and transmitted by the post to me.

MY LADY!—

But it would be highly incongruous to begin my letter at the bottom of the page. Adieu, therefore, till next post.

491.

To Lord Sheffield.

Lausanne, March 2nd, 1784.

Your despatch of Feb. 13th arrived safe yesterday, March 1st, and notwithstanding the winter obstacles of seas and roads there is, upon the whole, more delay than danger in the transactions of the posts. I am glad that my last appearance in Downing Street put an end to a course of abuse; but in spite of my profound veneration for dreams and omens, I flatter myself that the silence of *one month* will not always be interpreted as a certain testimony that I no longer exist. Before I quit the subject of dispatches, one word on Miss Firth's scissors whose operation you have so prudently checked. Their use was not intended to be daily but occasional, on some great and memorable debate in the Pandemonium. Such occasions might occur twenty or thirty times in the winter, and at one shilling each time the annual expence might have exceeded *one* Guinea. I had computed that such expence might be supported; but if you persist in a contrary opinion, I must submit.

You had given me notice that the purchase money of Lenborough would be paid in February, and as the title was so perfectly clear, I suppose the surplus (far beyond the amount of the Paris draught) is already in Gosling's hands, payable to my order. In that case I shall have no obligations to them for obeying my Commands. But as I was aware of the delays of the law, and of their narrow mercantile temper, I did conceive that they might scruple paying Mr. de Lessert's draught for 30,000 Livres *some days* before my money was actually in their shop. The French banker will draw at sight, but instead of the 20th of March, I have postponed his draught till the 20th of April. In due time I shall write to the Goose to give them notice not to ask a favour. It is to you only that I wish to be obliged, and if you inform them that you consider yourself as answer for the money, I cannot suspect that even their grovelling spirit will have any scruples. If instead of your word they should require your bond, you can give it in five minutes, and a few days when the purchase money is paid will release you from the obligation. The general comparison of the French and English funds I have not time to discuss. I think them more able, and ourselves more willing, to support our national faith, but if a man must trust his money to the Ocean, I think it more advisable to embark it on two separate bottoms. With regard to the scruples of the two Tabbies, I can only say that first they need not know anything of the matter, and secondly they will be so good as to allow me to think and act for myself.

A HAPPY WINTER OF STUDY AND SOCIETY.

With regard to the purchase of Lee's farm I am serious, and if I am abused for my follies I must have some credit for the more rational parts of my Conduct. At least you will give me credit when I declare that in a happy winter of study and society I have not once regretted the noise of St. Stephen's and the tiresome suspense of your incomprehensible politics, but I do most sincerely regret the decreasing value of my Senatorial commodity. As soon as you can, and as much as you can, is the advice which you will follow without my having the trouble of giving it. But in the meanwhile do not let us quarrel about the disposal of the Bearskin. I am not mad, nor do I mean to settle here for life. A small part of the indefinite price of my seat was destined to embelish my habitation, and if, after enjoying the comforts three or four years, I should leave my friend's house somewhat improved, I can see nothing very extravagant in the idea.

Thus far I have written before the departure of the post, and am preparing to pass the evening at a private representation of the Barbier de Seville, which will be followed by a lively and excellent supper. Embrace My Lady. I think of her often, especially every post day. Say a kind word to Kitty, I shall soon dream that she is dead likewise.—Gosling need not be apprized of the object of the Paris draught.—The additional £1500 which I wished to retain is superfluous, as I have already observed in my last.

You are or will be astonished with some farther orders for the march of plate, linnen, books, &c., but I am of opinion that the present moment is worth enjoying, and that carriage, even double carriage, is less expensive than purchase.—You have nothing to do with Wedgewood, but I shall soon consult My lady. The spring is delightful. I often snatch a walk on Deyverdun's terrace, and visit my books, which are already deposited, but I fear the house will not be accessible before the first of May. He says I am not patient, I say he is indolent; you know that the most harmonious pairs will sometime squabble.

492.

To Lord Sheffield.

Lausanne, April 31st, 1784.

Not a post has elapsed without my thinking of Sheffelina and intending her separate letter. This day which had been peremptorily fixed is now so far advanced that I have barely time to relieve my mind from some anxious *English* thoughts, the only ones that disturb the tranquil, chearful scenes of my well-judged retreat.—I have this moment perused the last English papers of the 20th instant, which contain by the bye your smart and as it seems successful dispute with the Minister.

Your adversaries (I fear they are the King, Lords and People) have now conquered, but at this distance I cannot discern the consequences of their victory, whether it will lead to treaty or dissolution. If the latter, adieu once more to my poor seat and all my little hopes of compensation. Can nothing, nothing be done in any way by direct or indirect, by humble or strenuous measures? Upon my soul, I should consider my election dinner, £100, or 200 pounds as a tolerable conclusion of my cursed political life. But in this business perhaps you can do nothing. I therefore turn to another, which would seriously alarm me, had I less confidence in your friendship. You know (and the Goslings are apprized) that on the 20th of April M. de Lessert of Paris will draw upon them for 30,300 French Livres, and I should feel the deepest shame and affliction if his draught in my name should meet with an unfavourable reception. I am in your hands, and can say no more. Perhaps I have been too hasty, yet you cannot forget that I might reasonably act on your assurance of the Lenborough purchase money being paid before the end of February. Since that notice you have never said a word on the subject. Is the business concluded? what occasions a delay? Have any difficulties arisen? Adieu. You grow an idle correspondent. The winter has been long but not extremely rigorous.—The person who occupies Deyverdun's house is an invalid; yet I think we shall migrate before my birthday, the 8th of May.

E. G.

493.

To Lord Sheffield.

Lausanne, May 11th, 1784.

Alas! alas! alas! We may now exchange our mutual condolence, and encourage each other to support with becoming fortitude the stroke of fate. Last Christmas, on the change of administration, I was struck with the thunderbolt of the unexpected event, and in the approaching dissolution I foresaw the loss of the little but precious stock which I had so foolishly embarked in the parliamentary bottom. *The long continuance and various changes of the tempest rendered me by degrees callous and insensible: when the art of the Mariners was exhausted, I felt that we were sinking; I expected the ship to founder; and when the fatal moment arrived, I was even pleased to be delivered from hope and fear, to the calmness of despair.

I now turn my eyes, not on the past, but on the present and the future; what is lost I try to consider as if it never had existed; and every day I congratulate my own good fortune, let me say my prudence and resolution, in migrating from your noisy stage to a scene of repose and content. But even in this separate state, I was still anxious for my friend upon English Earth, and at first was much delighted with your hint, that you were setting off for Coventry, without any prospect of an opposition. Every post, Wednesdays and Saturdays, I eagerly looked for the intelligence of your victory; and in spite of my misbehaviour, which I do not deny, I must abuse *My Lady*, rather than you, for leaving me in so painful a situation. Each day raised and increased my apprehension; the Courier de l'Europe first announced the contest, the English papers proclaimed your defeat, and your last letter, which I received four days ago, showed me that you exerted first the spirit, and at last the temper, of a hero. Lord B[eauchamp] behaved as I should have expected, and I am not much surprized that you should have been swept away in the general unpopularity, since even in this quiet place, your friends are considered as a factious crew, acting in direct opposition both to the King and People.

For yourself I am at a loss what to say. If this repulse should teach you to renounce all connexion with Kings and Ministers, and patriots, and parties, and parliaments; for all of which you are by many degrees too honest; I should exclaim, with Teague, your respectable countryman, "By my Shoul, Dear Joy, you have *gained* a loss." Private life, whether contemplative or active, has surely more solid and independent charms; you have *some* domestic comforts; Sheffield is still susceptible of useful and ornamental improvements, (alas! how much better might even the last £1500 have been laid out!) and if these cares are not sufficient to occupy your leisure, I can trust your restless and enterprizing spirit to find new methods of preserving yourself from the insipidity of repose. But I much fear your discontent and regret at being excluded from that Pandæmonium which we have so often cursed, as long as you were obliged to attend it. The leaders of the party will flatter you with the opinion of their friendship and your own importance; the warmth of your temper makes you credulous and unsuspicious; and, like the rest of our species, male and female, you are not absolutely blind to your own merit, or deaf to the voice of praise. Some place will be suggested, easy, honourable, certain, where nothing is wanted but a man of character and spirit to head a superior interest; the opposition, if any, is contemptible, and the expence cannot be large. You will go down, find almost every circumstance falsely stated, repent that you had engaged yourself, but you cannot desert those friends who are firmly attached to your cause; besides, the Money you have already spent would have been thrown away; another thousand will compleat the business: deeper and deeper will you plunge, and the last evil will be worse than the first.

A FREE-SPOKEN COUNSELLOR.

You see I am a free-spoken Counsellor; may I not be a true prophet! Did I consult my own wishes, I should observe to you, that as you are no longer a Slave, you might soon be transported, as you seem to desire, to one of the Alpine hills. The purity and calmness of the air is the best calculated to allay the heat of a political feaver; the education of the two princesses might be successfully conducted under your eye and that of my Lady; and if you had resolution to determine on a residence, not a visit, at Lausanne, your worldly affairs might repose themselves after their late fatigues. But you know that *I* am a friend to toleration, and am always disposed to make the largest allowance for the different natures of animals; a lion and a lamb, an eagle and a Worm. I am afraid we are too quiet for you; here it would not be easy for you to create any business; you have for some time neglected books, and I doubt whether you would not think our suppers and assemblies somewhat trifling and insipid.

For myself I am happy to tell, and you will be happy to hear, that this place has in every respect exceeded my best and most sanguine hopes. How often have you said, as often as I expressed any ill-humour against the hurry, the expence, and the precarious condition of my London life, "Ay, that is a nonsensical scheme of retiring to Lausanne that you have got into your head—a pretty fancy; you remember how much you liked it in your youth, but you have now seen more of the World, and if you were to try it again, you would find yourself most woefully disappointed"? I had it in my head, in my heart; I have tryed it; I have not been disappointed; and my knowledge of the World has only served to convince me, that a Capital and a Crowd may contain much less real society, than the small circle of this gentle retirement. The winter has been longer, but, as far as I can learn, less rigorous than in the rest of Europe. The spring in all its glory is now bursting upon us, and in our garden it is displayed in all its glory. I already occupy a temporary apartment, and we live in the lower part of the house; before you receive this our lodgers will be gone and we shall be in full possession. We have much to enjoy and something to do, which I take to be the happiest condition of human life.

Now for business, the kind of subject which I always undertake with the most reluctance, and leave with the most pleasure.* I do not thank you for standing between me and Gosling, you would despise my thanks. I know your sentiments, and you are not ignorant of mine. But the step on your side was necessary: even with your security Gosling has not done the thing in a graceful way, and even the letter which informs me that he will honour M. de Lessert's draught is written with unnecessary pertness. In a post or two I shall probably hear the payment acknowledged from Paris. The Goose hopes he shall soon be reimbursed: so do I likewise, and as no difficulties can arise with regard to the title, I should imagine that before you leave town the business, that is the payment, may be finally concluded.

ENGLISH FRIENDS AT LAUSANNE.

Of the persons who already cast a Hawk's eye on the poor surplus. There is one Harris whose bond, since he calls for it, must undoubtedly be discharged, though I should be glad if you could persuade him to be contented with the interest, and trust me some time longer with the principal. I write to Whitehead, the hirer of horses, by this post, and suppose you will hear no more of him. But I must confess that Richard Way's demand of one hundred Guineas fills me with surprize and indignation, and, unless you are decidedly of a contrary opinion, I do most absolutely refuse it. Had he only been useless something might be pleaded; but if you recollect that his entire service was the recommending me to Lovegrove, it would not be easy to compute the damages (for thousands) for which I might equitably sue that Land Jobber. Though I am not very favourably disposed to the Goslings, the surplus money, when the just demands are cleared, must be left in their hands, till I can employ it, but I am serious in my hint about Lee's farm, and wish you would correspond with Hugonin in the summer; by the bye, he has not pressed my tenants this winter. A Swiss Carrier by name Pache will call in a few days to send away the boxes of plate, linnen, china, which are probably packed for foreign service. The ornamental China was never intended to be sent.

Postscript.

I cannot as yet hear anything of a certain box left at my departure in Downing-place, and repeatedly and vainly demanded; by this time I hope that it is on the road. Elmsley, to whom it was peculiarly committed, is an ingenious, an honest, but a very idle fellow. The box contains some absolute necessaries, such as paper in particular, and you are a sufferer by the delay, as you will pay a double letter for the value, or at least the size, of a single one. The stationer's paper here is so extremely thin that I turned over two leaves at once, and the error is now irreparable. Adieu.

*And now, My Lady.

Let me approach your gentle, not grimalkin, presence, with deep remorse. You have indirectly been informed of my state of mind and body; (the whole winter I have not had the slightest return of the Gout, or any other complaint whatsoever;) you have been apprized, and are now apprized, of my motions, or rather of my perfect and agreeable repose; yet I must confess (and I *feel*) that something of a direct and personal exchange of sentiment has been neglected on my side, though I still *persuade* myself that when I am settled in my new house I shall have more subject, as well as leisure to write. Such tricks of lazyness your active spirit is a stranger to, though Mrs. Frazer complains that she has never had an answer to her last letters.* That aforesaid little Donna Catharina arrived here three or four days with her sister Miss Bristow: the widow is impatient to reach England: the maiden, who is much better, proposes staying here the whole summer with her dear Doctor Tissot, and returning on the approach of Winter to pass another season at Nice. *Poor Lady Pembroke! *you* will feel for her; after a cruel alternative of hope and fear, her only daughter, Lady Charlotte, died at Aix at Provence; they have persuaded her to come to this place, where she is intimately connected with the Cerjat family. She has taken an agreeable house, about three miles from the town, and lives retired. But I have seen her; her behaviour is calm, but her affliction——

I accept with gratitude your friendly proposal of Wedgewood's ware, and should be glad to have it bought and packed, and sent without delay through Germany.* To you I leave the absolute and *sole* command, but if you have a mind to consult the Baron with regard to the ornamental, the creature is not totally devoid of taste: the number, choice, pattern, sizes,

&c. you will determine, and *I shall only say, that I wish to have a very compleat service for two courses and a desert, and that our suppers are numerous, frequently fifteen or twenty persons. Adieu. I do not mean this as your letter. You are very good to poor Kitty. With you I do not condole about Coventry.*

May 11th, 1784. I wrote the first page of my letter last week.

———————————

494.

To his Stepmother.

Lausanne, May 28th, 1784.

DEAR MADAM,

*I begin without preface or Apology, as if I had received your letter by the last post. In my own defence I know not what to say; but if I were disposed to recriminate, I might observe that you yourself are not perfectly free from the sin of laziness and procrastination. I have often wondered why we are not fonder of letter-writing: we all delight to talk of ourselves, and it is only in letters, in writing to a friend, that we can enjoy that conversation, not only without reproach or interruption, but with the highest propriety and mutual satisfaction; sure that the person whom we address feels an equal, or at least a strong and lively interest in the consideration of the pleasing subject. On the subject therefore of *self* I will entertain a friend, to whom none of my thoughts or actions, none of my pains or pleasures can ever be indifferent.

When I first cherished the design of retiring to Lausanne, the loss I can hardly call it of your society, but at least of your neighbourhood, and the fear of your anxiety and disapprobation have always stood before me as the most powerful objections, and I was much more apprehensive of wounding your tender attachment, than of offending Lord Sheffield's manly and vehement friendship. In the abolition of the board of trade, the motives for my retreat became more urgent and forcible; I wished to break loose, yet I delayed above a year before I could take my final resolution; and the letter in which I disclosed it to you cost me one of the most painful struggles of my life. As soon as I had conquered that difficulty, all meaner obstacles fell before me, and in a few weeks I found myself at Lausanne, astonished at my firmness and my success.

THE REIGN OF SINECURES AT AN END.

Perhaps you still blame or still lament the step which I have taken. If on your own account, I can only sympathize with your feelings, the recollection of which often costs me a sigh; If on mine, let me fairly state what I have escaped in England, and what I have found at Lausanne. Recollect the tempests of this winter, how many anxious days I should have passed, how many noisy, turbulent, hot, unwholesome nights, while my political existence, and that of my friends, was at stake; yet these feeble efforts would have been unavailing; I should have lost my seat in Parliament, and after the extraordinary expence of another Year, I must still have pursued the road of Switzerland, unless I had been tempted by some selfish Patron, or by Lord S.'s aspiring spirit, to purchase at a most inconvenient price a new seat; and once more, at the beginning of an opposition, to engage in new scenes of business. As to the immediate prospect of any thing like a quiet and profitable retreat, I should not know where to look; my friends are no longer in power. With *Pitt* and his party I have no connection; and were he disposed to favour a Man of letters, it is difficult to say what he could give, or what I would accept. The reign of pensions and sinecures is at an end, and a commission in the Excise or customs, the summet of my hopes, would give me bread at the expence of leisure and liberty. When I revolve these circumstances in my mind, my only regret, I repeat it again and again, is, that I did not embrace this salutary measure three, five, ten years ago.

Thus much I thought it necessary to say, and shall now dismiss this unpleasing part of the subject. For my situation here, health is the first consideration, and on that head your tenderness had conceived some degree of anxiety. I know not whether it has reached you that I had a fit of the Gout the day after my arrival. The deed is true, but the cause was accidental; carelessly stepping down a flight of stairs, I sprained my ancle; and my ungenerous enemy instantly took advantage of my weakness. But since my breaking that double chain, I have enjoyed a winter of the most perfect health that I have perhaps ever known, without any mixture of the little flying incommodities which in my best days have sometimes disturbed the tranquillity of my English life. You are not ignorant of Dr. Tissot's reputation, and his merit is even above his reputation. He assures me, that in his opinion, the moisture of England and Holland is most pernicious, the dry pure air of Switzerland most favourable, to a Gouty constitution: that experience justifies the Theory; and that there are fewer martyrs of that disorder in this, than in any other country in Europe.

THE PAVILION AND TERRACE, LAUSANNE.

To face p. 108, Vol. II.

HIS HOUSE, TERRACE, AND GARDEN.

This winter has every where been most uncommonly severe; and you seem in England to have had your full share of the general hardship: but in this corner, surrounded by the Alps, it has rather been long than rigorous; and its duration stole away our spring, and left us no interval between furs and silks. We now enjoy the genial influence of the Climate and the Season; and no station was ever more calculated to enjoy them than Deyverdun's house and garden, which are now become my own. You will not expect that the pen should describe, what the pencil would imperfectly delineate. A few circumstances may, however, be mentioned. My library is about the same size with that in Bentinck Street, with this difference, however, that instead of looking on a paved court twelve feet square, I command a boundless prospect of vale, mountain, and water, from my three windows; my apartment is compleated by a spacious light closet, or store-room, with a bed-chamber and dressing-room. Deyverdun's habitation is pleasant and convenient, though less extensive: for our common use we have a very handsome winter apartment of four rooms; and on the ground-floor, two cool saloons for the summer, with a sufficiency, or rather superfluity, of offices, &c. A Terrace, one hundred yards long, extends beyond the front of the House, and leads to a close impenetrable shrubbery; and from thence the circuit of a long and various walk, carries me round a meadow and vineyard. The intervals afford abundant supply of fruit, and every sort of vegetables; and if you add, that this villa (which has been much ornamented by my friend) touches the best and most sociable part of the town, you will agree with me, that few persons, either princes or philosophers, enjoy a more desirable residence.

Deyverdun, who is proud of his own works, often walks me round, pointing out, with knowledge and enthusiasm, the beauties that change with every step and with every variation of light. I share, or at least I sympathize, with his pleasure: he appears content with my progress, and has already told several people, that he does not despair of making me a Gardener. Be that as it may, you will be glad to hear that I am, by my own choice, infinitely more in motion, and in the open air, than I ever have been formerly. Yet my perfect liberty and leisure leave me many studious hours; and as the circle of our acquaintance retire into the Country, I shall be much less engaged in company and diversion. I have seriously resumed the prosecution of my history; each day and each month adds something to the completion of the great work. The progress is slow, the labour continual, and the end remote and uncertain. Yet every day brings its amusement, as well as labour; and though I dare not fix a term, even in my own fancy, I advance, with the pleasing reflection, that the business of publication (should I be detained here so long) must enforce my return to England, and restore me to the best of mothers and friends.

With health and competence, with a full independence of mind and action, a delightful habitation, a true friend, and many pleasant acquaintance, you will allow, in the meanwhile, that I am rather an object of envy than pity; and if you were more conversant with the use of the French language, I would seriously propose to you to repose yourself with us in this fine country. But my indirect intelligence (on which I sometimes depend with more implicit faith than on the kind dissimulation of your friendship) gives me reason to hope that the last winter has been more favourable to your health than the preceding one. Assure me of it yourself honestly and truly, and you will afford me one of the most lively pleasures* that I am capable of receiving. Write soon, and *indeed* I will not be so tardy in my answer. Caplin presents his duty to you. You will be sorry to hear that he *seems* tolerably satisfied, and talks French (when I am not present) like a magpye. The English who have passed the Winter at Nice, Lady Pembroke, &c., are flocking here. I am civil without living among them, but you will rejoyce to hear that Mr. and Madame Necker pass the summer in our neighbourhood. I must request a short delay in your Midsummer draught as I am ignorant whether some money is paid in, but it need not exceed a fortnight or three weeks. Adieu.

495.

To Lord Sheffield.

Lausanne, June 19th, 1784.

The Goslings cannot do a handsome thing with a tolerable grace. They have accepted and paid Lessert's draught, but instead of taking your word or note or bond, for the entire sum as a separate loan, they have eked it out by squeezing to the last drop of between £300 and 400 of my cash in their hands without leaving me a shilling to supply the necessary and current demands. Alas, poor Lymington!! By this post I write to them, as well as to the Darrels, and one way or another I must create some temporary credit till the business of Lenborough is settled. When in the Devil's name (for to him most rightfully belong all money transactions) will it be concluded? Originally the purchase-money was to be paid in February, we are now in the middle of June. You have never suggested any impediments; even in your last you say it is in a fair way, yet surely four or five extraordinary months exceed even the common forms and delays of lawyers, auctioneers, and all that unfeeling race of men. I cannot suspect your friendship or diligence, yet possibly the Coventry election and your more early retreat to Sheffield may have thrown you a little out of the road: but I trust that you will soon recover your lost ground (if any) and finish the race with speed and success. You are sensible that it will deliver me from the remnant of my Worldly anxieties. If the purchaser is an honest and responsible man, might he not be persuaded to advance £500 on the purchase-money; no uncommon favour, and which now would be most singularly acceptable. If, on the other hand, he shuffles through weakness of mind or purse, I could support (in my present regular economy) the idea of reserving the Estate till more prosperous times, and of finding some real or *personal* security for the money which the Goslings have advanced.

HIS HOSPITALITIES.

*In this glorious season I frequently give tea and supper to a dozen men and women with ease and reputation, and heartily wish you and My Lady were among them. In this corner of Europe we enjoy, or shall speedily enjoy, (besides threescore English, with Lady Pembroke, and forty French, with the Duchess de Sivrac at their head), M. et Madame Necker, the Abbé Raynal, the Hereditary prince of Brunswick, Prince Henry of Prussia, perhaps the Duke of Cumberland; yet I am still more content with the humble natives, than with *most* of these *illustrious names.* Adieu. The post is on the wing, and you owe me a long Epistle. I am, as usual, in the firm intention of writing next week to my lady.* I hear from Ostend of the landing of four boxes: but I know not whether the Wedgewood is among them. If not, I hope it will soon follow. Adieu.

Could you not write to Gosling to release my poor Cash, and to take the whole of Lessert's sum on yourself?

496.

To Lord Sheffield.

Lausanne, October 18th, 1784.

*Since my retreat to Lausanne our Correspondence has never received so long an interruption; and as I have been equally taciturn with the rest of the English World, it may now be a problem among that sceptical nation, whether the historian of the decline and fall be a living substance or an empty name. So tremendous is the sleepy power of laziness and habit, that the silence of each post operated still more strongly to benumb the hand, and to freeze the *Epistolary* ink. How or when I should have naturally awakened, I cannot tell; but the pressure of my affairs, and the arrival of your last letter, compell me to remember that you are entrusted with the final amputation of the best limb of my property. The subject is in itself so painful, that I have postponed it, like a child's physic, from day to day; and losing whole mornings, as I walked about my library, in useless regret and impotent resolution. You will be amazed to hear that (after peeping to see that you were well, and returned from Ireland) I have not yet had the courage to peruse your letter, for fear of meeting with some gloomy intelligence; and I will now finish what I have to say of pecuniary matters, before I know whether its contents will fortify or overthrow my unbyassed sentiments.*

About three weeks ago I received the conveyance of Lenbourough, and immediatly executed the deeds in the presence of the Honble and Reverend Edward Conway, and Mr. Jones of Ireland, a nephew of Lord Tyrone. A coach was setting off, and the writings properly packed were directed to Mr. Elmsley, and in the inner Cover to Ld Sheffield to be left till called for: before this time they should be safe in London; the purchaser is said to be impatient. I am so likewise, and nothing (I should apprehend) can prevent you from delivering the land and receiving the Money. The miserable state of the funds must excuse the lowness of the price, and annihilate any probable benefit of a short delay: but when I look back (a foolish retrospect!) to our moderate expectation of £20,000 and calculate the interest, money, costs, vexations, &c., of eleven Years, I cannot look upon myself as a *very* successful man. Consider that since my departure I have fairly or foully lost at least £2000 on which I might depend with the most rational confidence, £1000 on the abatement of the Lenborough price, and £1000 by the dissolution of Parliament. *To what purpose (you will say) are these tardy and useless repinings? To arraign your manager? No, I am satisfied with the skill and firmness of the pilot, and only complain of the untoward violence of the tempest. To repent of your retreat into Switzerland? No, surely, every subsequent event has tended to make it as necessary as it has proved agreeable. Why then these lamentations? Hear and attend.

HIS PECUNIARY AFFAIRS.

It is to interest (if possible more strongly) your zeal and friendship, to justify a sort of avarice, of a love of money, very foreign to my character, but with which I cling to these last fragments of my fortune.* According to the terms of the conveyance, £12,000 are destined for the Goslings and £3500 for me, in all £15,500: yet I am almost sure that you mentioned £15,650 as the entire price. Of this remainder, Gosling will instantly seize his reimbursement of the Paris sum, £300 bond and, as I fear, some small arrears of interest. Besides this Harris's heirs have made a just claim; Way's damned hundred Guineas I cannot digest, and a long unknown bill of Newton rises to my imagination in all its horrors. Of tradesmen's debts I have left none behind me except about 300 pounds for the hire of horses to Whitehead and the purchase of books to Elmsley. When all these demands are summed and discharged, I tremble at the balance, and indeed I have found through life that I had always more to pay, and less to receive, than I expected. *As far as I can judge from the experience of a year, though I find Lausanne much more expensive than I imagined, yet my style of living (and a very handsome style it is) will be brought *nearly* within my ordinary revenues. I wish our poor Country could say as much! But it was always my favourite and rational wish, that at the winding up of my affairs I might possess a sum from one to two thousand pounds, neither buried in land, nor locked up in the funds, but free, light, and ready to obey any call of interest, or pleasure, or virtue; to defray any extraordinary expence, support any delay, or remove any obstacle. For the attainment of this object, I trust in your assistance.*

First, I must desire you to call in the bills (particularly Newton's) to cast up the amount of all the deductions on the £3500, and to send me the list, but to pay as little of it as you possibly can (except the Goslings), till you have heard again from me. I am sensible however that the residue can scarcely by any contrivance be brought even to the smallest of the above-mentioned sums (£1000), and here your friendship must again interpose to engage the Goslings to supply that deficiency on our Joint-bond. The money (I could wish it were £1500 in all) I should probably vest in India bonds, and the difference of ½ or of 1 per Cent. would be no formidable tax. At the end of three or four years I should be sure of replacing the principal from the profits of my history, without indulging any fanciful expectations from Aunt Hester, who complains a little of your silence. *Thus much of this money transaction; to you I need add no other stimulative, than to say that my ease and comfort very much depend on the success of this plan.*

I have now opened your letter; send them to the Devil if they talk of their moneys lying dead. Have I not been saddled with the interest of my mortgage? From whom has the delay proceeded? did *they* not insist on sending the deeds to Lausanne? Have *I* not returned them with uncommon diligence? Since Hugonin will not write to me himself, I must press and conjure him through you to get the rents paid on or before the 1st of December. I know not what may be this College business, but am glad to hear no more of the scruples of the Chief tenant. Cannot Hug. pick me up some odd money from Wooddyer?

On folding my Epistle, it turned out so minute that a cover became decent, and you will expect a few lines for your additional postage. First of *me*. I cannot esteem myself totally foolish when I reflect on the success of a scheme executed in opposition to the wisest of my friends. I have now given this place a year's tryal, and find that the climate agrees with my health, (I have not had a single return of the gout) and the people, their manners, their way of life, are suited to my Genius: some rubs will intervene, and even in my domestic life neither Deyverdun nor myself are Angels, but on the whole, I shall number *this* among, or rather above, the Happiest of my years, and nothing but your salutary hand to clear and establish my pecuniary concerns is now wanting.

As I thought every man of sense and fortune in Ireland must be satisfied, I did not conceive the cloud so dark as you represent it. If the growth of the Papists could awaken the fears and prejudices of the Protestants, it might be lucky, and the discovery of French gold would do more good than mischief. *I will seriously peruse the 8º, and in due time the 4º Edition; it would become a Classic book, if you could find leisure (will you ever find it?) to introduce some kind of order and ornament. You must negotiate *directly* with Deyverdun; but the State will not hear of parting with their only Reynolds. I embrace My Lady; let her be angry, provided she be well. Adieu. Yours.

P.S. The saving Ireland may have amused you in the Summer; but how do you mean to employ the Winter? Do you not cast a longing, lingering look at St. Stephen's Chappel? With your fiery spirit, and firm judgment, I almost wish you there; not for your benefit, but for the public. If you resolve to recover your seat,* pay a specific sum for a certain election,—

rather than *listen to any fallacious and infinite projects of interest, contest, return, petition, &c. Dixi.*

497.

To Lady Sheffield.

Lausanne, October 22nd, 1784.

*A few weeks ago, as I was walking on our Terrace with Mr. Tissot, the celebrated Physician, Mr. Mercier, the author of the Tableau de Paris; the Abbé Raynal, Mr., Madame, and Mademoiselle Necker, the Abbé de Bourbon, a natural son of Lewis the fifteenth, the hereditary prince of Brunswick, Prince Henry of Prussia, and a dozen Counts, Barons, and extraordinary persons, among whom was a natural son of the Empress of Russia——

Are you satisfied with this list? which I could enlarge and embellish, without departing from truth; and was not the Baron of Sheffield (profound as he is on the subject of the American trade) doubly mistaken with regard to Gibbon and Lausanne? Whenever I used to hint my design of retiring, that illustrious Baron, after a proper effusion of damned fools, condescended to observe, that such an obscure nook in Switzerland might please me in the ignorance of youth, but that after tasting for so many years the various society of Paris and London, I should soon be tired with the dull and uniform round of a provincial town. In the winter, Lausanne is indeed reduced to its native powers; but during the summer, it is possibly, after Spa, one of the most favourite places of general resort. The voyage of Switzerland, the Alps, and the Glaciers, is become a fashion; Tissot attracts the Invalids, especially from France; and a Colony of English have taken up the habit of spending their winters at Nice, and their summers in the Pays de Vaud. Such are the splendour and variety of our summer Visitors; and *you* will agree with me more readily than the Baron, when I say that this variety, instead of being a merit, is, in my opinion, one of the very few objections to the residence of Lausanne. After the dissipation of the winter, I expected to have enjoyed, with more freedom and solitude, myself, my friend, my books, and this delicious paradise; but my position and character make me here a sort of a public character, and oblige me to see and be seen. However, it is my firm resolution for next summer to assume the independence of a Philosopher, and to be visible only to the persons whom I like.

MDLLE. NECKER AND PRINCE HENRY OF PRUSSIA.

On that principle I should not, most assuredly, have avoided the Neckers and Prince Henry. The former have purchased the Barony of Copet near Geneva; and as the buildings were very much out of repair, they passed this summer at a country-house at the gates of Lausanne. They afford a new example, that persons who have tasted of greatness, can seldom return with pleasure to a private station. In the moments when we were alone he conversed with me freely, and I believe truly, on the subject of his administration and fall; and has opened several passages of modern history, which would make a very good figure in *the* American book. If they spent the summers at the Castle of Copet, about nine leagues from hence, a fortnight's or three weeks' visit would be a pleasant and healthful excursion; but, alas! I fear there is little appearance of its being executed. *Her* health is impaired by the agitation of her mind: instead of returning to Paris, she is ordered to pass the winter in the southern provinces of France, and our last parting was solemn; as I very much doubt whether I shall ever see her again. They have now a very troublesome charge, which you will experience in a few years—the disposal of a Baroness. Mademoiselle Necker, one of the greatest heiresses in Europe, is now about eighteen—wild, vain, but good-natured, and with a much larger provision of wit than beauty; what encreases their difficulties is their Religious obstinacy of marrying her only to a Protestant. It would be an excellent opportunity for a young Englishman of a great name and a fair reputation. Prince Henry must be a man of sense; for he took more notice, and expressed more esteem for me, than any body else. He is certainly (without touching his military character) a very lively and entertaining companion. He talked with freedom, and generally with contempt, of most of the princes of Europe; with respect of the Empress of Russia; but never mentioned the name of his brother, except once, when he hinted that it was *he himself* that won the battle of Rosbach.

His nephew, and our nephew, the hereditary prince of Brunswick, is here for his education, a soft and heavy piece of German dough. Of the English, who have lived very much as a national colony, you will like to hear of Mrs. Fraser and *one* more. Donna Catherina pleases every body by the perfect simplicity of her state of Nature, and I am glad to see that her giddyness is often checked by a sad remembrance of the General. You know she has had resolution to return from England (where she told me she saw you) to Lausanne, for the sake of Miss Bristow, who is in a very bad way, and in a few days they set off for Nice. *The other* is the Eliza; she passed through Lausanne, in her road from Italy to England; poorly in health, but still adorable, (nay, do not frown!) and I enjoyed some delightful hours by her bedside. She wrote me a line from Paris, but has not executed her promise of visiting Lausanne in the month of October.

My pen has run much faster, and much farther, than I intended on the subject of others; yet, in describing them, I have thrown some light over myself and my situation. A Year, a very short one, has now elapsed since my arrival at Lausanne; and after a cool review of my sentiments, I can sincerely declare, that I have never, during a single moment, repented of having executed my *absurd* project of retiring to Lausanne. It is needless to dwell on the fatigue, the hurry, the vexation which I must have felt in the narrow and dirty circle of English Politics. My present life wants no foil, and shines by its own native light. The chosen part of my library is now arrived, and arranged in a room full as good as that in Bentinck Street, with this difference indeed, that instead of looking on a stone Court, twelve feet square, I command, from three windows of plate glass, an unbounded prospect of many a league of vineyard, of fields, of wood, of lake, and of mountains; a scene which Lord S. will tell you is superior to all you can imagine. The climate, though severe in Winter, has perfectly agreed with my constitution; and the year is accomplished without any return of the gout. An excellent house, a good table, a pleasant garden, are no contemptible ingredients in human happiness. The general style of society hits my fancy; I have cultivated a large and agreeable circle of acquaintance, and am much deceived if I have not laid the foundations of two or three more intimate and valuable connections; but their names would be indifferent, and it would require pages, or rather volumes, to describe their persons and characters.

With regard to my standing dish, my domestic friend, I could not be much disappointed, after an intimacy of eight and twenty years. His heart and his head are excellent; he has the warmest attachment for me, he is satisfied that I have the same for him: some slight imperfections must be mutually supported; two batchelors, who have lived so long alone and independent, have their peculiar fancies and humours, and when the mask of form and ceremony is laid aside, every moment in a family life has not the sweetness of the honey moon, even between the husbands and wives who have the truest and most tender regard for each other.

Should you be very much surprized to hear of my being married? Amazing as it may seem, I do assure you that the event is less improbable than it would have appeared to myself a twelfthmonth ago. Deyverdun and I have often agreed, in jest and in earnest, that a house like ours would be regulated, and graced, and enlivened, by an agreeable female Companion; but each of us seems desirous that his friend should sacrifice himself for the public good. Since my residence here I have lived much in women's company; and, to your credit be it spoken, I like you better the more I see of you. Not that I am in love with any particular person. I have discovered about half a dozen *Wives* who would please me in different ways, and by various merits: one as a Mistress (a Widow, vastly like *the* Eliza: if she returns I am to bring them together); a second, a lively entertaining acquaintance; a third, a sincere good-natured friend; a fourth, who would represent with grace and dignity at the head of my table and family; a fifth, an excellent economist and housekeeper; and a sixth, a very useful nurse. Could I find all these qualities united in a single person, I should dare to make my addresses, and should deserve to be refused.*

THE LOSS OF HIS VALET.

In the meanwhile I have experienced a separation from a more humble companion with whom I expected to pass the remainder of my life: in a few days Caplin departs for England. He had long complained of his health, and though he made some progress in French, he could not reconcile himself to the people and country, and his personal attachment to me was less forcible than gratitude perhaps would have required. As he has saved some money in my service he proposes to set up in London in the Upholstery business, and will be a very useful correspondent, as he has been a very able assistant here in my first arrangements. I shall advise him to go down to Sheffield, and you may question him about a thousand little particulars. It is an heavy loss, yet I have the good luck to procure in his place a Valet de Chambre, a man of substance and reputation of this Country, but who has lived some years at Paris: he has passed three months in the school of Caplin, and as I am assured of his honesty and diligence I have very good hopes of his address and intelligence.

*You hint in some of your letters, or rather postscripts, that you consider me as having renounced England, and having fixed myself for the rest of my life in Switzerland, and that you suspect the sincerity of any vague or insidious schemes of purchase or return. To remove, as far as I can, your doubts and suspicions, I will tell you, on that interesting subject, fairly and simply as much as I know of my own intentions. There is little appearance that I shall be suddenly recalled by offer of a place or pension. I have no claim to the friendship of your young Minister, and should he propose a Commissioner of the Customs, or Secretary at Paris, the former objects of my low ambition, Adam in Paradise would refuse them with contempt. *Here* therefore I shall certainly live till I have finished the remainder of my history; an arduous work, which does not proceed so fast as I expected amidst the avocations of Society, and miscellaneous Study. As soon as it is compleated, most probably in three or *four* years, I shall infallibly return to England, about the month of May or June; and the necessary labour of printing with care two or three quarto Volumes, will detain me till their publication, in the ensuing Spring. Lord Sheffield and yourself will be the loadstone that most forcibly attracts me; and as I shall be a vagabond on the face of the earth, I shall be the better qualified to domesticate myself with you, both in town and country. Here, then, at no very extravagant distance, we have the certainty (if we live) of spending a year together, in the peace and freedom of a friendly interest; and a year is no very contemptible portion of this mortal existence.

HIS INVITATION TO THE SHEFFIELDS.

Beyond that period (I mean of the year, not of the existence, though it be true enough of that likewise) all is dark, but not gloomy. Whether, after the final completion of my history, I shall return to Lausanne, or settle in England, must depend on a thousand events which lye beyond the reach of human foresight, the state of public and private affairs, my own health, the health and life of Deyverdun, the fate of two elderly Ladies, the various changes which may have rendered Lausanne more dear, or less agreeable, to me than at present. But without losing ourselves in this distant futurity, which perhaps we may never see, and without giving any positive answer to Maria's parting question, whether I should be buried in England or Switzerland, let me seriously and earnestly ask you, whether you do not mean to visit me next summer? The defeat at Coventry would, I should think, facilitate the project; since the Baron is no longer detained the whole winter from his domestic affairs, nor is there any attendance on the house that keeps him till Midsummer in dust and dispute. I can send you a pleasant route, through Normandy, Paris, and Lyons, a visit to the Glaciers, and your return down the Rhine, which would be commodiously executed in three or four months, at no very extravagant expence, and would be productive of health and spirits to you, of entertainment to you both, and of instruction to the Baronessa. Without the smallest inconvenience to myself, I am able to lodge Yourselves and family, by arranging you in the winter apartment, which in the summer season is not of any use to us. I think you will be satisfied with your habitation, and already see you in your dressing-room; a small but pleasant room, with a delightful prospect to the West and South. If poor Aunt Kitty (you oblige me beyond expression by your tender care of that excellent Woman) if she were only ten years younger, I would desire you to take her with you, but I much fear we shall never meet again.

You will not complain of the brevity of this Epistle; I expect, in return, a full and fair account of yourself, your thoughts and actions, soul and body, present and future, in the safe, though unreserved, confidence of friendship. The Baron in two words hinted but an indifferent account of your health; you are a fine machine; but as he was absent in Ireland, I hope

I understand the cause and the remedy. Next to yourself, I want to hear of the two Baronesses. You must give me a faithful picture (and though a mother you can give it) of their present external and internal forms; for a year has now elapsed, and in *their* lives a year is an age.* Has the gentle Louisa (though you had discovered some marks of fire) expanded as much as you could expect in knowledge and understanding? I see Maria an accomplished and elegant young Woman, and only wish to know whether you have smoothed away some of the asperities of that fine diamond. Adieu.

Remember me to Miss Firth: My Wedgewood's China. But Caplin will put everything in motion.

Ever yours,
E. GIBBON.

I hear from Mrs. Frazer but an indifferent account of Mrs. Holroyd of Bath. I want to have a *cool* and faithful state of Mrs. G., her health and spirits: our correspondence is languid, but indeed it is rather her fault than mine.

498.

To his Stepmother.

Lausanne, October 27th, 1784.

MY DEAR MADAM,

If ever the excuse of procrastination be allowable it is when we ourselves are expecting a letter to which we are entitled in the due course of correspondence. Not that among friends the cold ideas of form and duty of debt and payment call find any admittance; but that every post that approaches and flyes away, seems to mark and postpone the natural opportunity of writing by alternately raising and disappointing our hopes. I am not indeed either surprized or angry at your long silence; the correspondence of distant friends will inevitably languish without any diminution of their mutual affection: their sentiments are still the same but their ideas become different; they no longer think or read or converse or act in the same sphere, and the object of their intercourse will be at last reduced to the reciprocal desire of being informed of each other's health and happiness. Could we persuade ourselves to convey that information every week or month in a billet of four lines, each friend would be satisfied: but the distance seems to require a longer Epistle, and the obligation of writing a great deal prevents us from writing at all, and leaves our friend in the doubt (which I now most anxiously feel) whether that silence be not occasioned by the want of health or spirits.

It is more particularly in a situation like ours that we are not prompted to write by the agitation and variety of the scenes which surround us. Nothing can be more uniform and tranquil than your Bath Life, except it be that which I lead at Lausanne. A regular alternative of Study and society carries away the hours and days in a smooth and pleasant Revolution, and I have scarcely commenced a month before I am astonished to find myself at the end of it—a sure indication of a quiet and domestic state of happiness. I am well satisfied with my union with a known and tryed friend, though (such are the infirmities of human nature) all our moments cannot partake of the Honey-moon. Among the people of the Country I have found some, I have formed many more Connections; their manners, their conversation, their style of living are perfectly adapted to my taste, and the sameness of the company is relieved in the Summer by a concourse of strangers whom health or curiosity or fashion invite to consult Tissot or to visit the Alps.

A TEMPERATE DIET AND EASY MIND.

As a kind of public character, a live Author, I am a little too much exposed to visits and compliments, but I was much delighted with the unexpected meeting of the Neckers. Tired of greatness and ambition (a polite phrase for a disgraced minister), they purchased an estate in Switzerland, and while the Castle was repairing they passed the summer in a country-house near Lausanne. Their society might diversify my life with occasional excursions; but, alas! *her* health is very much affected, and I think it extremely doubtful whether she will be able to revisit this country again. Of myself I can give you a much more pleasing account, nor do I remember a year in which I have enjoyed a more perfect state of health; the air though sharp is pure; it may be dangerous for weak lungs, but is excellently suited to a gouty constitution, and during the whole twelfth month I have never once been attacked by my old Enemy. Of Dr. Cadogan's three rules, I can observe two, a temperate diet and a easy mind. I am not agitated by the hopes and fears, and *regrets* of my London life, and whatever cares still pursue and overtake me are blown over by an English wind. I am afraid you sometimes sigh over me as an Exile. If I were fixed as a foreign Minister at Naples, or Petersburgh, you would be reconciled to my situation, yet such a splendid situation would be corroded by many a secret anxiety, and content is surely preferable to greatness. Adieu, My Dear Madam; give me a *satisfactory line*, and ever believe me,

Yours,
E. G.

499.

To Lord Sheffield.

Lausanne, March 13th, 1785.

*My long silence (and it has been long) must not, on this occasion, be imputed to lazyness, though that little Devil may likewise have been busy. But you cannot forget how many weeks I remained in suspence, expecting every post the final sentence, and not knowing what to say in that passive uncertainty. It is now something more than a fortnight since your last letter, and that of Gosling informed me of the event. I have intended every day to write, and every day I have started back with reluctance and disgust, from the consideration of the wretched subject. Lenborough irrecoverably gone, for three-fourths of its real, at least of its ancient, Value; my seat in Parliament (for the subject now presses home upon me) sunk without the smallest equivalent in the abyss of your cursed politics, and a balance neatly cyphered and summed by Gosling, which shews me a very shallow purse, in which others have a clearer right to dip than myself.

March 21st.

Another week has now elapsed, and though nothing is changed in this too faithful state of my affairs, I feel myself able to encounter them with more spirit and resolution; to look on the future, rather than the past; on the fair, rather than on the foul side of the prospect. I shall speak in the confidence of friendship, and while you listen to the more doleful tale of my wants and wishes, You will have the satisfaction of hearing some circumstances in my present situation of a less unpleasing nature.

1. In the first place, I most heartily rejoyce in the sale, however unfavourable, of the Bucks Estate. Considering the dullness of the times, and the high interest of money, it is not a little to obtain even a tolerable price, and I am sensible how much your patience and industry have been exercised to extort the payment* from a knavish or obstinate purchaser. Without supposing a shilling of balance in Gosling's hands, my circumstances are improved by the sale to the annual amount of £150; of £50 which I was obliged to add for the interest of the mortgage, of £100 which I received from my French annuity.

2. Your resistance to my Swiss expedition was more friendly than wise. Had I yielded, after eighteen months of suspense and anxiety, I should now, a still poorer man, be driven to embrace the same resource, which has succeeded according to, or even beyond, my most sanguine expectation. I do not pretend to have discovered the terrestrial paradise, which has not been known in this World since the fall of Adam; but I can truly declare, (now the charms of novelty are long since faded,) that I have found the plan of life the best adapted to my temper and my situation. I am now writing to you in a room as good as that in Bentinck Street, with three large windows of plate glass which command the country, the lake, and the mountains, and the opening prospect of the spring. The aforesaid room is furnished without magnificence, but with every conveniency for warmth, ease, and study, and the walls are already covered with more than two thousand volumes, the choice of a chosen library. I have health, friends, an amusing society, and perfect freedom. (A Commissioner of the Excise! the idea makes me sick). Even in Trifles, though it is not a Trifle, I have been singularly lucky, and you will conceive an high opinion of Blondel, my new Valet de Chambre, when I assure you that, except in the knowledge of books and the Upholstery business, I no longer regret Caplen. He probably related all the minute circumstances of my state, and I find, that without any prejudice for the Country and people, he has not represented them in an unfavourable light. *If you ask me what I have saved by my retreat to Lausanne, I will fairly tell you (in the two great articles of a Carriage and a house in town, and breathing place at Hampton Court, both which were indispensable, and are now annihilated, with the difference of Clubs, public places, servants' wages, &c.) about four hundred pounds, or Guineas, a year; no inconsiderable sum, when it must be annually found as addition to an expence which is somewhat larger than my present revenue.

HIS ESTABLISHMENT AT LAUSANNE.

3. *"What is then,"* you will ask, *"my present establishment?"* This is not by any means a cheap Country; and, except in the article of wine, I could give a dinner or make a coat, perhaps for the same price in London as at Lausanne. My chief advantage arises from the things which I do not want; and in some respects my style of living is enlarged by the encrease of my relative importance—an obscure batchelor in England, the master of a considerable house at Lausanne. Here I am expected to return entertainments, to receive Ladies, &c. and to perform many duties of society, which, though agreeable enough in themselves, contribute to inflame a Housekeeper's bills. From the disbursements of the first year I cannot form any just estimate; the extraordinary expences of the journey, carriage of heavy goods from England, the acquisition of many books, which it was not expedient to transport, the purchase of furniture, wine, fitting up my library, and the irregularity of a new Ménage, have consumed a pretty large sum. But in a quiet, prudent, regular course of life, I think I

can support myself with comfort and honour for six or seven hundred pounds a year, instead of a thousand or eleven hundred in England.* I can look forward with strong and rational hope. The departure of the two matrons, or not to build on the ice, the mere suppression of the Bath jointure will give me more than that income, which may even be enlarged by turning Buriton into an annuity.

Besides these uncertainties, (uncertain at least as to the time,) I have a sure and honourable supply from my own pen. I continue my history with pleasure and assiduity; the way is long and laborious, yet I see the end, and I can almost promise to land in England next September twelfthmonth, with a Manuscript of the current value of three thousand pounds, which will afford either a small income or a large capital. It is in the meanwhile that my situation is somewhat painful and difficult. From the French and English funds and the various produce on my Copper share, I receive between two or three hundred pounds: the rent of Buriton is between six and seven hundred, but when you have deducted taxes, repairs, Mrs. G.'s jointure (£300 clear) &c., weigh the residue; it will not break down the scale. It happens unluckily enough that this year there will be an extraordinary deduction (at least one hundred guineas) of the fine which is paid every seven years for the renewal of Horn farm. Since my arrival here, I have never received a line from Hugonin, to whom I wrote a long letter last summer, and I fear his eyes and infirmities disqualify him a little for business. The sums which he has remitted to Gosling the last and the present winter fall below the most moderate computation, and I see no reason or account of the deficiency. I wish you would write to him in my name or your own, and make yourself master of that same part of my affairs. Richard Andrews, an honest attorney of Petersfield, is allowed my quitrents for holding my courts, and he might surely, without more trouble or wages, receive and remit the rents of three or four farms.

Such are the services and revenues of the year; proceed we now, in the style of the budget, to the ways and means of extraordinary supplies. Payne's valuation of the remaining part of my library has not perfectly answered my expectation. Yet it is approved by my friend, Elmsley, who offers on his own account to change the pounds into Guineas, and as I want the money, and esteem his integrity, I shall signify my acceptance if he will allow me to make another moderate draft from the Catalogue. That transaction (all accounts settled) will put some money in my pocket: but as I understand that kind of business I will not trouble you or myself with any farther details. A circumstance which surprized me in Gosling's account is the last six months from Lady day to Michaelmas last, during which I pay interest for the Mortgage without receiving rent from the Estate: surely that is not just or reasonable. If that half year is properly excepted in the

Conveyance, you my omnipotent Attorney may draw it from the tenants, and it will serve at least to discharge Harris's bond. If it is not, I must submit with a sigh to this new deduction of two or three hundred pounds from the poor price of poor Lenborough. But this deficiency must somewhere be supplied: as I now pay interest to the *Job* for my horses, I can make the man wait a Couple of years till my return. But this cursed account of Newton! He is pathetic, you say, on the score of money advanced; a draft for £200 which I send you inclosed would surely discharge that advance, and you will try to manage him to stay till my labours are finished for the payment of his own. Yet perhaps the clearest and most honourable way would be to borrow £500 of the Goslings on my account and your own bond. *I will not affront your friendship, by observing that you will incur little or no risk on this occasion. Read, consider, act, and write.

PITT A FAVOURITE ABROAD.

It is the privilege of friendship to make our friend a patient hearer, and active Associate in our own affairs; and I have now written five pages on my private affairs, without saying a word either of the public, or of yourself. Of the public I have little to say; I never was a very warm Patriot, and I grow every day a Citizen of the World. The scramble for power and profit at Westminster or St. James's, and the names of Pitt and Fox, become less interesting to me than those of Cæsar and Pompey. You are not a friend of the young Minister, but he is a great favourite on the Continent, as he appears to be still; and you must own that the fairness of his character, his eloquence, his application to business, and even his youth, must prepossess at least the ignorant in his favour. Of the merit or defects of his administration I cannot pretend to speak; but I find, from the complaints of some interested persons, that his restraints on the smuggling of tea have already ruined the East India Companies of Antwerp and Sweden, and that even the Dutch will scarcely find it worth their while to send any ships to China. Your Irish friends appear to be more quiet, at least the Volunteers and national Congress seem to subside. How far that tranquillity must be purchased on our side, by any pernicious sacrifices, you will best decide; and from some hints in your last letters, I am inclined to think that you are less affected than might be supposed with national or local prejudice. Your introduction I have attentively read; the matter, though most important in itself, is out of the line of my studies and habits, and the subordinate beauties of style and arrangement you disclaim. Yet I can say with truth, that I never met with more curious and diligent investigation, more strong sense, more liberal spirit, and more cool and impartial temper in the same number of pages.

By this time you have probably read Necker's book on the Finances. Perhaps for you there is too much French enthusiasm and paint; but in many respects you must have gained a knowledge of his country, and on the whole, you must have been pleased with the picture of a great and benevolent mind. In your attack on Deyverdun for my picture I cannot promise you much success; he seems resolved to maintain his right of possession, and your only chance would be a personal assault. The next summer (how time slips away!) was fixed for your visit to Lausanne. We are prepared at all points to receive *you*, My lady, and a princess or two, with their train; and if you have a proper contempt for St. Stephen's chappel, you are perfectly free, and at leisure (can you ever be at leisure?) for the summer season. As you are now in a great measure disengaged from my affairs, you may find time to inform me of your proceedings and your projects. At present I do not even know whether you pass the winter at Sheffield-place or in Downing-street. My lady revenges herself of my long silence. Yet I embrace her and the Infants. In a few weeks we expect Miss Bristow and Mrs. Fraser from Nice. Adieu. You have deranged the decline and fall this morning. I have finished my Epistle since dinner, and am now going to a pleasant party and good supper.*

I send you enclosed a promissory note for £500. If you do not borrow the money of Gosling, you may throw it into the fire; if you do, in case of death it will serve as a remembrance. You will find that before and since the receipt of their balance I have drawn this year for £300. The change is most amazingly in my favour, and a banker of credit and substance at Lausanne allows me 4 per Cent. for all the money I leave on his hands.

500.

To his Stepmother.

Lausanne, July 15th, 1785.

Indeed and indeed, my Dear Madam, I will never go to sleep again; my next letter shall be short and speedy, and I will not always put myself under the shameful necessity of employing the first page in worthless Apologies. On the present occasion I will not excuse myself by saying (what is true enough) that I waited week after week in hopes of hearing from you. As our last letters crossed each other, you might reasonably entertain the same expectation, and thus it is that poor miserable mortals try to provide a decent colour for their own lazyness. You will expect some account of the time of silence, and that account will be short and satisfactory. I am no longer in the illusions of the Honey-moon, when every deformity is concealed, and a smooth deceitful gloss is given to every object.

A YOUNG MAN AT FIFTY.

In the space of two and twenty months, the Climate and Society of Lausanne, my own situation and expence, the character of my companion and of my looser connections of both sexes are perfectly understood. The Climate in these two Winters has shewn itself to all Europe, more strongly perhaps to us, under the most hideous form, severe cold, and a continuance or repetition of snow till the middle of April. In general my health has perfectly sustained the rigour of the season; good spirits, good appetite, good sleep are my habitual state, and though verging towards fifty I still feel myself a young man. I was in hopes that my old Enemy the Gout had given over the attack, but the Villain, with his ally the winter, convinced me of my error, and about the latter end of March I found myself a prisoner in my library and my great chair. I attempted twice to rise, he twice knocked me down again, and kept possession of both my feet and knees longer (I must confess) than he had ever done before. My recovery has been proportionably tedious, and I am hardly yet in possession of my full strength; this admonition calls for some extraordinary care, and without running into sudden extremes, I consult both my reason and my taste by abstaining at night from wine and meat, and contenting myself with a bason of milk.

Such are the drawbacks on the comforts of life, yet I am pleased to think that my gout, though it has adhered somewhat longer than usual, is neither sharp nor frequent, and respectfully confines itself to the lower extremities of the Machine. Of the Country I must not complain, this dry Climate is particularly favourable to gouty constitutions; Dr. Tissot and my own observation inform me that it is rare among the natives, and among my acquaintance I can only name one old Gentleman, who by free living acquired it about the age of three score. My unpleasant and sometimes painful confinement was soothed not only by the mercenary aid of Servants and Physicians (the fee of a visit is about half a crown), but by the assiduous offices of my friends, and instead of the lonesome time an invalid who has not a family must pass amidst the crowds of London, I had the frequent visits of agreable men and women and a party of cards every evening that I chose it.

I do not suppose that real affection, especially to a stranger, is a very plentiful commodity, but here there are much fewer avocations of business or pleasure, and my style of living, my house, my table, &c., make me a man of mark and consequence. With the recovery of my strength, I now return civilities, relax my studies, and visit my acquaintance who are not gone; but so well do I like this habitation, and such is my sedentary disposition, that I have not yet lain from Home, nor gone five miles from Lausanne. You will give me credit when I say, that, though a lover of society, my library is the room to which I am the most attached. I almost hesitate whether I shall tell you that the prospect and furniture are equally agreable, that a reasonable number of my books is arrived from England, and that my whole establishment is formed upon a comfortable yet œconomical plan: in the single articles of house-rent, carriage, servants' wages, clubs, and public places I save between four and five hundred a year. And let me appeal to your reason and spirit whether such a saving be not as real and a much more honourable addition of income, than a pityful, precarious place or pension to be held or lost by the caprice of a Minister or the Revolutions of politics. When I was flattered with a *distant* hope of a seat at the boards of customs or excise, I was told that I need not work above five days in the week, and that I should sometimes enjoy the respite of Holydays and Vacations. Without any attendance or obligation I have given myself a state of leisure and independence, in which my labour is only employed on litterary pursuits, the objects of my choice and the foundation of my fame.

As every white spot in this life is clouded with a shade of black, I can only lament that this state is so far remote from the best and most faithful of my friends, so faithful and so true that they will enjoy my happiness though they cannot be witnesses or partakers of it. On my side, I think *of* them much oftener than I write *to* them, and warmly cherish the hope of an English Journey to them; the time must depend on the completion of my history, and I am sorry to observe that as I advance on my Journey "New

Alps on Alps arise;" and I know not when I shall reach the shelter of my Inn.

CHANGES IN ENGLISH POLITICS.

After yourself and Mrs. Porten, Lord and Lady Sheffield are the persons whom I most desire to see. Among my companions of the World are undoubtedly several whom I regard and of whose good wishes I am persuaded; yet those slighter tyes are insensibly relaxed by the distance of time and place, by the interposition of new objects. My political connections have undergone such astonishing changes, a new Parliament, a new Administration, Patriots whom I left Ministers, Ministers whom I left Boys, the whole Map of the Country so totally altered, that I sometimes imagine I have been ten years absent from England. That incessant hurry of Politicks was indeed one of the things which disgusted the most, and there is nothing pleases me so much in this country as to enjoy all the blessings of a Good Government without ever talking or thinking of our Governors. In my domestic Government a great though not unexpected Revolution has happened. Caplen, unable to accustom himself to the language or manners of this country, resigned his employments and returned to England the beginning of last winter. You may easily conceive my loss and apprehension, and you will rejoyce in my good fortune that I was able to fill his place with no unworthy successor; a servant of this country, but who had lived with a Lady at Paris till her death—a man of substance and reputation, and who on the tryal of some months appears to deserve my confidence and good opinion. We are already thoroughly accustomed to each other. Adieu. My Dear Madam, may our correspondence be more frequent, and may I find you on my return in the possession of every blessing.

Most truly yours,
E. G.

501.

To Lord Sheffield.

Lausanne, September 5th, 1785.

*Extract from a weekly English paper, September 5th, 1785.—"It is reported, but we hope without foundation, that the celebrated Mr. Gibbon, who had retired to Lausanne in Switzerland to finish his valuable history, lately died in that city."

The hope of the News writer is very handsome and obliging to the historian; yet there are several weighty reasons which would incline me to believe that the intelligence may be true. *Primo*, It must one day be true; and therefore may very probably be so at present. *Secundo*, We may always depend on the impartiality, accuracy, and veracity of an English newspaper. *Tertio*, which is indeed the strongest argument, we are credibly informed that for a long time past the said celebrated historian has not written to any of his friends in England; and as that respectable personnage had always the reputation of a most exact and regular correspondent, it may be fairly concluded from his silence, that he either is, or ought to be, dead. The only objection that I can foresee, is the assurance that Mr. G—— himself read the article as he was eating his breakfast, and laughed very heartily at the mistake of his brother historian; but as he might be desirous of concealing that unpleasant event, we shall not insist on his apparent health and spirits, which might be affected by that subtle politician. He affirms, however, not only that he is alive, and was so on the fifth of September, but that his head, his heart, his stomach, are in the most perfect state, and that the Climate of Lausanne has been congenial both to his mind and body. He confesses, indeed, that after the last severe winter, the Gout, his old enemy, from whom he hoped to have escaped, pursued him to his retreat among the mountains of Helvetia, and that the siege was long, though more languid than in his precedent attacks; after some exercise of patience he began to creep, and gradually to walk; and though he can neither run, nor fly, nor dance, he supports himself with grace and firmness on his two legs, and would willingly kick the impertinent Gazetteer; impertinent enough, though more easily to be forgiven than the insolent Courier du Bas Rhin, who about three years ago amused himself and his readers with a fictitious Epistle from Mr. Gibbon to Dr. Robertson.

A CURIOUS QUESTION OF PHILOSOPHY.

Perhaps now you think, Irish Baron, that I shall apologize in humble style for my silence and neglect. But, on the contrary, I do assure you that I am truly provoked at your Lordship's not condescending to be in a passion. I might really have been dead, I might have been sick; if I were neither dead nor sick, I deserved a volley of curses and reproaches for my infernal laziness, and you have defrauded me of my just dues. Had I been silent till Christmas, till Doomsday, you would never have thought it worth your while to abuse me. "Why, then," (let me ask in your name and language, 'you damned beast'), "did you not write before?" That is indeed a very curious question of natural and moral Philosophy. Certainly I am not lazy; elaborate quartos have proved, and will abundantly prove my diligence. I *can* write; spare my modesty on that subject. I like to converse with my friends by pen or tongue, and as soon as I can set myself a going, I know no moments that run off more pleasantly. I am so well convinced of that truth, and so much ashamed of forcing people that I love to forget me, that I have now resolved to set apart the first hour of each day for the discharge of my obligations; beginning *comme de raison*, with yourself, and regularly proceeding to Lord Loughborough and the rest. May Heaven give me strength and grace to accomplish this laudable intention! Amen.

Certainly (yet I do not know whether it be so certain) I should write much oftener to you, if we were not linked in business, and if my business had not always been of the unpleasant and mortifying kind. Even now I shove the ugly monster to the end of this epistle, and will confine him to a page by himself, that he may not infect the purer air of our correspondence. Of my situation here I have little new to say, except a very comfortable and singular truth, that my passion for my wife or mistress (Fanny Lausanne) is not palled by satiety and possession of two years. I have seen her in all seasons and in all humours, and though she is not without faults, they are infinitely over-balanced by her good qualities. Her face is not handsome, but her person, and every thing about her, has admirable grace and beauty: she is of a very chearful, sociable temper; without much learning, she is endowed with taste and good sense; and though not rich, the simplicity of her education makes her a very good economist; she is forbid by her parents to wear any expensive finery; and though her limbs are not much calculated for walking, she has not yet asked me to keep her a Coach.

Last spring (not to wear the metaphor to rags) I saw Lausanne in a new light, during my long fit of the Gout; and must boldly declare, that either in health or sickness I find it far more comfortable than your huge metropolis. In London my confinement was sad and solitary; the many forgot my existence when they saw me no longer at Brookes's; and the few, who sometimes cast a thought or an eye on their friend, were detained by business or pleasure, the distance of the way, or the hours of the house of commons; and I was proud and happy if I could prevail on Elmsley to enliven the dullness of the Evening. Here the objects are nearer, and more distinct, and I myself am an object of much larger magnitude. People are not kinder, but they are more idle, and it must be confessed that, of all nations on the globe, the English are the least attentive to the old and infirm; I do not mean in acts of charity, but in the offices of civil life. During three months I have had round my chair a succession of agreeable men and women, who came with a smile, and vanished at a nod; and as soon as it was agreeable I had a constant party at cards, which was sometimes dismissed to their respective homes, and sometimes detained by Deyverdun to supper, without the least trouble or inconvenience to myself. In a word, my plan has most compleatly answered; and I solemnly protest, after two years' tryal, that I have never in a single moment repented of my transmigration.

HIS COUNTRYMEN AT LAUSANNE.

The only disagreeable circumstance is the encrease of a race of animals with which this country has been long infested, and who are said to come from an island in the Northern Ocean. I am told, but it seems incredible, that upwards of 40,000 English, masters and servants, are now absent on the continent; and I am sure we have our full proportion, both in town and country, from the month of June to that of October. The occupations of the Closet, indifferent health, want of horses, in some measure plead my excuse; yet I do too much to please myself, and probably too little to satisfy my Countrymen. What is still more unlucky is, that a part of the Colony of this present year are really good company, people one knows, &c.; the Astons, Hales, Hampdens, Trevors, Lady Clarges and Miss Carter (*her Sappho*), Lord Northington, &c. I have seen Trevor several times, who talks of you, and seems to be a more exact correspondent than myself. *His wife* is much improved by her diplomatic life, and shines in every company, as a woman of fashion and elegance. But those who have repaid me for the rest were Lord and Lady Spencer. I saw them almost every day, at my house or their own, during their stay of a month; for they were hastening to Italy, that they might return to London next February. He is a valuable man, and where he is familiar, a pleasant Companion; she a charming woman, who, with sense and spirit, has the simplicity and playfulness of a child. You are not ignorant of her talents, of which she has left me an agreable specimen, a drawing of the Historic muse, sitting in a thoughtful posture to compose.

So much of self and Co. Let us now talk a little of your house and your two Countries. Does my Lady ever join in the abuse which I have merited from you? Is she satisfied with her own behaviour, her unpardonable silence, to one of the prettiest, most obliging, most entertaining, most &c. Epistles that ever was penned since the Epistles of Paul of Tarsus? Will she not *mew* one word of reply? I want some account of her spirits, health, amusements, of the womanly accomplishments of Maria, and the opening graces of Louisa: of yourself I wish to have some of those details which she is much more likely to transmit. Are you patient in your exclusion from the House? Are you satisfied with legislating with your pen? Do you pass the whole winter in town? Have you resumed the pursuits of farming, &c.? What new connexions, public or private, have you formed? A tour to the Continent would be the best medicine for the shattered nerves of a soldier and politician. By this expression you will perceive that your letter to Deyverdun is received; it landed last post, after I had already written the two first pages of this composition. On the whole, my friend was pleased and flattered: but instead of surrendering or capitulating, he seems to be making preparations for an obstinate defence. He already talks of the right of possession, of the duties of a good Citizen, of a writ *ne exeat Regno*, and of a vote of the two hundred, that whosoever shall, directly or indirectly, &c., is an Enemy to his Country. Between you be the strife, while I sit with my scales in my hand, like Jupiter on Mount Ida.

SENSE OR NONSENSE OF IRISH PARLIAMENTS.

I begin to view with the same indifference the combat of Achilles Pitt and Hector Fox; for such as it should now seem, must be the comparison of the two Warriors.* Lord Northington, who is firm in his party, assures me that the popularity of the young Minister, and even the opinion of his abilities, have considerably diminished; but he confesses that such, or much greater, diminution will not weaken his influence in the Parliament, and must tend to promote his favour and confidence in a certain place. *At this distance I am much less angry with bills, taxes, and propositions, than I am pleased with Pitt for making a friend and a deserving man happy, for releasing poor Batt from the shackles of the law, and for enhancing the gift of a secure and honourable competency, by the handsome unsolicited manner in which it was conferred. This I understand to be the case, from the unsuspicious evidence of Lord N. and Chief Baron Skinner; and if I can find time (*resolution*) I will send him a hearty congratulation; if I fail, you may at least communicate my intentions. Of Ireland I know nothing, and while I am Writing the decline of a great Empire, I have not leisure to attend to the affairs of a remote and petty province. I see that your friend Foster has been hooted by the Mob, and unanimously chosen Speaker by the House of Commons. How could Pitt expose himself to the disgrace of withdrawing his propositions after a public attempt? Have ministers no way of computing beforehand the sense or nonsense of an Irish parliament? I am quite in the dark; your pamphlet, or book, would probably have opened my eyes; but whatever may have been the reason, I give you *my word of honour* that I have never seen nor heard of it. Here we are much more engaged with Continental politics. In general we hate the emperor, as the enemy of peace, without daring to make War. The old Lyon of Prussia acts a much more glorious part, as the Champion of public tranquillity, and the independence of the German states.

And now for the bitter and nauseous pill of pecuniary business, upon which I shall be as concise as possible in the two articles of my discourse, land and money.* And concise indeed I may be according to the slender proportion of either that is now left. You sometimes accuse me of not reading or remembering the most important points of your despatches: may I not equally complain that you pass in silence all my enquiries and requests on the subject of Buriton? In the space of two years I have never received a line of intelligence from Hugonin concerning the state of that last and dearest possession. And as far as I can judge from Gosling's confused account, which records only dates and names, a portion, not a very small one, of the rent remains unpaid, or has been sunk in unknown charges and expences. Let me therefore repeat perhaps more clearly what I have already desired.

1. That you would correspond with Hugonin, and obtain from him a correct mercantile account of debtor and creditor of rents and payments for the aforesaid two years.

2. That if there remains any arrears, you would propose and enforce the most vigorous measures for my prompt and entire satisfaction.

3. That as there must be deducted from this year's rents a considerable fine to Magdalen College for Horn, Hugonin at your instigation would cast about to see whether he cannot perceive any extraordinary means of supply in the timber way. A dozen years have now elapsed since the first Cut of the Hanger. May not those *underwoods* be again ripe for the Axe? You know I consider only present profit, and disregard all future improvements and rural beauty. A beast, you will say. Alas, why do hard circumstances force me to be one?

4. That you would manage, if it can be done without *offence* or expence, the substitution of Richard Andrews, in the place of Hugonin, a clear-sighted Agent for a blind Gentleman. I fear nothing more is to be expected from Lenborough, but as you seem quiet, I entertain a faint hope that Harris's bond has been discharged from the rent or purchase money. You have done no more than I expected in assuring me that the £500 shall be ready at Goslings', but I should be sorry to distress you, or to lay your generous spirit under any obligations to a purse-proud Cit. If they will readily take

your bond, and allow me credit for the sum before the 1st of December for January next, it will be the readiest and most private way. Otherwise I can have recourse to another expedient, of desiring the Darrels either to sell an equivalent part of my short annuity, or, if the funds are too low, to advance me the *desideratum* on a security which is in their own hands. When I am possessed of the money in one way or another I will take a view of my former credit with Gosling (a small credit, I trow) of this additional supply of my debts, expences, and resources, and I hope I shall be able to discharge at least the remainder of Newton's bill. But I must not impoverish myself too, and I have some thoughts of keeping the rest of my library (if not troublesome to Downing Street) till my return to England.

DELAYS IN HIS HISTORY.

*It is impossible to hate more than I do this odious necessity of owing, borrowing, anticipating; and I look forwards with impatience to the happy period when the supplies will always be raised within the year, with a decent and useful surplus in the treasury. Had it not been for the cursed dissolution of Parliament, such would already have been the case. I now trust to the conclusion of my History, and it will hasten and secure the principal comforts of my life. You will believe I am not lazy; yet I fear the term is somewhat more distant than I thought. My long gout lost me three months in the spring; in every great work unforeseen [obstacles], and difficulties, and delays will arise; and I should be rather sorry than surprized if next autumn was postponed to the ensuing spring. If My Lady (a good creature) should write to Mrs. Porten, she may convey news of my life and health, without saying anything of this *possible* delay. Adieu. I embrace, &c.*

502.

To Lord Sheffield.

Lausanne, January 17th, 1786.

*Hear all Ye nations! An Epistle from Sheffield-place, received the 17th of January, is answered the same day; and to say the truth, this method, which is the best, is at the same time the most easy and pleasant. Yet I do not allow that in the last past silence and delay you have any more right to damn than myself. Our letters crossed each other, our claims were equal, and if both had been stiffly maintained, our mutual silence must have continued till the day of judgment. The balance was doubtless in my favour, if you recollect the length, the fullness, the variety of pleasant and instructive matter of my last dispatch. Even at present, of myself, my occupations, my designs, I have little or nothing to add; and can only speak dryly and briefly to very dry and disagreeable business demands and want of money. But we shall both agree that the true criminal is My Lady; and though I do suppose that a letter is on the road, which will make some amends, her obstinate, contumacious, dilatory silence, after so many months or years since my valuable letter, is worthy not of a Cat but of a Royal Tygress.

Notwithstanding your gloomy politicians, I do love the funds; and were the next war to reduce them to half, the remainder would be a better and pleasanter property, than a similar value in your dirty acres. We are now in the height of our winter amusements; balls, great suppers, comedies, &c.; and, except St. Stephen's, I certainly lead a more gay and dissipated life here, among the Alps, (by the bye, a most extraordinary mild winter,) than in the midst of London. Yet my mornings, and sometimes an afternoon, are diligently employed, my work advances, but much remains, indeed much more than I imagined; but a great book, like a great house, was never yet finished at the given time. When I talk of the spring of '87, I suppose all my time well bestowed; and what do you think of a fit of the gout, that may disqualify me for two or three months? You may growl, but if you calmly reflect on my pecuniary and sentimental state, you will believe that I most earnestly desire to compleat my labour, and *visit* England. Adieu.*

With regard to the three old Ladies, I behave like a fool to one, and like a beast (though they too are silent) to the other two. But all shall be speedily rectified. The portrait seems to be firmly rooted here. You know you have no right, and Deyverdun seems not disposed to shew you any indulgence.

Yours,
E. G.

I shall probably hear from you and the Goslings before the end of next month, and you may depend on an immediate answer. You will probably have corresponded with Hugonin. It is surely hard to be obliged to a man, who in two years and four months, has not condescended to send me a line of information or account. If you talk of credit, you must allow that it is unpleasant to desire the Darrels to sell a part of my short Annuity.

503.

To his Stepmother.

Lausanne, May 3rd, 1786.

DEAR MADAM,

Shall I begin by a complaint or an apology? Without much injustice I might complain of your long silence, which between other correspondents than ourselves might seem to indicate some degree of forgetfulness, the too frequent consequences of absence and distance. Between us, however, it indicates no such thing, and in the confidence of our mutual regard our silence is more eloquent than the loquacity of others. I might even add that the constant expectation on every post-day of a letter from Bath, has suspended my not very vigorous efforts to renew the correspondence. Some truth there undoubtedly may be in this assertion, but you will much more readily believe, that in my strange compound of industry and lazyness, I have very often formed the design, and as often found some excellent reason of delay till the very next post, when I would most undoubtedly write to the best and dearest of my friends. Perhaps it would not be a bad method on both sides, a note of four lines, a certificate of health and remembrance, without computing of debtor or creditor, or any formal attempt to produce a regular Epistle. But as even this project may fail, I must seriously beg that you would never allow yourself to be made uneasy by any flying reports, or newspaper. Be assured that if any untoward accident should stop my breath, or disable my hand, my friend M. Deyverdun will send the early and authentic Gazette to Sheffield place, from whence it will be imparted with proper speed to my other friends in England. At the same time, I can affirm with truth, that my sole reason for this advertisement is derived from some foolish Articles, that were very familiar last year to the home and foreign papers. Since I have known you or myself I never had more pleasing inducements to cherish life, or less apprehension of too speedily quitting it.

IMPROVEMENT IN HIS HEALTH.

My health is certainly better than when I left England, and this improvement I partly ascribe to the climate, and partly to the temperance of my diet. I had long ago shaken off the bad habits of the Hampshire Militia, but a London life, in the best Company, is a life of fullness and intemperance; which cannot be separated from the lateness and irregularity of our hours, the variety of wines and dishes, and the English practise of setting after dinner, with the bottle and glasses on the table. Since my last fit of the Gout, I avoid the temptation without losing the pleasure of suppers, by confining myself to a mess of boiled milk, and in companies of twenty or thirty men and women, my frugal bason has often been placed on the tables: my dinners are moderate, and breakfast still continues to be my favourite repast. This regimen appears to have succeeded; I have passed the winter without hearing of the enemy, and last month, after a short and slight visit or rather menace, he politely retired, and has left me free to enjoy the beauties of an incomparable spring, which rapidly treads on the heels of a very mild winter.

The glories of the landskip I have always enjoyed; but Deyverdun has almost given me a taste for minute observation, and I can dwell with pleasure on the shape and colour of the leaves, the various hues of the blossoms, and successive progress of vegetation. These pleasures are not without cares; and there is a white Acacia just under the windows of my library, which in my opinion was too closely pruned last Autumn, and whose recovery is the daily subject of anxiety and conversation! My romantic wishes led sometimes to an idea which was impracticable in England, the possession of an house and garden, which should unite the society of town with the beauties and freedom of the country. That idea is now realized in a degree of perfection to which I never aspired, and if I could convey in words a just picture of my library, apartments, terrace, wilderness, vineyard, with the prospect of land and water, terminated by the mountains; and this position at the gate of a populous and lively town where I have some friends and many acquaintance, you would envy or rather applaud the singular propriety of my choice.

During the first year of my residence I often compared the tumult of London and the house of Commons, with the studious social tranquillity of Lausanne, and felt with complacency that I had chosen the better part. Those busy scenes are now far from me, like the remembrance of a noisy and troublesome dream, and though I possess from nature or reflection a happiness of temper that can be easy almost in any situation, I am at a loss to conceive how I could support so long a way of life so ill-suited to my mind and circumstances. What I particularly disliked was the alternative of a batchelor, large accidental dinners abroad, or my solitary chicken at home. Here I can keep a regular table and establishment equal to the best families of the place; we seldom dine alone, and I have often agreable suppers of men and women. The habits of female conversation have sometimes tempted me to acquire the piece of furniture, a wife, and could I unite in a single Woman, the virtues and accomplishments of half a dozen of my acquaintance, I would instantly pay my addresses to the Constellation.

In the mean while I must content myself with my other wife, the decline and fall of the Roman Empire, which I prosecute with pleasant and constant industry. I had some hopes of compleating it this year, but let no man who builds a house, or writes a book, presume to say when he will have finished. When he imagines that he is drawing near to his journey's end, Alps rise on Alps, and he continually finds something to add, and something to correct. Yet I *now* think myself sure of bringing over two or three Volumes in quarto (down to the taking of Constantinople by the Turks) in the course of next summer, I mean the summer of eighty-seven, and as the business of impression will require many months, I may long enjoy the company of my English friends. Of private friends I hope to find many in the *vulgar*, and some in the *pure* and *genuine* sense of the word, but I shall be totally bewildered. About three months after my departure, an Earthquake threw down all the men and systems of which I had any knowledge, and the country seems to be governed by a set of most respectable boys, who were at school half a dozen years ago. I see in the papers that young Eliot is become the brother and privy-Counsellor of Pitt, and that the independent father has no objection either to titles or places.

And now, My Dear Madam, after so much about myself, let me conclude with a word of enquiry on a subject very near to my heart, your health and happiness. The only apprehension from your silence relates to want of activity and spirits, and from those fears I hope you can honestly deliver me. Remember me with kindness to Mrs. Gould, and Mrs. Holroyd, and let me hear if any thing good has befallen them, more especially the former, whose situation was more susceptible of change: when I mention her I include her family. Is Mr. Melmoth still alive? I saw young Coxe last year, with a very decent and reasonable Bear, whom he leads from North to South. Adieu, Dear Madam, my paper fails.

Most truly yours,
E. G.

504.

To Lord Sheffield.

Lausanne, May 10th, 1786.

*By the difference, I suppose, of the posts of France and Germany, Sir Stanier's letter, though first written, is still on the road, and yours, which I received yesterday morning, brought me the first account of poor Mrs. P[orten]'s departure. There are few events that could affect me more deeply, and I have been ever since in a state of mind more deserving of your pity than of your reproaches. I certainly am not ignorant that we have nothing better to wish for ourselves than the fate of that best-humoured woman, as you very justly style her. A good understanding, and an excellent heart, with health, spirits, and a competency, to live in the midst of her friends till the age of fourscore, and then to shut her eyes without pain or remorse. Death can have deprived her only of some years of weakness, perhaps of misery; and for myself it is surely less painful to lose her at present, than to find her in my visit to England next year sinking under the weight of age and infirmities, and perhaps forgetfull of herself and of the persons once the dearest to her.

All this is perfectly true: but all these reflections will not dispell a thousand sad and tender remembrances that rush upon my mind. To her care I am indebted in earliest infancy for the preservation of my life and health. I was a puny child, neglected by my Mother, starved by my nurse, and of whose being very little care or expectation was entertained; without her maternal vigilance I should either have been in my grave, or imperfectly lived a crooked ricketty monster, a burthen to myself and others. To her instructions I owe the first rudiments of knowledge, the first exercise of reason, and a taste for books, which is still the pleasure and glory of my life; and though she taught me neither language nor science, she was certainly the most useful preceptor I have ever had. As I grew up, an intercourse of thirty years endeared her to me, as the faithful friend and the agreeable companion. You have seen with what freedom and confidence we lived together, and have often admired her character and conversation, which could alike please the young and the old. All this is now lost, finally, irrecoverably lost! I will agree with My Lady, that the immortality of the soul is on some occasions a very comfortable doctrine. A thousand thanks to her for her constant kind attention to that poor woman who is no more.

I wish I had as much to applaud and as little to reproach in my own behaviour towards Mrs. P. since I left England; and when I reflect that my letters would have soothed and comforted her decline, I feel more deeply than I can express, the real neglect, and seeming indifference, of my silence. To delay a letter from the Wednesday to the Saturday, and then from the Saturday to the Wednesday, appears a very slight offence; yet in the repetition of such delay, weeks, months, and years will elapse, till the omission may become irretrievable, and the consequence mischievous or fatal. After a long lethargy, I had rouzed myself last week, and wrote to the three old Ladies; my letter for Newman Street went away last post, Saturday night, and yours did not arrive till Monday morning. Sir Stanier will probably open it, and read the true picture of my sentiments for a friend who, when I wrote, was already extinct. There is something sad and awful in the thought, yet on the whole, I am sorry that even this tardy Epistle preceded my knowledge of her death. But it did not precede (you will observe) the information of her dangerous and declining state, which I conveyed in my last letter, and her anxious concern that she should never see or *hear* from you again.

This idea, and the hard thoughts which you must entertain of me, press so hard on my mind, that I must frankly acknowledge a strange and inexcusable supineness, on which I desire you would make no comment, and which in some measure may account for my delays in corresponding with you. The unpleasant nature of business, and the apprehension of finding something disagreeable, tempted me to postpone from day to day, not only the answering, but even the opening, your penultimate epistle; and when I received your last, yesterday morning, the seal of the former was still unbroken. Oblige me so far as to make no reflections; my own may be of service to me hereafter. Thus far (except the last sentence) I have run on with a sort of melancholy pleasure, and find my heart much relieved by unfolding it to a friend. And the subject so strongly holds me, so much disqualifies me for other discourse, either serious or pleasant, that here I would willingly stop, and reserve all miscellaneous matter for a second volunteer Epistle. But we both know how frail are promises, how dangerous are delays, and there are some pecuniary objects on which I think it necessary to give you an immediate, though now tardy, explanation.

I do not return you any formal thanks for* securing me the £500 at Gosling's. We are sufficiently acquainted with each other's sentiments, nor can I be surprized that you should do for me what in a similar situation you would have found and accepted without hesitation on my part. But I must remove the appearance of duplicity which might not give you pleasure, that

I should complain of urgent poverty, and doubt whether my draught would be paid, while I had £400 in Gosling's hands. A part of this wealth is only ideal, as I had reckoned on Mrs. Gibbon's Christmas half-year (£150), which was really drawn for a few days afterwards. For the rest of the difference, I can only say that I reckoned from memory (having mislaid their last year's account), that my fears preponderated, and that I am glad to find myself for once, a richer man than I expected. To show you that I am in earnest, as I shall not want to draw for some months, I am very willing that you should divert a part of your supply to the most pressing occasions. Of that nature is certainly the Buckinghamshire bond to the man who married Harris's daughter, and I beg you would pay both principal and interest immediately. The Jobbman for horses should, I think, be the next, and when these two are satisfied, upwards of £200 must remain. When I consider the large amount and easy earning of Newton's bill, he surely may wait for my return. If you are too much plagued with his importunities, silence him with another sop of £100. Whatever you do, you will send me the account, that I may know the exact quantity of my provision. You know my attachment to my little deposit in the funds, but if I should be pressed before my return by any further expences or demands, I will transact the business with the Darrels either by sale or loan. Apropos of Newton, were it perfectly convenient, I would not clear his whole bill, till I had extracted from his hands all the writings of my Hampshire Estate. I wish you would seriously undertake that extraction, the importance of which you feel more strongly than myself.

I have really an hundred things to say of myself, of you and Co., of your works, of mine, of my books in Downing Street, of Lausanne, of Politicks, &c. &c. After this, some Epistolary debts must and SHALL be paid; and to proceed with order, I have fixed this day fortnight (May 25th) for the date and dispatch of your second Epistle. Give me credit once more. Pray, does My Lady think herself absolved from all obligation of writing to me? To *her*, at least, I am not in arrear. Adieu.

505.

To Lord Sheffield.

Lausanne, July 22nd, 1786.

This general order will, I presume, remove all the unforeseen difficulties, which I should have thought must have given way to your name, and the knowledge of our connection. Use the power according to your own discretion, even to the full amount of your £500 which I have not yet violated, but remember not to satisfy Newton till he has disgorged my writings, of which, as you will easily believe, I have no list. *I suppose you have sworn (I have sworn myself) at my long silence and delay. The *plena Epistola* I have postponed from post to post, and as I see no end of waiting (though I think it will not run beyond the end of the month), it seemed most prudent to dispatch this needful missive. I am well, happy, and diligent; but your kind hint of the London house is perfectly superfluous; as instead of the *spring*, we must already read the *summer* of next year.* Do not be childish or passionate; trust me, I wish to appear in England; but it must be with my book in my hand; and a book takes more time in making than a pudding. Adieu. Will my Lady never write?

E. G.

*Since I have another page, and some leisure moments, we may as well employ it in friendly converse; the more so, as the great letter to which I alluded is most wonderfully precarious and uncertain; the more so likewise, as our correspondence for some time past has been of an abrupt, dark and disagreeable cast. Let us first talk of Sheffield's works; they are of two sorts: *primo*, two nymphs, whom I much desire to see; the stately Maria and the gentle Louisa. I perfectly represent them both in the eye of fancy; each of them accomplished according to her age and character, yet totally different in their external and internal forms. *Secundo*, three pamphlets; pamphlets I cry you mercy; three weighty treatises, almost as useful as an enquiry into the state of the primitive Church; and here let me justify, if I have not before, my silence on a subject which we authors do not easily forgive. The first, whose first editions had seen the light before I left England, followed me here in a more compleat condition; and that Treatise on the American Trade has been read, judged, approved, and reported. The second, on Ireland, I have seen by accident, the copy you had sent Mr. Trevor, who passed last summer (85) in this [place]. The third, and in my present situation the most interesting, on the French Commerce, I have not yet seen by any means whatsoever, and you who know what orders you have given to Elmsley or others, will best discern on whom should be laid the fault and the blame.* By the bye, Mrs. Trevor is now here without her husband—so much the better—and I am just going to see her, about a mile out of town: she is judged elegant and amiable; but in health and figure most lamentably declined since last year. *But to return to your books, all that I have seen must do you honour, and might do the public service; you are above the trifling decorations of style and order, but your sense is strong, your views impartial, and your industry laudable. I find that your American tract is just translated into German.

HIS CONTEMPLATED VISIT TO ENGLAND.

Do you still correspond with* Eden? *If he could establish a beneficial intercourse between the two first nations in the World, I could excuse him some little political tergiversation. At some distance of time and place, those domestic squabbles lose much of their importance; and though I should not forgive him any breach of private friendship or confidence, I cannot much blame him if he chose rather to serve his family and his country, than to persevere in a hopeless and, as I suspect, an unpopular opposition. You have never told me clearly and correctly how you support your inactive retreat from the house of Commons; whether you have resumed your long forgotten taste for rural and domestic pleasures, and whether you have never cast a look towards Coventry, or some other borough equally pure and respectable. In the short space that is left I will only repeat more distinctly, that in the present contemplation of my work, June or July of next year is the earliest term at which I can hope to see England*; and if I have a fit of the Gout—I have, indeed, been free from the monster this last twelvemonth; but he is most arbitrary and capricious. Of my own situation let me say with truth that it is tranquil, easy, and well adapted to my character. All enthusiasm is now at an end; I see things in their true light, and I applaud the judgment and choice of my retirement.

You see why I have left a blank in the first page; and when I begun I had no design of going beyond it; and now, unless I have some extraordinary fit of diligence and zeal, shall probably wait till the return of your Epistle. A word before we part, about the least unpleasant of my business; my library in Downing-street. Excuse the accidental derangement; I shall send for no more books, and only beg you to give them shelter in your stinking parlour till my arrival. Two or three mornings will suffice for a personal review, and the subsequent steps of sale or travel will most properly be executed under my own eye. Ours and the foreign papers announce the distress and reformation of the P. of W. Are you one of the Noblemen who offer him their houses? As papa is tenacious and poor, I suppose Fox next session will celebrate his economy, and Parliament will pay his debts. Once more adieu.

506.

To Lord Sheffield.

Lausanne, Jan. 20th, 1787.

*After some sallies of wrath, you seem at length to have subsided in sullen silence, and I must confess not totally without reason. Yet if your mind be still open to truth, you will confess that I am not quite so black as I appear. 1. Your Lordship has shewn much less activity and eloquence than formerly, and your last letter was an answer to mine, which I had expected some time with impatience. Bad examples are dangerous to young People. 2. Formerly I have neglected answering your Epistles on essential, though unpleasant, business; and the *Res-publica* or *-privata* may have suffered by my neglect.* At present, when you have paid away the £500 of your own creation in Gosling's hands, satisfied Newton and *Job* (I do not mean the most patient of men), and withdrawn my writings from the Attorney's paw, I do not recollect any matter of interest remaining in your hands to exercise your industry, vex my temper, or sully your dispatches. That sum of £500 you will find entire and intact in Fleet Street; you may exhaust, but in spite of my general credit I hope you will not exceed it.

*Supposing, therefore, we had no transactions, why should I write so often? To exchange sentimental compliments, or to relate the various and important transactions of the Republic of Lausanne? As long as I do not inform you of my death, you have good grounds to believe me alive and well: you have a general, and will soon have a more particular, idea of my system and arrangement here. One day glides away after another in tranquil uniformity. Every object must have sides and moments less luminous than others; but, upon the whole, the life and the place which I have chosen are most happily adapted to my character and circumstances; and I can now repeat, at the end of three years, what I soon and sincerely affirmed, that never, in a single instant, have I repented of my scheme of retirement to Lausanne; a retirement which was judged by my best and wisest friend a project little short of insanity. The place, the people, the climate, have answered or exceeded my warmest expectations: and I truly rejoice in my approaching visit to England. Mr. Pitt, were he your friend and mine, would not find it an easy task to prevent my return.

BUILDING A GREAT BOOK.

3. And now let me add a third reason, which often diverted me from writing; namely, my impatience to see you this next summer. I am building a great book, which, besides the three stories already exposed to the public eye, will have three stories more before we reach the roof and battelments. You too have built or altered a great Gothic Castle with Baronial battlements; did you finish it within the time you intended? As that time drew near, did you not find a thousand nameless and unexpected works that must be performed; each of them calling for a portion of time and labour? and had you not despised, nobly despised, the minute diligence of finishing, fitting up, and furnishing the apartments, you would have discovered a new train of indispensable business. Such, at least, has been my case. A long while ago, when I contemplated the distant prospect of my work, I gave you and myself some hopes of landing in England last Autumn; but, alas! when autumn grew near, hills began to rise on hills, Alps on Alps, and I found my journey far more tedious and toilsome than I had imagined.

When I look back on the length of the undertaking, and the variety of materials, I cannot accuse, or suffer myself to be accused, of idleness; yet it appeared that unless I doubled my diligence, another year, and perhaps more, would elapse before I could embark with my complete manuscript. Under these circumstances I took, and am still executing, a bold and meritorious resolution. The mornings in winter, and in a country of early dinners, are very concise; to them, my usual period of study, I now frequently add the evenings, renounce cards and society, refuse the most agreeable evenings, or perhaps make my appearance at a late supper. By this extraordinary industry, which I never practised before, and to which I hope never to be again reduced, I see the last part of my history growing apace under my hands; all my materials are collected and arranged; I can exactly compute, by the square foot, or the square page, all that remains to be done; and after concluding text and notes, after a general review of my time and my ground, I can now decisively ascertain the final period of the decline and fall, and can boldly promise that I will dine with you at Sheffield-place in the month of August, or perhaps of July, in the present year; within less than a twelfthmonth of the term which I had loosely and originally fixed; and perhaps it would not be easy to find a work of that size and importance in which the workman has so tolerably kept his word with himself and the public. But in this situation, oppressed with this particular object, and stealing every hour from my amusement, to the fatigue of the pen and the eyes, you will conceive, or you might conceive, how little stomach I have for the Epistolary style; and that instead of idle, though friendly, correspondence, I think it far more agreeable to employ my time in the effectual measures that may hasten and exhilarate our personal interview.

About a month ago I had a voluntary, and not unpleasing Epistle from Cadell; he informs me that he is going to print a new octavo edition, the former being exhausted, and that the public expect with impatience the conclusion of that excellent work, whose reputation and sale increases every day, &c. I answered him by the return of the post, to inform him of the period and extent of my labours, and to express a reasonable hope that he would set the same value on the three last as he had done on the three former Volumes. Should we conclude in this easy manner a transaction so honourable to the author and bookseller, my way is clear and open before; in pecuniary matters I think I am assured for the rest of my life of never troubling my friends, or being troubled myself; a state to which I aspire, and which I indeed deserve, if not by my management, at least by moderation.

A CITIZEN OF THE WORLD.

In your last, you talk more of the French treaty than of yourself and your wife and family; a true English *Quid nunc!* For my part, in this remote, inland, neutral country, you will suppose, that after a slight glance on the papers, I have neither had the means or the inclination to think very deeply about it. As a Citizen of the World, a character to which I am every day rising or sinking, I must rejoyce in every agreement that diminishes the separation between neighbouring countries, which softens their prejudices, unites their interest and industry, and renders their future hostilities less frequent and less implacable. With regard to the present treaty, I hope both nations are gainers; since otherwise it cannot be lasting; and such double mutual gain is surely possible in fair trade, though it could not easily happen in the mischievous amusements of war and gaming.* I am much pleased with our great patriots who write to you for sense as schoolboys on an exercise day. *What a delightful hand have these great statesmen made of it since my departure! without power, and, as far as I can see, without hope. When we meet I shall advise you to digest all your political and commercial knowledge, (England, Ireland, France, America,) and, with some attention to style and order, to make the whole a Classic book, which may preserve your name and benefit your Country. I know not whether you have seen Sir Henry Clinton since his return: he passed a day with me, and seemed pleased with my reception and place. We talked over you and the American War. Mrs. Trevor passes the winter here: she is pleasing and fashionable. I embrace the *silent My Lady* and the two honourable Misses, whom I sigh to behold and admire. Adieu. Ever yours.*

I have three or four things to add of meaner importance.

1. My Journey to England costs me a good servant: he has a farm, a shop, and a wife: absence from these frightens him, and he takes this opportunity of retiring from the domestic state.

2. *Though I can part with land, you find I cannot part with books: the remainder of my library has so long embarrassed your stinking room that it may now await my presence and final judgment.*

3. All my coloured handkerchiefs are worn out: I wish My Lady would get me a couple of dozen of the best sort from Ireland: an elegant Poplin would likewise be acceptable for a fur Coat. *Has the said My Lady read a novel intitled Caroline de Lichfield, of our home manufacture? I may say of ours, since Deyverdun and myself were the judges and patrons of the Manuscripts. The author, who is since married a second time, (Madame de Crousaz, now Montolieu), is a charming woman. I was in some danger.* Once more, bar a long fit of the Gout, and the historian will land at Dover before the end of July. Adieu.

507.

To Lord Sheffield.

Lausanne, June 2nd, 1787.

INTENTION TO ARRIVE IN LONDON.

*I begin to discover that if I wait till I could atchieve a just and satisfactory Epistle, equally pleasant and instructive, you would have a poor chance of hearing from me. I will therefore content myself with a simple answer to a question, which (I love to believe) you repeat with some impatience: "When may we expect you in England?" My great building is, as it were, compleated, and some slight ornaments, the painting and glazing of the last finished rooms, may be dispatched without inconvenience in the autumnal residence of Sheffield-place. It is therefore my sincere and peremptory intention to depart from Lausanne about the 20th of July, and to find myself (*me trouver*) in London on or before the glorious first of August. I know of nothing that can prevent it but a fit of the gout, the capricious tyrant, who obeys no laws either of time or place; and so unfortunately are we circumstanced, that such a fit, if it came late and lasted long, would effectually disable me from coming till next spring; since thereby I should lose the season, the monsoon, for the impression of three quarto volumes, which will require nine months (a regular parturition), and cannot advantageously appear before the beginning or middle of May.

At the same time do not be apprehensive that I mean to play you a dog's trick. From a thousand motives it is my wish to come over this year; the desire of seeing you, and the *silent sullen* My lady; the family arrangements, discharge of servants, which I have already made; the strong wish of settling my three youngest children in a manner honourable to them and beneficial to their parent. Much miscellaneous matter rises to my pen, but I will not be tempted to turn the leaf. Expect me therefore at Sheffield-place, with strong probability, about the 15th of August.* You say nothing of your final settlement with Newton: if the Attorney refuses to give parchments for money he must have some bad intention. Adieu. Yours.

508.

To his Stepmother.

DEAR MADAM,

After a long silence which I will no longer attempt to excuse, I have the pleasure of informing you that when you receive this letter I shall be on my way to England, and that I hope to reach London on or before the 9th of next month. I need not say that by the first post you shall be apprized of my arrival. I bring over the remainder of my history, and only regret that instead of running down to Bath, the necessary cares of an author will detain me in the neighbourhood of London and the press. But my impatience will be alleviated by the convenience of a near and frequent intercourse, and I sincerely hope that you can return the assurance which I give, that I have been long happy and am now well.

I am, My Dear Madam,
Ever yours,
E. G.

509.

To Lord Sheffield.

Lausanne, July 21st, 1787.

*The 20th of July is past, and I am still at Lausanne; but the march of heavy bodies, such as armies and historians, can seldom be foreseen or fixed to a precise day. Some particular reasons have engaged me to allow myself another week; and the day of my departure is now (*I believe*) determined for Sunday the 29th instant. You know the road and the distance. I am no rapid English traveller, and my servant is not accustomed to ride post. I was never fond of deeds of darkness, and if the weather be hot, we must repose in the middle of the day. Yet the roads are in general good: between Sun and Sun the interval is long; and, barring the accidents of winds and waves, I think it possible to reach London in ten or twelve days; *viz.* on or before the ninth of August. With your active spirit, you will scarce understand how I can look on this easy journey with some degree of reluctance and apprehension; but after a tranquil, sedentary life of four years, (having lain but a single night out of my own bed,) I see mountains and monsters in the way; and so happy do I feel myself *at home*, that nothing but the strongest calls of friendship and interest could drag me from hence.*

HIS ARRIVAL IN LONDON.

You ingeniously propose that I should turn off at Sittenbourn, and seem to wonder what business I can find, or make, for an immediate residence in the Capital. Have you totally forgot that I bring over three quarto volumes for the press? and are you ignorant that not a moment must be lost, if we are desirous of appearing at a proper season? I must ratify and sign my agreement with Cadell and Strahan, deliver the first part of the manuscript, settle some preliminaries with the printer and corrector, revise the first sheets, procure some necessary books, consult others, and set the machine in motion before I can secede to Sheffield-place with an easy mind, and for a reasonable term. Of this be assured, that I shall not be less impatient than yourself, and that, of human two-legged animals, yourself and yours are the first, though not the sole, whom I shall wish to see in England.

For myself, I do not regret the occupancy of Downing Street; in my first visit to London, a lodging or hotel in the Adelphi will be more convenient; but I have some anxiety about my books, and must try whether I can approach those holy relicks, without offending the delicacy of an amiable Dutchess.

Our interview is so near, that I have little more to add, except a single caution about my own concerns, in which you will confess, that from Lovegrove, and Winton, to Newton, I have been generally unlucky. If any thing remains, present or future, it must be agitated and decided; but all retrospects are useless and painful, and we have so many pleasant subjects of conversation, that all such odious matters may be buried in oblivion. Adieu. I embrace My Lady and Louisa, but I no longer presume, even on paper, to embrace the tall and blooming Maria.

Ever yours,
E. G.

Let me find a letter at Elmsley's, and inform me of the direction of your agent Purden. I may possibly have a commission for him.

510.

To Lord Sheffield.

Adelphi Hotel, August the 8th, 1787.

Intelligence extraordinary.—This day (August the 7th) the celebrated E. G. arrived in the Adelphi with a numerous retinue (one Servant). We hear that he has brought over from Lausanne the remainder of his history for immediate publication. The post had left town before my arrival. I am pleased, but indeed astonished, to find myself in London, after a journey of six hundred miles, and hardly yet conceive how I had resolution to undertake it. I find myself not a little fatigued, and have devoted this hot day to privacy and repose, without having seen any body except Cadell and Elmsley, and my neighbour Batt, whose civility amounts to kindness and real friendship. But you may depend on it, that instead of sauntering in town, or giving way to every temptation, I will dispatch my necessary work, and hasten with impatience to the groves of Sheffield-place; a project somewhat more rational than the hasty, turbulent visit which your vigour had imagined. If you come up to quicken my diligence, we shall meet the sooner; but I see no appearance of my leaving town before the end of next week. I embrace, &c. Adieu.

511.

To his Stepmother.

MY DEAR MADAM,

At length, after a pleasant journey, I again breathe the air of my native country; and though I quitted with some regret my friends, my house, my garden, my library at Lausanne, I already find many objects that compensate my losses. I reached the Adelphi Hotel *Wednesday* the 8th instant, after the departure of the post. The first arrangements of my litterary business, and some social meetings will detain me here till the middle or end of next week, after which I shall bury myself at Sheffield-place to revise and correct. The printer mutters some complaints of the distance, but it is not possible at this time of year to confine myself to a sultry and solitary metropolis. Adieu, my dear Madam, let me soon have an account, and a favourable account, of yourself.

I am
Ever yours,
E. G.

512.

To Lord Sheffield.

Tuesday, 1787.

Two lines to say that you dine with Mrs. Hanley Thursday, visit Pall Mall between eight and nine in the evening, and dine on Friday with Lord L[oughborough]. Lady L., if agreable, will be glad to see Maria, and to call on her in her carriage. All's well. Adieu. I wish we had My lady with us. I am impatient to see her.

513.

To his Stepmother.

Sheffield-place, Sept. 23, 1787.

MY DEAR MADAM,

THE TWO MR. GIBBONS.

I am extremely happy that by Mrs. Holroyd's kind enquiries in my name, the veil is at length withdrawn, and a mistake is removed which has given us, with an appearance of reason, some mutual anxiety. No one doubtless is less entitled than myself to confound the indolence of the pen with the coldness of the heart, yet I must confess that I was surprized and grieved, that you should not take the smallest notice of the letter in which I had announced my arrival in England. Each post encreased my uneasiness, which was at the same time aggravated and soothed by the assurance from Mrs. H. that illness could not be the cause of your silence, and this day was the last which I had fixed for asking the favour of a line of comfort and explanation. By this you will understand that I have never received your kind answer directed to me in town, and, though the loss of a letter by the post is a rare, and to many, an incredible event, I can explain it in this instance by a singular concurrence of circumstances. Two Hotels which bear the name of the Adelphi stand opposite to each other, and two Mr. Gibbons were lodged at the same time in the adverse houses, as Lord Sheffield perceived on his coming up to find me out. Your direction was applied to my rival, and as he had already departed into the country, his letter must have been sent after him, and he alone is guilty for not acknowledging and rectifying the error.

I have now passed some weeks with our friends Lord and Lady Sheffield, who wish me to express in their name every sentiment of attachment and regard; they both lament the disappointment of their wishes of enjoying your company in this place, and would promise that during your stay, it should not be profaned by any American rebels, or any fashionable females whose conduct may be less calculated to edify than to please. I am here, very idle and very busy. After building a great house, a thousand little alterations, improvements and ornaments present themselves to the architect, and besides the trouble of painting and glazing some of the last apartments, I have the daily duty of receiving, correcting, and returning a printed sheet which is sent me from London. Impatient as I am to visit

Bath, I must defer my journey till I am in a great measure got out of my litterary brick and mortar; and if I can postpone it till the beginning of December, Lord Sheffield gives me hopes of his company. The moments I can pass with you will be some of the most pleasing of my life, and it will give me real concern, that I shall find it impossible to prolong my visit as I could wish, much less to fix my winter residence at Bath.

I am, Dear Madam,
Most truly yours,
E. GIBBON.

514.

To his Stepmother.

Sheffield-place, Nov. 11th, 1787.

DEAR MADAM,

HIS VISIT TO MRS. GIBBON.

Besides my usual dislike to letter-writing for which you so obligingly account, I have had an additional reason or excuse for my silence in the weekly dispatches which are transmitted from hence to Bath, and by which you are frequently apprized of my health and good spirits, the only circumstances which I could transcribe from this peaceful and uniform scene. It is with real pleasure that I see the approaching period of my journey to Bath. I leave this place next Sunday, and as I hope that a fortnight *may* suffice for some litterary business (consulting books, &c.) which can only be dispatched in town, I reckon with confidence on the satisfaction of embracing you at the Belvidere within a month from the present time. As to my old enemy the gout, it is impossible to answer for his motions, but I have not the slightest grounds to suspect him of any hostile intentions. Lord Sheffield wishes to accompany me in the journey and return, but so many obstacles may impede a man of business, that I must not depend on him with any degree of assurance. Will you be so good as to inform his sister how much I am obliged to her for thinking so often and so kindly of me?

I wish it were in your power to give me a more favourable account of your health, or at least of your strength, for I flatter myself that it is in the latter you are chiefly deficient. I am not without apprehension that the sight of a long-lost friend may exhaust your spirits by too much painful pleasure. Be persuaded, my Dear Madam, that you are the sole object of my journey, that I most sincerely request that you will not contrive any dinners or parties for my amusement, that my time will be most agreably spent in your conversation, and that I could wish to enlarge the number of days which my avocations in life and litterature will allow me to enjoy at Bath. Do not give yourself the trouble of an answer, and expect a line from town, as soon as I can fix the exact time of my departure.

Lord and Lady Sheffield wish me to convey in their names every wish and sentiment of friendship.

I am, Dear Madam,
Ever yours,
E. G.

515.

To Lord Sheffield.

Wednesday, Nov. 27.

The assurance that neither giants nor dragons were to be feared between Sheffield Place and Pall Mall had induced me to leave to your fancy or judgment the well-known circumstances of changing horses, alighting from the chaise, surveying the lodging (bad and dear), ordering a fowl from the Cocoa-tree, &c., &c., and I feel every day the awkwardness of the six o'clock post. The first evening I passed at home and had scarcely dined when the Poet Hayley was announced: he embraced, forgave me, and we entered on a pleasant conversation of two hours. I mentioned to him your Christmas plan: he is grateful, but seems to decline it. However I shall see him again, and possibly he may fall in your way.

You would make me vain; nor am I less touched by the growlings of my lady, than by the praises of the Maria, whose probable excursion I applaud. As yet I have chiefly attended to my litterary concerns, and have only seen Crauford, the Lucans, Sir Joshua, &c. I have knocked without success at Lord Loughborough's door, but shall dine with him before the end of the week, perhaps with M. de Calonne, who is a favourite with all parties. Pitt in the *general* opinion seems to be the Hero of the day, and Lord Lucan, fresh from Paris, says that nothing can equal the conscious shame of the French, except their public abhorrence of the Queen, and their wild resolutions of freedom. Take care of Severy, I had rather he did not go to Lewes: a set of drunken dragoons.

As I may not write again (do not be furious) I can positively say that my departure for Bath is fixed for Saturday sennight, and that I shall expect you, &c., on Thursday at latest. For the possession of your house, I believe the Dutchess would scruple at few sacrifices either pecuniary or *personal.* Could you resist? Do not imitate my negligence in forgetting the herald John G. He will make a great figure at Bath. Adieu.

516.

To Lord Sheffield.

Monday afternoon, 1787.

A MISERABLE CRIPPLE.

I precipitate! I inconvenience! Alas! alas! I am a poor miserable cripple, confined to my chair. Last Wednesday evening I felt some flying symptoms of the gout: for two succeeding days I struggled bravely, and went in a chair to dine with Batt and Lord Loughborough: but on Saturday I yielded to my conqueror. I have now passed three wearisome days without amusement, and three miserable nights without sleep. Yet my acquaintance are charitable; and as virtue should never be made too difficult, I feel that a man has more friends in Pall Mall than in Bentinck Street. This fit is remarkably painful; the enemy is possessed of the left foot and knee, and how far he may carry the war, God only knows. Of futurity it is impossible to speak; but it will be fortunate if I am able to leave town by the end, not of this, but of the ensuing week. Pity me, magnanimous Baron; pity me, tender females; pity me, Swiss exile, and believe me, it is far better to be learning English at Uckfield. I write with difficulty, as the least motion or constraint in my attitude is repeated by all the nerves and sinews in my knee. But in the daily papers *you shall find each day a note or bulletin of my health. To-morrow I must give pain to Mrs. G. Adieu.* Caplin's servant has other offers, and grows impatient for a speedy and final answer.

Ever yours,
E. G.

517.

To his Stepmother.

Saturday, Nov. 30th, 1787.

DEAR MADAM,

I must reluctantly mention, what I could still wish to conceal: but the month of December approaches, and I may have been already betrayed by the Sheffield gazette. Your suspicions were but too just, and both my feet have been for some days past in the iron fetters of the gout. This obstacle must retard, though it shall not prevent my journey to Bath, and as soon as I am able to travel I shall summon Lord S., who with his daughter Maria is impatient to start. No term can be possibly assigned, but I feel with pleasure that the bitterness of the fit is past or passing, and the gouty tide now appears to ebb; whether its retiring motions will be slow or rapid, fluctuating or regular, I cannot foresee, but I wish you to believe that my pain is not a little aggravated by my disappointment. You will excuse my brevity, as I cannot write in a pleasant attitude, but in the course of next week you shall receive some account of my proceedings, either from me or Caplen. Adieu.

Ever yours,
E. G.

518.

To Lord Sheffield.

I resume the pen for a few moments, and with some difficulty, to say that I am not insensible of the complaints, exclamations, projects, &c., of the natives of Sheffield. Your daily missives have been uncomfortable, but when things are at the worst they begin to mend, and I flatter myself that the gouty tide is now ebbing. Last night (with some foreign aid) was the best I have known, and this day my pain is rather less severe. *What may be the future progress, whether slow or rapid, fluctuating or steady, time alone will determine, and to that master of human knowledge I must leave our Bath journey.*—Adieu. Lord Guilford is neither dead nor has been ill.— The D[uchess] of G[ordon] is in treaty for a house in Piccadilly.—The public voice is harmony and applause. Remember me to Severy. Perhaps next week.

I hear this moment from my landlady, Mrs. Crauford, the Gordon milliner, that the Dutchess has absolutely taken the house, and is removing without delay from Downing Street. Huzza.

519.

To Lord Sheffield.

Saturday, 8th December.

DISARRANGEMENT OF HIS PLANS.

I thought we might have safely depended on Caplin's *daily* diligence, but you could fairly conclude from his silence that we advance with a fair wind. The venom of the Gouty humour is almost dispelled, and I am going on to reduce the size and recover the strength of my feet. Mama cannot be more impatient than myself for the signal of weighing anchor: this unlucky check has disarranged all my social and litterary projects: in a lodging I am destitute of a thousand comforts: my books are few, my society precarious, my days long and often tedious, nor is any thing less pleasant than to be left solitary and motionless while the world is flying round and round me. In point of kind, civil, assiduous attendance of male and female friends Lausanne had quite spoilt me.

In the course or chain of my winter designs, I most ardently wish to hasten the Bath journey, that I may urge our family settlement in Downing street, for I have felt by experience the difference between town and country with regard to the press. But wishes are not hopes, nor are hopes equivalent to assurances. Yet I think (should no reverse of fortune take place) that I can promise to ascend my post-chaise painfully enough either Friday or Saturday next, the 14th or 15th instant, and therefore, if you hear nothing to the contrary, your Lordship *cum mamma amabili* may find yourself in town the Wednesday or Thursday, and we will contrive, if I am strong enough, some dinner with Lord L., Batt, or elsewhere. I am much obliged to Severy for his letter and Lausanne news. I hope he is somewhat less miserable. Adieu, I am tired. Salutations to My lady, &c. Do you know anything more of the house?

520.

To his Stepmother.

Dec. 10th, 1787.

DEAR MADAM,

I have the pleasure of informing you, that according to our last arrangements Lord S. comes to town next Thursday with Maria: that on Saturday we set out for Bath, and that on Sunday, about four or five o'clock, I hope to have the pleasure of visiting the Belvidere. This gouty impediment has been most unseasonable and disarranges the whole chain of my projects: but you may rest assured that I am not rash or precipitate: the disorder is leaving me in the most gentle and regular manner; the easy journey must do me good and cannot do me any possible harm, and I shall have the benefit of the adroit and faithful services of Caplen, who accompanies me. It is only unlucky that my old lodgings should be taken; but your prime minister will provide me with others as near as possible to the sole object of my journey.

I am, Dear Madam,
Ever yours,
E. G.

Depend on my taking the utmost care of myself.

521.

To Lady Sheffield.

Bath, December 18th, 1787.

*Alas! alas! alas! How vain and fallacious are all the designs of man. This is now the 18th of December, precisely one month since my departure from Sheffield-place; and it was firmly my wish, my hope, my resolution, that after dispatching some needful business in London, and accomplishing a pious duty at Bath, I should by this day be restored to the tranquil leisure, and friendly society, of S. P. A cruel tyrant has disconcerted all my plans; my business in town has been neglected, my attendance at Bath is just begun, and my return is yet distant. I was not a little edified to hear of some expressions of regret and discontent on my departure; and though I am not able to produce as good evidence, you will perhaps believe that in the solitude of a London lodging I often railed at the gout for maliciously delaying his attack till I was removed from a place where my sufferings would have been alleviated by every kind and comfortable attention. I grew at last so desperately impatient, as to resolve on immediate flight, without waiting till I had totally expelled the foe, and recovered my strength. I performed the journey with tolerable ease, but the motion has agitated the remains of the humour. I am very lame, and a second fit may possibly be the punishment of my rashness.

AN ACT OF DUTY AT BATH.

As yet I have seen nothing of Bath except Mrs. G.; and weakness, as well as propriety, will confine me very closely to her.* I am carried over the way in a chair about one o'clock, maintain a conversation till ten o'clock in the evening, and am then reconveyed to my lodging. *Lord S., with Mrs. Holroyd and Maria, dined with us yesterday* on the haunch of venison, but such reliefs are not always to be expected, and I chearfully perform an act of duty which is necessary and cannot be long. I am astonished to see Mrs. Gibbon so well, and though undoubtedly weaker, she seems in the last five years to be very little altered either in mind or person. *We begin to throw out hints of the shortness of our stay, and indispensable business; and, unless I should be confined by the gout, it is resolved in our cabinet to leave Bath on Thursday the 26th, and passing through Lord Loughborough's and town, to settle at Sheffield, most assuredly, before the end of the year.* Maria, to whom every object is new and pleasant, and who begins to undraw the curtain of the great theatre, wonders and almost murmurs at our impatience. *For my own part I can say with truth, that did not the press loudly demand my presence, I could, without a sigh, allow the Dutchess to reign in Downing Street the greatest part of the winter, and should be happy in the society of two persons (no common blessing) whom I love, and by whom I am beloved.* I understand with pleasure and gratitude that with the assistance of two Ushers (Miss Firth and Mrs. Moss) you have undertaken the care of Severy's English studies, from whence I expect a most rapid progress. I know not whether yours in Trisset will be equal. Pray inform our pupil, that I shall write from hence to his parents, that I am much obliged to him for his letter, which I hope to answer in a fortnight at Sheffield-place.

Adieu, Dear Madam, and believe me, with the affection of a friend and brother, ever Yours.

522.

To Lady Sheffield.

Bath, January 4th, 1788.

I congratulate you and myself on what I now consider as certain, the evacuation of Downing Street. Col. Fullarton, a cousin of the Dutchess, informed me yesterday, that after sending her children I know not where, perhaps to the parish, she had indignantly fled into the country. By this day's post I expect an official confirmation from Lord S., and as he will probably reach you as soon as this letter, the communication will inform him of my intended motions. You will admire the triumphant Maria, and your observation will soon discern whether it will be easy to brush the powder out of her hair, and the world out of her heart, or to shut her eyes after they have been once opened to the light of pleasure. This excursion will render our scheme still more necessary, and in my letter from hence I sound Madame de S. on the subject: the more I revolve it, I think the exchange will be pleasant and beneficial to my English and Swiss friends, whose mutual advantage I shall have the advantage of promoting. You have already understood that my precipitation in leaving London has been justly punished by a second and worse fit of the gout and a fortnight's confinement.

I now begin to crawl again on two crutches, and my first sally in a chair will be to return the charitable visits of the Dutchess and her friend the Ætherial of poor Lord North, &c. Were I capable of listening to experience or common sense, I should remain here a week or ten days longer; but I am so impatient to leave this place and to reach London and S. P. that I mean to escape next Monday: Tuesday afternoon and all Wednesday will be the least that my litterary business in town will require, and I have hopes of dining at S. P. on Thursday the 10th instant, after an absence twice as long and ten times as disagreeable as I expected. As I now run, not from you, but to you, you will view my rashness with indulgence, and nurse my infirmities with compassion.—Excuse me to Severy for not answering his two letters, and let him be in readiness to receive me. Adieu.

Ever yours,
E. G.

523.

To his Stepmother.

Tuesday, the 14th January, about 1788.

Andover five o'Clock in the afternoon.—Safe, well, and hungry. Not a single Lyon or Giant to be seen on Salisbury plain.—Very odd!

524.

To Lady Sheffield.

Bentinck Street, Thursday, Feb. 24th.

The Gibbon with his friend Nic (a very proper companion) still proposes to visit Sheffield Place, on Saturday next the 26th instant, but as he travels slowly and prudently with his own horses, they dine at Godstone and cannot reach the mansions of bliss before the dusk of evening. The Gibbon presume that the most amiable Lara means to allow *him* some extraordinary days.

525.

To his Stepmother.

Downing Street, March 1st, 1788.

MY DEAR MADAM,

HIS WORK AND FRIENDS.

As long as it was necessary that you should be informed of my motions and those of the gout, my letters succeeded each other with sufficient rapidity. The establishment of my health and strength has allowed me, from these unnatural efforts, to sink into my usual indolence, but I now begin to feel that my silence has lasted too long, and that you may entertain some doubts of my present state, unless I assure you by a line that it still continues easy and prosperous. I use with moderation the society of this great town, and although I do not lead a solitary life, yet my principal attention is bestowed on my domestic friends, and on the progress of my work, which is drawing fast to a conclusion. My own brevity will encourage you not to fatigue yourself by a long letter, but I wish to hear directly from *you* and about *yourself*, the object most truly interesting to your filial friend.

I am, Dear Madam,
Ever yours,
E. GIBBON.

526.

To his Stepmother.

Downing Street, May 28th, 1788.

DEAR MADAM,

Both as an author and as a friend I am delighted with your kind approbation: and I enjoy the pleasing assurance that the perusal of my history may sometimes beguile a solitary hour, and recall the historian still more forcibly to your mind. For my own part I now feel as if a mountain was removed from my breast; as far as I can judge, the public unanimously applauds my compliment to Lord North, and does not appear dissatisfied with the conclusion of my work. I look back with amazement on the road which I have travelled, but which I should never have entered had I been previously apprized of its length.

In your last letter you express some joy at the approach of summer, as it is connected with my second visit to Bath which I had promised to make before my departure for the Continent. On my side the promise will be most chearfully performed, and in the prospect of embracing a dear and valuable friend I shall ever esteem fatigue and expence as of small account. The Sheffields leave town in the beginning of next week; I must continue some days after them to pack up my books and dispatch some necessary business, and in about a fortnight I could undertake the journey to Bath. Yet before you resolve, I wish you coolly to weigh whether prudence should advise us to gratify or restrain our inclination. In my Christmas visit, confined as I was by the gout, I could not but observe how much my presence and your desire of inviting company to amuse me deranged the privacy of your life and the distribution of your hours. Delicate health and spirits like yours are agitated even by the pleasure, the tumultuous pleasure, of an interview; and that pleasure is embittered by the painful foresight of an approaching separation. According to my arrangements, which it is no longer in my power to break, I *must* return to Lausanne early in the month of July, nor can I indulge my wishes at the Belvidere beyond the term of a week. That week is perfectly at your service, and I only hope to receive your commands as soon as possible. Lord and Lady S. beg to be remembered to you in the kindest manner.

I am, Dear Madam,
Ever yours,
E. G.

527.

To Lord Sheffield.

Hampton Court, Wednesday, June 16th, three o'clock.

Whether you mean to abuse or applaud me, you must postpone that pleasure from Sunday the 20th to Saturday the 26th. I have some literary accounts to settle before I shut my shop for some months, and they have run, as it commonly happens, to a greater length than I had expected. This delay happens likewise to be very convenient to my agreeable companion Mr. Nicholls, who salutes the whole Barony with proper respect.

528.

To Lord Sheffield.

Downing-street, Saturday (June 17th, 1788).

*I have but a moment between my return home and my dressing, and heartily tired I am; for I am now involved in the horrors of shopping, packing, &c.; yet I must write four lines to prevent a growl and a damn, which might salute the arrival of an empty-handed post on Sunday. I hope the whole caravan, Christians and pagans, arrived in good health at the castle; that the Turrets begin to rise to the third Heaven; that each has found a proper occupation; and that Tuft enjoys the freedom and felicity of the lawn.

Yesterday the august scene was closed for this year. Sheridan surpassed himself; and though I am far from considering him as a perfect orator, there were many beautiful passages in his speech, on justice, filial love, &c.; one of the closest chains of argument I ever heard, to prove that Hastings was responsible for the acts of Middleton; and a compliment, much admired, to a certain historian of your acquaintance. Sheridan, in the close of his speech, sunk into Burke's arms; but I called this morning, he is perfectly well.* A good Actor!

I fear that I shall not be able to dine at home a single day. To-morrow Severy and myself go to Bushy. I hope to be with you by Sunday the 22nd Instant, but I find I have much to do, and the most important business of my Magdalen farms is not concluded. You know Hugonin's method of writing most when there is least occasion for it. I have not had a line from him since I sent the College license. *The casing of my books is a prodigious operation. Adieu.*

529.

To Lord Sheffield.

Downing-street, June 21st, 1788.

Instead of the historian, you receive a short letter; in your eyes an indispensable tribute. This day, at length, after long delay and frequent expostulation, I have received the writings, which I am now in the act of signing, sealing, and delivering, according to the lawyer's directions. They return to-night by the Mail Coach into Hugonin's hands, from which they will not depart till the money is paid. I hope to receive it next Tuesday; next Wednesday must be employed with the Darrels in proper investments, and the Thursday I hope to be at Sheffield. *You see my departure is not postponed a moment by idleness or pleasure, but the precise day still hangs on contingencies, and we must all be patient, if our wishes should be thwarted. I say our wishes, for I sincerely desire to be with you. I have had many dinners, some splendid and memorable, with Hastings last Thursday, with the Prince of Wales next Tuesday,* both by special desire. *But the town empties, Texier is silent, and in an evening, I *desiderate* the resources of a family or a club. Caplen has finished the Herculean labour, and seven Majestic boxes will abdicate on Monday your hall. Severy has likewise dispatched his affairs, and secured his Companion Clarke, who is arrived in town; but his schemes are abridged by the inexorable rigour of Lord Howe, who has assured our great and fair Intercessors, that by the king's orders the dock-yards are shut against all strangers. We therefore give up Portsmouth, and content ourselves with two short trips; one to Stowe and Oxford, the other to Chatham; and if we can catch a launch and review, *encore vit-on.* He (Severy, not Lord Howe) salutes with me the Christians and Pagans of the family. Adieu. Yours.*

530.

To Lord Sheffield.

Downing street, Saturday, June 25th, 1788(?).

*According to your imperious law I write a line, to postpone my arrival to Friday, or perhaps Saturday, but I hope Friday, and I promise you that not a moment shall be wasted.

And now let me add a cool word as to my final departure, which is irrevocably fixed between the 10th and 15th of July. After a full and free enjoyment of each other's society, let us submit, without a struggle, to reason and fate. It would be idle to pretend business at Lausanne; but a compleat year will elapse before my return. Severy and myself are now expected with some impatience.* I desire to see *my own* house; *my own* library; *my own* garden, whose summer beauties are each day losing something. *I am thankful for your hospitable entertainment; but I wish you to remember Homer's admirable precept:

"Welcome the coming, *speed* the parting guest."

Spare me, therefore, spare yourself, the trouble of a fruitless contest, in which (according to a great author) I foresee a certain loss of time, and a probable loss of temper. The Petersfield business is terminated, and I have received the money; but Darrel will not come to town from Richmond. I believe we shall have both Craufurd and Hugonin at Sheffield-place. Adieu.*

531.

To his Stepmother.

Sheffield place, June 29th, 1788.

MY DEAREST MADAM,

I must indeed be incorrigible, since I could delay an answer to your last kind and generous letter: but you will again exercise that kind indulgence, nor shall I aggravate my old offence by a formal and foolish apology. I am now at Sheffield-place preparing for my departure, which is only delayed by an excursion of my young friend to Oxford and perhaps to Bath, in which case he will certainly request of Mrs. Holroyd the favour of presenting him to you. The Sheffields have not been so firm and reasonable as yourself, and in the bitter mixture of our last interview I strongly feel the propriety of your choice.—I propose setting out between the 10th and 15th of next month, and, as long as the journey can inspire you with the smallest doubt or apprehension, you may depend on hearing punctually from me. After I subside in the calm of a Lausanne life, my diligence will probably be relaxed: yet I hope more than I dare promise.

POSSIBLE SALE OF BERITON.

With Lord Sheffield's advice I begin to entertain some thoughts of disposing of Buriton. A landed Estate, to me an useless incumbrance, is attended with many drawbacks and expences: and as several rich neighbours, Lord Egremont, Lord Stawell, and Mr. Bonham are eager for the purchase, it is probable that while I diminish my cares, I may almost double my income. Before any serious steps are taken in the business, your ease and interest will be first consulted, and as I propose leaving a considerable part of the purchase money on the Estate, your jointure may be secured on the same kinds as firmly as before. Lord Sheffield, in whose honour and abilities you have a perfect confidence, will correspond with you on the subject, and you may be assured that nothing shall be done without your full and chearful approbation. Lord and Lady Sheffield beg me to communicate in their name all the wishes of regard and friendship.

I am, Dear Madam,
Ever yours,
E. GIBBON.

532.

To his Stepmother.

Sheffield-place, July the 18th, 1788.

MY DEAR MADAM,

A kind and generous behaviour is what I always expect from you; and your obliging condescension with regard to Buriton, the sale of which would place me in so desirable a situation, excites rather gratitude than surprize in my breast. I agree with you in wishing to refer the detail of this business to your correspondence with Lord Sheffield, who will weigh every circumstance and every objection, who will consider in the first place your satisfaction, and my interest in the second. Let me only say that the idea of a Mortgage was partly for your security and partly from an apprehension of trusting my whole fortune to the public credit; that such an investment of money unites, when it is carefully made, the solidity of land with the clear ready payment of the funds, and that I am not less averse than yourself to any connection, open or clandestine, with the member for Petersfield.

To-morrow I shall leave this place, where I have been detained much longer than I intended by an indisposition of poor Severy which prevented him from waiting on you at Bath. I dine to-morrow at Tunbridge-Wells with Lord North, reach Dover Sunday, pass the water, if possible, Monday, and repose myself at Lausanne about Wednesday sevennight the 30th instant. You are too well acquainted with the World and with me not to smile at the report of my approaching marriage, of which you might be sure of having the earliest and most direct information. Cadell is too discreet to have opened his mouth on a subject, on which for particular reasons we had mutually promised secrecy. The public, where it costs them nothing, are extravagantly liberal; yet I will allow with Dr. Johnson "that booksellers in this age are not the worst patrons of litterature."

I am, Dear Madam,
Ever yours,
E. G.

533.

To Lord Sheffield.

Lausanne, July 30, 1788.—Wednesday, 3 o'clock.

I have but a moment to say, before the departure of the post, that, after a very pleasant journey, I arrived here about half an hour ago; that I am as well arranged, as if I had never stirred from this place; and that dinner on the table is just announced. Severy I dropt at his country-house about two leagues off. I just saluted the family, who dine with me the day after to-morrow, and return to town for some days, I hope weeks, on my account. The son is an amiable and grateful Youth; and even this journey has taught me to know and to love him still better. My satisfaction would be compleat, had I not found a sad and serious alteration in poor Deyverdun; but thus our joys are checkered! I embrace all; and at this moment feel the last pang of our parting at Tunbridge. Convey this letter or information, without delay, from Sheffield-place to Bath. In a few days I shall write more amply to both places.

534.

To his Stepmother.

Lausanne, August the 16th, 1788.

DEAR MADAM,

RETURN TO LAUSANNE.

The day and indeed the moment of my arrival in this place I announced the event by a short missive to Sheffield-place, and desired that the intelligence might be forwarded without delay to the Belvidere. The perils of the ocean and the road, imaginary perils, are now over, and I am again seated in the elegant repose of my library and garden: free to enjoy all the pleasures of study, my first pleasures, but no longer chained to the regular performance of a laborious task. At this time of the year small as well as great cities are emptied of their most dignified inhabitants: yet if I were not rather disposed to a sedentary life, I could find in the town and adjacent country what Mr. Christie (?) calls a very respectable vicinage. But their names and characters would be uninteresting to you, and with the best intentions a correspondence with a distant friend must degenerate into mutual questions and answers concerning each other. The only person here with whom you are acquainted, poor Deyverdun, is, I much fear, in a state of decline, though I hope not of actual danger: that would indeed be a loss.

Present my kindest remembrance to Mrs. Holroyd, and if they are with you, to the Goulds. I lament that I never saw them during my stay in England.

I am, Dear Madam,
Ever yours,
E. GIBBON.

535.

To Lord Sheffield.

October 1, 1788.

*After such an act of vigour as my first letter, composed, finished, and dispatched within half an hour after my landing, while the dinner was smoking on the table, your knowledge of the animal must have taught you to expect a proportionable degree of relaxation; and you will be satisfied to hear, that, for many Wednesdays and Saturdays, I have consumed more time than would have sufficed for the Epistle, in devising reasons for procrastinating it to the next post. At this very moment I begin so very late, as I am just going to dress, and dine in the Country, that I can take only the benefit of the date, October the first, and must be content to seal and send my letter next Saturday.

October the 4th.

Saturday is now arrived, and I much doubt whether I shall have time to finish. I rose, as usual, about seven; but as I knew I should have so much time, you know it would have been ridiculous to begin any thing before Breakfast. When I returned from my breakfast-room to the library, unluckily I found on the table some new and interesting books, which instantly caught my attention; and without injuring my correspondent, I could safely bestow a single hour to gratify my curiosity. Some things I found in them insensibly led me to other books, and other enquiries; the morning has stolen away, and I shall be soon summoned to dress and dine with the two Severys, father and son, who are returned from the Country on a disagreeable errand, an illness of Madame, from which she is, however, recovering. Such is the faithful picture of my mind and manners, and from a single day *disce omnes*.

ILLNESS OF DEYVERDUN.

After having been so long chained to the oar, in a splendid galley indeed, I freely and fairly enjoy my liberty as I promised in my preface; range without controul over the wide expanse of my library; converse, as my fancy prompts me, with poets and historians, philosophers and Orators, of every age and language; and often indulge my meditations in the invention and arrangement of mighty works, which I shall probably never find time or application to execute. My garden, *berceau*, and pavillion often varied the scene of my studies; the beautiful weather which we have enjoyed exhilarated my spirits, and I again tasted the wisdom and happiness of my retirement, till that happiness was interrupted by a very serious calamity, which took from me, for above a fortnight, all thoughts of study, of amusement, and even of correspondence. I mentioned in my first letter the uneasiness I felt at poor Deyverdun's declining health, how much the pleasure of my life was embittered by the sight of a suffering and languid friend. The joy of our meeting appeared at first to revive him; and, though not satisfied, I began to think, at least to hope, that he was every day gaining ground; when, alas! one morning I was suddenly recalled from my berceau to the house, with the dreadful intelligence of an Apoplectic stroke; I found him senseless: the best assistance was instantly collected; and he had the aid of the genius and experience of Mr. Tissot, and of the assiduous care of an ordinary Physician, who for some time scarcely quitted his bedside either night or day.* You will understand his danger when I recapitulate the operations of a few hours—leeches, six bleeding vomits, purges, clysters, blisters to his thighs, warm baths, and mustard to his feet. *While I was in momentary dread of a relapse, with a confession from his physicians that such a relapse must be fatal, you will feel that I was much more to be pitied than my friend. At length, Art or Nature triumphed over the enemy of life. I was soon assured that all immediate danger was past: and now for many days I have had the satisfaction of seeing him recover, though by slow degrees, his health and strength, his sleep and appetite. He now walks about the garden, and receives his particular friends, but has not yet gone abroad. His future health will depend very much upon his own prudence: but, at all events, this has been a very serious warning; and the slightest indisposition will hereafter assume a very formidable aspect.

But let us turn from this melancholy subject.—The man of the people escaped from the tumult, the bloody tumult of the Westminster Election, to the lakes and mountains of Switzerland, and I was informed that he was arrived at the Lyon d'Or. I sent a compliment; he answered it in person;* we returned together to the Inn, brought away the fair Mrs. Armstead, *and settled at my house for the remainder of the day. I have eat and drank, and conversed and sat up all night with Fox in England; but it never has happened, perhaps it never can happen again, that I should enjoy him as I did that day, alone,* for his fair Companion was a cypher,* from ten in the morning till ten at night. Poor Deyverdun, before his accident, wanted spirits to appear, and has regretted it since. Our conversation never flagged a moment; and he seemed thoroughly pleased with the place and with his Company. We had little politicks; though he gave me, in a few words, such a character of Pitt, as one great man should give of another his rival: much of books, from my own, on which he flattered me very pleasantly, to

Homer and the Arabian nights; much about the country, my garden (which he understands far better than I do), and, upon the whole, I think he envies me, and would do so were he Minister. The next morning I gave him a guide to walk him about the town and country, and invited some company to meet him at dinner. The following day he continued his journey to Berne and Zurich, and I have heard of him by various means. The people gaze on him as a prodigy, but he shows little inclination to converse with them.* The wit and beauty of his Companion are not sufficient to excuse the scandalous impropriety of shewing her to all Europe, and you will not easily conceive how he has lost himself in the public opinion, which was already more favourable to his Rival. Will Fox never know the importance of character?

Far different has been the conduct and success of *our friend Douglas; he has been curious, attentive, agreeable; and in every place where he has resided some days, he has left acquaintance who esteem and regret him: I never knew so clear and general an impression.

After this long letter I have yet many things to say, though none of any pressing consequence. I hope you are not idle in the deliverance of Buriton, though the late events and edicts in France begin to reconcile me to the possession of dirty acres. What think you of Necker and the States generals? Are not the public expectations sanguine? Adieu. I will write soon to My Lady separately, though I have not any particular subject for her ear.

Ever yours,*
E. GIBBON.

536.

To Lord Sheffield.

Lausanne, Nov. 29, 1788.

INSANITY OF GEORGE III.

As I have no Correspondents but yourself, I should have been reduced to the stale and stupid communications of the papers, if you had not most gloriously dispatched me a sketch of the strange revolution that three Kingdoms should depend on the brain of one man! *In so new a case the *Salus populi* must be the first law; and any extraordinary acts of the two remaining branches of the Legislature must be excused by necessity, and ratified by general consent.* Yet I cannot any more than yourself understand this speedy and peremptory sentence of the Medical tribe. The apprehension or rather hope of his death may admonish the reigning ministers not to irritate the heir apparent: otherwise, since they have a Majority, what should prevent them from shackling him with a Counsel, or from tacking to the address of support a request that he would not change his servants? They have the confidence (aye growl) of the Country and of Europe: by *them*, I mean Pitt. *Till things are settled, I expect a regular Journal.

From kingdoms I descend to farms,* and the latter in a selfish consideration are not the least important and interesting. You seem to have made a considerable progress in the Buriton affair, since you would not have fixed the price without a careful survey and valuation of each particular founded on your own judgement and that of some able professor. You do not however mention that you have employed any such person. I submit to your science, but I cannot say that I am fond of this mode of auctions: besides the publicity, which on this occasion may be dangerous, you expose yourself either to let the estate go for an inadequate price or to an improper purchaser; or else by purchasing it in, you incur the expences, tax, &c., to a large amount. Since we know the persons whom Buriton best suits, suppose Bonham, Lords Stawell, and Egremont, might not the same end be answered with less inconvenience by writing at the same time a public circular letter to each, and desiring that by a certain day they would send in sealed proposals? Would they not have the same inducement to bid against one another? Upon the whole the 18,000 pounds would make me happy for life. Yet I would not proceed hastily in this momentous business. What is the motive of Hugonin's sudden migration, is it health, distress, fancy? Where does he settle? Who will take care of my affairs? A year's rent is now due, besides some arrears.

I have written to my two old Ladies without receiving answers. What are your accounts from Bath? I hope you have satisfied *her* about the sale of Buriton, which I would much sooner delay than give her any uneasiness. I wish we had a correspondent at Stamford (that Attorney whose name I have forgot, who called upon me in Downing Street) to give you notice in case it should please Almighty God, &c.—Deyverdun is not worse. Yet I much doubt whether you will see him next year. Do you still persist? Thinking as you do, I feel the force of a certain objection, and must own that a small circle is often more dangerous than a large one. I likewise fear for yourself the want of occupation in winter, and am now apprehensive of the views of Parliament, office, &c., that may open themselves under a new and friendly reign. As soon as you are *absolutely* determined let me know; as the arrangement of a proper house would not be easy.

The Severys are well and *all* impatient to see you. I have passed three weeks with them at Rolle, as comfortably as at S.P.: we made a tour to Geneva. The youth is perfectly reconciled to his little Country. If My Lady, in the paradise of Brighton, could find leisure for a line, it would be gracious. Adieu.

537.

To Lord Sheffield.

Lausanne, Dec. 13, 1788.

DEATH OF HUGONIN.

Poor Hugonin! I can assure you that my thoughts, my first thoughts at least when I read your letter, turned much more on himself. I knew him from my youth: he was an honest useful friend, and though he could never be much of a companion to me, I always loved and esteemed him. His death is a loss if an auction at Petersfield was ever an advisable measure. You have considered and must have determined before this can reach you. But if it be not too late, revolve the advantages and inconveniences of auctions.

Buriton is no elegant villa which may catch the eye and fancy of a stranger; it is an heap of dirty acres which can only derive their extraordinary value from local merit. Will any man give so much as Mr. Bonham and Lord Stawell, and in that case would not a private treaty with them be more easy and effectual? I again repeat that Mrs. Gibbon must be perfectly satisfied. I hope you will not let it go under £18,000. We once talked of twenty.

*Of public affairs I can only hear with curiosity and wonder: careless as you may think me, I feel myself deeply interested. You must now write often; make Miss Firth copy any curious fragments; and stir up any of my well-informed acquaintance, Batt, Douglas, Adam, perhaps Lord Loughborough, &c., to correspond with me; I *will* answer them.

We are now cold and gay at Lausanne. The Severys came to town Yesterday. I saw a good deal of Lords Malmsbury and Beauchamp and their Ladies; Ellis, of the Rolliad, was with them; I like him much: I gave them a great dinner.

Adieu for the present. Deyverdun is not worse.*

Will you direct Richard Andrews to collect and remitt my year's rent which is now payable? I suppose he can be trusted, and that you can authorize him. H.'s departure seems to be a new reason for disposing of Buriton.

538.

To Lord Sheffield.

December 31st, 1788.

HUGONIN'S DISHONESTY.

This moment I receive and answer your Epistle. We are in the midst of the hardest winter I ever felt, and three English mails are arrived at once this morning. A black prospect indeed of public and private affairs, and such is my patriotism that I must fairly own the latter are predominant in my thoughts. Is it possible that my old friend poor Hugonin should turn out a rogue? I thought him both an honest and a frugal man, but the facts you mention are strongly against him. Is it possible that his landed property, which was considerable, should be insufficient to satisfy my demands and those of all his creditors? Is it possible that, living retired in the Country, he should have deranged his affairs? I still flatter myself that his executors must and can repay any sums which he may have *borrowed* in my name, and though there should be some delay, I still hope that, with proper steps on your side, there will not finally be much loss. If all is indeed desperate down to Hugonin's strange receipt in full, it is not a year but a year and a half's rent that I have miserably lost, as I had been persuaded or compelled to allow six months' grace, and to be satisfied with receiving before Christmas the year's rent which had been due the preceding Lady-day. There is besides some arrear of rent from the College farms which was due at the time of the sale, and which Hugonin has never clearly settled. Such a blow, at least of seven or eight hundred pounds, will most essentially distress me, and derange those schemes of comfort and order which I now thought most firmly established. You are my only refuge. Could I hope (I may wish, I must not ask) that you would get into your post-chaise in Downing Street and run down to Petersfield? Your eagle-eye and active firmness would see more and do more in eight and forty hours than all the agents and letters in the World. If this be too much, a man of confidence (is Purden fit for the commission?) might be sent to make a full observation and report of the state of accounts, and of the farm at Beriton with respect both to present arrangements and final operations. Andrews has a fair character, but an Attorney!

This unforeseen and unfortunate blow encreases my desire of getting rid of such dangerous and ungovernable property; and from the produce of any sum between 18 and 15,000 pounds I could certainly draw a larger and safer income than I enjoy at present. But how to proceed. Is Mrs. G. of Bath perfectly satisfied? I have not heard from her nor do you mention her name. Have you heard of the Northamptonshire Saint? You wait for my instructions, I can send none. You are an able and active friend, and I shall acquiesce in all you think right, even in the auction, which does not thoroughly suit my taste. I should prefer a fair Gentlemanlike private address to Bonham either by letter or in person. For God's sake, or rather for friendship's sake, comfort and extricate me. I am in low spirits. Adieu.

Ever yours,
E. G.

Write soon—I think the earliest and most vigorous steps should be taken for making my demand on H.'s executors. Is there no allusion between him and the Tenant? if there is would it not invalidate his *unusual* receipt?

539.

To Lord Sheffield.

Lausanne, Feb. 4th, 1789.

If Hugonin's debt be desperate I must submit, but there is no *imbecillity* in saying that the loss will derange my plans, since I must sell out of the funds to supply the deficiency. The amount of my fruitless demand I cannot specify, but you may easily make it out by comparing Hugonin's remittances to the Goslings with the rent-roll of the Estate. Mrs. G. of Bath must doubtless be satisfied and secured in any way and on any fund which her prudence or fancy may prefer. You had once dropt something of giving *her* a security on your Estate. That method, which could not be attended with any risk or inconvenience to yourself, would perhaps be most agreable to all parties. I most sincerely hope that the sale may be already dispatched by private contract, before the decisive 18th of February. Why should you confine yourself to so short a day, since the town is equally full in March and April? and you are sensible how much the failure of the auction would blast any other operations. Is it yet too late for a delay? I mean only of some weeks, for I am very desirous of terminating this winter, in the *present* prosperous state of the Country: and indeed so desirous that I could patiently submit to a much larger abatement, to be at last possessed of a much better income free from those accidents and deductions to which land is so woefully exposed. You talk of £18,000, but if you could not get more than 17 or even 16, I might afterwards repent your refusal. I would certainly vest part in a mortgage, but I would rather chuse my man and my county, and should like to have the security of a larger estate than that of Buriton. While such an one was looking for, the part of the purchase money not secured to Mrs. G. might lye safely in the funds.

I have not heard from either of the old Ladies, and wish you could inform yourself of the state of the Northamptonshire Saint. If you will apply to my good friend Lord Spencer, he could easily find you a correspondent in that neighbourhood who without noise or scandal might send you regular and early notice of her decline and fall.—On smaller matters you are too earnest and almost angry: the continuance of the foreign papers I could not foresee and will try to rectify. Jones's bill, a trifle of about ten pounds, I will settle——

Had I the least idea of the 25 guineas of the Royal society, I should not have solicited so useless a title: but the dye is now cast, and I will write to Elmsley to satisfy that demand as well as the Antiquarian and African. I certainly did not give him any orders about newspapers, magazines, &c., as I cannot devise any method of getting them in any reasonable time without an extravagant expence. Your copiousness on my affairs makes you concise on those of the public. The debates and the outside transactions I can read in English and foreign papers, but from you, as Cicero says to his friend Cœlius (ad familiares, L. ii. Ep. 8) *nec præterita nec præsentia, sed ut ab homine longe in posterum prospiciente futura exspecto, ut ex tuis litteris, cum formam Rei publicæ viderim, quale ædificium futurum sit scire possim.* Above all I wish to hear what part you are likely yourself to act in the new regency, your hopes, your wishes, and whether you intend next winter to breathe the free and pleasant air of Lausanne or to tug at the parliamentary and official oar, amid the fogs of London.

DEYVERDUN'S SECOND ATTACK.

Of my book I have not leisure or inclination to talk. Its genuine reputation will rise or fall without any regard to the barking critics who always attend the heels of any popular work. Two translations are printing at Paris, and two English editions in Germany. I embrace My lady, &c., and still hold my *intention* of writing. Adieu. Severy tells his own story. I believe he is a tolerable correspondent. Poor Deyverdun has had another, a slighter, attack; he is now better, but I fear that his days will be neither long nor happy. A melancholy theme. Once more Adieu.

E. G.

540.

To his Stepmother.

Lausanne, February 28th, 1789.

DEAR MADAM,

Immediately on my return to this place, I wrote to inform you of my safe arrival: but some months have now elapsed without hearing from you. I should not have patiently acquiesced under this silence, had I not in the mean time obtained, through the channel of Mrs. Holroyd and Lord Sheffield, such frequent and authentic information as gave me tolerable though not perfect satisfaction on the very interesting subject of your health and happiness. With regard to my own I have no reason to complain. I have supported without inconvenience the short but severe cold of this winter; the gout has not yet invaded my tranquillity, and I again enjoy the life of society and study which renders Lausanne so agreable to my taste. The heaviest drawback is the state of poor Deyverdun. Besides a gradual and visible decline he has had two strokes of an Apoplexy, and as these dreadful warnings cannot teach him a lesson of temperance, his physicians do not allow me to entertain a hope of his recovery.

My desire to get rid of Buriton is much confirmed by a very disagreable proof of the danger of distant and landed property. Hugonin is just dead, and dead insolvent: his real estate is entailed on his brother, his personals will not satisfy his bond creditors, and as he had given receipts to my tenants down to Michaelmas last, I must lose without hopes of redress the rent and arrears of a year and a half. An heavy and unseasonable loss! Yet notwithstanding my ardour to shake off the incumbrance, I have made it my first condition with Lord Sheffield that in the progress of the business he shall obtain not only your legal consent, but your free and chearful approbation. Since you dislike a mortgage, the security of your jointure may be transferred to an adequate part of the purchase money, vested in the funds, or if you prefer land I am persuaded that Lord S. will not refuse the broad basis of his Sussex estate. May you long enjoy an income which I have often wished it were in my power to enlarge to the full measure of my affection.

Let me hear from you soon; if writing be inconvenient, I am persuaded that Mrs. or Miss Gould would discharge with pleasure the office of secretary.

I am, Dear Madam,
Ever yours,
E. G.

541.

To Lord Sheffield.

Lausanne, April 25, 1789.

THE SALE OF BERITON.

*Before your letter, which I received yesterday, I was in the anxious situation of a King, who hourly expects a courier from his general, with the news of a decisive engagement. I had abstained from writing, for fear of dropping a word, or betraying a feeling, which might render you too cautious or too bold. On the famous 8th of April, between twelve and two, I reflected that the business was determined; and each succeeding day I computed the speedy approach of your messenger, with favourable or melancholy tidings. When I broke the seal I expected to read, "What a damned unlucky fellow you are! Nothing tolerable was offered, and I indignantly withdrew the estate." I *did* remember the fate of poor Lenborough, and I was afraid of your magnanimity, &c.* Well, then, I have £16,000 pounds instead of Buriton! upon the whole I rejoyce in the exchange, although the sum has fallen short of our expectations, and I feel the weight of the reasons which kept it down. But if Lord Stawell was the only bidder, why in God's name could he not make the same offer by private contract, and save me the expences of the Auction, which I fear are considerable? Pray who pays the tax, the buyer or the seller, and what deduction will occur on the gross sum?

What I am specially pleased with is the character of the purchaser, or rather of his agent, whom I still suppose to be my old acquaintance, Mr. Sainsbury, a man of sense, experience, and a fair reputation. He was bred an Attorney at Petersfield, knows every inch of the estate, and would not have suffered his Lord to purchase without having the money, or to give a price above the real value. From him we shall have no captious difficulties or evasive delays—he will be content with a fair title, and I flatter myself that the whole business will be terminated with ease and despatch. But as many things fall out between the cup and the lip, your friendship I am sure will not be asleep, you will goad the slow-paced lawyers, and settle Mrs. G.'s security for her jointure in the manner most convenient and agreable for herself. By what time do you probably suppose that I may have the money in my pocket? It would be generous, too generous perhaps, in Lord S. and his agent, if they would make the payment and take possession of the estate on your act and guarantee without waiting for the return of the writings from Lausanne. I have sketched a short paper which you may shew them if you think it will be of any use.

It is whimsical enough, but it is in human nature, that I now begin to think of the deep-rooted foundations of land, and the airy fabrick of the funds. I not only consent, but even wish, to have eight or ten thousand pounds on a good mortgage; but I think the whole of that sum too large for Buriton, and conceive that Lord Stawell should reinforce it by some collateral security. How often have I regretted my dear New-river share which the Goslings so rudely tore from me. I should not be unwilling to repurchase it for the same money, I mean instead of the mortgage.—I forgot to say, indeed it is needless, that I suppose all proper care has been taken about a deposit, and to secure my receipt of the rents till the payment of the money. A propos of the rents, half a year is now due since that worthy general discharge of last Michaelmas, and I desire that Andrews may instantly exact it, it will be a seasonable supply, and if Heartfee suffers any inconvenience it will be no more than a just punishment for his scandalous and manifest collusion with poor Hugonin, whose merits I am more inclined to remember than his faults.

Mrs. G[ibbon] of Cliffe has not answered my letters, and I am anxious to learn the state of her health. Her correspondent in town is Mr. Law, I know not of what trade, in Sun Court, Cornhill or Cheapside: if you call on him in one of your morning walks you may gain and transmit some information.—When you see your Madeira friends (is not his name Millighan?) of John Street, pray thank him in my name; the wine proves excellent, it is a credit to my table, and a comfort to my health. I want a pipe that he can answer for, and as bottles almost double the expence, I think it should be packed carefully in a double cask, and sent with all convenient speed to Messieurs Romberg at Ostend, the greatest voituriers in Europe: they must be instructed to forward it with all proper precaution to their correspondent at Basil or Basle in Switzerland, who must keep it safe till he has received from me a permit for its admission into the Canton of Berne, which I shall be able to send beforehand if Messieurs Romberg inform me of his name and direction. For want of such a permit my former wine *was seized, and would have been confiscated, if the Government of Berne had not treated me with the most flattering and distinguished civility: they not only released the wine, but they paid out of their own pocket the shares to which the Bailiff and the informer were entitled by law. I should not forget that the Bailiff refused to accept of his part.

Poor Deyverdun's constitution is quite broken; he has had two or three attacks, not so violent as the first: every time the door is hastily opened, I expect to hear of some fatal accident: the best or worst hopes of the

Physicians are only that he may linger some time longer; but, if he lives till the summer, they propose sending him to some mineral waters at Aix, in Savoy. You will be glad to hear that I am now assured of possessing, during my life, this delightful house and garden. The act has been *lately* executed in the best form, and the handsomest manner.

RECOVERY OF GEORGE III.

I know not what to say of your miracles at home: we rejoyce in the king's recovery, and its ministerial consequences; and I cannot be insensible to the hope, at least the chance, of seeing in this Country a first Lord of trade, or Secretary at War. In your answer, which I shall impatiently expect, you will give me a full and true account of your designs, which by this time must have droppt, or be determined at least, for the present year. If you come, it is high time that we should look out for a house—a task much less easy than you may possibly imagine.*

I embrace My Lady with warm affection, and still cherish the firm intention of writing to her soon. But the Dame pays more attention to the Epistles which she does not, than to those which she does, receive. At her request Madame de Severy wrote her a long letter about the two *Tufts* and many other important matters, and Mademoiselle at my desire added a scrap for Mademoiselle. They begin to wonder at her silence, and accuse the negligence of the post. By her correspondence with Severy I rejoyce to find that the clouds are dispelled, and hope that she leads Maria into the winter pleasures of the World.

*Among new books, I recommend to you the Count de Mirabeau's great work, *sur la Monarchie Prussienne*; it is in your own way, and gives a very just and compleat idea of that wonderful machine. His *Correspondence secrette* is diabolically good. Adieu. Ever yours.*

542.

To Lord Sheffield.

Lausanne, June 13, 1789.

*You are in truth a wise, active, indefatigable, and inestimable friend; and as our virtues are often connected with our faults, if you were more tame and placid, you would be perhaps of less use and value. A very important and difficult transaction seems to be nearly terminated with success and mutual satisfaction: we seem to run before the wind with a prosperous gale; and, unless we should strike on some secret rocks, which I do not foresee, we shall, on or before the 31st July, enter the harbour of content; though I cannot pursue the metaphor by adding we shall *land*, since our operation is of the very opposite tendency. I could not easily forgive myself for shutting you up in a dark room with parchments and attornies, did I not reflect that this probably is the last material trouble that you will ever have on my account; and that, after the labours and delays of near twenty years, I shall at last attain what I have always sighed for, a clear and competent income, above my wants, and equal to my wishes. In this contemplation you will be sufficiently rewarded. I hope Sainsbury will be content with our title-deeds, for I cannot furnish another shred of parchment.*

ANXIETY FOR HIS STEPMOTHER.

What difficulty can arise about our family Wills? My father made none, and I took out letters of administration as heir at law: my grandfather's may be found at the Commons for a shilling: but it is not worth that shilling, since I joyned on coming of age with my father to cut off the entail. Our fine and recovery (in the year 1758) are doubtless registered in the proper courts. I as little understand the want of my father's marriage settlement. With his first wife? she has been dead above forty years, and I am her sole representative. With his second, the present Mrs. Gibbon? From her it may be easily procured, and you are not ignorant that *her jointure of £200 a year is secured on the Buriton estate, and that her legal consent is requisite for the sale. Again and again I must repeat my hope that she is perfectly satisfied, and that the close of her life may not be embittered by suspicion, or fear, or discontent. What new security does she prefer,—the funds, the mortgage, or your land? At all events she must be made easy. I wrote to her again some time ago, and begged that if she were too weak to write, she would desire Mrs. Gould or Mrs. Holroyd to give me a line concerning her state of health. To this no answer; I am afraid she is displeased.* By the channel of Mrs. H. you might convey some idea of my *real* anxiety.

The Saint seems ripe for heaven: could you not learn from Law, what people are about her, and what measures can be taken to have the earliest intelligence of her departure to prevent a Will being secreted, &c.? Yet I am her heir-at-law.

Now for the disposal of the money: I approve of the £8000 mortgage on Buriton; and honour your prudence in not showing them, by the comparison of the rent and interest, how foolish it is to purchase land. If you can obtain from Lord S[tawell] the four and a half, *tant mieux*. In case you cannot, I will suggest an odd but I think a rational scheme. Let four and a half, or rather five per cent. be stipulated in the mortgage deed, with a proviso in a separate act that, as long as the interest shall be paid on or before the day appointed, I will be satisfied with four per cent. As long as Lord S. is punctual (and this will be a stimulus) he will pay no more; and should I ever be forced by his neglect to transfer the mortgage, which will, I suppose, be in my power, I shall easily find a substitute at the advanced interest. For how many years do I lend? Do I reserve a right of putting in my own receiver? Six thousand more will be vested in the three per cents, and if Mrs. G. chuses them, that sum will not be too large a basis for her jointure of £200 a year. The additional hundred which I pay her is a separate account. The remainder, between two and three thousand, may be trusted to private security.

Did you wish for the whole, or part, or more? it is perfectly at your service; but as you are indifferent, I write to you in the third person.

"I have some knowledge of the Lord Sheffield whom you mention, and though he is poor, I believe him to be honest, and I should therefore prefer his four and a half regularly paid at Gosling's, without trouble or application, to a more doubtful five per cent. which might perhaps be found on bond security."

But I had rather wait some weeks before I absolutely determine, as *there is a chance of my drawing the greatest part of the sum into this country, for an arrangement which you yourself must approve, but which I have not time to explain at present. For the sake of dispatching, by this evening's post, an answer to your letter which arrived this morning, I confine myself to the *needful*, but in the course of a few days I *will* dictate to Severy a more familiar Epistle. I embrace, &c. Adieu. Ever yours.*

543.

To Lord Sheffield.

Lausanne, July 14, 1789.

DEATH OF DEYVERDUN.

*Poor Deyverdun is no more: He expired Saturday the 4th instant: and in his unfortunate situation, death could only be viewed by himself, and his friend, in the light of a consummation devoutly to be wished for. Since September he has had a dozen Apoplectic strokes, more or less violent: in the intervals between them his strength gradually decayed; every principle of life was exhausted; and had he continued to drag a miserable existence, he must probably have survived the loss of his faculties. Of all misfortunes this was what he himself most apprehended: but his reason was clear and calm to the last; he beheld his approaching dissolution with the firmness of a philosopher. I fancied that time and reflection had prepared me for the event; but the habits of three-and-thirty years' friendship are not so easily broken. The first days, and more especially the first nights, were indeed painful. Last Wednesday and Saturday it would not have been in my power to write. I must now recollect myself, since it is necessary for me not only to impart the news, but to ask your opinion on a very serious and doubtful question, which must be decided without loss of time. I shall state the facts, but as I am on the spot and as new lights may occur, I do not promise implicit obedience.

Had my poor friend died without a Will, a female *first* cousin settled somewhere in the north of Germany, and whom I believe he had never seen, would have been his heir at law. In the next degree he had several cousins; and one of these, an old companion, by name Mr. de Montagny, he has chosen for his heir. As this house and garden was the best and clearest part of poor Deyverdun's fortune; as there is an heavy duty or fine (what they call *Lods*) on every change of property out of the legal descent; as Montagny has a small estate and a large family, it was necessary to make some provision in his favour. The will therefore leaves me the option of enjoying this place during my life, on paying the sum of £250 (I reckon in English money) at present, and an annual rent of £30; or else of purchasing the house and garden for a sum which, including the duty, will amount to £2500. If I value the rent of £30 at twelve years' purchase, I may acquire my enjoyment for life at about the rate of £600; and the remaining £1900 will be the difference between that tenure and absolute perpetual property. As you have never accused me of too ardent a zeal for the interest of posterity, you will easily guess which scale at first preponderated. I deeply felt the advantage of acquiring, for the smaller sum, every possible enjoyment, as long as I myself should be capable of enjoying: I rejected, with scorn, the idea of giving £1900 for ideal posthumous property; and I deemed it of little moment whose name, after my death, should be inscribed on my house and garden at Lausanne. How often did I repeat to myself the philosophical lines of Pope, which seem to determine the question:

Pray Heaven, cries Swift, it last as you go on;

I wish to God this house had been your own.

Pity to build without or son or wife:

Why, you'll enjoy it *only* all your life.

Well, if the use be mine, does it concern one,

Whether the name belong to Pope or Vernon?

In this state of self-satisfaction I was not much disturbed by the unanimous advice of all my real or nominal friends, who exhort me to prefer the right of purchase: among such friends, some are careless and some are ignorant; and the judgment of those, who are able and willing to form an opinion, is often byassed by some selfish or social affection, by some visible or invisible interest. But my own reflections have gradually and forcibly driven me from my first propensity; and those reflections I will now proceed to enumerate:

1. I can make this purchase with ease and prudence. As I have had the pleasure of *not* hearing from you very lately, I flatter myself that you advance on a carpet-road, and that almost by the receipt of this letter (July the 31st) the acres of Buriton will be transmuted into Sixteen thousand pounds: If the payment be not absolutely compleated by that day, Sainsbury will not scruple, I suppose, depositing the £2500 at Gosling's, to meet my draught. Should he hesitate, I can desire Darrel to sell off *quantum sufficit* of my short annuities. As soon as the new settlement of my affairs is made, I shall be able, after deducting this sum, to square my expence to my income.* The decay of the Belvidere *must* place me in easy, and the bounty of the Cliffe *may* establish me in affluent circumstance. If this Lausanne purchase should seem a violent measure, at the worst I can make Cadell repay me the money in three or four years. I am revolving the means. I am beginning to be a rich man.

*2. On mature consideration, I am perhaps less selfish or less philosophical than I appear at first sight: Indeed, were I not so, it would now be in my power to turn my fortune into life-annuities, and let the Devil take the hindmost. I feel, (perhaps it is foolish,) but I feel that this little paradise will please me still more when it is absolutely my own; and that I shall be encouraged in every improvement of use or beauty, by the prospect that, after my departure, it will be enjoyed by some person of my own choice. I sometimes reflect with pleasure that my writings will survive me: and that idea is at least as vain and chimerical.

"FIERCE AND ERECT, A FREE MASTER."

3. The heir, Mr. de Montagny, is an old acquaintance* of mine. I *believe* him to be a man of honour: but I *know* him to be a man of a passionate quarrelsome disputatious temper. *My situation of a life-holder is rather new and singular in this country: the laws have not provided for many nice cases which may arise between the Landlord and tenant: some I can foresee, others have been suggested, many more I might feel when it would be too late. His right of property might plague and confine me: he might forbid my lending to a friend, inspect my conduct, check my improvements, call for securities, repairs, &c. But if I purchase, I walk on my own terrace, fierce and erect, the free master of one of the most delicious spots on the Globe.*

4. You will perhaps think £2500 a very smart price for a moderate house and three or four acres of land (I fancy that is about the measure). You will be much more surprized to hear that poor Deyverdun has valued it in my favour at least £1000 below the real value and market price. Of this I must inform myself more correctly, but I am much inclined to believe it, from the general opinion, from the comparison of other sales and purchases, from the peculiar merits of the situation, and from the scarcity of ground. If it were divided into three houses and gardens and sold to builders, I know not what it would produce.

*Should I ever migrate homewards, (You stare, but such an event is less improbable than I could have thought it two years ago,) this place would be disputed by strangers and natives, and the difference would perhaps clear the expences of my removal.

Weigh these reasons, and send me without delay a rational, explicit opinion, to which I shall pay such regard as the nature of circumstances will allow. But, alas! when all is determined, I shall possess this house, by whatsoever tenure, without friendship or domestic society. I did not imagine, six years ago, that a plan of life so congenial to my wishes, would so speedily vanish. I cannot write upon any other subject. Adieu, yours ever.*

544.

To Lord Sheffield.

July 22nd, 1789.

Am I not an exact man! The power is executed, attested, and dispatched the same day (July 22) on which it was received. The appearance of liberality confirms my belief that we are transacting with a fair willing purchaser, and inclines me to hope that the small defects of deeds will be supplied or excused. Surely a great part of our strict formalities is calculated for the emolument of the lawyers rather than the security of the parties. In this simple country we are far less rigid, and a quiet possession of some years (all mortgages are registered) is admitted as a sufficient title. But at all events, as this letter will not reach you before the third or fourth of next month, I see that the day of payment will be postponed beyond the 31st of July. Before this time you will have received, weighed and answered my important missive of the 15th. I am still in a state of doubt and suspense from which your opinion may possibly relieve me, but I must know whether, in case of farther delay, Sainsbury will advance the £2500, or rather £2800, and whether I may draw on the Goslings, from whom I must never expect any favour.

You say nothing of the Belvidere. Have you her legal acquiescence? What security has she chosen? I think she cannot last very long, but I should be hurt if her last days were embittered by any fears or scruples. As to the money destined for the funds you had better consult with David. He is friendly and knowing.

I embrace my lady, but no longer dare talk of writing to her. Maria must now be in all the glories of Lewes races. At Severy's we often talk of the *famille*. I rejoyce in the Douglas match: it is just such a wife as I should chuse, but I hope she will still live with her father.—Is your picture on the road? Mine shall set out whenever you please. Are you not amazed at the French revolution? They have the power, will they have the moderation to establish a good constitution? Adieu.

Ever yours,
E. G.

545.

To Lord Sheffield.

Lausanne, July 25th, 1789.

*After receiving and dispatching the power of attorney, last Wednesday, I opened, with some palpitation, the unexpected missive which arrived this morning. The perusal of the contents spoiled my breakfast: they are disagreeable in themselves, alarming in their consequences, and peculiarly unpleasant at the present moment, when I hoped to have formed and secured the arrangements of my future life. I do not perfectly understand what are these deeds which are so inflexibly required; the wills and marriage-settlements I have sufficiently answered. But your arguments do not convince Sainsbury, and I have very little hope from the Lenborough search. What will be the event? If his objections are only the result of legal scrupulosity, surely they might be removed, and every chink might be filled, by a general bond of indemnity, in which I boldly ask you to joyn, as it will be a substantial important act of friendship, without any possible risk to yourself or your successors. Should he still remain obdurate, I must believe what I already suspect, that Lord Stawell repents of his purchase, and wishes to elude the conclusion. Our case would be then hopeless, *Ibi omnis effusus labor,* and the Estate would be returned on our hands with the taint of a bad title. The refusal of mortgage does not please me; but surely our offer shows some confidence in the goodness of my title. If he will not take £8000 at *four per cent.* we must look out elsewhere; new doubts and delays will arise, and I am persuaded that you will not place an implicit confidence in Woodcock or any other Attorney. I know not as yet your opinion about my Lausanne purchase.

If you are against it, the present posture of affairs gives you great advantage, &c., &c.* The purchase money of Buriton will not be paid in time. Sainsbury, if false, will not advance a shilling, and with the prospect of living or rather starving on a landed estate, I cannot afford to sell out £2500 of my short annuities. For my own part I hang in suspense, but if the money could be easily found I rather incline to the *property* as simple and beneficial.

I am ignorant of your picture: mine shall depart by the first proper occasion: but should not some precautions be taken with regard to duties?

the importation of foreign pictures is heavily taxed, but a work of Sir Joshua's may surely return home.

*The Severys are all well; an uncommon circumstance for the four persons of the family at once. They are now at Mex (pronounce May), a country-house six miles from hence, which I visit to-morrow for two or three days: they often come to town, and we shall contrive to pass a part of the Autumn together at Rolle. I want to change the scene; and beautiful as the garden and prospect must appear to every eye, I feel that the state of my own mind casts a gloom over them; every spot, every walk, every bench, recalls the memory of those hours, of those conversations, which will return no more. But I tear myself from the subject. I could not help writing to-day, though I do not find I have said any thing very material. As you must be conscious that you have agitated me, you will not postpone any agreeable, or even *decisive* intelligence. I almost hesitate, whether I shall not run over to England, to consult with you on the spot, and to fly from poor Deyverdun's shade, which meets me at every turn. I did not expect to have felt it so sharply. But six hundred miles! why are we so far off?

Once more, what is the difficulty of the title? Will men of sense, in a sensible Country, never get rid of the tyranny of lawyers? more oppressive and ridiculous than even the old yoke of the Clergy. Is not a term of seventy or eighty years, near twenty in my own person, sufficient to prove our legal possession? Will not the record of fines and recoveries attest that *I* am free from any bar of entails and settlements? Consult some Sage of the Law, whether their present demand be necessary and legal. If our ground be firm, force them to execute the agreement or forfeit the deposit. But if, as I much fear, they have a right, and a wish, to elude the consummation, would it not be better to release them at once, than to be hung up five years, as in the case of Lovegrove, which cost me in the end four or five thousand pounds? You are bold, you are wise; consult, resolve, act.

In my penultimate letter I dropped a strange hint, that a migration homeward was not impossible. I know not what to say; my mind is all afloat; yet you will not reproach me with caprice or inconstancy. How many years did you damn my scheme of retiring to Lausanne! I executed that plan; I found as much happiness as is compatible with human nature, and during four years (1783-1787) I never breathed a sigh of repentance. On my return from England the scene was changed: I found only a faint semblance of Deyverdun, and that semblance was each day fading from my sight. I have passed an anxious year, but my anxiety is now at an end, and the prospect before me is a melancholy solitude. I am still deeply rooted in this country; the possession of this paradise, the friendship of the Severys, a mode of society suited to my taste, and the enormous trouble and *expence* of a migration. Yet in England (when the present clouds are dispelled) I could form a very comfortable establishment in London, or rather at Bath; and I have a very noble country-seat about ten miles from East Grinstead in Sussex. That spot is dearer to me than the rest of the three kingdoms; and I have sometimes wondered how two men, so opposite in their tempers and pursuits, should have imbibed so long and lively a propensity for each other.

IDEA OF ADOPTING CHARLOTTE PORTEN.

Sir Stanier Porten is just dead. He has left his widow with a small pension, and two children, my nearest relations: the eldest, Charlotte, is about Louisa's age, and one of the most amiable, sensible young creatures I ever saw. I have conceived a romantic idea of educating and adopting her; as we descend into the vale of years, our infirmities require some domestic female society: Charlotte would be the comfort of my age, and I could reward her care and tenderness with a decent fortune. A thousand difficulties oppose the execution of this plan, which I have never opened but to you; yet it would be less impracticable in England than in Switzerland. Adieu. I am wounded, pour some oil into my wounds: Yet I am less unhappy since I have thrown my mind upon paper. Adieu, ever yours.*

546.

To Lord Sheffield.

Lausanne, Sept. 9, 1789.

*Within an hour after the reception of your last, I drew my pen for the purpose of a reply, and my exordium ran in the following words: "I find by experience, that it is much more rational, as well as easy, to answer a letter of real business by the return of the post." This important truth is again verified by my own example. After writing three pages I was called away by a very rational motive, and the post departed before I could return to the conclusion. A second delay was coloured by some decent pretence: three weeks have slipped away, and I now force myself on a task, which I should have dispatched without an effort on the first summons. My only excuse is, that I had little to write about English business, and that I could write nothing definitive about my Swiss affairs. And first, as Aristotle says, of the first,

1. I was indeed in low spirits when I sent what you so justly style my dismal letter; but I do assure you, that my own feelings contributed much more to sink me, than any events or terrors relative to the sale of Buriton. But I again hope and trust, from your consolatory epistle, that* the purchasers are willing and honest, that the deeds have been produced or excused, and that on or before the reception of this despatch (alas, it will be the 23rd perhaps of September) the money has been paid. In all this I must be passive, but with regard to Mrs. Gibbon's, before it is again vested, I am sure she will be satisfied with your security, as mine on the stock which I already hold would require new powers of Attorney, and must be productive of fresh delay. But it is a whimsical circumstance in my fate, that I happen to receive the largest sum which can ever fall to my lot at the time, when money is the most plenty and consequently bears the lowest value, when good mortgages are so difficult to be found, and when the funds scarcely yield four per cent. interest. I wish Lord Stawell would take the £8000 on Buriton even at four per cent., perhaps his proud stomach may be come down. Should he still disdain it, I listen with pleasure and gratitude to the proposal of your Yorkshire mortgage on the same terms, though in general it is more advisable for friends to abstain from any pecuniary concerns with each other. If you no longer adhere to that idea, some sound good mortgage, if possible in a register county, must be found, and I would even stretch the loan to £10,000, in which case my property would be nearly divided between landed and monied security without

reckoning my copper share or my poor annuity in the French funds. In the meanwhile, that the portion destined to the mortgage may not lye dead, I suppose with you that there is nothing more commodious than India-bonds. Will you consult Darrel?

LIFE-INTEREST IN DEYVERDUN'S HOUSE.

*2. My Swiss transaction has suffered a great alteration. I shall not become the proprietor of my house and garden at Lausanne, and I relinquish the fantom with more regret than you could easily imagine. But I have been determined by a difficulty, which at first appeared of little moment, but which has gradually swelled to an alarming magnitude. There is a law in this country, as well as in some provinces of France, which is styled "*le droit de retrait, le retrait lignager*" (Lord Loughborough must have heard of it), by which the relations of the deceased are entitled to redeem an house or estate at the price for which it has been sold; and as the sum fixed by poor Deyverdun is much below its known value, a crowd of competitors are beginning to start. The best opinions (for they are divided) are in my favour, that I am not subject to "*the droit de retrait,*" since I take not as a purchaser, but as a legatee. But the words of the Will are somewhat ambiguous, the event of law is always uncertain, the administration of justice at Berne (the last appeal) depends too much on favour and intrigue; and it is very doubtful whether I could revert to the life-holding, after having chosen and lost the property. These considerations engaged me to open a negotiation with Mr. de Montagny, through the medium of my friend the Judge; and as he most ardently wishes to keep the house, he consented, though with some reluctance, to my proposals. Yesterday he signed a covenant in the most regular and binding form, by which he allows my power of transferring my interest, interprets in the most ample sense my right of making alterations, and expressly renounces all claim, as landlord, of visiting or inspecting the premises. I have promised to lend him 12,000 Livres, (between seven and eight hundred pounds), secured on the house and land. The mortgage is four times its value; the interest at four per cent. will be annually discharged by the rent of thirty guineas, and I shall have an additional hold on his good behaviour. So that I am now tranquil on that score for the remainder of my days. I hope that time will gradually reconcile me to the place which I have inhabited with my poor friend; for in spite of the *cream* of London, I am still persuaded that no other residence is so well adapted to my taste and habits of studious and social life.

Far from delighting in the whirl of a Metropolis, my only complaint against Lausanne is the great number of strangers, always of English, and now of

French, by whom we are infested in summer. Yet we have escaped the *damned* great ones, the Count d'Artois, the Polignacs, &c. who slip by us to Turin. What a scene is France! While the assembly is voting abstract propositions, Paris is an independent Republic; the provinces have neither authority nor freedom, and poor Necker declares that credit is no more, and that the people refuse to pay taxes. Yet I think you must be seduced by the abolition of tythes. If Eden goes to Paris you may have some curious *confidential* information. Give me some account of Mr. and Mrs. Douglas; do they live with Lord North? I hope they do. When will parliament be dissolved? Are you still Coventry mad? I embrace My Lady, the stately Maria, and the smiling Louisa. Alas! Alas! you will never come to Switzerland. Adieu, ever yours.*

547.

To Lord Sheffield.

Lausanne, Sept. 25th, 1789.

*Alas! what perils do environ

The man who meddles with cold iron.

Alas! what delays and difficulties do attend the man who meddles with legal and landed business! yet if it be only to disappoint your expectation, I am not so very nervous at this new provoking obstacle. I had totally forgotten the deed in question, which was contrived by the two trustees to tye his hands and regulate the disorder of his affairs (in the last year of my father's life); and which might have been so easily cancelled by Sir Stanier, who had not the smallest interest in it, either for himself or his family. The amicable suit which is now become necessary must, I think, be short and unambiguous, yet I cannot help dreading the crotchets that lurk under the Chancellor's great wig; and, at all events, I foresee some additional delay and expence. The golden pill of the £2800 has soothed my discontent; and if it be safely lodged with the Goslings, I agree with you in considering it as an unequivocal pledge of a fair and willing purchaser. It is, indeed, chiefly in that light that I now rejoyce in so large a deposit, which is no longer necessary in its full extent. You are apprized by my last letter that I have reduced myself to the life enjoyment of the house and garden, and, in spite of my feelings, I am every day more convinced that I have chosen the safer side. I believe my cause to have been good, but it was doubtful: law in this country is not so expensive as in England, but it is more troublesome. I must have gone to Bern, have solicited my Judges in person—a vile custom! the event was doubtful, and during at least two years, I should have been in a state of suspense and anxiety: till the conclusion of which it would have been madness to have attempted any alteration or improvement.

According to my present arrangement I shall want no more than eleven hundred pounds of the £2000, and I suppose you will direct Gosling to lay out the remainder in East India bonds, that it may not lye quite dead, while I am accountable to Sainsbury for the interest.* I presume that I am entitled till the consummation to the rents of Buriton: a little drop of honey is collected from Lady-day to Michaelmas, and Andrews is I hope instructed to squeeze the bag without delay or mercy: the Tenant deserves none.

*The elderly Lady in a male habit, who informed me that Yorkshire is a register County, is a certain Judge, one Sir William Blackstone, whose name you may possibly have heard. After stating the danger of purchasers and creditors, with regard to the title of estates on which they lay out or lend their money, he thus continues: "In Scotland every act and event regarding the transmission of property is regularly entered on record; And some of our own provincial divisions, particularly the *extended county of York* and the populous county of Middlesex, have prevailed with the Legislature to erect such registers in their respective districts." (Blackstone's Commentaries, Vol. ii. p. 343, Edition of 1774, in quarto.) If I am mistaken, it is in pretty good company; but I suspect that we are all right, and that the register is confined to one or two Ridings. As we have, alas! two or three months before us, I should hope that your prudent sagacity will discover some sound land, in case you should not have time to arrange your own Mortgage.

I now write in a hurry, as I am just setting out for Rolle, where I shall be settled with cook and servants in a pleasant apartment till the middle of November. The Severys have a house there, where they pass the Autumn. I am not sorry to vary the scene for a few weeks, and I wish to be absent while some alterations are making in my house at Lausanne. I wish the change of air may be of service to Severy the father, but we do not at all like his present state of health. How compleatly, alas, how compleatly! could I now lodge you: but your firm resolve of making me a visit seems to have vanished like a dream. Next summer you will not find five hundred pounds for a rational friendly expedition: and should parliament be dissolved, you will perhaps find five thousand for ****. I cannot think of it with patience. Pray take serious strenuous measures for sending me a pipe of excellent Madeira in cask, with some dozens of Malmsey Madeira. It should be consigned to Messrs. Romberg, Voituriers, at Ostend, and I must have timely notice of its march. We have so much to say about France, that I suppose we shall never say anything. That country is now in a state of *dissolution.* Adieu.*

548.

To his Stepmother.

Lausanne, December 5th, 1789.

MY DEAR MADAM,

I need not repeat what we have both so often felt and acknowledged, that between us silence is never the effect of coldness or forgetfulness, yet when I recollect that your second letter is still unanswered, a conscious blush rises to my cheek. Our mutual friendship we have no occasion to express, of our health and situation we may have frequent accounts by the channel of Lord Sheffield and Mrs. Holroyd; mere topics of Epistolary conversation do not readily occur between distant friends, but you ask me some questions of an interesting nature and your kind curiosity it is incumbent on me to satisfy.

The disposal of Buriton I think you cannot disapprove. A distant landed estate is the worst kind of property, and you will not be surprized to hear that after the payment of every expence and every deduction, the remainder of the clear income was little more than sufficient for the annual supply, which I hope will be long, very long, offered to the Belvidere at Bath. The neglect, I will not give it an harsher name, of Hugonin cost me last year above seven hundred pounds; yet after his death, where could I have found a more creditable agent? At sixteen thousand pounds Lord Sheffield does not think Buriton ill sold, especially as four or five thousand more must be added which I had already received from the sale of Horn and Harris's farms. Some forms of law have delayed the final conclusion, but I expect to hear every post of the payment of the money, and you will rejoyce to hear, what I assure on my honour is true, that every shilling is my own, and that prudence, without any pressure of distress or debt, is the sole motive of my conduct. The entire sum I mean to divide between the stocks and a good mortgage, that at all events I may have a sound leg to stand upon. I hope you are satisfied with the arrangement of your jointure: Lord Sheffield cannot forget the burthen of every one of my letters, "Unless Mrs. G. be safe and easy, I cannot be so."

IRREPARABLE LOSS OF A FRIEND.

When I had the pleasure of seeing you at Bath two years ago, you may remember the melancholy account which I gave you of poor Deyverdun. On my return to Lausanne I found him much altered for the worse; he was attacked by a succession of Apoplectic fits, and after a general decay, he died last July, when his life could be no longer desirable for himself or his friends. The loss of a friend of five and thirty years is irreparable, and each day I feel the comfortless solitude to which I am reduced. By his will he designed that I should possess the delightful house and garden which I inhabit: and which have not, I believe, their equal in Europe; by a subsequent arrangement with his heir, in which both find their advantage, I have secured the free and indisputable enjoyment for my life, and have already made some agreable and useful alterations. I still like the people and the country, and here I shall probably spend the latter season of life, with the resolution however of visiting England every three or four years. I have often regretted that your imperfect knowledge of the French language never allowed me to seduce you to this place. I am sure you would have pleased and been pleased in the circle of my familiar acquaintance.

My health was never so good as it is at present, and since my unseasonable attack at Bath I have not felt the slightest return of the gout. You may possibly hear that Mr. Gibbon has undertaken some new history; be persuaded, if I know his intentions, that after six weighty quartos, he now reads and writes for his own amusement, though I will not answer for what those amusements may one day produce. You may likewise hear of tumults and rebellions in Switzerland. Be persuaded, that the popular madness of France and Flanders has not reached these tranquil regions, and that the Swiss have sense enough to feel and maintain their own happiness, which is endeared to them by the disorders of the neighbouring countries.

Adieu, Dear Madam; I grieve for you and for myself that we are now entering into the cold and dreary season, but I sincerely hope that you will find strength and spirits to lay this and many other winters at your feet.

Ever yours,
E. G.

549.

To Lord Sheffield.

Lausanne, December 15th, 1789.

*You have often reason to accuse my strange silence and neglect in the most important of *my own* affairs; for I will presume to assert, that in a business of yours of equal consequence, you should not find me cold or careless. But on the present occasion my silence is, perhaps, the highest compliment I ever paid you. You remember the answer of Philip of Macedon: "Philip may sleep, while he knows that Parmenio is awake." I expected, and, to say the truth, I wished that my Parmenio would have decided and acted, without expecting my dilatory answer, and in his decision I should have acquiesced with implicit confidence. But since you will have my opinion, let us consider the present state of my affairs. In the course of my life I have often known, and sometimes felt, the difficulty of getting money, but I now find myself involved in a much more singular distress, the difficulty of placing it, and if it continues much longer, I shall almost wish for my land again.

I perfectly agree with you, that it is bad management to purchase in the funds when they do not yield four per cent.,* and I incline every day more and more to the encrease of the mortgage. I am much mistaken if in my last letter I did not extend the sum as £10,000 pounds, which would make, as I remember to have said, about an equal partition of my property. Can that sum be called, even in your wealthy island, so very inconsiderable? I would even give somewhat larger latitude (even as far as £12,000 if I preserve a right of calling in a fourth or a moiety on reasonable notice). Is it possible that in seven or eight months no good and clear security can be found, especially if I am forced to be content with the scanty interest of four per cent.? Yet I approve your diffidence and caution: in the concerns of our friends even cowardice is a virtue. The doubtful title of a mortgage might distress and perplex me for the remainder of my life, and you would not easily forgive yourself for having been the innocent author of my calamities. Rather than expose myself to such a risk, I would try whether some *great* banker would not be disposed to give low interest and firm security for my money till it should be called for, or at all events I would deposit it in the Bank for six months or a year, and live on the principal till you could find an unquestionable opportunity of placing it on landed property. *Some of this money I can place safely and advantageously by means of my banker here; and I shall possess, what I have always desired, a command of cash, which I cannot abuse to my prejudice, since I have it in my power to supply by my pen any extraordinary or fanciful indulgence of expence. And so much—much, indeed—for pecuniary matters.

GLORIOUS OPPORTUNITY OF FRANCE.

What would you have me say of the affairs of France? we are too near, and too remote, to form an accurate judgment of that wonderful scene. The abuses of the court and government called aloud for reformation; and it has happened, as it will always happen, that an innocent, well-disposed prince has paid the forfeits of the sins of his predecessors; of the ambition of the Lewis XIV., of the profusion of Lewis XV. The French nation had a glorious opportunity, but they have abused, and may lose their advantages. If they had been content with a liberal translation of our system, if they had respected the prerogatives of the crown, and the privileges of the Nobles, they might have raised a solid fabric, on the only true foundation, the natural Aristocracy of a great Country. How different is the prospect! Their King brought a captive to Paris, after his palace had been stained with the blood of his guards; the Nobles in exile; the Clergy plundered in a way which strikes at the root of all property; the capital an independent Republic; the union of the provinces dissolved; the flames of discord kindled by the worst of men; (in that light I consider Mirabeau;) and the honestest of the Assembly a set of wild Visionaries, (like our Dr. Price,) who gravely debate, and dream about the establishment of a pure and perfect democracy of five-and-twenty millions, the virtues of the golden age, and the primitive rights and equality of mankind, which would lead, in fair reasoning, to an equal partition of lands and money. How many years must elapse before France can recover any vigour, or resume her station among the powers of Europe! As yet, there is no symptom of a great man, a Richelieu or a Cromwell, arising, either to restore the Monarchy, or to lead the Commonwealth. The weight of Paris, more deeply engaged in the funds than *all* the rest of the Kingdom, will long delay a bankrupcy; and if it should happen, it will be, both in the cause and effect, a measure of weakness, rather than of strength.

FRENCH EXILES AT LAUSANNE.

You send me to Chamberry, to see a prince and an Archbishop. Alas! we have exiles enough here, with the Marshal de Castries and the Duke de Guignes at their head: and this inundation of strangers, which used to be confined to the summer, will now stagnate all the winter. The only ones whom I have seen with pleasure are M. Mounier, the late president of the

National Assembly, and the Count de Lally; they have both dined with me. Mounier, who is a serious dry politician, is returned to Dauphiné. Lally is an amiable man of the World, and a poet: he passes the winter here with his *female friend* the Princess d'Hénin. You know how much I prefer a quiet select society to a crowd of names and titles, and that I always seek conversation with a view to amusement rather than information. What happy countries are England and Switzerland, if they know and preserve their happiness.

I have a thousand things to say of My Lady, Maria, and Louisa, but I can add only a short postscript about the Madeira and picture.

1. Good Madeira is now become essential to my health and reputation. May your hogshead prove as good as the last; may it not be intercepted by the rebels or the Austrians. What a scene again in that country! Happy England! happy Switzerland!* I again repeat I must have early notice of my wine's approach, that I may send a permit to meet it at Basil.

2. To whom did you entrust the picture and Rennel's maps? I have not heard of either. Was it to Elmsley? I have expected these many months a box of books, &c., which he announced. Will you not clear up the point? My picture expects a safe occasion. Adieu.

550.

To Lord Sheffield.

Lausanne, January 27th, 1790.

Your two last epistles, of the 7th and 11th instant, were somewhat delayed on the road; they arrived within two days of each other, the last this morning, (the 27th); so that I answer by the first, or at least by the second post. Upon the whole, your French method, though sometimes more rapid, appears to me less sure and steady than the old German highway.

I will not deny (for it was probably too visible) that your proposal, which arose from the kindest motives, of your Yorkshire mortgage embarrassed me from the beginning, and whatever faint signs of acquiescence I may have given, they proceeded from the apprehension of wounding your honourable feelings by anything that might bear the appearance of doubt and distrust. I could not reconcile the two characters of debtor and friend, and I was shocked by the idea, however distant or unlikely, that in a serious concern our interests might possibly become opposite to each other. Your first letter relieved me from that weight, and I viewed with much less horror the chance of leaving the purchase money for some time idle and unproductive in the bank: yet I could not entirely subscribe to your charge that I had changed my *principles.* Eight thousand pounds had been always designed for the mortgage: you object (to my great surprize) that good landed security cannot easily be found for so *small* a sum; I agree to enlarge it; where is the change or contradiction? I confess however that the very high price of the Stocks has rendered me less eager for an investment which at present will not even produce the four per cent., and which rather affords the danger of a fall than the hopes of a rise. You are likewise inaccurate when you accuse me of having already drawn near £2000 of the purchase money.

But enough of these altercations. *A new and brighter prospect seems to be breaking upon us, and few events of *that kind* have ever given me more pleasure than your successful negotiation and Sainsbury's satisfactory answer. The agreement is, indeed, equally convenient for both parties: no time or expence will be wasted in scrutinizing the title of the estate; the interest will be secured by the clause of five per cent., and I lament with you, that no larger sum than £8000 can be placed on Beriton, without asking (what might be somewhat impudent) a collateral security, &c., &c.* As I do not mean to entrap them, the allowance of a month is perfectly right and in truth immaterial. As the purchase money is by this arrangement very much reduced, they will now pay it, I suppose, whenever you please, and perhaps (you will judge) it may be as well to consummate on Lady Day, that I may be entitled to another half year's rent from the Tenant. The power of calling in the Mortgage, I only meant as a superfluous precaution, but I suppose there will be some restraint on their paying it off whenever they please, perhaps at a time inconvenient to the creditor. After Lord Stawell has paid or secured £10,800 there will still remain (subject to I know not what charges) £5200. While the stocks are so very high as not to yield four per cent., might it not be expedient to trust it in two or three loans in good personal bond security at four and a half? Would not the Goslings for the consideration of the half per cent. bind themselves to answer for the interest and principal. In their business they have always a command of money, and if the security be such as I ought to accept, the risk for themselves must be very inconsiderable. *But I wish you to chuse and execute one or the other of these arrangements with sage discretion and absolute power.

DIRTY LAND AND VILE MONEY.

I shorten my letter, that I may dispatch it by this post. I see the time, and I shall rejoyce to see it at the end of twenty years, when my cares will be at an end, and our friendly pages will be no longer sullied with the repetition of dirty land and vile money; when we may expatiate on the politics of the World and our personal sentiments. Without expecting your answer of business, I mean to write soon in a purer style, and I wish to lay open to my friend the state of my mind, which (exclusive of all worldly concerns) is not perfectly at ease. In the mean while, I must add two or three short articles. 1. I am astonished at Elmsly's silence, and the immobility of your picture. Mine should have departed long since, could I have found a sure opportunity.* It had almost started last week had I not been afraid of rolling it, but I think that a person on whom we may depend will undertake the journey and commission about the middle of next month. 2. I shall expect the Madeira with impatience if it is remarkable. I have not any objection to the *two* hogsheads, but perhaps one may suffice, as I have a promise from Sir Ralph Payne, with whom you may confabulate on the subject if you excurse to London. 3. Give me some account of the two old Ladies. I no longer write to Cliffe, as I suppose her (perhaps erroneously) incapable of correspondence. I embrace My Lady, &c. When shall I see them at Lausanne or Sheffield Place? the one must take place if the other does not. Adieu.

Yours,
E. G.

P.S.—If you met with another neat, safe, little mortgage of £2000 I have no objection. Since I have again opened my letter, I will ask you how the property of an Ecclesiastical differs from that of a lay Corporation, and whether you think Parliament could legally seize and appropriate the lands of the City of London. If either Corporation was mischievous, Government might indeed extinguish it in time, by prohibiting a supply of new members, and the vacant property would perhaps devolve to the public. No change of events or opinions in France: next month will be critical from the Provincial Assemblies.

551.

To Lord Sheffield.

Lausanne, May 15th, 1790.

LEGAL FORMS BENEFIT LAWYERS.

*Since the first origin (*ab ovo*) of our connection and correspondence, so long an interval of silence has not intervened, as far as I remember, between us.* Yet on the present occasion neither is materially to blame, nor has either been materially injured. My conscience was easy, since my last letter, I felt myself in the proud security of a creditor, and though after a certain space I waited every post for an answer, yet I waited with little impatience and no anxiety, in the firm persuasion that Lady-day would finally settle the whole transaction of the mortgage and the payment. I now find that the delay is involuntary and indefinite, and that it is not so easy to escape even from the amicable grip of the Court of Chancery. Can such superstitious forms be of any use except to the Lawyers? whose bill I much apprehend. Might not such an obsolete deed which I had perfectly forgot, have been thrown into the fire with the consent of all parties? However we must follow the stream, and I trust that neither Sussex nor Africa, nor Reading nor Bristol will relax your diligence in the cause of your friend. In the winding up an arrangement of twenty years, it is vexatious to be stopped by a little knot: but otherwise my nerves are not so much discomposed as you might suspect. As I believe the purchasers to be honest and sincere, the difference is only between the rent and the interest: the tenant deserves no mercy, and I hope your orders are absolute for distraining the next day on failure of payment. I trust that the £8000 mortgage is settled with Sainsbury, nor do I dislike your last resolution of pouring the whole residue into the funds.

*From my silence you conclude that the moral complaint, which I had insinuated in my last, is either insignificant or fanciful. The conclusion is rash. But the complaint in question is of the nature of a slow lingering disease, which is not attended with any immediate danger. As I have not leisure to expatiate, take the idea in three words: "Since the loss of poor Deyverdun, I am *alone*; and even in paradise, solitude is painful to a social mind. When I was a dozen years younger, I *scarcely* felt the weight of a single existence amidst the crowds of London, of Parliament, of Clubs; but it will press more heavily upon me in this tranquil land, in the decline of life, and with the encrease of infirmities. Some expedient, even the most desperate, must be embraced, to secure the domestic society of a male or female companion. But I am not in a hurry; there is time for reflection and advice." During this winter such finer feelings have been suspended by the grosser evil of bodily pain. On the ninth of February I was seized by such a fit of the Gout as I had never known, though I must be thankful that its dire effects have been confined to the feet and knees, without ascending to the more noble parts. With some vicissitudes of better and worse, I have groaned between two and three months; the debility has survived the pain, and though now easy, I am carried about in my chair, without any power, and with a very distant chance, of supporting myself, from the extreme weakness and contraction of the joints of my knees. Yet I am happy in a skilful physician, and kind assiduous friend: every evening, during more than three months, has been enlivened (except when I have been forced to refuse them) by some chearful visits, and very often by a chosen party of both sexes. How different is such society from the solitary evenings which I have passed in the tumult of London! It is not worth while fighting about a shadow, but should I ever return to England, Bath, not the Metropolis, would be my last retreat.

Your portrait is at last arrived in perfect condition, and now occupies a conspicuous place over the chimney-glass in my library. It is the object of general admiration; good judges (the few) applaud the work; the name of Reynolds opens the eyes and mouths of the many; and were not I afraid of making you vain, I would inform you that the original is not allowed to be more than five-and-thirty. In spite of private reluctance and public discontent, I have honourably dismissed *myself*. I shall arrive at Sir Joshua's before the end of the month; he will give me a look, and perhaps a touch; and you will be indebted to the president one guinea for the carriage. Do not be nervous, I am not rolled up; had I been so, you might have gazed on my charms four months ago. I want some account of yourself, of My lady, (shall we never directly correspond?) of Louisa, and of the soft, the stately Maria. How has the latter since her launch supported a quiet Winter in Sussex? I so much rejoice in your divorce from that b—— Kitty Coventry, that I care not what marriage you contract. The second City in England would suit your dignity, and the duties of a Bristol Member, which would kill me in the first session, would supply your activity with a constant fund of amusement. But tread softly and surely; the ice is deceitful, the water is deep, and you may be soused over head and ears before you are aware. Why did not you or Elmsly send me the African pamphlet by the post? it would not have cost much. You have such a knack of turning a nation, that I am afraid you will triumph (perhaps by the force of argument) over justice and humanity. But do you not expect to work at Beelzebub's sugar plantations in the infernal regions, under the tender government of a negro-driver? I should suppose both My lady and Miss Firth very angry with you.

As to the bill for prints, which has been too long neglected, why will you not exercise the power, which I have never revoked, over all my cash at the Goslings'? I have no further claims either for quarto or octavo copies, but I am persuaded that Cadell's liberality will credit your applications in my name for one of each. The Severy family has passed a very favourable winter; the young man is impatient to hear from a family which he places something above the Holy family: yet he will generously write next week, and send you a drawing of the alterations in the house. Do not raise your ideas; you know *I* am satisfied with convenience in architecture, and some elegance in furniture. I hear nothing decisive either from Sir Ralph Payne about Madeira, and if I do not receive a supply in the course of the summer, I shall be in great shame and distress. I would write to the Bath Knight if I knew his address. That is serious business, but I admire the coolness with which you ask me to epistolize Reynell and Elmsly, as if a letter were so easy and pleasant a task; it appears less so to me every day.*

552.

Lord Sheffield to Edward Gibbon.

Sheffield Place, 28th July, '90.

LORD SHEFFIELD RETURNED FOR BRISTOL.

I wish I had better paper, but this is good enough for a foreigner. At length I have obtained an attested copy of Hester's Will, but no further letter or information from Mr. Law.

I find the Will was made in November, 1786, and is of considerable length, altho' her nephew Edward Gibbon takes up not much more than two lines of it. The rest says much about the family of Law, and the heirs of the Rev. Wm. Law. It gives the Sussex Estate to Edward Gibbon and his heirs for ever, and one thousand pounds to the said Edward, and one hundred pounds to her niece Lady Eliot, but the *chat d'enfer*, by a codicil dated 18th February, 1788, when her nephew resided in Downing Street, took the trouble of reducing the thousand pounds to one hundred pounds, to be paid within 12 months after her decease. When there is an opportunity I shall send the composition to you. And now you are once more a landed man. But I wonder I have not had a summons lately to attend Messrs. Sainsbury and Rhodes to conclude the Buriton business. I have furnished them with every paper, &c., they have desired, and I verily believe they are proceeding, yet it seems in a truly Chancery style. They plagued me lately about a deed for which it was necessary to ransack the boxes.

My last letter was from Clifton near Bristol (I believe) after my return from Coventry, and I also believe I therein mentioned Proceedings at Reading, Bristol, and Coventry. I was detained some time among my constituents for the purpose of incorporating a due quantity of Turtle, and on leaving them I subscribed somewhat above £300 to Infirmary, Magdalens, Small Debtors, &c. but that was all my expence at Bristol. I suppose I mentioned in my last that my expences at Coventry did not exceed £150.

Sir Joseph Banks and family have been here several days, and inquired much after you. They are just gone, and Batt is just arrived, and stays till Brighthelmstone Races next week. Lord North and family are at Tunbridge Wells, and will make a visit here as soon as we are settled after Races.

HESTER GIBBON'S WILL.

Perhaps it may be needful to mention to you that the rent of your Newhaven, alias Meeching Farm, is £225. The Manor is considerable, the quit-rents and profits above £40—the latter uncertain. The deductions on account of Land-tax and Sackville College rent and expenses of collecting quit-rent about £29. I shall not readily approve of your selling it, but if you should be desperately disposed to increase your income, what do you think of taking double or treble the clear rent for your life, for the said Estate? I suppose about £550 per annum, which allows for outgoings, including repairs of sea-walls and every deduction but moderately—they have been of late years somewhat immoderate.

If you do not think of making little ones, it may suit you and it would me, although I am poor, because it would be a very respectable addition to my Sussex Estate. It would give me marshland of which I have none, also the mouth of the River Ouse, &c.: and perhaps a small house on the sea-shore. I do not know that it would be a good bargain for you and your heirs, but I think it would be a good one for the House of Holroyd, except that I should not like to be benefitted by the Devil taking you—yet I do not suspect I should wish it. In case of his taking me or not, you would have a collateral security besides that of the Estate itself. The best argument for your doing it is that I shall with-hold my consent to your selling it. On this subject you will give your mind without ceremony. It will furnish you with subject matter for a letter.

Yours ever,
S.

Remember us to the house of Severy.

553.

To Lord Sheffield.

Lausanne, August 7, 1790.

*I answer at once your two letters; and I should probably have taken earlier notice of the first, had I not been in daily expectation of the second. I must begin on the subject of what really interests me the most, your glorious election for Bristol. Most sincerely do I congratulate your exchange of a cursed expensive jilt, who deserted you for a rich Jew, for an honourable connection with a chaste and virtuous matron, who will probably be as constant as she is disinterested. In the whole range of election from Caithness to St. Yves, I much doubt whether there be a single choice so truly honourable to the member and the constituents. The second Commercial city invites, from a distant province, an independent Gentleman, known only by his active spirit, and his writings on the subject of trade; and names him, without intrigue or expence, for her representative: even the voice of party is silenced, While factions strive which shall applaud the most.

You are now sure, for seven years to come, of never wanting food—I mean business; what a crowd of suitors or Complainants will besiege your door! what a load of letters and memorials will be heaped on your table! I much question whether even you will not sometimes exclaim, *Ohe! jam satis est!* but that is your affair. Of the excursion to Coventry I cannot decide, but I hear it is pretty generally blamed: but, however, I love gratitude to an old friend; and shall not be very angry if you damned them with a farewell to all eternity. But I cannot repress my indignation at the use of those foolish, obsolete, odious words, Whig and Tory. In the American War they might have some meaning; and then your Lordship was a Tory: since the coalition, all general principles have been confounded; and if there ever was an opposition to men, not measures, it is the present. Luckily, both the Leaders are great men; and, whatever happens, the country must fall upon its legs. What a strange mist of peace and war seems to hang over the ocean! We can perceive nothing but secrecy and vigour; but those are excellent qualities to perceive in a Minister. From yourself and politics I now return to my private concerns, which I shall methodically consider under the three great articles of mind, body, and estate.* And first, as Aristotle says, of the first.

COMFORTLESS STATE OF DOMESTIC SOLITUDE.

*1. I am not absolutely displeased at your firing so hastily at the hint, a tremendous hint, in my last letter. But the danger is not so serious or imminent as you seem to suspect; and I give you my word, that, before I take the slightest step which can bind me either in law, conscience, or honour, I will faithfully communicate, and we will freely discuss, the whole state of the business. But at present there is not any thing to communicate or discuss; I do assure you that I have not any particular object in view: I am not in love with any of the Hyænas of Lausanne, though there are some who keep their claws tolerably well pared. Sometimes, in a solitary mood, I have fancied myself married to one or other of those whose society and conversation are the most pleasing to me; but when I have painted in my fancy all the probable consequences of such an union, I have started from my dream, rejoyced in my escape, and ejaculated a thanksgiving that I was still in possession of my natural freedom. Yet I feel, and shall continue to feel, that domestic solitude, however it may be alleviated by the world, by study, and even by friendship, is a comfortless state, which will grow more painful as I descend in the vale of years. At present my situation is very tolerable; and if at dinner-time, or at my return home in the evening, I sometimes sigh for a companion, there are many hours, and many occasions, in which I enjoy the superior blessing of being sole master of my own house. But your plan, though less dangerous, is still more absurd than mine: such a couple as you describe could not be found; and, if found, would not answer my purpose; their rank and position would be awkward and ambiguous to myself and my acquaintance; and the agreement of three persons of three characters would be still more impracticable. My plan of Charlotte Porten is undoubtedly the most desirable; and she might either remain a spinster (the case is not without example,) or marry some Swiss of my choice, who would increase and enliven our society; and both would have the strongest motives for kind and dutiful behaviour. But the mother has been indirectly sounded; and will not hear of such a proposal for some years. On my side, I would not take her, but as a piece of soft wax which I could model to the language and manners of the Country: I must therefore be patient.

2. Young Severy's letter, which may be now in your hands, and which, for these three or four last posts, has furnished my indolence with a new pretence for delay, has already informed you of the means and circumstances of my resurrection. Tedious indeed was my confinement, since I was not able to move from my house or chair, from the ninth of February to the first of July, very nearly five months. The first weeks were accompanied with more pain than I have ever known in the Gout, with anxious days and sleepless nights; and when that pain subsided, it left a weakness in my knees, which seemed to have no end. My confinement was however softened by books, by the possession of every comfort and

convenience, by a succession each evening of agreeable company, and by a flow of equal spirits and general good health. During the last weeks I descended to the ground floor, poor Deyverdun's apartment, and constructed a chair like Merlin's, in which I could wheel myself in the house and on the terrace. My patience has been universally admired; yet how many thousands have passed those five months less easily than myself. I remember making a remark perfectly simple, and perfectly true: "At present," I said to Madame de Severy, "I am not positively miserable, and I may reasonably hope a daily or weekly improvement, till sooner or later in the summer I shall recover new limbs, and new pleasures, which I do not now possess: have any of you such a prospect?" The prediction has been accomplished, and I have arrived to my present condition of strength, or rather of feebleness: I now can walk with tolerable ease in my garden and smooth places; but on the rough pavement of the town I use, and perhaps shall use, a sedan chair. The Pyrmont waters have performed wonders; and my physician (not Tissot, but a very sensible man) allows me to hope, that the term of the interval will be in proportion to that of the fit.*

3. And so Aunt Hester is gone to sing Hallelujahs, a glory which she did not seem very impatient to possess. I received the news of this dire event with much philosophic composure: she might have done better, she might have done worse, and I was always prepared for the worst. By this time you have probably a copy of the Will, and will take (as I suppose you are authorized) the proper and necessary steps. I most wish to learn whether she has left me the fee simple, the absolute disposal of her Sussex estate; the power of selling or the necessity of keeping that costly piece of property will make a wonderful difference in the value of her gift. From a motive of curiosity I wish to learn what she has done with her personal fortune; her four copper shares were worth at least five or six thousand pounds. Has she given them to the Laws? If in the bequeathing what was absolutely in her power she has postponed relations for friends, I think her determination both honourable and wise. If in the entailed estate she has preferred a poor though unbelieving nephew to a rich niece, she was likewise right. I speak with the impartiality of a third person.

And now let me seriously address you on the most important of my temporal concerns, Buriton. You will do me the justice to allow that I have not been either impatient or nervous: but the Estate was sold in April, 1789: this is now August, 1790, and the money is not yet paid, nor the purchase concluded. Is Lord Stawell perfidious, is he poor, is he unwilling? is the delay only produced by the ingenious forms of the lawyers? How many terms do they require for an amicable suit in Chancery? In the meanwhile I lose interest, the estate must suffer by neglect, and what will be the event? Exert your vigour, argue, persuade, consummate! On the 10th of November next my father will have been dead twenty years: let it not be said that with the counsel and aid of such a friend, I have not been able to settle my affairs in twenty years. What can I say more? the conclusion an Indian Epistle.

Yes, I have more or rather nothing more to say about the disposal of the money. I hope the Buriton mortgage for £8000 still holds: nothing else can be so easy or good. The remainder you will throw into the funds, and I wish we could take advantage of the present fall, but if a sure bond or neat mortgage from £2500 to £4000 should offer itself, I should be very well pleased.

SWISS SENSIBLE OF THEIR HAPPINESS.

Have you read in the English papers, that the Government of Bern is overturned, and that we are divided into three Democratical leagues; true as the Gospel: true as what I have read in the French papers, that the English have cut off Pitt's head, and abolished the house of Lords. The people of this country are happy; and in spite of some malcontents, and more foreign Emissaries, they are sensible of their happiness.

My MADEIRA is almost exhausted, and I must receive before the end of the Autumn a stout cargo of wholesome exquisite wine with proper *previous* notice which may prevent all accidents at the Custom House. Your Bristol connection must give you great advantages, but (if I could procure his direction) I would not neglect Sir Ralph Payne's favours.

Inform My lady, that I am indignant at a false and heretical assertion in her last letter to Severy, "that friends at a distance cannot love each other, if they do not write." I love her better than any woman in the world; indeed I do; and yet I do not write. And she herself—but I am calm. We have now nearly one hundred French exiles, some of them worth being acquainted with; particularly a Count de Schomberg, who is become almost my friend; he is a man of the World, of letters, and of sufficient age, since in 1753 he succeeded to Marshal Saxe's regiment of Dragoons. As to the rest, I entertain them, and they flatter me: but I wish we were reduced to our Lausanne society. Poor France! the state is dissolved, the nation is mad! Adieu.

554.

Lord Sheffield to Edward Gibbon.

Sheffield Place, 21st Sept., '90.

I approve your observations on the Bristol Election, and I do not believe you heard the Excursion to Coventry pretty generally blamed. I knew nothing of an Opposition till two days after the Poll began. A man who had been useful to me in the same line being concerned, I had no difficulty nor hesitation as to what was to be done.

On the subject of Buriton I acknowledge you have been as Philosophic as could be expected. There seems to be something supernatural attending all your worldly concerns. In answer to a repeated remonstrance to Mr. Sainsbury, the last information is from Mr. Rhodes the Attorney, dated Sept. 4th instant. He says (Mrs. Sainsbury desired him to write, Mr. Sainsbury being in Ireland), "The matter in Chancery remains unfinished by the Master. When we obtained the Deed and laid it before him, he said that he had then so many other reports to prepare that he was apprehensive that he should not be able to prepare ours. We said and did everything in our power to induce him to do it, but we could not prevail. He has promised to let us have it before the ensuing Term, which will begin on the 6th of November next, and the other business cannot be completed before the first week in the term." It is difficult to believe these delays are intentional, as a considerable sum remains dormant as to the Land in the hands of the Auctioneers, Messrs. Skinners, and as so great a proportion of the purchase money is to remain in Mortgage. The only thing I can firmly object to, is an over nicety on the part of Sainsbury or his Lawyers as to the title, but I shall go to London as soon as Term begins and reiterate every measure that can speedily bring matters to a conclusion. In the meantime I shall be very troublesome until I am assured every paper is ready for signature. As to the Estate it does not suffer by neglect; a new Tenant recommended by Sainsbury has taken it from the poor flimsy creature that held it in a fright, and Andrewes stoutly exacts the rent when due.

LORD SHEFFIELD'S OFFER FOR NEWHAVEN.

We almost howled when we read the tremendous account of nearly five months' confinement—the weakness in your traces affrighted me most, but I rejoiced exceedingly in your last, which says that you have advanced to nearly your usual condition of strength. I never heard of Pyrmont waters for the gout—but I grieve to tell you that notwithstanding repeated applications I find your Hogshead of Madeira (which is on its travels) may not arrive sooner than 4, 5, or 6 months. I must spare you all I can of my Old Madeira which is in London, but I do not know that it will amount to a quantity worth the trouble of sending. I shall make every effort and inquire everywhere for you. As to Sir Ralph Payne, surely a letter directed to him in London would find him, if you think that mode preferable.

Your plan as to Charlotte Porten might be the most desirable, but nothing could be more fancifull than to suppose it could possibly succeed, unless you could send a Demon cracked from Paris to hang the mother to a Lanthern.

My last letter answers your question whether Hester had left you the fee-simple of the Sussex Estate. I have learned nothing more concerning that Holy woman since the receipt of the Copy of her Will, nor am I likely, unless I should find some of the family of the Laws in London next winter. I think you should inclose to me an order to the Executors, Messrs. William Law, Senior, of Kings Cliffe, and William Law of Stamford, to deliver to me all the Writings, Papers, Surveys, Plans, &c., relating to the Sussex Estate, and you may add, those which relate to the Family of Gibbon.

When Batt was here not long since, I mentioned to him your old Aunt's Bequest and my proposition to you; at first, he did not object, but next day he scouted my folly and extravagance in diminishing my Income. My observations that I should and could easily cut down annually more timber than would pay the difference, and that in case I went to glory, those who came after me would be fully compensated in the end for loss of Income— I say, these observations seemed to make little impression on him. However, I was somewhat chilled, yet I cannot help thinking it or something of the kind might answer to both of us, if you should be desperately disposed to sell to increase your Income. I should acquire a position on the Sea-Shore—but you may have thought of something that would answer your purpose better.

You admire the Minister's secrecy and vigour. There is no secrecy in the case, but surely he has made a desperate plunge, and it appears to me a very wanton one—and if it is right to take an advantage, he is losing the opportunity. It is difficult to suppose that Spain will engage *single-handed* with us, but we may bully them into it, and although France cannot at present do much, yet the adherence of the National Assembly to the Family compact may help the Spaniards to be stout, and above all it would be good policy in the French Aristocrats to dash France into a war at all events.

You are incorrigible, but we desire that you will encourage De Severy to write. It is surprising he can write and remember English so well. The alterations in your Chateau pleased us very much. I have enquired more than once whether you would have the provision for Mrs. Gibbon to be £200 or £300. You pay the latter, but I understand.

Everybody is looking into Bruce's Travels. Part takes the attention, but they are abominably abused. Banks objects to the Botany, Reynell to the Geography, Cambridge to the History, The Greeks to the Greek, &c., &c.; yet the work is to be found on every table. Bruce printed the work, and sold 2000 copies to Robertson for £6000. He sells to the booksellers at 4 guineas, and they to their customers at 5 guineas.

555.

This letter is apparently written to M. Langer, *the Librarian of the Ducal Library of Wolfenbuttel. A translation of part of it was found with Gibbon's manuscript of the* Antiquities of the House of Brunswick, *and published by Lord Sheffield* (Gibbon's Miscellaneous Works, vol. iii. pp. 353-558).

À Rolle, ce 12 Octobre, 1790.

Je vous aurois plutot remercié, Monsieur, des soins obligeans que vous avez bien voulû vous donner pour me procurer les Origines Guelficæ, si d'un côté notre honnête libraire Mr. Pott ne m'avoit pas appris que vous etiez en voyage, si de l'autre je n'avois pas été moi même en proye à l'acces de goutte le plus rigoureux et le plus long que j'aye encore éprouvé.

Nous revoici à present dans notre état ordinaire, je marche, et vous ne courez plus. Je vous suppose bien etabli, bien enfoncé dans votre immense bibliotheque dans un endroit qui fournit peut-être un choix plus étendu et plus interessant des morts que des vivans. Comme vous êtes également propre à vivre avec les uns et les autres, je desirerois pour votre bonheur aussi bien que pour celui de vos amis, que vous pûssiez enfin executer comme moi le projet de chercher une douce retraite sur les bords du lac Leman. Il s'en faut de beaucoup que vous n'y soyez oublié: nous parlons souvent de vous surtout dans la famille de Severy, nous regrettons votre absence et en nous rappellant l'aimable franchise, la vivacité piquante de *l'Esclave*, nous cherisons l'esperance de vous revoir parmi nous en homme libre, ne dependant que de vos gouts et pouvant vous donner tout entier aux lettres et à la societé.

Vous aurez sans doute appris la perte irreparable que j'ai faite du pauvre Deyverdun. En vertu de son testament et de mes arrangemens avec son heritier Mr. le Major de Montagny, je me suis assuré ma vie durant la jouissance de sa maison et de son jardin. Vous en connoissez tous les agrémens qui se sont encore augmentés par une dépense assez considerable et assez bien tendu que j'y ai faité depuis sa mort. Je dois être content de ma position mais on ne peut pas remplacer un ami de trente ans. Votre curiosité, peut-être votre amitié, desirera de connoitre mes amusemens, mes travaux, mes projets pendant les deux ans qui se sont écoulé depuis la dernière publication de mon grand ouvrage. Aux questions indiscretes qu'on se permet trop souvent vis-à-vis de moi, je responds avec une mine renfrognée et d'une manière vague, mais je ne veux rien avoir de caché pour vous et pour imiter la franchise que vous aimez, je vous avouerai naturellement que ma confidence est fondée en partie sur le besoin que j'aurai de votre secours.

Après mon retour d'Angleterre les premiers mois ont été consacrés à la jouissance de ma liberté et de ma bibliotheque, et vous ne serez pas étonné si j'ai renouvellé une connoissance familière avec vos auteurs Grecs et si j'ai fait vœu de leur reserver tous les jours une portion de mon loisir. Je passe sous silence ces tristes momens dans lesquels je n'ai été occupé qu'à soigner et à pleurer mon ami: mais dès que j'ai commencé à me retrouver un esprit moins agile, j'ai cherché à me donner quelque distraction plus forte et plus interessante que la simple lecture. Le souvenir de ma servitude de vingt ans m'a cependant effrayé et je me suis bien promis de ne plus m'embarquer dans une entreprise de longue haleine que je n'acheverois vraisemblablement jamais. Il vaut bien mieux, me suis je dit, choisir, dans tous les pays et dans tous les siecles, des morceaux historiques que je traiterai separément suivant leur nature et selon mon gout. Lorsque ces opuscules (je pourrai les nommer en Anglais, *Historical Excursions*) me fourniront un volume, je le donnerai au public: ce don pourroit etre renouvellé jusqu'a ce que nous soyons fatigués ou ce public ou moi même: mais chaque volume, complet par lui même, n'exigera point de suite, et au lieu d'être borné comme la diligence au grand chemin, je me promenerai librement dans le champ de l'histoire en m'arrêtant partout où je trouve des points de vue agreables. Dans ce projet je ne vois qu'un inconvenient,—un objet interessant s'étend et s'aggrandit sous le travail: je pourrois être entrainé au dela de mes bornes, mais je serai doucement entrainé sans prevoyance et sans contrainte.

THE HISTORY OF THE GUELFS.

Mes soupçons ont été vérifiés dans le choix de ma première *excursion*. Ce que j'avois si bien prevu n'a pas manqué d'arriver à mon premier choix et ce choix vous expliquera pourquoi j'ai demandé avec tant d'empressement les Origines Guelficæ. Dans mon histoire j'avois rendu compte de deux alliances illustres, d'un fils du Marquis Azo d'Este avec une fille de Robert Guiscard, d'une princesse de Brunswick avec l'Empereur Grec. Un premier apperçu de l'antiquité et de la grandeur de la maison de Brunswick a excité ma curiosité, et j'ai cru me pouvoir interesser les deux nations que j'estime le plus par les mémoires d'une famille qui est sortie de l'une pour regner sur l'autre. Mes recherches, en me devoilant la beauté de ce sujet, m'en ont fait voir l'étendue et la difficulté. L'origine des Marquis de Ligurie et peut-être de Toscane a été suffisament eclaircie par Muratori et Leibnitz; l'Italie du moyen age, son histoire et ses monumens, me sont très connus et je ne suis pas mécontent de ce que j'ai déjà écrit sur la branche cadette d'Este qui est demeurée fidelle a garder ses cendres casanières. Les anciens Guelfs ne me sont point étrangers, et je me crois en etat de rendre compte de la puissance et de la chute de leurs heritiers, les Ducs de Bavière et de Saxe.

La succession de la maison de Brunswick au trône de la Grande Bretagne sera très assurément la partie la plus interessante de mon travail; mais tous les materiaux se trouvent dans ma langue, et un Anglois devroit rougir s'il n'avoit pas approfondi l'histoire moderne et la constitution actuelle de son pays. Mais entre le premier Duc et le premier Electeur de Brunswick il se trouve un intervalle de quatre cent cinquante ans, je suis condamné à suivre dans les ténèbres un sentier étroit et raboteux, et les divisions, les sous divisions, de tant de branches et de territoires repandent sur ce sentier la confusion d'un labyrinthe Genealogique. Les événemens sans éclat et sans liaison sont bornés à une province d'Allemagne et ce n'est que vers la fin de cette periode que je serois un peu ranimé par la reformation, la guerre de trente ans, et la nouvelle puissance de l'Electorat. Comme je me propose de crayonner des Memoires et non pas de composer une histoire, je marcherois sans doute d'un pas rapide, je presenterois des resultats plutot que des faits, des observations plutot que des récits: mais vous sentez, combien un tableau general exige de connoissances particulières, combien l'auteur doit être plus savant que son livre.

Or cet auteur, il est à deux cent lieues de la Saxe, il ignore la langue et il ne s'est jamais appliqué à l'histoire de l'Allemagne. Eloigné des sources, il ne lui reste qu'un seul moyen pour les faire couler dans sa bibliotheque. C'est de se menager sur les lieux même un correspondant exact, un guide eclairé, un oracle enfin qu'il puisse consulter dans tous ses besoins. Par votre caractère, votre esprit, vos lumières, votre position, vous êtes cet homme precieux et unique que je cherche, et quand vous m'indiquerez un *suppléant* aussi capable que vous même je ne m'addresserois pas avec la même confiance à un étranger. Je vous accablerois librement de questions, et de nouvelles questions naitroient souvent de vos reponses; je vous prierois de fouiller dans votre vaste depôt; je vous demanderois des notices, des livres, des extraits, des traductions, des renseignements sur tous les objets qui peuvent intéresser mon travail. Mais j'ignore si vous êtes disposé à sacrifier votre loisir, vos études chéries à une correspondance pénible sans agrémens et sans gloire. Je me flatte que vous feriez quelque chose pour moi, vous feriez encore davantage pour l'honneur de la maison à laquelle vous êtes attaché, mais suis-je en droit de supposer que mes ecrits puissent contribuer de quelque chose à son honneur?

J'attends, Monsieur, votre reponse qu'elle soit prompte et franche. Si vous daignez vous associer à mon entreprise, je vous envoyerai sur le champ mon premier interrogatoire. Votre refus me decideroit à renoncer à mon dessein, ou du moins à lui donner une nouvelle forme. J'ose en même tems vous demander un profond secret: un mot indiscret seroit repeté par cent bouches et j'aurois le desagrement de voir dans les journaux, et bientôt dans les papiers Anglois, une annonce, peut-être défigurée, de mes projets littéraires, qui ne sont confiés qu'à vous seul.

J'ai l'honneur d'être,
E. G.

556.

To Lord Sheffield.

[Oct. 17, '90.]

You call me incorrigible: but I never was less disposed than at present to plead guilty. Have you forgot the general picture of mind, body and estate which I sent you since my recovery? in the tranquil life of Lausanne a long interval might elapse without affording any features to alter or any colours to vary. On the most interesting topic, poor Buriton, it is mine to hear rather than to write, and most ardently indeed do I now desire to hear of the conclusion of that incomprehensible business. Is it possible, are we under such servitude to the lawyers that an obsolete act without force or meaning should have hung us up for a year in Chancery? If I do not learn before the end of the year that the money is paid and placed, I shall be as miserable as pecuniary events can make me; when it is done I am easy and happy for life. In the midst of your arduous affairs I do not suspect any failure of zeal, but I now call upon you to redouble your speed, and to strain every nerve till we have reached the goal. Till the present business I never imagined that it was difficult to find people who would take your money. It is lucky that Sainsbury has consented to leave £8000 on Buriton: with regard to the remainder I leave it absolutely to your judgement, but since you distrust with reason private bond security, I see no other way than throwing it into the funds; a short delay might be allowed in expectation of their sinking, but the rise and fall are so uncertain, that it might be the 'rusticus expectat dum defluat amnis.' In the mean while Buriton rent must be paid, and as the two quarters due at Lady day had been neglected, the whole year till last Michaelmas must be rigorously exacted. I do not believe (though I would not give a gentleman the lye) that you ever asked me the question about Mrs. G.'s jointure: it will be an handsome, an easy compliment to give her a right to the three hundred which I pay her in fact.

Let us now make a tour to Newhaven. Upon the whole I am very well satisfied. You remark that about February, 1788, the old Saint decimated her nephew: but have you forgot that her atheistical nephew had neglected to accept her invitation and would not even write her a civil letter? surely *he* has no right to complain. I am ignorant of the character and behaviour of the Laws, but in the general principle of preferring friends to relations, I think her perfectly right.—You were not surely impatient for an answer to your proposal: it demands the coolest deliberation, and there cannot be the smallest occasion for dispatch. I will however impart such ideas as have arisen.

1. I agree with Batt in thinking it an unwise measure for yourself. Is this a time to diminish your income when you must enlarge or at least support your expence, when you know that for seven years to come you will not enjoy the benefit of a single winter fallow? If you have timber it will be sufficiently wanted for your annual supplies.

2. The balance of my fortune and my wishes depends on a contingency which I have neither power nor inclination to hasten. As soon as the Belvidere subsides, I am rich beyond all my plans of expence at Lausanne. Every winter such an event is probable, and it is highly probable that it will happen in three or four winters. It is indeed possible that a fine thread may be drawn to a great length without breaking, and if I turned a landed estate into an annuity, I should never be at a loss to employ the superfluity. If my heir, the creature of my choice does not think he has enough, the dog has too much.

557.

Lord Sheffield to Edward Gibbon.

Sheffield Place, 3rd Jan., 1791.

It occurs to me in the midst of much hurry, that you may have a wish for further information on the subject of the Madeira. It was shipped for Ostend on the 3rd Dec., with full and ample instructions (according to your own directions) for its conveyance to Basle, where it is to wait your further orders. I suppose that on the receipt of my former letter you wrote to your correspondent there.

The Wine is gone in one hogshead and one tierce, marked & No. E. G. No. 1 & 2.

The Bill as follows—

	£	s.	d.
No. 1. 6 doz. finest Malmsey sealed red—			
on board	17	4	0
6 doz. Bottles	1	1	0
No. 2. One Hogshead best Old Madeira—			
on board	39	0	0
1 Hogshead—1 Tierce—1 Case &			
Bills of Lading	1	10	8
	59	5	8

Probably it is the best wine of the kind that ever reached the centre of Europe. You will remember that an Hogshead is on his travels through the torrid zone for you. I suppose you do not mean to decline it when it arrives. No wine is meliorated to a greater degree by keeping than Madeira, and you latterly appeared so ravenous for it, that I must conceive you wish to have a stock.

I have had a Congress with Sainsbury, &c. The business has been referred to the Master of the Rolls. I have talked with the Master. It seems in good train. The conveyance is preparing. The message of young Porten is very troublesome. Sainsbury wished to avoid taking the £8000 on mortgage. I remonstrated strongly. He agreed, handsomely, to take it rather than embarrass. I have promised £4000 on a Yorkshire mortgage. I have been very busy in Town. I am glad I cannot finish *the Paper*, because you are such a worthless fellow, that you do not answer even on business.

Yours ever,
S.

N.B.—The Birth of Maria, & the Justices are waiting for me at the Inn.

558.

To Lord Sheffield.

1791.

Your indignation will melt into pity, when you hear that for several weeks past I have been again confined to my chamber and my chair. Yet I must hasten, generously hasten, to exculpate the Gout, my old enemy, from the curses which you already pour on his head. He is not the cause of this disorder, although the consequences have been somewhat similar. After some days of fever and a most violent oppression in my head and stomach, the morbid humour forced itself into my right leg, which was covered from my knee to my toe with a strong inflammatory *Erisipèle* or Rash. I was gradually relieved by a plentiful discharge of pus *atque Venenum* (excuse the indelicacy) which, according to my Physician, has surpassed that of fifty blisters. The skin has been compleatly renewed, and I now crawl about the house upon two sticks. *I am satisfied that this effort of nature has saved me from a very dangerous, perhaps a fatal, crisis; and I listen to the flattering hope that it may tend to keep the Gout at a more respectful distance.* You will determine whether it ought to raise or sink the purchase of my annuity.

I must confess that I am disappointed, vexed, harrassed, fatigued with the strange procrastination of the Buriton affairs which are now verging to the end of the second year. In former transactions while we were fighting with knaves and madmen nothing could surprise, but in this amicable connection with a willing and able purchaser, it is indeed provoking that term after term we should be hung up (a most proper expression) in the forms of the Court of Chancery. You are now on the spot, and I conjure you by every tye of friendship and humanity to steal some moments from the service of Bristol, to strain every nerve of your active genius, and to send me a speedy and satisfactory account that the business is terminated, and the money paid. The funds are indeed so very high, that I agree with you in preferring a clear four per cent. which *they* do not yield, on the solid basis of the Earth, I mean on good landed security. I therefore much approve of your holding Sainsbury to his engagement of retaining the £8000 on the mortgage of Buriton's own self, and hope you will not fail of success in registering £4000 more in Yorkshire. Should any loose hundreds remain, they may be best added to my India bonds in Gosling's hands. I much fear that another half year from Buriton will become due (at Lady-day), and hope you will order Andrews to exact it without mercy or delay.

I feel myself much embarrassed how to define or establish my claims on Hugonin. We always treated with the confidence of friends, and the ease of Gentlemen, and his short accounts, from art or accident, were always so vague, that I could never discern to what half year his remittances applied. I am satisfied that two years or at least eighteen months have never been accounted for; but on the most moderate footing I may demand the year's rent which ended at Michaelmas 1788, and which was not paid when I left England. The agency of Hugonin will not be disputed, the Tenant's receipt will prove that it was paid into his hands, and even the silence of Gosling's books will afford some evidence that it never was remitted for my use. Besides, will not the *onus probandi* rest on Hugonin's heirs, who ought to produce my discharge? On recollection I may even state my damages at eighteen months, since according to a vile abuse, the tenant only paid at Michaelmas the year's rent which had been due the previous Lady-day.

ACCEPTS ANNUITY FOR NEWHAVEN.

I now proceed to the important business of Newhaven, and am not sorry that we have both of us taken sufficient time to avoid the reproach of rash and precipitate measures. As you are not an infant I will decline any farther remonstrance of what may be proper or improper for yourself, and will think solely of my own interest. After mature consideration I am *resolved* to amplify my income by the sale of Newhaven, leaving one half of the purchase money to sink in an Annuity and the other half to swim in a Mortgage. My old scruples against pecuniary transactions with a friend are much diminished by my experience of the delays and difficulties which occur in a treaty with a stranger, and I flatter myself that you will not think it necessary to ascertain my title to the Estate by an amicable suit in Chancery. Your statement is impartial and your terms are liberal: Twenty-eight years' purchase appears a fair price for an Estate circumstanced like mine, and I am not ambitious of paying more than twelve years for the chance of my earthly existence. But I do not perfectly acquiesce in your striking off the casual profits to balance the casual losses and repairs, and I must request that you would try a very simple calculation: Supposing the three per Cents at eighty, your landed estate, after deducting every possible outgoing, would pay you as good interest as your money in the funds. Is such an equality reasonable? Should you pay nothing for the solid security of land? Is the National Debt less exposed than the Sussex acres to be swallowed in the Ocean? The calculation is easy.

	£	s.	d.
Clear rent of Newhaven after deducting			
Land-tax and quitrents	234	17	10
Interest paid by the Tenant on £154 at			
4 per cent.	6	0	0
Casual profits on an average	19	13	4
	£260	11	2
	28		

£7280,

of which

£	£
4000	mortgage 160
3280	annuity 273

£433

Suppose we reduce this sum to £7000 and divide it equally, the produce will be £430 (£140 for the Mortgage, £290 for the Annuity). I cannot think my expectations quite unreasonable, but I leave the final arbitration to yourself, as if we were treating with a third person, and I authorize you to conclude with Lord Sheffield on such conditions as I ought to ask and he will be disposed to give. The farm itself will never answer for the Mortgage, and you will obtain a good and sufficient security for the annuity. In the meanwhile I should be glad to know when I may expect the payment of some rent, and from what date it will begin to accrue to me.

N.B.—Your own offer is £4200, the Mortgage; £280 Annuity. But arithmetic is erroneous: 3052 divided by 12 do not produce 280 but only 254. You are a pretty man of business. So much for Newhaven.

Since we are talking of Wills, I must request that you would commit mine to the flames. By the first opportunity I will send you the duplicate of another which I have constructed on more rational principles. You will not disapprove the preference which I now give to the children of Sir Stanier Porten: they are the nearest, the most indigent and the most deserving of my relations.

*The whole sheet has been filled with dry selfish business; but I must and will reserve some lines of the cover for a little friendly conversation. I passed four days at the castle of Copet with Necker; and could have wished to have shown him, as a warning to any aspiring youth possessed with the Dæmon of ambition. With all the means of private happiness in his power, he is the most miserable of human beings: the past, the present, and the future are equally odious to him. When I suggested some domestic amusements of books, building, &c. he answered, with a deep tone of despair, "Dans l'état où je suis, je ne puis sentir que le coup de vent qui m'a abbattu." How different from the careless chearfulness with which our poor friend Lord North supported his fall! Madame Necker maintains more external composure, *mais le Diable n'y perd rien.* It is true that Necker wished to be carried into the Closet, like old Pitt, on the shoulders of the people; and that he has been ruined by the Democracy which he had raised. I believe him to be an able financier, and know him to be an honest man; too honest, perhaps, for a minister. His rival Calonne has passed through Lausanne, in his way from Turin; and was soon followed by the Prince of Condé, with his son and grandson; but I was too much indisposed to see them. They have, or have had, some wild projects of a counter-revolution: horses have been bought, men levied, and the Canton of Berne has too much countenanced such foolish attempts which must end in the ruin of the party.

PRAISE OF BURKE'S *REFLECTIONS.*

Burke's book is a most admirable medicine against the French disease, which has made too much progress even in this happy country. I admire his eloquence, I approve his politics, I adore his chivalry, and I can forgive even his superstition. The primitive Church, which I have treated with some freedom, was itself at that time an innovation, and I was attached to the old Pagan establishment. The French spread so many lyes about the sentiments of the English nation, that I wish the most considerable men of all parties and descriptions would join in some public act, declaring themselves satisfied with and resolved to support our present constitution. Such a declaration would have a wonderful effect in Europe; and, were I thought worthy, I myself should be proud to subscribe it. I have a great mind to send you something of a sketch, such as all thinking men might adopt.

I have intelligence of the approach of my Madeira, and on its receipt will despatch a draught for the payment. I accept with equal pleasure the second, now in the torrid zone. Send me some pleasant details of your domestic state, of Maria, &c. If my lady thinks that my silence is a mark of indifference, my lady is a goose. I *must* have you all at Lausanne next summer.* Apropos, I must have £3000 on Annuity and £3000 on Mortgage: the surplus you may divide as you like best. I wish you would not enclose your letters to Paris. I have no longer any connections with Lessert, and they desire not to be troubled with them.

559.

Lord Sheffield to Edward Gibbon.

Downing Street, 5th Feb., 1791.

We remained in the country to the last moment, & I came to Town furious against you on account of your neglect of writing, but on reaching Lord Guilford, I learned that you had been very ill, & I was completely softened and no longer abusive. His information came from Major Frank North, who added that you were recovering.

Now are you not a damned good-for-nothing fellow for not recollecting that we might hear you were ill, & therefore not desiring De Severy to write a line to mention that you were recovering? I have for a long time exhorted my Lady to write to him. I think she will now favour him with a Philipick. What has been the matter? for my account does not say whether it has been the gout only or something more. I shall be really sulky if you do not write one line. We are much annoyed. I went to Elmsley & he knew nothing.

THE CORN LAWS AND SLAVE TRADE.

I will not write to you on business until a fragment arrives from you, except to say the Business has stopped in hopes of information from you relative to the amount of Hugonin's debt to you. You know I had nothing to do with the affairs between you and him, and of course could not make out the ballance. Andrews has stated it to me at £347 2*s*. 3*d*. I supposed it to be more, therefore waited to hear from you; but I have an Affidavit ready prepared to make before a Master for that amount; that operation is necessary before any further progress can be made. In addition to my other occupations I am more busied than ever I was in my life about a Corn Bill now depending, (as great a business as I have ever undertaken). I examined it well during the Recess, and made ample notes on my arrival; I have shewn them to Batt and Sir Joseph, and they recommend strenuously that I should publish them with my name. They say it is too argumentative, it requires too much consideration, for a speech. They think it will do me great credit. They add it is impossible even for a very able man in the art of speaking and in the habit, to do it justice in a speech. In short, I am obliged to undertake publication in such an hurry as will not produce your commendation. The question comes on in a week. I find the first Edition of my *Observations on the Project for Abolishing the Slave Trade* was not sent to you. I have delivered the second Edition to Elmsley to be forwarded when there is an opportunity. I learned from him that you had not received Burke's *Pamphlet*.

If you had not been ill I should have talked to you as you deserve about the addition to your History. It is as it should be, that I am to hear of that addition for the first time from Newspapers or accidental correspondents. I did not believe the circumstance until everybody was convinced of it, and Mr. Cadell's information was general. It is intolerable.

560.

Lord Sheffield to Edward Gibbon.

Downing Street, 15th March, 1791.

Your manuscript at last received exhilarated us very considerably. We heard you were better, but did not exactly know the state of things. We had almost made up our minds to go to see you in a snug party for a month or two in the summer, but now you are well we do not care so much about you. Maria says the allowance of a year's purchase is a fair offer, and my Lady is still more eager to go than Maria.

I know not how I made the mistake in saying the annuity should be £280 instead of £254, but on the receipt of your letter, I desired Woodcock to make out the conveyance for £3000 in an annuity at 12 years' purchase (£250) and £4000 on Mortgage at 4 per cent., £160 together with £410. You will observe that I have somewhat diminished the sum to be laid out on an annuity and encreased the sum on Mortgage, thinking it better for you. Unfortunately for you, since the above arrangement, I have discovered that besides the outgoings I mentioned to you there is a Fee Farm rent of £5 8s. 0d. payable out of the Estate, which at 28 years' purchase makes a deduction of £151 4s. 0d. Be assured that you are a damned Jew, otherwise you would have been content with the £6700 which I profferred to you, and I think you ought still. I propose that the annuity and mortgage interest shall begin from Lady-day ensuing, and the Deeds shall be sent to you whenever I can prevail on Woodcock to prepare them. The Annuity shall be payable out of certain farms at Sheffield, and the £4000 mortgage shall be on the Newhaven Estate. The Mortgage Deeds, &c., shall be left in Batt's hands for your account. It is observable that I am paying you £4000 for the reversion of the Estate, and in the meantime more than the annual clear income of it. I am purchasing Lord Heathfield's House and Estate in Sussex, 14 miles from Sheffield, for Sir Henry Clinton. Only 25 years' purchase, deducting every outgoing, is asked, and the timber (which will be very advantageous) is rated very moderately.

You have often remarked how singular your ill-luck is as to sales and titles to Estates. Be it known to you that the conveyance of the Newhaven Estate to your Grandfather is lost. All the other old writings belonging to it were found carefully tyed up and transmitted to me by Mr. Law. The Lawyers say, as I know the circumstances of the Estate and Family, it is such a title as I may take if I please. Yet that I should not be able to sell it again but to disadvantage. I answer that I do not wish it to be sold again. Thus it appears you could not easily sell to anybody but me. As to the Buriton business, I have been almost afraid to tell you that it is still hung up. It is again referred to a Master in Chancery. However, there is no step neglected that can bring it to a conclusion, and I hope it cannot hold on much longer. I have made out that Hugonin was indebted to you to the amount of a year and a half of Buriton. I have sworn to the account, and you will receive at least ten shillings in the pound. Hugonin, his Mistress and daughter are all dead within two years. You will have £8000 on Mortgage in Hampshire, £4000 in Sussex, and £4000 in Yorkshire. All good strings to your bow.

THE LABOURING OAR IN THE HOUSE.

The account of your undergoing a drain equal to fifty blisters furnishes me with some satisfaction, as we think it will be serviceable to your fat carcase. You have proven me busy, but I was comparatively at leisure. I have illuminated the Corn Laws. The subject was not understood. The Pamphlet written in a few days is in great repute. You will abuse it because I only attended to the sense in writing it. I have the labouring oar in the House of Commons. I shall write again soon. In the meantime you must write by return of post, if you wish any other distribution of the money.

I am on a Committee every day from ten to four.

561.

To Lord Sheffield.

Lausanne, April 9th, 1791.

I *will* say no more, because I can say no more on the unfortunate subject of Buriton, the most unlucky because the least expected of all my worldly embarrassments. Tell me fairly whether you suspect any secret management, or any legal chicanery, &c., on the side of the purchasers. If they are sincere and willing as ourselves, what hinders that we should give possession, we of the land and they of the money, and let the Master in Chancery make his report whenever it may amuse him? If such a scheme be impracticable, goad, I conjure you, the lawyers and fix a day, a definite day, a short day for the final conclusion, for my release from a state of suspense which keeps me hanging between heaven and earth.

You say nothing of what rent may be due from Newhaven, and of the payment of my wretched legacy. My repairs and improvements have now run away with a great deal of money, and my cash account with the Goslings has seldom been so low. It would, however, suffice to pay for the Madeira which is arrived in perfect health: but with my usual accuracy I have lost the account.

After mature consideration I accept your terms of £250 annuity and four thousand mortgage with the security which you propose; the former on some farms at Sheffield (doubtless of a more ample produce), the latter on the Newhaven estate, the imperfect title of which it will not become me to dispute. Notwithstanding your recent discovery of a fee farm rent, I think you will still have a very good bargain; but if you are obstinate, you may strike off ten pounds a year from the Annuity, for your chance of getting back any money would be a very poor one indeed.—With regard to the writings, I have no objection to the method which you propose of lodging them in Batt's hands. I do not recollect anything more on the subject of business, since I have already approved of the distribution of the purchase money. £8000 on Buriton, £4000 in Yorkshire, the loose residue, if any, in the funds. We may therefore proceed to more interesting and less interested topics.

*First, of my health; It is now tolerably restored: my legs are still weak, but the animal in general is in a sound and lively condition; and we have great hopes from the fine weather and the Pyrmont waters. I most sincerely wished for the presence of Maria, to embellish a ball which I gave the 29th of last month to all the best company, natives and foreigners, of Lausanne, with the aid of the Severys, especially of the mother and son, who directed the œconomy, and performed the honours of the *Fête*. It opened about seven in the evening; the assembly of men and women was pleased and pleasing, the music good, the illumination splendid, the refreshments profuse: at twelve, one hundred and thirty persons sat down to a very good supper; at two, I stole away to bed, in a snug corner; and I was informed at breakfast, that the remains of the Veteran and young troops, with Severy and his sister at their head, had concluded the last dance about a quarter before seven. This magnificent entertainment has gained me great credit; and the expence was more reasonable than you can easily imagine. This was an extraordinary event, but I give frequent dinners; and in the summer I have an assembly every Sunday evening. What a wicked wretch! says Lady Pantile.

I cannot pity you for the accumulation of business, as you ought not to pity *me*, if I complained of the tranquillity of Lausanne: we suffer or enjoy the effects of our own choice. Perhaps you will mutter something of our not being born for ourselves, of public spirit (I have formerly read of such a thing), of private friendship, for which I give you full and ample credit, &c. But your parliamentary operations, at least, will probably expire in the month of June; and I shall refuse to sign the Newhaven conveyance, unless I am satisfied that you will execute the Lausanne visit this summer. On the 15th of June, suppose lord, lady, Maria, and maid, (poor Louisa!) in a post coach, with Etienne on horseback, set out from Downing-street, or Sheffield-place, cross the Channel from Brighton to Dieppe, visit the national assembly, buy caps at Paris, examine the ruins of Versailles, and arrive at Lausanne, without danger or fatigue, the second week in July; you will be lodged pleasantly and comfortably, and will not perhaps despise my situation. A couple of months will roll, alas! too hastily away: you will all be amused by new scenes, new people; and whenever Maria and you, with Severy, mount on horseback to visit the country, the Glaciers, &c., My lady and myself shall form a very quiet tête-à-tête at home. In September, if you are tired, you may return by a direct or indirect way; but I only desire that you will not make the plan impracticable by grasping at too much. In return, I promise you a visit of three or four months in the autumn of ninety-two: you and my booksellers are now my principal attractions in England. You had some right to growl at hearing of my supplement in the papers: but Cadell's indiscretion was founded on a loose hint which I had thrown out in a letter, and which in all probability will never be executed. Yet I am not totally idle. Adieu.*

562.

Lord Sheffield to Edward Gibbon.

Downing Street, 21st April, 1791.

A BARGAIN WITH THE SHEFFIELDS.

At length the Buriton business is almost concluded, and all your and my cares on that subject will be at an end, the moment I receive the Deeds which were sent to you early this morning for signature. The Masters in Chancery are the Devils, and I should not have expressed myself much more amiably of the Master of the Rolls, if he had not been at last particularly attentive to my exhortations to dispatch. All difficulties are at end, the conveyances, &c., engrossed, and one part of them are gone to you, because Lord Stawell's Lawyers wish you to sign that part, notwithstanding they drew up the Power of Attorney which you signed to enable me.

At the same time are gone the Deeds which convey Newhaven from Ed. Gibbon to Lord Sheffield, reciting the £4000 on Mortgage and the annuity of £250 per Ann. The conveyance is to J. T. Batt to the use of Lord Sheffield. Batt is Trustee; and the Deeds, when returned with the other writings belonging to the Estate, must be left in his hands as such, not only on account of the Mortgage of £4000, but also because the Newhaven Estate is made subject to the Annuity, notwithstanding a greater proportion of the Sheffield Estate is chargeable with it than is necessary to pay the whole. It was unnecessary to send you the Deed which grants the Annuity of £250 chargeable on Sheffield and Newhaven. It is signed by me and left in Batt's hands. He has perused and examined the drafts of the Conveyance and of the grant of the annuity before they were engrossed.

There are four deeds sent for your signature—and with them directions as to the parts where to be signed, which parts are marked with pencil. It is also mentioned that you should have English witnesses. Frank North might be one, and I suppose you may find at any time another fit English witness at Lausanne. You will despatch as soon as you can and return the writings immediately. If you give me a line of notice as soon as they are signed it will be still better, and will forward, and in reality conclude, matters.

SNUGNESS OF GIBBON'S AFFAIRS.

We have not been able to get any intelligence of the conveyance of the Newhaven Estate to your Grandfather, which is somewhat strange. I mentioned in my last that I had given directions for forming the conveyance from you to me, previous to the discovery of a Quit-rent, and that I thought you had better pay me the value of that Quit-rent than alter the even sum of £4000 Mortgage or £250 annuity. I must therefore take 28 years' purchase for the Quit-rent, and I flatter myself you are too much of a gentleman and too little of the Jew to make any objection. You have a good bargain, and I would sooner have seen you at the Devil than have given you so much, if you did not seem to be under my direction in these matters.

I almost envy you the snugness of your affairs. You will be a rich fellow. What a damned long letter on such matter, to make things easy to the meanest capacities.

Perhaps I may write soon on the Russian War, the Slave Trade, and the Corn Bill. The first has been an extraordinary business. On the second I was a considerable prop to good sense against nonsense and the most eloquent declamation on humanity. What think you of shutting the Ports of the West Indies? It would not have succeeded better than the experiment at Boston. I have beaten Pitt 3 times on the Corn Bill.

563.

Lord Sheffield to Edward Gibbon.

Downing Street, 13th May, 1791.

Nothing could be more unfair and insidious than the proposition that you would come here in 1792, if we would go to you in 1791. It raised the whole Family, and everybody one knows, against me. It raised me against myself. It is true in a weak season, when we supposed you poorly, I exhibited a disposition to go to you, but when you recovered *insurmountable* difficulties occurred. The Great Navigation in Sussex which is at its crisis depends on me, and a thousand other matters, besides expence when I have not got a shilling to spare. However, the Idea is entertained. I am much conciliated, as I should be to anything that binds you to a compact to be here in 1792. I cannot prevail on myself at once to say—I will, altho' I apprehend I must. Therefore say by the return of the post, whether you can accommodate the Louisa, if she should make a fifth in the Coach with My Lady, her woman, Maria and myself. I suppose she might, if necessary, sleep with Maria or the Woman. I have not mentioned this letter to the Ladies, but Maria is anxious that Louisa should go, and we think she is at an age to receive improvement even in a visit for a couple of months. I cannot go sooner than the beginning of July, and I must be here early in October. Desire our Friend De Severy to write detail to me on the subject of the journey.

It just occurred to write this letter. A Committee is waiting for me, but to make you amends, I send you Woodfall's account of one of the most extraordinary debates in Parliament.

Yours ever,
S.

564.

To Lord Sheffield.

Lausanne, May 18th, 1791.

DANGER OF RUSSIAN WAR.

I write a short letter, on small paper, to inform you, that the various deeds, which arrived safe and in good condition, have this morning been sealed, signed, and delivered, in the presence of respectable and well known English witnesses, though out of compliment to you I inserted one Irish evidence, a protégé of Sarah's, and considering all things a very pretty gentleman. I am very well behaved to him. *To have read the aforesaid acts, would have been difficult; to have understood them, impracticable. I therefore signed them with my eyes shut, and in that implicit confidence, which we freemen and Britons are humbly content to yield to our lawyers and ministers. I hope, however, most seriously hope, that every thing has been carefully examined, and that I am not totally ruined. It is not without much impatience that I expect an account of the payment and investment of the purchase-money,* and am somewhat afraid of the high charges of auctioneers and attornies. The writings well secured are delivered to a trusty carrier, who promises to begin his Journey Monday next, the 23rd instant, and to deposit them in Downing Street about a fortnight afterwards. *It was my intention to have added a new edition of my Will: but I have an unexpected call to go to Geneva to-morrow with the Severys, and must defer that business a few days, till after my return. On my return I may possibly find a letter from you, and will write more fully in answer: my posthumous work, contained in a single sheet, will not ruin you in postage. In the meanwhile, let me desire you either never to talk of Lausanne, or to execute the journey this summer; after the dispatch of public and *private* business, there can be no real obstacle but in yourself, and if you deceive me I shall insist on the additional year's purchase for Newhaven, which I had given up in consideration of the visit. Pray do not go to War with Russia: it is very foolish: I am quite angry with Pitt. Adieu.* Pray inform Mrs. G. of our conclusion and her security. I write to her this post after a long pause. I am a sad dog.

565.

To his Stepmother.

Lausanne, May 18th, 1791.

DEAR MADAM,

*As much as I am accustomed to my own sins, I am shocked, really shocked, when I think of my long and most inexcusable silence; nor do I dare to compute how many months I have suffered to elapse without sending a single line—(Oh shame! shame!)—to the best and dearest of my friends, who indeed has been very seldom out of my thoughts. I have sometimes imagined, that if the opportunities of writing occurred less frequently, they would be seized with more diligence; but the unfortunate departure of the post twice every week encourages procrastination, and each short successive delay is indulged without scruple, till the whole has swelled to a tremendous account. I will try, alas! to reform; and although I am afraid that writing grows painful to you, I have the confidence to solicit a *speedy line*, to say that you love and forgive me. After a long experience of the unfeeling doubts and delays of the law, you will probably soon hear from Lord S. that the Buriton transaction is at last concluded, and I hope you will be satisfied with the full and firm security of your annuity. That you may long continue to enjoy it is the first and most sincere wish of my heart.

LIKE ADAM ALONE IN PARADISE.

In the placid course of our lives, at Lausanne and Bath, we have few events to relate, and fewer changes to describe; but I indulge myself in the pleasing belief that we are both as well and as happy as the common order of Nature will allow us to expect. I should be satisfied, had I received from time to time some indirect, but agreeable information of the general state of your health. For myself, I have no complaint, except the Gout; and though the visits of my old enemy are longer, and more enfeebling, they are confined to my feet and knees; the pain is moderate, and my imprisonment to my chamber, or my chair, is much alleviated by the daily kindness of my friends. I wish it were in my power to give you an adequate idea of the conveniency of my house, and the beauty of my garden: both of which I have improved at a considerable expence since the death of poor Deyverdun. But the loss of a friend is indeed irreparable, and I sometimes feel, that like Adam I am alone in Paradise. Were I ten years younger, I might possibly think of a female companion; but the choice is difficult, the success doubtful, the engagement perpetual, and at fifty-four a man should never think of altering the whole System of his life and habits. The disposal of Buriton, and the death of my aunt Hester, who has left me a small estate in Sussex, makes me very easy in my worldly affairs; my income is equal to my expence, and my expence is adequate to my wishes. You may possibly have heard of litterary projects which are ascribed to me by the public without my knowledge: but it is much more probable that I have closed the account: and though I shall never lay aside the pleasing occupations of study, you may be assured that I have no serious settled thoughts of a new work. Next year I shall meditate, and I trust shall execute, a visit to England, in which the Belvidere is one of my powerful loadstones. I often reflect, with a painful emotion, on the imperious circumstances which have thrown us at such a distance from each other.

In the moving picture of the World, you cannot be indifferent to the strange Revolution which has humbled all that was high, and exalted all that was low, in France. The irregular and lively spirit of the Nation has disgraced their liberty, and instead of building a free constitution, they have only exchanged Despotism for Anarchy. This town and country are crowded with noble Exiles; and we sometimes count in an assembly a dozen princesses and dutchesses. Burke, if I remember right, is no favourite of yours; but there is surely much eloquence and much sense in his book. The prosperity of England forms a proud contrast with the disorders of France; but I hope we shall avoid the folly of a Russian War. Pitt, in this instance, seems too like his father.*

I am, My Dearest Madam,
Ever most affectionately Yours,
E. GIBBON.

566.

To Lord Sheffield.

Lausanne, May 31st, 1791.

*At length I see a ray of sunshine breaking from a dark cloud. Your Epistle of the 13th arrived this morning, the 25th instant, the day after my return from Geneva; it has been communicated to Severy; we now believe that you intend a visit to Lausanne this summer, and we hope that you will execute that intention. If you are a man of honour, you shall find me one; and, on the day of your arrival at Lausanne, I will ratify my engagement of visiting the British isle before the end of the year 1792, excepting only the fair and foul exception of the Gout. You rejoyce me by proposing the addition of dear Louisa; it was not without a bitter pang that I threw her overboard, to lighten the vessel and secure the Voyage: I was fearful of Mrs. Moss, a second carriage, and a long train of difficulty and expence, which might have ended in blowing up the whole scheme. But if you can bodkin the sweet creature in the coach, she will find an easy welcome at Lausanne. The first arrangements which I must make before your arrival, may be altered by your own taste, on a survey of the premises, and you will all be commodiously and pleasantly lodged. You have heard a great deal of the beauty of my house, garden, and situation; but such are their intrinsic value, that, unless I am much deceived, they will bear the test even of exagerated praise. From my knowledge of your Lordship, I have always entertained some doubt how you would get through the *French* society of a Lausanne winter: but I am satisfied that, exclusive of friendship, your summer visits to the banks of the Leman Lake will long be remembered as one of the most agreeable periods of your life; and that you will scarcely regret the amusement of a Sussex Committee of Navigation in the dog days. You ask for details: what details? a map of France and a post-book are easy and infallible guides. If the Ladies are not afraid of the Ocean, you are not ignorant of the passage from Brighton to Dieppe: Paris will then be in your direct road; and even allowing you to look at the Pandæmonium, the ruins of Versailles, &c., a fortnight diligently employed will clear you from Sheffield-place to Gibbon Castle. What can I say more?

As little have I to say on the subject of my worldly matters, which seems now, Jupiter be praised, to be drawing towards a final conclusion; since, when people part with their money, they are indeed serious. I do not perfectly understand the ratio of the precise sum which you have poured into Gosling's reservoir, but suppose it will be explained in a general account;* as that reservoir is unproductive, I hope the Yorkshire mortgage will soon be in motion. I had not a doubt of the Law's (in either sense of the word) delaying to the last moment the payment of Hester's paltry legacy, but I conceive that you are in possession of Newhaven, and that you have obtained for me the year's or at least the nine months' rent to which I must have been entitled last Lady-day. I do not perfectly understand whether my share of Hug, or to what amount, has actually been paid. By this time you must have received the Deeds.—*Act.*

BURKE A RATIONAL MADMAN.

*You have been very dutiful in sending me, what I have always desired, a cut Woodfall on a remarkable debate; a debate, indeed, most remarkable! Poor Burke is the most eloquent and rational madman that I ever knew. I love Fox's feelings, but I detest the political principles of the man, and of the party. Formerly you detested them more strongly, during the American War, than myself. I am half afraid that you are corrupted by your unfortunate connections. Should you admire the National assembly, we shall have many an altercation, for I am as high an Aristocrate as Burke himself; and he has truly observed, that it is impossible to debate with temper on the subject of that cursed Revolution. In my last excursion to Geneva I frequently saw the Neckers, who by this time are returned to their Summer residence of Copet. He is much restored in health and spirits, especially since the publication of his last book, which has probably reached England. Both parties who agree in abusing him, agree likewise that he is a man of virtue and Genius: but I much fear that the purest intentions have been productive of the most baneful consequences. Our military men, I mean the French, are leaving us every day for the camp of the princes at Worms, and support what is called —— representation. Their hopes are sanguine; I will not answer for their being well grounded: it is *certain*, however, that the emperor had an interview the 19th instant with the Count of Artois at Mantua; and the Aristocrates talk in mysterious language of Spain, Sardinia, the empire, four or five armies, &c. They will doubtless strike a blow this summer: May it not recoil on their own heads! Adieu. Embrace our female travellers. A short delay.*

567.

To Lord Sheffield.

Lausanne, June 12th, 1791.

I now begin to see you all in real motion, swimming from Brighton to Dieppe, according to my scheme, and afterwards threading the direct road which you cannot well avoid, to the turbulent capital of the late Kingdom of France. I know not what more to say, or what further instructions to send; they would indeed be useless, as you are travelling through a country which has been sometimes visited by Englishmen: only this let me say, that, in the midst of Anarchy, the roads were never more secure than at present. As you will wish to assist at the national assembly, you will act prudently in obtaining from the French in London a good recommendation to some leading member; Cazalès, for instance, or the Abbé Maury. I soon expect from Elmsly a cargo of books; but you may bring me any new pamphlets of exquisite flavour, particularly the last works of John Lord Sheffield, which the dog has always neglected to send. You will have time to write once more, and you must endeavour, as nearly as possible, to mark the day of your arrival. You may come either by Lyons and Geneva, by Dijon and Les Rousses, or by Dole and Pontarlière. The post will fail you on the edge of Switzerland, and must be supplied by hired horses. I wish you to make your last day's journey easy, so as to dine upon the road, and arrive by tea-time. I rejoyce in the approaching conclusion of my affairs, though the residue of the purchase money has suffered and will suffer most heavy evacuations.

*The pulse of the contre-Revolution beats high, but I cannot send you any certain facts. Adieu. I want to *hear* My lady abusing me for never writing. *All* the Severys are very impatient.

Notwithstanding the high premium, I do not absolutely wish you drowned. Besides all other cares, I must marry and propagate, which would give me a great deal of trouble.*

568.

Lord Sheffield to Edward Gibbon.

Downing Street, Tuesday, 14th June, 1791.

Your letter of May 31 was received last Friday. As soon as this letter is finished the Family is to set out for Sheffield Place, and from thence we shall move as soon as we can towards Lausanne. We are pressed to pass through France before the Confederation or Commemoration of the 14th July, and if possible we shall be with you before that day. I have much to do in Sussex, but I shall hasten. I shall wish to pass one day at Rouen and three or four at Paris. I hope to quit Sheffield Place about the 28th instant. We expect the Borders of France to be troubled, perhaps Besançon may not be perfectly tranquil. Take care to send a few lines to meet me at the Post Office, Paris.

Louisa is delighted with your *empressement* to see her. All My Lady's sagacious friends have assured her that it is absolutely necessary to have two men servants on our Travels. Etienne was dismissed six months ago on account of his indecorous conduct towards My Lady's woman. A Swiss was hired in his place, in Livery, another is now hired out of Livery, both of them of the neighbourhood of Lausanne. One may be dismissed when we arrive there, if we can get a place for him.

The chief disagreement I experience is a disappointment about your £4000 mortgage in Yorkshire. The owner sold the Estate. However I insist on compensation, he having engaged the money. I am in treaty about a mortgage near my Yorkshire Estate for £3000. I must do the best I can with the other £1000. It will be extravagant to buy into the Stocks. They never will be higher, and are likely to be lower. If I could get £1000 Subscriptions in the Lewes Navigation at 5 pr. Ct., it would be well secured and well paid, but money is too plentiful; I fear I shall not be able to get it.

LORD SHEFFIELD AN ANTI-DEMOCRAT.

You exceedingly mistake my Politicks. I am as great an Anti-Democrat as Mr. Burke, and so are most of the party; but you are deceived by Burke's speeches. I hold the French proceedings in such abhorrence and dislike as an English Politician, that I shall be in danger of the Lantern.

Remember us with many thanks to de Severy.

Yours ever,
S.

The Ladies are impatient for their voyage. The writings were not received till three days ago, and it is impossible for the greatest Philosopher to have signed them with a greater degree of ignorance, &c. Especially those relating to Buriton I must carry to you again.

569.

Lord Sheffield to Edward Gibbon.

Sheffield House, 27th June, 1791.

Your letter of the 12th June was graciously received two days ago, and notwithstanding the intelligence we received yesterday morning of the Royal Escape, and notwithstanding the probable confusion and warfare that will take place in France, the ardour of the Ladies to go to you is redoubled. My Lady seems scared lest prudence should induce me to halt for intelligence, and cannot endure a delay even for the packet, which will sail on Saturday. No, we must set out after dinner for Brighton, and sail from thence to-morrow for Dieppe. This I should not have undertaken if I had not received a letter from Pelham dated Paris, two days after the elopement, which mentioned that on the second day all was quiet, the National Assembly cool and united, but that he should take care a letter should meet me at Rouen, which would inform me whether it would be advisable to pass thro' Paris. He thinks it may not be easy to get from thence. It is probable I shall be glad to avoid Paris, if so, I may be at Lausanne in a very short time, especially if I find a tolerable road from Rouen to Fontainebleau. From thence I have travelled to Dijon and Besançon to Lausanne. I think there is most danger of difficulty in passing thro' a considerable garrison such as Besançon. If we can approach you we shall wish to arrive in the evening at the time you mention.

Finally, such an undertaking just at this moment will not allow us to be deemed by our acquaintance *compos mentis*, but we are going to you and may arrive sooner than this letter. I shall write from Rouen however, where I shall stop one day at least.

Yours ever,
S.

Alas! just after I had finished I heard the King and Queen are captives. I must go to Rouen before I determine, but I incline to a rapid pass thro' France.

570.

To Lord Sheffield.

Lausanne, July 1st, 1791.

FLIGHT AND ARREST OF LOUIS XVI.

*In obedience to your orders, I direct a flying shot to Paris, though I have not any thing particular to add, excepting that our impatience is increased in the *inverse ratio* of time and space. Yet I almost doubt whether you have passed the sea. The news of the King of France's escape must have reached you before the 28th, the day of your departure, and the prospect of strange unknown disorder may well have suspended your firmest resolves. The Royal animal is again caught, and all may probably be quiet. I was just going to exhort you to pass through Brussels and the confines of Germany; a fair Irishism, since if you read this, you are already at Paris. The only reasonable advice which now remains, is to obtain, by means of Lord Gower, a sufficiency, or even superfluity, of forcible passports, such as leave no room for cavil on a jealous frontier. The frequent intercourse with Paris has proved that the best and shortest road, instead of Besançon, is by Dijon, Dole, Les Rousses, and Nyon.* As my larder cannot always be furnished for the doubtful day of your arrival, I must desire that you would make your first appearance, not at dinner time, but at the hour of tea; you may dine at Rolle or Morges. *Adieu. I warmly embrace the ladies. It would be idle now to talk of business.*

571.

Lord Sheffield to Edward Gibbon.

Paris, Tuesday, 5th July, 1791.

Neither the Royal Flight or Capture prevented or even interrupted for a day our travels to the Historian. We passed two nights at sea, and we have passed two nights at the Castle of Navarre with the Duke of Bouillon, near Evreux, much more to our satisfaction. Nothing could be more handsome than our reception there. I was glad of the opportunity of shewing to the Ladies, the style of living of one of the first men in France, and at one of the finest places. I came here last night. I have already had an opportunity of good intelligence. Matters of the highest consequence are *this moment* in agitation. *They* are determined to get rid of the King, but how, is not so easy a business. Many of his enemies are sorry he was retaken, because they know not what to do with him (a Council will be appointed). I believe they would be glad to let him go, if they did not fear the Parisian mobility. The Judges agree that the Gardes de Corps, who acted as couriers, cannot be tried. They will be suffered to depart whenever it will be safe. As to the Queen, when I said I was surprised they did not send her home (that is to the Pais Autrichiennes) to avoid mischief to her Person, and also to avert a disagreeable demand, I was told there is no doubt that she will be allowed to go if she pleases. De Bouillé has emitted an invitation to Officers and Soldiers to join him. His letter to the National Assembly might have been well enough for a Captain of Grenadiers, but it does not smell of the grand Politician. I understand that scarce a General Officer remains with the Army on the Austrian Border towards ——, and that numbers, even whole corps of officers, have deserted, but this I know not with any precision. I think we may go from hence in 4 or 5 days. Matters are coming to a Crisis—therefore you may be sure I shall not stay long lest we should be stopped and not suffered to go from this city, but I expect an introduction to Cazalès, La Fayette, and some others.

Lausanne has the honour of containing Lady Webster before this time. People are apt to spoil her. I desire you will not, because it gives me a great deal of trouble to set her right afterwards. Milady writes to her. She and her daughters are well and entertained. We are just come from the Comédie Francoise.

Yours ever,
S.

I shall not write again before our departure.

———

572.

Lord Sheffield to Edward Gibbon.

Paris, July 8th, 1791.

The system of getting rid of the King will not do. The night before last the principal men of the Committees, the Chiefs of the National Assembly, about 100 in number, met, and after a considerable debate, they resolved that the Constitution should be maintained, and that the person of the King is inviolable. Only two of them, Messrs. Dumont and Petier, were of a different opinion, and they argued for a tryal. La Clos, the friend of the Duke of Orleans, the night preceding the Jacobins, vigorously insisted on a Tyral and a Regency, but it is known that a great majority of the National Assembly wish to restore the King and to put him in the situation he held before his flight, and to give him a Council. The Queen not being a part of the Constitution, they do not intend to take any notice of her; much management is necessary to keep the people quiet, and the Chiefs dare not as yet bring forward moderate measures. The National Guard wish to get rid of the King. The resolution I mention in the beginning of this letter is intended to be kept secret as much as possible for the present. The measure will be carried with some difficulty. I have scarce a moment. On Monday we attend the Apotheosis of Voltaire. On Tuesday next we go to the National Assembly for the last time (having the President's Box), and on Wednesday we talk of setting out for La Suisse, but I must stop a day or two at Dijon and one or two perhaps at Besançon. We suppose the Websters lost, because we have not heard from them.

Yours,

S.

573.

Lord Sheffield to Edward Gibbon.

Paris, 13th July, 1791.

LORD SHEFFIELD AT THE JACOBINS.

We are going at 8 o'clock this morning to the Assembly, lest we should be too late for places to hear the report and debate on the King's Flight. It is not likely to finish in one day, but we are not disposed to stay more than 2 or 3 days longer on any account. It will be proper to remain here a day or two just to see whether they really will cut one another's throats. I do not expect it. It does not seem to be their genius to do more than Fishwomen, to scratch and tear one or two to pieces in a cattish fury. Since my last the Democratic *enragé* seems to have gained ground. I have been placed high on a chair next the President at the Jacobins, having been introduced by Noailles as a good English Patriot amidst much *applaudissement*. Brissot de Warville made (as *on m'a dit*) the greatest speech that ever was heard. It was well calculated to inflame Frenchmen, but he forgot to use any argument, and utterly omitted to shew that the King had committed any crime against the Law, and finished by moving that the King should be tried. The word *enragé* does not half describe a French Democrate. The modern men think the speech has made a great impression, and think matters are not in so good train for the King as they were. I have not a moment to say more than that I have seen men and things to great advantages, and I shall write again.

Yours,

S.

574.

The Hon. Maria Holroyd to Edward Gibbon.

Berne, Oct. 7th, 1791.

The truth is, that I attempted to write to you, the day we arrived here, & found myself unequal to a longer account of things, than just to say—we are eighteen Leagues from Lausanne, & I have made the family lift up their hands & eyes in astonishment, by wishing to walk back that distance. I ought to express my Gratitude for all the kindness and attentions we have met with, during our stay in Switzerland, & if I was less sensible of it, I could compose a fine speech—but I can only say, I can feel, & I hope you will never find me ungrateful. Tuesday we slept at Avenches & arrived here at two o'clock on Wednesday. If you wish to know how we amused ourselves on the Road, I will tell you, by Meditation & Silence. If you wish to know what was the Subject of our Meditations I will answer for myself—Lausanne. Indeed, my Thoughts have not quitted that place, for five minutes, & I begin to wonder, whether I shall ever think of any thing else. Our horse, that had one Wooden & one broken Leg, fell down, & rather damaged a third Leg—so that, as Papa thought if any accident should happen to the fourth, we might find some difficulty in proceeding on our journey, & being rather indignant at their slow method of moving, he has dismissed them, rather too precipitately, as we are now uncertain whether we shall leave this Town to-morrow or a fortnight hence. No horses to be had at present.

Yesterday we went to the Lac de Thun—the day was very fine, & we crossed the Lake to Mr. Fischer's house, where we found his Lady and Mother. We stopped at Mr. de Mulhinen's house in our return—& saw Made. de Mulhinen, who is a very pleasing Woman. Papa was so much pleased with the Lake that he lamented very much that he had not persuaded you & Severy to come with us there & stay two or three days. Perhaps you might have been inexorable, but I wish the other part of the scheme had been thought of a little sooner. I liked the expedition upon the lake very well, but it was not the Lake of Geneva, nor was the Boat St. J. Legard's; & yet, as there was a Lake & a Boat, there was resemblance enough, for me to make comparisons, to the disadvantage of the present time. Mr. Coxe gave Papa a Letter to Mr. Wyttenbach; he has been here, & walked about the Town with us on Wednesday evening, & has made me very happy by promising to send me a Collection of Alpine Plants. He is to take us this morning to shew us the World. Papa is gone with Mr. Fischer on horseback to see Farms. After dinner we are to go to the library, & to-morrow, if we can get horses, we shall go to Bienne. Mon^r. Fredennick was here this morning, & every body seems to try who shall pay most attention. I wish they would try & be disagreeable, to make me rejoice at being on my return to England. Mon^r. Wyttenbach is come & prevents me adding any more, than to assure you that I am your ever obliged & affec.

M. T. HOLROYD.

575.

The Hon. Maria Holroyd to Edward Gibbon.

Strasbourgh, Thursday, Oct. 13th, '91.

SAFE IN THE LAND OF LIBERTY

I felt a strong inclination to write from Basle, but as you said, Berne *or* Basle & not Berne *&* Basle, I was afraid of being troublesome. However I take the first moment of my arrival at the next station from whence you desired to hear from me, to tell you we are safe in the Land of Liberty, where the People may sing *Ça ira* all day & all night, if they like it. Friday, the day I wrote from Berne, we went to Wyttenbach's house, to see his curiosities—& he has made me *Wild* again about Botany, by giving me a Collection of Alpine Plants—so that now, instead of admiring Nature in general, I have no eyes but for Weeds, & I have made a considerable Collection in my Journey from Lausanne here. The Advoyer came before dinner, & from his suit of Black Powdered Wig & Gold headed cane, I began to be afraid I was ill, & that the Physician was come to give his Opinion. Mr. Fischer dined with us, Mr. Fredennick came after dinner, and they went with us to the Library & walked upon the ramparts. In a part of the Ditch we saw two of the Sovereign Lords of the Pays de Vaud. Their Excellencies were very quiet and rather Rheumatic, but there were two young ones very frisky and playful.

Saturday. We were rather unfortunate in a very rainy Day—& in one of the Springs of the Carriage breaking near Arberg, which delayed us some time. If it had been a fine day, we should have been very disagreeable, but as it was impossible to go to the Island of St. Pierre that day, we made up our minds very tolerably. Sunday. The Weather was very favorable, & we went upon the Island, wrote our names in Rousseau's Bed chamber, returned to Bienne to dinner, & went to Moutier the same day. Mama had an opportunity of shewing her heroism—for the last three Leagues we performed by moonlight, & Coxe describes the Road as so narrow, that one Wheel rubs against the Rocks & the other hangs over the Precipice— though this description is poetical, yet there is some foundation for it. We regretted passing thro' such picturesque scenes in the dark, but the next day the Country we passed thro' from Moutier to Basle was exactly the same. I thought after the Tour to the Glaciers, that I should think nothing equal to that part of the World, but the Valley of Munster pleased me more than anything I have seen. Tuesday, we saw the Gardens of Arlesheim, the Library & the dance of death. Mr. Ochs was the only one of Mr. Levade's friends who was at Basle—the others were both in France. The *higgledy-piggledy* Party came to Basle on Tuesday & were very much in our way on the Road. Papa determined to go to Strasbourgh on the french side of the River, as the Horses on the other side are quite knocked up by transporting Aristocrates to Coblentz. The Craven family with their Guardians, Lord Molyneux and Mr. Nott, took all the horses at the first Post, & tho' they left Basle two hours before us, when we got to St. Louis we were obliged to wait an hour and a half, for the return of the horses—during which time we amused ourselves by walking to Huningue—which I was very glad of, as it gave me a better Idea of Scarps & Counter-Scarps, Ravelines & Bastions, than I should have had without it.

STRANGE CHARM IN SWITZERLAND.

This day's journey was rather long. We left Basle at eight o'clock & we arrived at Krafft, where we slept, at ½ past eleven—quite in despair at the dirt of the French Inns; having met with such excellent ones in Switzerland, we had quite forgot what a bad Inn was. We are just arrived here to breakfast, & expect to meet with some information as to the superiority of Navigation over Land carriage. Papa was so much out of humour with the delay, occasioned by want of horses upon the road yesterday, that he is very much inclined to take a Boat here. The people at Lausanne, judging I suppose by themselves, assured me I should forget that place by the time I got to Basle. I am at Strasburgh, which is still farther; and I can say from Experience, which is the only thing that ever convinces me, that notwithstanding the variety of Scenes that I have passed through, & the amusement I have found on the road, I *still* regret the Terrace & the Pavillion. I do not know what strange Charm there is in Switzerland that makes everybody desirous of returning there; you know I did not go there with any prejudice in its favor. As to Mama, she owes it such a Spite for fascinating you, that she will never do it common Justice, till the Democrates have obliged you to be content with our little Island; then perhaps her obligations to them will change her sentiments.

Indeed I am ashamed of myself, to have taken up so much of your time. You will, I am afraid, repent of our Engagement, & think that reading my Letters is even more tremendous than answering them. I live in hopes, that we shall hear something of, or from, you at Coblentz. Remember us all, but me in particular, to every one of the Severy family. *Et dite à ma chère Angletine que je pense bien souvent d'elle & du dernier jour que nous avons passées ensemble.* I dread exposing even that short sentence to your criticizing eye, but I wish to shew her that, in promising to write to her, I have undertaken what I am very unequal to perform, in order to keep up some remembrance of me. I cannot bear the thoughts of being forgot by those I love. Mama desires to be most affectionately remembered to you.

Believe me,
Ever sincerely & affec^y yours,
MARIA T. HOLROYD.

I just find I am too late for the Post to-day, & that my Letter must wait till Saturday. To-morrow we stay here. Papa is happy in the Idea of seeing the Troops exercise.

576.

The Hon. Maria Holroyd to Edward Gibbon.

Coblentz, Oct. 21st, 1791.

Our Adventures since I wrote from Strasbourgh have been very numerous, & if every body had been equally disposed with myself to be entertained with them, they would have lost much of their unpleasant circumstances. Papa had determined to go from Strasburgh to Manheim by Rastadt; but the Inn keeper advised us to go on the other side of the Rhine, as we should find the Inns all full in Germany & the Post horses very bad. The Rain was incessant all day & had continued for two days before. We found the Roads very bad & lost our way in a large forest; quite dark; amidst many ejaculations from Mama. When we at last arrived at Girmenheim, where we were to sleep, we found the Inn quite full. A Commission was there from Manheim to keep the Rhine in order, who has heard so much lately of Liberty on both sides, that he had a mind to make the experiment, & has strayed over the neighbouring meadows, unmindful of the excellent Caution given to a Brother River—"Thames, ever while you live, keep between your banks." We were put into a small room, where a Company had just finished supper. Travellers are not often, I imagine, so unfortunate as to go that road, if I may judge from the astonishment and, I hope, admiration our Appearance caused. The Doors were opened and the Room was lined with Spectators, who gazed at us in silence for near a quarter of an hour—more to my amusement than Mama's. There was only one Room where we could sleep—& we *all* arranged ourselves in three Beds, after having quieted some delicate scruples of Papa's, who proposed sleeping in the Coach—however by putting out the Candles nobody found it necessary to blush.

We left this charming place very early, breakfasted at Spire and arrived at Manheim early enough to see all the Lyons before dinner. I was much entertained with the Gallery of Pictures in the Elector's Palace. It was much superior to anything I had seen. The Library is very handsome. Papa went to the Play in the evening & made an acquaintance there, who he brought home with him, & talked Commerce and Agriculture, till near one in the morning. The next day we went to Mayence, & the day after saw the Castle, the Provost's house, the Cathedral, &c., and left Mayence at two o'clock in a very tolerable Boat. But the Wind was quite contrary, & it was very late when we arrived at Bingen. Mama did not take a fancy to Navigation in the least. For my part I enjoyed it very much, as the Banks of the Rhine, particularly from Bingen to Coblentz, are very picturesque. The great number of Castles made me imagine myself in the Age of Chivalry, & I almost persuaded myself I was a distressed Damsel carried away against my Will. The next thing, of course, was to expect a brave Knight to set me free, but as none made their appearance, I was obliged to quit my romantic Ideas, & my *Castles in the Air*, of which I had plenty, as well in my head, as around me. In plain English, I was much pleased with the day's journey, & Mama was pretty well reconciled to seeing Water all round her, which was at first a great grievance.

COBLENTZ AND WHITE COCKADES.

Our famous Adventures begin here. We arrived at Coblentz at five o'clock last Wednesday, & found every Inn in the Town full of *Panaches blancs*. After staying three hours in the Boat, with difficulty Papa found one Room, with one Bed, without Curtains & no other furniture of any kind in it. We preferred this to sleeping in the Boat, the only alternative, & accordingly we females slept on Mattresses upon the ground. As there were no curtains it was impossible to admit Papa of the Party, & he remained all Night in the Boat. The Account that was brought us of the Room we were to sleep in, was that between forty and fifty Officers were in two Rooms at each end of ours, which opened with Folding Doors. Upon a nearer enquiry, the number was reduced between 10 & 20—but they are tolerably quiet, considering they are *Frenchmen*. Yesterday was passed enquiring for Lodgings, & by the help of the Duc de Guiche, the Woman of the house was prevailed upon to give us three Garrets, perfectly unfurnished—but this we considered as charming accommodation compared to the *higgledy piggledy* Style we had been accustomed to—but the Ground is still our Bed.

Papa has found out a great deal of amusement for himself. He was presented yesterday to the Elector, Monsieur, Madame, the Comte d'Artois, the P. of Condé and his Son; to-day he dined at a very large dinner at the Prince of Nassau's—& is now at the Play in Mad^e. de Nassau's Box, who was very desirous of our Company, but Mama is not fond of *violent measures*. The Comte de Romanzov is here, Ambassador to the Princes from the Empress Cat. The Bishop of Arras is not here; but the Duc de Guiche is every thing that is delightful, & Papa has not been at a loss for the Bishop. Our amusements may be mentioned in very few words. We have seen the citadel. We go from here early to-morrow morning—in our Boat. The Weather is very unfavorable to us. Only that you might justly make the Observation, "If you are sensible of your fault, why do you continue to offend?" I would apologize for the length of my Letter. But while you allow me to write to you, I do not think I have quite left Lausanne—& I never know how to leave off. Distribute our Love and comp^{ts} properly.

Believe me
Ever affec. yours,
MARIA T. HOLROYD.

I forgot to say we found our Letters here. Mama desires her Love to Severy & many thanks for his Letter. I have taken a great deal of pains to persuade her to write to him; but she has not resolution enough to take up her pen. I must whisper to you we were disappointed at not hearing a few lines from you.

577.

The Hon. Maria Holroyd to Edward Gibbon.

Brussels, October 29th, 1791.

It is probable that this my fourth Letter may remain unopened in your Pocket, but I shall leave that to Fate, & only think of convincing you, that I still remember Lausanne & my promise. I like to let People know how *unreasonable* I am, & therefore I will tell you I had faint hopes of finding a few Lines here, either written or dictated by you. I frequently ask Mama, do you think they are talking of us at Lausanne? & she generally answers—I daresay not; so I should have had a great deal of satisfaction in shewing her, that you thought so much of us as to make a *violent effort* to tell us so. We have proceeded on our journey with great success from Coblentz to Brussells, & to-morrow go to Antwerp. We arrived here on Thursday from Louvain—the Road was so bad & the Post-horses moved in such a *Swiss* manner, that we were four days coming from Cologne.

The first day we slept at Juliers, the second at Liège, the third at Louvain, & the fourth (as I had the *honour* of telling you) we came to Brussells, & fortunately arrived at 'L'Imperatrice,' the only Hotel where there was a single Room unoccupied, just as the Princesse de Salms was moving off— & took possession of her apartments with great satisfaction, as we expected Coblenz accomodations.

THE SIGHTS OF BRUSSELS.

We stayed but one night at Cologne, as the Maréchal de Castries was not there, & the Town possessed no other Charms to tempt us to stay, for it is the most dismal place I have seen. The Maréchal is here, & Papa has had a long conference with him. Luckily for us, Papa has neither met with a Quarter Master nor a Commercial man, nor a Farmer here, so we have seen a great deal and been very much amused. We saw the Palace of the Archduchess, a league out of Town, yesterday—& it is fitted up with more Taste than any thing we have seen in our travels. The rest of our time has been spent in Churches, the Arsenal, & some good Collections of Pictures. I have not time to be *prolix* in my narration, which you will perhaps not be sorry for, as you are not as fond of a long letter as I am. Mama is pretty well, but will not be sorry to find herself at her own fire side again.

Remember us to those who remember our existence—you will not have much trouble, for I suppose you will only deliver the message to yourself— I suspect nobody else of thinking of us. Louisa desires I will not forget her best Comp^ts to *M. Mentrond*; she does not choose to suppose he can *forget her*. I expect to hear a great deal of *Mrs. Wood*—or if any body else has supplied her place in your *heart*. When you do write, if such an unlikely event should ever take place, pray tell me something of everybody; I shall like to see the names of those I was acquainted with, & while I read y^r letter, shall fancy myself at Lausanne.

Believe me,
Ever sincerely y^rs,
MARIA T. HOLROYD.

I write in such haste that you must excuse faults of Style, Writing, &c.

578.

Lord Sheffield to Edward Gibbon.

Calais, 5th Nov., 1791.

After various and sundry embarrassments, here we are safe. The pleasure of the visit being over and the sorrow of departure come on, it naturally occurred in aid of my concern what a damned Fool I was to undertake such an operation. To correct such cogitation, the *distractions* of the Rhine were some relief. The state of its neighbourhood is at this time very interesting. It was curious to find the Princes and prime Nobility of France thankfull to be allowed to exist on a small angle formed by the Moselle and the Rhine. An army of officers, but not a common man. For the sake of visiting the Garrisons of Alsace, I went the whole length of that Province. Levade's letters were of essential service to me. I thankfully wrote to him when I had proceeded far down the Rhine. Probably I furnished some details, with which he probably has furnished you. I know not whether I mentioned that Huninge and Brisach are in good condition. An incompleat Regiment of two battalions in each place and some Dragoons, not sufficient garrisons, but some cantoned Troops might be thrown in if required.

MILITARY FORCES ON FRENCH FRONTIER.

The Regulars at Strasburgh are 6760, including 1100 Horse and 1300 artillery. They say they have some 7000 National Guards, I doubt it. They are the best I have seen; and yet they are very poor stuff for Soldiers, and many are not cloathed. I dined with the Colonel of Carbineers, and saw the finest regiment of France in detail, and also a Swiss Regiment (Viguier), one of the best. Some of the regiments are not more soldier-like than the National Guards. The Democrates say that the officers, being Aristocrates, neglect the men on purpose, and wish the regiments to be ruined; 40 officers had quitted one regiment in Alsace. In short, only seven remained with it, including the Colonel. The Park of Artillery at Strasburgh seems very compleat. It is the second in the Kingdom. A Train is ready for 40 Battalions. The Province of Alsace is at least half Aristocrate. I passed the evening and supped at the Mayor's while at Strasburgh. He and his Lady (a clever dame) thorough Republicans. Observe the Regulars in the two departments of the Rhine are commanded by a German, and the National Guards by a Lt.-Colonel who is a Livonian. Mirabeau's Corps seems a miserable collection; several deserters came from it while I was at

Strasburgh. Finally I flattered myself there would be a compleat *Brouillerie* between the regulars and the National Guards before I left that place. The officers of the latter are naturally disposed to be very absurd. The double pay of these troops *soldès* is likely to have an excellent effect on the *Troupes de ligne.* I found about 100 French officers at Manterin. Towards 900 at Worms. Bouillé and a certain number are at Mayence.

Including upwards of 900 of the Gardes du Corps and near 20 Generals, there are 2500 Officers at Coblentz. I was very graciously received by the Princes. They give a supper every night, where I had the amusement of being introduced to Marshal Broglie, &c., &c. The Prince of Condé and Duc de Bourbon were there on a visit. Romanzov has brought credentials and two millions of livres French from the Empress; Calonne is at Baths not far distant for his health; Burke's son had been sometime at Coblentz and was gone to England with Cazalés. Our King has written a very amicable letter to the Princes promising neutrality. I went to Cologne to see the Marshal de Castries. He was gone to Brussels, where I found him. At every inn I found 20 or 30 French Officers, the road is covered with them from Brussels to Coblentz. Nothing can be worse timed than this desertion. It is a Phrenzy and was like wildfire. They would be much better with their regiments and ready in the country to protect Friends and to avail themselves of circumstances. The most sensible of the French disapprove this migration. The officers leave their Regiments without concert with the Princes, who have not lately encouraged it. There seems to be no particular plan at present but to wait events. I unfortunately missed the Abbé Maury passing to Coblentz. I wished to know him. He is a Cardinal *in petto.* He is to have the Arch-Bishop of Sens's Hat. The regular regiments were long ago ordered to be completed to the war establishment, but on an average they have not above half their complements, and on the frontier of the Low Countries there is not an officer left except Soldiers of Fortune.

L'Esprit de Revolution is not likely to flourish again for some time in the Pais Bas. I found Imperial and Electoral troops in possession of Liège, and new taxes laid to pay expenses, viz. on Dogs, Servants, bachelors, &c. The Discontents in the Austrian Netherlands are not likely to be of much consequence, a great part of the country was miserably duped and the whole thrown into such an execrable state, that none but the lowest of the creation can wish for another experiment at a Revolution. The leading party among the enemies of the House of Austria being Clergy and Aristocrates cannot coalesce easily with the Democrates of France. All the Provinces except Brabant are content. Many say a counter-revolution in France is impossible, because the Mass of the People are of one mind. Not near so much as the Austrian Netherlands were. There almost every man was a

Patriot, yet the moment an army appeared there was not a struggle. The different extent of country, &c., prevent a correct comparison.

However, it may be observed that France has not a neighbour that is not unfriendly to the Revolution. I have the worst opinion of the French Army. The National Guard behaved execrably at Nancy, where alone they have been tried. We indeed were told the contrary. Some Swiss officers (Democrates) who acted against the regiment of Chateau Vieux have given me details. You may be sure that the Regulars and National Guards will not agree. I am satisfied that of those officers who remain with the Regiments, almost all except soldiers of fortune are aristocrates. The soldiers do *not desert*, but they say they will go to Paris. They will enter into the *Gardes Nat. soldès*, and they go where they please; nobody can stop them. Yet with such a King the situation of the Aristocrates is very difficult. Divisions will naturally take place, the Kingdom is *en traine* to be torn to pieces. A foreign army on the Frontier or advancing to Paris might unite them, therefore it may be better to wait events. At the same time I have not a notion that a French army would fight under its present circumstances.

THE MEETING AT PILNITZ.

It was a comfort to see the excellent Bohemian and Hungarian Infantry in the Austrian Netherlands. They are in fine order. The Treaty of the 23rd of July last between the Emperor and the King of Prussia has been well concealed. It is defensive. The supposition is that Prussia is dissatisfied with England. If Russia should accede to the Treaty (which is not thought unlikely), we shall be compleatly left in the lurch.

Maria has been alert and well-disposed to your correspondence. She seemed pleased with the office, but she will expect an answer. She has saved me from writing sooner. From Brussels we went to Antwerp, Ghent, Bruges, Ostende, and Dunkirk to this place. Mi Ladi continues the same. I should have stopped more than three days at Brussels if I had not been afraid of the division of Mrs. Maynard. Say everything kind for us to the de Severy family. If Mi Ladi does not reply soon to the Fils, I shall. I found letters at Brussels by which I learn that your £2000 is accepted by the Navigation Society, that Mr. Taylor has found a mortgage for £5000 in Yorkshire. He says somewhat of its being more convenient if the money is not paid till a little time hence, and I also learn that my worldly affairs, and the Navigation, have gone on as badly as might be expected from my absence.

Remember us to Mrs. Grevers.

579.

Lord Sheffield to Edward Gibbon.

[Incomplete in original.]

The increase of Mi Ladi's woman, and apprehensions thereon, made it necessary to shorten my visits. You have heard of the little accident on board the Packet. You know dear Puff has a great dislike to cats. About midnight, midway between France and England, an hideous noise like that of a cat in the act of being strangled was heard. Puff barked and was furious. I looked out of my den, and beheld it was an human kitten that proceeded from Mrs. Maynard who was prostrate on the floor. My Lady also incumbent there. Maria contemplative and Louisa astonished. Not a creature on board the Packet but ourselves and the crew. We never know what we may come to, and above all we should not have guessed that Mi Ladi was to become a mid-wife. The mother and child could not have been better, (and have continued so,) if all the obstetric Faculty of Paris and London had attended. The mother was so well that she expressed the greatest anxiety to go with us the day following above 80 miles across the country to this place. We left her in good lodgings and in good care. The want of her prevented the Ladies from passing two days at Lord Guilford's. We found two letters from him at Dover and a dozen messages. I went and had a pleasant dinner with him, and returned at night to the Ladies.

I must now come to the unpleasant part, your business. Immediately on my return I wrote to Taylor about the £5000 mortgage. I have a letter full of disappointment. The person to be paid off has accepted low interest. He complains of being frequently thus treated. Don't bother yourself. I still hope soon to settle the business.

I wrote you a long letter from Calais.

580.

The Hon. Maria Holroyd to Edward Gibbon.

Sheffield Place, Nov. 13th, 1791.

It is with a mixture of satisfaction & regret, that I complete my part of our engagement in writing this Letter. I find great pleasure in being returned to dear, precious Sheffield, & in telling you so, because I am sure you will be glad to hear we are safe and well; but writing to you the last letter is like a second taking leave, & tho' I have been near six weeks upon the journey from Lausanne, that moment is still as fresh in my memory as it was the next day, & the recollection of it as unpleasing. If I *dared* I would ask to be allowed to tell you we were alive, now & then when Papa & Mama were in an idle mood, & to be allowed to *hope* for an answer *once* in *two* or *three years*, in your own hand or not, as you thought proper or found convenient.

DISTRESSES UPON THE SEA.

I was very glad Papa wrote a long letter from Calais, as his information about things in general would be more interesting to you than mine, as I suppose he gave you a full account of our route from Brussells to Calais. I will only tell you that I was very much amused at Antwerp, & that I *catch* myself, now & then, *making believe* to know a good Picture from a bad one—having seen so many excellent ones lately. We left Calais last Sunday at 9 in the morning, having waited three days for a favorable wind, & at last in despair, set off in a perfect Calm, which prolonged our passage 24 hours—which was uncommonly tedious, & very bad luck, as our Passage from Brighton was as tiresome in coming over. However to pass the time, or to diversify the amusements of the Passage, which from the sickness of the Company would have preserved some degree of sameness, Mrs. Maynard with Mama's assistance, half way between Calais & Dover, presented the cabbin boy with a *Sea Nymph*; which with its Mother are now *as well as can be expected*, at Cap^n Sampson's house at Dover. I have heard that Sailors, when they come from a voyage, find great pleasure in talking of & recollecting Toils & Dangers past—such is our case; for we have laughed very heartily here, at our Distresses upon the Sea—which certainly at the time was no laughing matter.

We found the inhabitants of S. P. in excellent preservation & quite rejoyced to see us returned—most of them, when we left England, being convinced we should be all massacred by the National Assembly in a very short time. I hope the quiet life of this place will soon restore Mama's health & spirits, who desires her kindest remembrances to you & those we love at Lausanne. Do not let anybody forget us, for we forget nobody.

Ever much y^{rs},
M. T. HOLROYD.

581.

Lord Sheffield to Edward Gibbon.

Sheffield Place, 13th Dec., 1791.

My Lady is getting quite well. Bratts very fond of their Swiss Tour. I have passed a week very pleasantly in London. King apparently quite well. Lally a great favourite with Lord Loughborough. He assisted at a copious dinner at Batt's, and said he never enjoyed one more interesting. He saw Lord Guilford on his passage through London, who was well pleased with him, as also is Douglas. Tell Mr. Trevor good care will be taken of him. La Comtesse de Lally seems to preserve a strict incognito. Lady Loughborough visits her. I can only collect that she doth not appear to like to go out. It is said, she has not confined her practices to Lally. Introduced him to Burke, who says the said Lally persists in his errors, and justifies all his mischievous conduct in the beginning, and the said Burke is as ridiculous and as absurd as may be imagined. I have been presented to Cazalés (who resides with Burke), but I had not an opportunity of seeing anything of him. England has supplied and has been paid for 36,000 stand of arms for the Emigrants. The Corps Diplomatique at London says that Spain has sent 5 millions of livres to the Princes, and Portugal 4 millions— Berlin 2 millions.

I have expectation of seeing Batt and Lally here at Christmas. Tell Levade I have only just learned where to find his son-in-law. I hope also to see him here. People begin to talk of 3½ per Cent. for money.

582.

Lord Sheffield to Edward Gibbon.

Sheffield Place, 25th Dec., 1791.

I am obliged to write to you, otherwise it would not be proper, because we are determined to starve you into a more decent deportment; not a fragment from you except the medley to Maria. She has been so zealous in your service, that she deserved more notice. The obligation to write is that a pipe of Madeira (which has travelled and is very good) is ordered to set out for Lausanne by the same consignment and way as the last, *ergo* you must give notice to your correspondent at Basle, &c.

MARRIAGE, BATTLE, FIRE, AND SCANDAL.

Nothing extraordinary has occurred in this family since my last. My Lady is better. We expect Batt to-morrow, probably Lally, and also Mr. Levade's son-in-law, with whom I have corresponded. The Duchess of York almost smothered the French Revolution in this country; Lord Cornwallis's operations almost suppressed the Duchess of York, and I daresay the Duke of Richmond's fire has afforded some relief to Lord Cornwallis. I should be happy to furnish you with as much scandal as possible, but I know of no event of the kind worth record, unless Lady Belmore's trip to the Continent incontinently with Lord Ancrum should be deemed so, and Lady Tyrconnell's Flight to Glamis Castle with Lord Strathmore. These amiable women have left behind them grown daughters. May the Mamas——

I have secured for you the famous Shakespear; Boydel is satisfied that I subscribed for two setts. It is by far the finest book ever printed. I have your first number and 5 large and 5 small prints in my possession, but I shall not send them—you must come for them.

As you care nothing about the good of the nation, it is almost unnecessary to mention that the gross produce of the Permanent Revenue last year, including Land and Malt, amounted to £20,355,380 exclusive of fines, forfeitures, Taxes on Places, First Fruits, &c., amounting to £125,476 and the profit of the Lottery. The Gross Excise last year £9,054,850, encrease this year £1,200,000, of which £800,000 are old and £400,000 new Duties. The British Shipping has increased 318,522 tons since 1773. The whole tonnage of France is not much more than a fourth more. Their tonnage in 1787 was little more than a fifth of ours.

Lord Cornwallis has been marching about in Tippoo's country for six weeks to prove that it was not the monsoon that obliged him to quit Seringapatam. Was it not a curious omission to have neither a minister nor a spy in the Maratta Camp, and was it not an extraordinary folly to risk an engagement for the purpose of besieging Seringapatam 9 days before there was an absolute famine in the English Camp? Abercrombie's cattle were all swept away by Tippoo's General, and neither Abercrombie nor any of his officers have a second coat or shirt.

We never had cavalry in an Indian Army before. It was the great strength of this famous army. It is all ruined.

583.

To Lord Sheffield.

Lausanne, December 28th, 1791.

THE DEMON OF PROCRASTINATION.

---

*Alas! alas! the Demon of procrastination has again possessed me. Three months have nearly rolled away since your departure; and seven letters, five from the most valuable Maria, and two from Yourself, have extorted from me only a single epistle, which, perhaps, would never have been written, had I not used the permission of employing my own tongue and the hand of a secretary. Shall I tell you, that, for these last six weeks, the eve of every post day has witnessed a *firm* resolution, and the day itself has furnished some ingenious delay? This morning, for instance, I had determined to invade you as soon as the breakfast things should be removed: they were removed; but I had something to read, to write, to meditate, and there was time enough before me. Hour after hour has stolen away, and I finally begin my letter at two o'Clock, evidently too late for the post, as I must dress, dine, go abroad, &c. A foundation, however, *shall be* laid, which will stare me in the face; and next Saturday I shall probably be rowzed by the awful reflection that it is the last day in the year.

After realizing this summer an event which I had long considered as a dream of fancy, I know not whether I should rejoyce or grieve at your visit to Lausanne. While I possessed the family, the sentiment of pleasure, with some occasional shades, highly predominated; and the last weeks of harmony and content were those which I the most truly enjoyed, when, just as we had subsided in a regular, easy, comfortable plan of life, the last trump sounded, and, without speaking of the pang of separation, you left me to one of the most gloomy, solitary months of October, which I have ever passed.

For yourself and daughter, however, you have contrived to snatch some of the most interesting scenes of this World. Paris, at such a moment, Switzerland, and the Rhine, have suggested a train of lively images and useful ideas, which will not be speedily erazed. The mind of the young Damsel, more especially, will be enlarged and enlightened in every sense; in four months she has lived many years; and she will much deceive and displease me, if she does not review and methodize her journal, in such a manner as she is capable of performing, for the amusement of her particular friends. Another benefit which will redound from your recent view is, that every place, person, and object, about Lausanne, are now become familiar and interesting to you. In our future correspondence (do I dare pronounce the word correspondence?) I can talk to you as freely of every circumstance as if it were actually before your eyes.

And first, of my own improvements.—All those venerable piles of ancient verdure which you admired, have been eradicated in one fatal day. Your faithful substitutes, William de Severy and Levade, have never ceased to persecute me, till I signed their death warrant. Their place is now supplied by a number of picturesque naked poles, the foster fathers of as many twigs of platanuses and acacias, which may afford a grateful but distant shade to the founder, or to his *seris nepotibus*. In the meanwhile I must confess that the terrace appears broader, and that I discover a much larger quantity of snow than I should otherwise do. The workmen admire your ingenious plan for cutting out a new bed-chamber and book-room; but, on mature consideration, we all unanimously prefer the old scheme of adding a third room beyond the library, with two spacious windows, and a fire-place between, on the Terrace. It will be larger (28 feet by 21), and pleasanter, and warmer: the difference of expence will be much less considerable than I imagined: the door of communication with the library will be artfully buried in the wainscot; and, unless it be opened by my own choice, may always remain a profound secret. Such is the design; but as it will not be executed before next summer, you have time and liberty to state your objections. I am much colder about the staircase, but it may be finished, according to your idea, for thirty pounds; and I feel they will persuade me. Am I not a very rich man? When these alterations are compleated, not forgetting the watercloset, few authors of six Volumes in quartos will be more agreeably lodged than myself.

Lausanne is now full and lively; all our native families are returned from the Country; and, praised be the Lord, we are infested with few foreigners, either French or English. Even our Democrates are more reasonable or more discreet; it is agreed to wave the subject of politics, and we all seem happy and cordial. I have a grand dinner this week, a supper of thirty or forty people on Twelfth-day, &c.; some concerts have taken place, some balls are talked of; and even Maria would allow (yet it is ungenerous to say even Maria) that the winter scene at Lausanne is tolerably gay and active. I say nothing of the Severys, as Angletine has epistolized Maria last post. She has probably hinted her brother meditates a short excursion to Turin; that worthy creature Trevor has given him a pressing invitation to his own house. Mrs. Trevor, who is one of us, does not envy him.

PEACE OR WAR IN EUROPE?

In the beginning of February I propose going to Geneva for three or four weeks. I shall lodge and eat with the Neckers; my mornings will be my own, and I shall spend my evenings in the society of the place, where I have many acquaintance. This short absence will agitate my stagnant life, and restore me with fresh appetite to my house, my library, and my friends. Before that time, the end of February, what events may happen, or be ready to happen! The National assembly (compared to which the former was a Senate of heroes and Demigods) seem resolved to attack Germany *avec quatre millions de bayonettes libres*; the army of the princes must soon either fight, or starve, or conquer. Will Sweden draw his sword? will Russia draw her purse? an empty purse! All is darkness and anarchy: neither party is strong enough to impose a settlement; and I cannot see a possibility of an amicable arrangement, where there are no heads (in any sense of the word) who can answer for the multitude. Send me your ideas, and those of Lord Guildford, Lord Loughborough, Fox, &c.

Before I conclude, a word of my vexatious affairs.—Shall I never sail on the smooth stream of good security and half-yearly interest? Will every body refuse my money? I had already written to Darell and Gosling to obey your commands, and was in hopes that you had already made large and salutary evacuations. During your absence I never expected much effect from the cold indifference of agents; but you are now in England—you will be speedily in London; set all your setting dogs to beat the field, hunt, enquire,—why should you not advertise? And let not the Goslings dine at my expence. I know not what to say at present of India bonds—do they not Sink? Our affairs in that Country seem in a very ticklish situation. At all events consult with Darrel, he has knowledge of that sort and is a real friend. Yet I am almost ashamed to complain of some stagnation of interest, when I am witness to the natural and acquired philosophy of so many French, who are reduced from riches, not to indigence, but to absolute want and beggary. A Count Argout has just left us, who possessed ten thousand a-year in the Island of St. Domingo; he is utterly burned and ruined; and a brother, whom he tenderly loved, has been murdered by the Negroes. These are real misfortunes.

AN AMAZING PUSH OF REMORSE.

I have much revolved the plan of the Memoirs I once mentioned; and, as you do not think it ridiculous, I believe I shall make an attempt: if I can please myself, I am confident of not displeasing; but let this be a profound secret between us: people must not be prepared to laugh; they must be taken by surprize. Have you looked over your, or rather my letters? Surely in the course of the year, you may find a safe and cheap occasion of sending me a parcel; they may assist me. Adieu. I embrace My Lady: send me a favourable account of her health and spirits. How happy might we have been, could she have preserved them at Lausanne! I kiss the Marmaille. By an amazing push of remorse and diligence I have finished my letter, three pages and a half, this same day since dinner; but I have not time to read it. Ever yours.*

half past six.

584.

To Lord Sheffield.

Lausanne, December 31st, 1791.
To-morrow a new year, *multos et felices.*

*I now most sincerely repent of my late repentance, and do almost swear never to renounce the amiable and useful practice of procrastination. Had I delayed, as I was strongly tempted, another post, your missive of the 13th, which did not reach me till this morning (three mails were due), would have arrived in time, and I might have avoided this second Herculean labour. It will be, however, no more than an infant Hercules. The topics of conversation have been fully discussed, and I shall now confine myself to the needful of the new business. *Felix faustumque sit!* May no untoward accident disarrange your Yorkshire Mortgage; the conclusion of which will place me in a clear and easy state, such as I have never known since the first hour of property.*

Considering the fragment which we had recovered from Hugonin's shipwreck, and the large autumnal payments, I should have imagined that the Goslings would have been somewhat fatter: your lawyers' bills, the last (as I flatter myself) that I shall ever know, must have cut deeper than you expected; but I shall see the detail of their account. If the Yorkshire friend should like £6000 instead of £5000, and if the estate would afford adequate and ample security, why should you not desire Darrel to sell the amount of £3800? I should then have exactly £20,000 firmly seated on land and water, besides your annuity of £250, and I would not touch the moderate residue of my short annuities, till poor Mrs. G.'s dismission from below (which cannot be a very distant event) shall release me from her annual tribute of £300.

*The three per cents are so high, and the country is in such a damned state of prosperity under that fellow Pitt, that it goes against me to purchase at such low interest. In my visit to England next autumn, or in the spring following, (alas! you *must* acquiesce in the alternative,) I hope to be armed with sufficient materials to draw upon Cadell for a loose sum of £1000 perhaps or £1500, which may be employed as taste or fancy shall dictate, in the improvement of my library, a service of plate, &c. I am not very sanguine, but surely this is no uncomfortable prospect.

This pecuniary detail, which has not indeed been so unpleasant as it used formerly to be, has carried me farther than I expected. Let us now drink and be merry. I flatter myself that your Madeira, improved by its travels, will set forwards for Messrs. Romberg, at Ostend, early in the spring; and I should be very well pleased if you could add a hogshead of excellent claret, for which we should be entitled to the Drawback. They must halt at Basle, and send notice to me for a safe conduct. Have you had any intelligence from Lord Awkland about the wine which he was to order from Bourdeaux, by Marseilles and the Rhone? The one need not impede the other; I wish to have a long stock. Corea has promised me a hogshead of his native Madeira, for which I am to give him an order on Cadell for a copy of the Decline and Fall: he vanished without notice, and is now at Paris. Could you not fish out his direction by Mrs. Wood, who by this time is in England? I rejoice in Lally's prosperity, but cannot think Burke so very mad. Have you reconsidered my proposal of a declaration of constitutional principles from the heads of the party? I think a foolish address from a body of Whigs to the national assembly renders it still more incumbent on you. The intelligence of my Lady's amendment has given us all most heartfelt pleasure. How very unlucky was the moment! Achieve my worldly concerns, *et eris mihi magnus Apollo.* Adieu, ever yours.*

585.

Lord Sheffield to Edward Gibbon.

Sheffield Place, 16th January, 1792.

The circumstance of your being already damned (in the opinion of all good people) has often checked expectoration, and has often been so far inconvenient as to deprive me of an Exordium, which occasion and fine feelings inspired. I have been boiling for some time, and was meditating some eminent degree of abuse when your letters of the 28th and 31st ultimo arrived this morning. They have so far softened, as to save me the trouble of examining your impudent excuses. Seven to one are great odds, especially in letter writing.

THE CAPACITY OF MARIA HOLROYD.

As to Lausanne, I do not like to talk of my visit there. I do not think I enjoyed it half enough. It is true I contrived to snatch some of the most interesting scenes of this world. France and Paris at such a moment—the truly Sovereign Proceedings of Berne. It was a comfort to see the whiskered Germans, that excellent contrast to the French National Guards. The Rhine and Austrian Flanders, though last, did not promote and assist less lively images or less usefull ideas. The young ladies are still full of their excursion, and they seem even more delighted with the recollection than they were with the enjoyment. I am glad you recommended to Maria to review and methodise her journal. Her capacity, if well directed, is equal to anything. I hear a superlative account from various parts of the letters she wrote to England. I have not seen them. I hear a good deal also of my own, and I wish I had some long letters I wrote to the Duke of Portland, Lord Guilford, and Lord Loughborough. I have no journal or memoranda of the subjects of them.

We have had some extra encitements to think of Lausanne. First came Francillon, smart, pleasing, and attentive, and although he has not a very imposing Parsonick gravity, I think I discover that he is a diligent pastor. There is a small matter which I flatter myself I may be able to do for him by means of the Arch-Bishop of Canterbury. N.B.—Levade's letter was a great treat to us, and Lavater's manuscript is considered by the Family as an acquisition. I shall write to the former speedily.

Francillon stayed here about ten days, but before his departure, the Lally Tollendal arrived. That lively, miserable, pleasant, mortified, pious, and ingenuous man has been here above a fortnight, and what is still more miraculous, he does not seem to have the least disposition to go; and yet I have walked him on foot over ploughed fields when very wet, and I have trotted him on horseback in the roughest lanes when frozen as hard as possible. He is delighted with the Library, where he finds a great variety of books he had not seen. He has made exhilirating discoveries in respect to Strafford, and he is become the most profound Antiquarian in Parliamentary history that I know. As it is not customary for him to wear breeches until he goes out, which is always late, or until he comes to dinner, I have just received a note from his apartment, which states that not being in condition to enter the Library (Mrs. Poole in her 83rd year is there) he prays me to send him certain folios. Poor fellow, his nerves are in a horrid state, but he says not worse than they have generally been since he had the small pox. Tell Mrs. Trevor I am particularly attentive to his health. I recommend regular meals instead of one enormous dinner, and earlier times of going to and rising from bed, to which in some degree he attends. My Lady, (who is infinitely better) takes to him amazingly, but that seems the custom with all Ladies. I have only one objection to him, namely, he reads in Bed and is eminently *distrait*; I am sorry, as it is a rule with me never to solicit a second visit from a person who has that practice, because there is some inconvenience in having the house burnt down in the middle of the night, unless it could be so contrived that all the inhabitants should be burnt at the same time without knowing anything of the matter. I wish his Malkin was re-established at Tournay—and so I believe does he. The expectations from the uncles are not flattering. I fancy he would like best to be with his Princesses of the Desert and Madame Trevor. Lord Loughborough is extremely pleased with him and is uncommonly kind to him. Lord Guilford likes him, and Lally was much satisfied with his visit of two days to Bushey Park. The King took a great deal of notice of him, and talked to him a long time. They conversed on the *Renversement de toutes les Idées que caracterisait La Revolution Francaise.* Lally said, *"Sire, Je quitte un des sujets de vôtre Majestie et certainement des plus distingués. Il a caracterisè à merveille par une seule plaisanterie ce que nous arrive."* *"Qui?"* *"M. Gibbon."* *"Et que dit il?"* *"Il dit, que la Revolution Francaise lui rappelle le tems de son enfance, où on lui faisait voir dans une grande estampe un cochon faisant rôtir un Cuisinier."* Lally adds, *"Sa Majestie Brittanique a ri de ce rire inextinguible que Homer nous donne pour un attribut des Dieux."*

Finally, the Count is likely to pass his time in London as well as can be expected in his burdened state. Everybody interests themselves about him. Yet I can discover no symptom of a commodious arrangement for him. I thought he would have gone to the Queen's Naissance, but I think he will now stay here till Parliament meets, viz. the 31st instant. On his passage to this Island, he had a long conversation with De Bouillè at Mayence. You will remember I have abused that general for not attempting to retake the King. I was unjust. He followed him with one thousand cavalry nine leagues in what is stated an incredibly short time (yet four hours are mentioned), and was stopped by a river, like Lord Cornwallis going to join Abercrombie, who complains that he had not been told of that river; but if they were afraid of being drowned *à la nage*, 500 of them might have gone into the river, and by holding themselves and their horses in a proper direction might have formed a temporary bridge for the other 500.

The flight failed through the King's departure a day later than he proposed. The attendance of a democratic woman on the Dauphin was to end on the day which had been fixed. The King had announced to Bouillè that it would be better to delay till the woman's time was out, but too late for him to give notice to the Person and Troops he had posted. Charles Damas and Choiseul had advanced to meet the King. He not coming on the day he was expected, they supposed the enterprise had failed, and retired two hours only before the King arrived. He expected to find a relay of horses on the Paris side of Varrennes. The horses were waiting on the other side, of which the King had no information. The Postillions would not pass the stage. The King, not meeting those persons he expected, despaired. The Queen was impatient, got out of the carriage, enquired at different places for the relay. Thence suspicions arose. Damas and Choiseul finding they had caused some jealousy, had returned by a cross road, otherwise the King would have overtaken them. They came into Varrennes after the King was seized. Bouillè says the flight was entirely planned by the King, that the Emperor had pressed the attempt. He excuses his letter, &c., by saying "His object was to turn the thoughts of the people from the King on him." What a reverse for poor Bouillè! If the King had reached Montmedi, I have not a doubt of his having been joined by the Army and of his being now re-established at Paris. Bouillè would have been in the highest situation. Now he is a vagabond in Germany.

THE HIDEOUS PLAGUE IN FRANCE.

Letters from Paris represent Pitt as the vilest Machiavel in respect to French affairs. Perhaps France has no great right to complain. When lately in London I dined in company with the Duke of Richmond, and was sitting next him. I whispered that the Princes were very well satisfied with our King's friendly letter to them, which promised neutrality on the part of Britain. The Duke said, twice, with eagerness, "No, no. It promised nothing." If the plague, comparatively a trifling misfortune, had broke out in France, the neighbouring countries would have formed a cordon round it—but now, when the most hideous plague that can be imagined, rages there, which no cordon ever will be able to contain, if it should continue, but which inevitably will spread over and contaminate all Europe, it is treated as a matter of ordinary policy. I do not understand these precious Sovereigns. They deserve their fate, and their ministers to be hanged, but I object to the several countries being torn to pieces; at the same time I must say that I do not see that there is sufficient ground to believe our ministers are acting a double part as is supposed. Finally, it is obvious that there is not at present the possibility of an arrangement between the two parties of France, because neither party can govern or answer for the multitude. Lally talks with much satisfaction of the manner in which Lord Guilford expressed himself in respect to Necker, his honour, honesty, &c., &c. He is greatly struck with his candour, moderation and good sense. Remember me in an handsome manner to M. and Madame Necker when you see them.

As you talk of being restored to your pristine tranquility at Lausanne, and that Politicks are waved, I suppose Mr. Commissioner Fischer is gone. Rather than part with him, I should have been content with your alarms and your Politicks. I should even have regretted the whiskers and my Friend Meluner. Maria says the Commissioner is gone, because you presume to mention a Ball. I hope Wilhelm de Severy was not obliged to make verses. Remember us to his excellent Pere, Mere, & Sœur.

Luckily it is not necessary to reserve much space for your affairs. They are in good train. It is a satisfaction when I can observe in you a dawning of intelligence in such matters, and that you see there is an advantage of 15 per cent. in changing at this time from the Funds to a Mortgage, besides the security against depreciation. I have already written to desire that your Fund in Yorkshire may be increased if it should suit. I should have remembered the Dowager. However, the interest of Stock now due and the money you have at Lausanne will be enough for two months. Remember it will be little more before considerable payments will be made. You are a rich old fellow. I shall leave the India Bonds if the price should be bad. The Lawyers' bills paid are only those I showed to you. I apprehend the Madeira has begun its travels. I think I discovered when I saw Lord Auckland lately, that he had done nothing respecting the claret, but I believe I can provide for you by another channel.

I have an imperfect recollection of having mentioned in a late letter some instances of British prosperity, but I know not what. The gross produce of the permanent Revenue of the year ending 5th Jany, 1791, including Land-Tax and Annual Malt, amounted to £20,355,380, exclusive of casual revenue, such as seizures, fines, taxes on Places & Pensions, First fruits, &c., amounting to £125,476, and exclusive also of the profits of the Lottery. The actual receipt of the Excise for the same year was

£9,054,850

Resting to be accounted for   194,245

_____

£9,249,096

Expense of management, £505,014. But allowances, Exports, Bounties, &c., reduced the nett payment into the Exchequer to £7,689,973; notwithstanding this ample amount, the net increase of the excise for the year ending 5th Jany, 1792, will not be less than £1,200,000, of which £800,000 are old, and £400,000 are new duties. The general expence of collecting all the Taxes is £5 13s. 7d. per cent. I understand the expence of collecting the Revenue in France previous to the Revolution was £11 17s. 0d. per cent.

You recollect that we ought to have been ruined by the Independence of America—*selon tous les regles*, except mine and a few others—yet since 1773, when the troubles in America began, the export of British manufactures have gradually increased upwards of four millions annually. British built commercial tonnage has increased since that period 318,522 tons, which is more than three-fourths of the whole Commercial tonnage of France. Thanks to that illustrious writer the Lord Sheffield. The total of French commercial tonnage is 426,121. Total of English, 1,527,240, English coasting tonnage 3,711,135, French ditto 1,004,729. There is more Foreign than French shipping employed in the trade of France. When their silly and crazy patriots have ruined their West India trade, they will have little occasion for sailors. Such considerations are beneath such elevated minds.

MASSA KING WILBERFORCE.

We are going to send 300 dismounted Light Dragoons to Jamaica and 600 foot from Nova Scotia. Hitherto all has been quiet there, but 3000 Negroes assembled in the parish of Westmoreland to celebrate Massa King Wilberforce's Birthday, lately raised some alarm. Happily they were quietly dispersed. Have you observed that the estimated expence of France for the last year was about 26 millions sterling, and the Ways and Means about 24 millions? (It is rather awkward to set out with a deficit of 2 millions.) On the 31st October last, only about 2,700,000 had been received, and it was not even supposed then that more than 2,400,000 more would be paid before the end of the year. The Arrear of Taxes since the Revolution is about 70,000,000. The Land-tax however is not to be considered as all lost. The imperfect receipt of it arises from an incomplete arrangement, I understand, as to the mode of collection. About 12 millions of that tax are behind.

I have not thought so bad of your taste, since I heard the vile unmeaning masses are removed from your Terrace, and I hope most of the vulgar flower-pots. You have not given a tolerable reason for preferring a bed-chamber which cannot have a good approach, without indeed a very great expence. What I propose, may be done without spoiling your Library, and without disturbing you in that comfortable room.

I have not forgot your poultry, I could have done the needfull for £7, instead of £70. You did not want a menagerie. The alteration of the staircase would do away the most awkward entrance I ever saw into an House at a very small expense—but if the French Revolution is not checked, I must flatter myself your Books will be used for cartridges. As to the letters, I thought you expressed indifference about them before I left you. I shall examine, altho' I do not believe there are many except of a late Times. Assure the Duchess of Biron (she is a great favourite here) that the parcel for Madame de Cambis was received safe.

586.

To Lord Sheffield.

Lausanne, April 4th, 1792.

*For fear you should abuse me, as usual, I will begin the attack, and scold at you, for not having yet sent me the long-expected intelligence of the completion of my mortgage. You had positively assured me that the second of February would terminate my worldly cares, by a consummation so devoutly to be wished. The news, therefore, might reach me about the 16th; and I argued with the gentle logic of lazyness, that it was perfectly idle to answer your letter, till I could chaunt a thanksgiving song of gratitude and praise. As every post disappointed my hopes, the same argument was repeated for the next; and twenty empty-handed postilions have blown their insignificant horns, till I am provoked at last to write by sheer impatience and vexation.

Facit indignatio versum. Cospetto di Baccho; for I must ease myself by swearing a little. What is the cause, the meaning, the pretence, of this delay? Are the Yorkshire Mortgagors inconstant in their wishes? are the London lawyers constant in their procrastination? Is a letter on the road, to inform that all is concluded, or to tell me that all is broke to pieces? In sober truth I am out of humour to think of all the dinners that the Goslings have given at my expence. Had the money been placed in the three per Cents last May, besides the annual interest, it would now have gained by the rise of stock nearly twenty per Cent. Your Lordship is a wise man, a successful writer, and a useful Senator; you understand America and Ireland, Corn and Slaves, but your prejudice against the funds, in which I am often tempted to joyn, makes you a little blind to their encreasing value in the hands of our virtuous and excellent minister. But our regret is vain; one pull more and we reach the shore; and our future correspondence will be no longer tainted with business. But shall I then be more diligent and regular? I hope and believe so; for now that I have got over this article of worldly interest, my letter seems to be almost finished.

A propos of letters, am I not a sad dog to forget My Lady and Maria? Alas! the dual number has been prejudicial to both. How happy could I be with either, were t'other dear charmer away. I am like the Ass of famous memory; I cannot tell which way to turn first, and there I stand mute and immoveable. The Baronial and maternal dignity of My Lady, supported by twenty years' friendship, may claim the preference. But the five incomparable letters of Maria!—Next week, however.—Am I not ashamed to talk of next Week?

A MONTH WITH THE NECKERS.

I have most successfully, and most agreeably, executed my plan of spending the month of March at Geneva, in the Necker house, and every circumstance that I had arranged turned out beyond my expectation; the freedom of the morning, the society of the table and drawing-room, from half an hour past two till six or seven; an evening assembly and card-party, in a round of the best company, and, except one day in the week, a private supper of free and friendly conversation. You would like Geneva better than Lausanne; there is much more information to be got among the men; but though I found some agreeable women, their manners and style of life are, upon the whole, less easy and pleasant than our own. I was much pleased with Necker's brother, Mr. de Germani, a good-humoured, polite, sensible man, without the genius or fame of the statesman, but much more adapted for private and ordinary happiness.

Madame de Stael is expected in a few weeks at Copet, where they receive her, and where, "to dumb forgetfullness a prey," she will have leisure to regret the pleasing anxious being, which she enjoyed amidst the storms of Paris. But what can the poor creature do? her husband is in Sweden, her lover is no longer Secretary of War, and her father's house is the only place where she can reside with the least degree of prudence and decency. Of that father I have really a much higher idea than I ever had before; in our domestic intimacy he cast away his gloom and reserve; I saw a great deal of his mind, and all that I saw is fair and worthy. He was overwhelmed by the hurricane, he mistook his way in the fog, but in such a perilous situation, I much doubt whether any mortal could have seen or stood. In the meanwhile, he is abused by all parties, and none of the French in Geneva will set their foot in his house. He remembers Lord Sheffield with esteem. His health is good, and he would be tranquil in his private life, were not his spirits continually wounded by the arrival of every letter and every newspaper. His sympathy is deeply interested by the fatal consequences of a Revolution, in which he had acted so leading a part; and he feels as a friend for the danger of Mr. de Lessart, who may be guilty in the eyes of the Jacobins, or even of his judges, by those very actions and dispatches which would be the most approved by all true Lovers of his Country.

THE MARCH OF THE MARSEILLAIS.

What a momentous event is the Emperor's death! In the forms of a new reign, and of the Imperial election, the Democrates have at least gained time, if they knew how to use it. But the new Monarch, though of a weak complexion, is of a martial temper; he loves the Soldiers, and is beloved by them; and the slow, fluctuating politics of his uncle may be succeeded by a direct line of march to the gates of Strasburgh and Paris. It is the opinion of the master-movers in France, (I know it most certainly,) that their troops will not fight, that the people have lost all sense of patriotism, and that on the first discharge of an Austrian cannon the game is up. But what occasion for Austrians or Spaniards? the French are themselves their greatest enemies; 4000 Marseillais are marched against Arles and Avignon, the *troupes de ligne* are divided between the two parties, and the flame of civil war will soon extend over the southern provinces. You have heard of the unworthy treatment of the Swiss regiment of Ernst. The canton of Bern has bravely recalled them, with a stout letter to the King of France, which must be inserted in all the papers.

I now come to the most unpleasant articles, our home politics. Rosset and La Motte are condemned to five and twenty years imprisonment in the fortress of Arbourg. We have not yet received their official sentence, nor is it believed that the proofs and proceedings against them will be published; an awkward circumstance, which it does not seem easy to justify. Some (though none of note) are taken up, several are fled, many more are suspected and suspicious. All are silent, but it is the silence of fear and discontent; and the secret hatred which rankled against Government begins to point against the few who are known to be well-affected.

I never knew any place so much changed as Lausanne, even since last year; and though you will not be much obliged to me for the motive, I begin very seriously to think of visiting Sheffield-place by the month of September next. Yet here again I am frightened, by the dangers of a French, and the difficulties of a German, route. You must send me an account of the passage from Brighton, with an itinerary of the Rhine, distances, expences, &c. As usual, I just save the post, nor have I time to read my letter, which, after wasting the morning in deliberation, has been struck off in a heat since dinner. No news of the Madeira. The views of Sh.-pl. are just received; they are admired, and shall be framed. Severy has spent the Carnival at Turin. Trevor is only the best man in the World.*

587.

Lord Sheffield to Edward Gibbon.

Downing Street, 18th April, 1792.

You will readily guess that I do not write to you because the Mortgage was not finished, but I cannot readily guess the cause of your not answering my letter, which according to the best of my recollection was long and amiable. Be assured that you are a worthless fellow.

When the Yorkshire business is finished you will have £20,000 as well placed as can be. N.B. The Buriton interest is not yet paid, but I suppose will in a few days. I have been at Sheffield Place near a fortnight during Easter.

I am engaged in numberless matters before the Commons, British business is not slack. I have been all night at a Ball. I am just returned from a Congress with Mr. Secretary Dundas on the subject of his Slave Bill. He and I are likely to agree. The innocence of Captain Kimber will be made as clear as will the extreme rascality of his surgeon who accuses. Louisa settled at Bath with Aunt about the middle of Febry. It was the best that could be done. Mrs. Moss set out this day for the neighbourhood of Geneva, where she is to pass the summer. She carries a letter to you in case she should pass thro' Lausanne, that you might show such attention to her as you can by selfe, Levade, or De Severy. She carries also 14 of your letters of the years 77, 78, 79.

588.

Lord Sheffield to Edward Gibbon.

Downing Street, 14 May, 1792.

The Plot thickens. Some information induces me to think that Switzerland, till lately the happy and peaceful, may be disquieted, especially the countries bordering on France. I can conceive it possible that the insane discontents of the Pais de Vaud may render Lausanne not altogether an eligible and comfortable residence to you. We hear that the National Guards have assembled on the borders towards Geneva and are trying to perform some manœuvres. I can suppose it reasonable for you to think of this Isle sooner than you intended,—that the border may be disquieted and travelling for such an unweildy creature neither commodious nor delightful. It is possible the Borders may be less tempting for Travellers at present than some time hence. In such case, if anything like turbulence should exist at Lausanne, Berne may afford you the best Asylum till the journey to old England may be safe and sure, that is void of embarrassments which might annoy you, altho' they might appear only curious events and agreeable Episodes to me and some others. I apprehend that a journey by Germany, unless you make a great detour, would be troublesome.

When we joked last Autumn about whiskers and Jacobins and the great utility of books for making cartridges, I did not think you so near disturbance as you possibly may be. The annihilation of your books might be a proper judgement upon you for the damned, parson-minded, inglorious idea of leaving books to be sold. A trumpery fellow, that after having made a good collection had not the idea of keeping them together by leaving them to Sheffield Place, where they would involve the books already there, and the whole be handed down *seris nepotibus* as the Gibbonian Library! I could hardly contain my indignation when you mentioned your sniverling notion. I have often fully and duly anathematized you since, but I do not flatter myself that barbarism is as yet arrived at the trouble of attacking the Library of an Aristocrate.

You will discover that I want to hear of you. At such a time a few lines might have been expected even from you—or anything ten times worse than you. How are the De Severy's? I should have attempted to make amends for my Lady's neglect of writing, if I had not been bothered in the extreme. I wish also to write to Levade. Is Mrs. Moss arrived? Altho' the new French art of War tends to enable to fight another day, yet it is to be hoped the execrable troops will not take that trouble. After I left you and had seen those warriors in Alsace, &c., I transmitted my opinion that they would take the very first opportunity of running away and murdering their officers. Our Associations here have now received a good brush. Your idea of signing Declarations would be adopted by many, if there was not an apprehension that Democrates would represent it as an Aristocrate Association against the People. Your Yorkshire Mortgage draws towards a conclusion. I have had an excellent letter of many pages from Lally at Paris which I must forthwith answer.

589.

To Lord Sheffield.

Lausanne, May 30th, 1792.

: -- :
: DEMOCRATIC PROCESS IN ENGLAND. :
: -- :

*After the receipt of your *penultimate*, eight days ago, I expected with much impatience, the arrival of your next-promised Epistle. It arrived this morning, but has not compleatly answered my expectations. I wanted, and I hoped for a full and fair picture of the present and probable aspect of your political World, with which, at this distance, I seem every day less satisfied. In the slave question you triumphed last session; in this you have been defeated. What is the cause of this alteration? If it proceeded only from an impulse of humanity, I cannot be displeased, even with an error; since it is very likely that my own vote (had I possessed one) would have been added to the Majority. But in this rage against slavery, in the numerous petitions against the Slave trade, was there no leaven of new democratical principles? no wild ideas of the rights and natural equality of man? It is these I fear. Some articles in newspapers, some pamphlets of the year, the Jockey Club,—have fallen into my hands. I do not infer much from such publications; yet I have never known them of so black and malignant a cast. I shuddered at Grey's motion, disliked the half-support of Fox, admired the firmness of Pitt's declaration, and excused the usual intemperance of Burke. Surely such men as* Grey, Sheridan, Erskine, *have talents for mischief.

I see a Club of reform which contains some respectable names. Inform me of the professions, the principles, the plans, the resources of these reformers. Will they heat the minds of the people? Does the French democracy gain no ground? Will the bulk of your party stand firm to their own interest, and that of their country? Will you not take some active measures to declare your sound opinions, and separate yourselves from your rotten members? or if you allow them to perplex government, if you trifle with this solemn business, if you do not resist the spirit of innovation in the first attempt, if you admit the smallest and most specious change in our parliamentary system, you are lost. You will be driven from one step to another; from principles just in theory, to consequences most pernicious in practice; and your first concessions will be productive of every subsequent mischief, for which you will be answerable to your country and to posterity. Do not suffer yourselves to be lulled into a false security; remember the proud fabric of the French Monarchy. Not four years ago it stood founded, as it might seem, on the rock of time, force, and opinion, supported by the triple Aristocracy of the Church, the Nobility, and the Parliaments. They are crumbled into dust; they are vanished from the earth. If this tremendous warning has no effect on the men of property in England; if it does not open every eye, and raise every arm, you will deserve your fate. If I am too precipitate, enlighten; if I am too desponding, encourage me.

My pen has run into this argument; for, as much a foreigner as you think me, on this momentous subject I feel myself an Englishman.

The pleasure of residing at Sheffield-place is, after all, the first and the ultimate object of my visit to my native country. But when or how will that visit be effected? Clouds and whirlwinds, Austrian Croats, and Gallic cannibals, seem on every side to impede my passage. You appear to apprehend the perils or difficulties of the German road, and French peace is more sanguinary than civilized War. I must pass through, perhaps, a thousand Republics or municipalities, which neither obey nor are obeyed. The strictness of passports, and the popular ferment, are much encreased since last summer: Aristocrate is in every mouth, Lanterns hang in every street, and an hasty word or a casual resemblance, may be fatal. Yet, on the other hand, it is probable that many English, men, women, and children, will traverse the country without any accident before next September; and I am sensible that many things appear more formidable at a distance than on a nearer approach. Without any absolute determination, we must see what the events of the next three or four months will produce. In the mean while, I shall expect with impatience your next letter: let it be speedy; my answer shall be prompt.

GALLIC WOLVES PROWL ROUND GENEVA.

You will be glad, or sorry, to learn that my gloomy apprehensions are much abated, and that my departure, whenever it takes place, will be an act of choice, rather than of necessity. I do not pretend to affirm, that secret discontent, dark suspicion, private animosity, are very materially asswaged; but we have not experienced, nor do we now apprehend, any dangerous acts of violence, which may compel me to seek a refuge among the friendly Bears, and to abandon my library to the mercy of the Democrates. The firmness and vigour of Government have crushed, at least for a time, the spirit of innovation; and I do not believe that the body of the people, especially the Peasants, are disposed for a revolution. From France, praised be the Demon of Anarchy! the insurgents of the pays de Vaud could not at present have much to hope; and should the *Gardes nationales*, of which there is little appearance, attempt an incursion, the country is armed and prepared, and they would be resisted with equal numbers and superior discipline. The Gallic wolves that prowled round Geneva are drawn away, some to the south and some to the north, and the late events in Flanders seem to have diffused a general contempt, as well as abhorrence, for the lawless savages, who fly before the enemy, hang their prisoners, and murder their officers. The brave and patient regiment of Ernest is expected home every day, and as Bern will take them into present pay, that veteran and regular corps will add to the security of our frontier.

I rejoyce that we have so little to say on that subject of Worldly affairs.* Since the interest of the Yorkshire is due from the mouth of February my complaints are silenced, but I am desirous of the consummation of the business. You seem to applaud your good fortune in finding an excellent settlement for £3000, with which you have purchased three unexceptionable Debentures, but you forget to mention who are my Creditors and in what part of the Globe my landed security is placed. I must confess some fears of Ireland or the West Indies, with neither of which I would willingly have any connection. As my property is now divided, I should much wish that you would draw up and sign a regular statement of the several objects, stating in whose hands and where the respective title deeds are deposited. With regard to those which are entrusted ―――― it could not surely be offensive to ask him for a written acknowledgment. I have no evidence whatsoever to produce to his Executors; this thought sometimes makes me rather uneasy. I thank you for the offer of supporting my Credit at Gosling's; but the stream now begins to flow faster than I draw, and they have been instructed to keep £500 India bonds from your talons. Notwithstanding the Darrel's caution, I wish you had seized the propitious moment when stocks were so ridiculously high. I am much surprized to have no account whatsoever of the approach of my Madeira, which has been so injudiciously paid for beforehand; enquiries must be made. Will you likewise inform yourself of the Wedgewood, why I have not been able to obtain their old account which was solicited by letter, a strong measure from me, when I paid Severy's bill two or three years ago? If they have waited scandalously for their money, it is not my fault; but I do not like it myself, as it is the only debt I have in the World. Mrs. Moss saw my house and garden in a rainy day, and her passage was so rapid that I could not even give her a dish of tea: she seems pleased with her situation at Geneva.

*This summer we are threatened with an inundation, besides many nameless English and Irish; the Dowager Lady Spencer is arrived, the Dutchess of Ancaster is expected, but I am less anxious about those matrons, than for the good Dutchess of Devonshire and the wicked Lady Elizabeth Foster, who are on their march. Lord Malmsbury, the *audacieux*

Harris, will inform you that he has seen me: *him* I would have consented to keep.*

THE DESTINY OF HIS LIBRARY.

Before I absolutely conclude, I must animadvert on the whimsical peroration of your last Epistle concerning the future fate of my library, about which you are so indignant. I am a friend to the circulation of property of every kind, and besides the pecuniary advantage of my poor heirs, I consider a public sale as the most laudable method of disposing of it. From such sales my books were chiefly collected, and when I can no longer use them they will be again culled by various buyers according to the measure of their wants and means. If indeed a true liberal public library existed in London, I might be tempted to enrich the catalogue and encourage the institution: but to bury my treasure in a *country* mansion under the key of a jealous master! I am not flattered by the Gibbonian collection, and shall own my presumptuous belief that six quarto Volumes may be sufficient for the preservation of that name. If however your unknown successor should be a man of learning, if I should live to see the love of litterature dawning in your grandson—— In the meanwhile I admire the firm confidence of our friendship that you can insist, and I can demur, on a legacy of fifteen hundred or two thousand pounds without the smallest fear of offence.

*One word more before we part; call upon Mr. John Nichols, bookseller and printer, at Cicero's head, Red-Lion-passage, Fleet-street, and ask him whether he did not, about the beginning of March, receive a very polite letter from Mr. Gibbon of Lausanne? To which, either as a man of business or a civil Gentleman, he should have returned an answer. My application related to a domestic article in the Gentleman's magazine of August, 1788, (p. 698,) which had lately fallen into my hands, and concerning which I requested some farther lights. Mrs. Moss delivered the letters into my hands, but I doubt whether they will be of much service to me; the work appears far more difficult in the execution than in the idea, and as I am now taking my leave for some time of the library, I shall not make much progress in the memoirs of P. P. till I am on English ground. But is it indeed true, that I shall eat any Sussex pheasants this autumn? The event is in the book of Fate, and I cannot unroll the leaves of September and October. Should I reach Sheffield-place, I hope to find the whole family in a perfect state of existence, except a certain Maria Holroyd, my fair and *generous* correspondent, whose annihilation on proper terms I most fervently desire. I must receive a copious answer before the end of next month, June, and again call upon you for a map of your political World. The Chancellor roars; does he break his chain? *Vale.**

590.

Lord Sheffield to Edward Gibbon.

Your former letter said you should be very sure, very high & select. You now say you are not merchants, &c. General Bude (a Genevois) recommended Dergueuse. The Duke of Leeds, hearing that he was known to me, desired Glover to enquire of me by letter. I advised Leigneur not to propose or trouble himself about terms, but to let General Bude do whatever was necessary of that kind. He has been at Moins sometime. He came from thence here, and is much pleased with his good fortune. Lord Carnarvon is older than we imagined. If there are the means at Lausanne of interesting Genl. Bude in favour of S[every], it might be usefull. I should make an agreement for S. or not according to the rank or character of the Principles; but I really do not know what salary should be thought of—you should give me some hint thereon. When I answered Glover, I told him if he should hear of any considerable Family who wished to have a friend to attend a son, that you and I could recommend one that would be very desireable. You are so awkward and careless about letters that I do not like to write to you except about matters that might be published at Charing-cross.

As to your £3000 debentures, I apprehend I have explained them to you before. Hammersley's Banking House has advanced £40,000 on Lord Barrymore's Estate in Ireland (£10,000 per annum at least); they have 6 per cent., and have raised the money by Debentures, giving the same security and £20,000 in the funds in addition. Their house and the £20,000 answerable for the interest. It is thought an *excellent thing*, and Pelham transferred it to me as a Friend. If you do not like it at any time you may have premium on selling. I wish you to indulge your own notions as to this matter and not to mind mine. I am not fond of being responsible as to other property than land. The Debentures are in the custody of Goslings, to enable them to receive at Hammersley's the interest half yearly.

GIBBON'S TABBY APPREHENSIONS.

Your Tabby apprehensions about your writings are silly enough—you have none except the mortgage on Buriton and Newhaven, and those being blended in your conveyance of the Estates, the Title of the purchaser and your security are the same, and if your counterpart were lost, the Title of the Purchaser would be your security. The Mortgage Deeds of Buriton are in my archive, very properly as Trustee. Instead of your curious notion of sending the writings in Batt's custody for the sake of safety to Lausanne, it will be better to send them in their Box to Gosling's Iron-room, to appease your fears. I had settled with Batt to examine the List when I go next to Town. Your Navigation Mortgage is in Gosling's hands. I had lately heard of a £3000 mortgage in this county that I thought would do, but they talked of only 3½ per Ct.

I have had a new care lately which has occupied me as much as possible. I mean the French clergy; above 1200 have landed in this country. I have exerted myself in their favour; I have succeeded pretty well in obviating prejudice in respect to the rise of provisions by the arrival of so many friends. There is little in respect to the arrival of so many popish priests.

Tell Lady Eliza I have written a very pretty letter long ago, & I am surprised she has not received it.

591.

Lord Sheffield to Edward Gibbon.

Sheffield Place, 30 July, 1792.

If I had not been bothered in a superlative degree since my return from London with much company, Navigation and County Meetings, &c., I should have favoured you with my opinion on the state of things. Twice each week I intended so to do at some length, and now I begin just before I set out for the Camp at Bagshot.

I have watched the origin, impression and progress of the French Revolution, both in France and in the other Governments in Europe, and I am fully convinced that if our Good Old Island had been drawn into the torrent of the new Philosophy, Holland, Germany, Spain, &c., would have followed her, and we should have seen all Europe involved in the extravagances of irreligion, immorality, anarchy, and barbarism. Our nature being at all times essentially the same, I presume that after a certain period of ferociousness and horrors, a resettlement of some sort, probably of the most despotic governments, would have taken place. The devastation of the Species might be repaired, and at the end of a couple of centuries it is possible that Science, the fine Arts, and the politeness and gentleness of Society, might again have been brought to the point at which they now are. Perhaps you may recollect that on the Decline and Fall of the Roman Empire a greater number of centuries were necessary for restoration. I really believe there is nothing exaggerated in this speculation.

OPPOSITION AND GOVERNMENT.

Having these opinions, I highly approved and cordially promoted the conduct of Opposition at such a crisis. They have come to the Aid of Government fairly and unreservedly, and many, even zealously, particularly the Dukes of Portland, Devonshire, Lord Fitzwilliam, Guilford, Spencer, Egremont, Ashburnham, Stormont, Loughborough, Windham of Norfolk, Sir Gilbert Elliott, in short almost everybody except about a score who had committed themselves with Mr. Grey, many of whom are heartily sick of the business. The attempt at an Association has in truth had an excellent effect. It has alarmed, roused and combined men in support of the Constitution and of good order. It will at last appear that there exists no great object or principle of party difference. It may lead to the formation of the strongest administration this country has ever known, and at a time when there should be no risk. It should be the first of all objects in these feverish times to guard against all possibility of phrenzy. At present there is very little amiss among men of property. The Dissenters however wait a good occasion for some change. The great care should be to prevent the mass of the people from being inflamed and made the tools of those who would risk anything to gain certain points or situations. It is essential to engage, to occupy the best of those.

There never was such an opportunity as at present of forming a good administration. Several openings can be easily made in the Cabinet and elsewhere without essential derangement. Lord Thurlow is gone, Lord Campden wishes to go, Marquis of Stafford is willing to go, and Dundas is only *locum tenens*. The concurrence in favour of the Constitution has greatly softened the asperity of party. I never observed so great a change, and I am convinced a junction would be generally liked by the respectable men of all parties and descriptions.

CAN PITT AND FOX COMBINE?

There is a difficulty and that is great. Whether insurmountable I cannot say. How to arrange Pompey and Caesar—Pitt and Fox. Government has candidly said it is not strong enough, the candour of the avowal has tended rather to conciliate than to animate opposition. Lord Loughborough has had a conversation with Pitt and Dundas. I scout the idea of the Party coming in without Fox. He has behaved, at all times, honourably to them and they will behave honourably towards him. Even if they were capable of quitting him, it would be foolish to leave him to bear the discontent of the country. Neither Fox nor Pitt should be suffered to be in that situation. Even if the King were to send for the Duke of Portland and desire him to form an administration, the best answer would be that he could not, without Mr. Pitt, form one which would be sufficiently firm and strong enough to carry on business as it should be, especially at this time. Both parties are too strong to suffer Government to go on efficaciously without them: but how to arrange Fox & Pitt, so that one should not seem to yield too much to the other, there is the rub. I should think it the most patriotick act to settle that matter. I discover no animosity, no rancour, no interest likely to make the parties disagree if once united, nothing that would dispose them to circumvent. I think it the interest of both our Orators to unite. I never supposed I should find it the wish of so many of the first men of the Country as I do. It appears to me to be greatly Pitt's interest. The regret of both King and Queen on the dismission of the Chancellor is well known. If Pitt should make an handsome fair offer to Fox (I do not know the latter is averse) and he should refuse, especially after the late business of Grey, it will prejudice Fox much with his party. If, on the other hand, Pitt should directly or indirectly aim at excluding him, the overture that has been made and the evident want of strength in Government would exasperate some, and encourage others to a redoubled spirit of opposition. Pitt must see that, if such an administration could be formed, there would be scarce a great family in opposition, and that distinction of party in that administration would soon be lost. Although the business is difficult I do not think it impossible. It is rather suspended than broke off. I should have supposed the Duke of Richmond most likely of all to be averse to it, but I find him much disposed to a junction.

Maria amuses herself very much with my conciliating and amiable moderation, but you will discover that my present disposition is perfectly consistent with the opinion I always had of the advantage to the Country at all times, and the necessity in these times, of a firm and strong Government.

I have now inflicted on you and myself a large *dose*.

Give us intelligence of you forthwith. When you set out. Which road you take. The French subject is too much to begin on. The Jacobins are *au comble*. Such execrable animals should be extirpated.

Pray acquaint Lady Elizabeth that I have this moment rec^d. her letter, that we wished it had been longer, and that I shall endeavour to collect something for her amusement very speedily. Present my best compliments also to the Duchess.

592.

To his Stepmother.

Lausanne, August 1st, 1792.

MY DEAREST FRIEND,

Notwithstanding all the arts of our great Enemy, the Demon of procrastination, I should not have postponed for so many months a pleasing duty, which may at any time be performed in a single hour, had I not for some time past entertained a lively and probable hope of visiting you this autumn in person; had I not flattered myself, that the very next post I might be able to fix the day of my departure from Lausanne, and almost of my arrival at the Belvidere. That hope is now vanished, and my journey to England is unavoidably delayed till the spring or summer of next year. *The extraordinary state of public affairs in France opposes an insuperable bar to my passage; and every prudent stranger will avoid that inhospitable land, in which a people of slaves is suddenly become a nation of tyrants and cannibals. The German road is indeed safe, but, independent of a great addition of fatigue and expence, the armies of Austria and Prussia now cover that frontier; and though the Generals are polite, and the troops well disciplined, I am not desirous of passing through the Clouds of Hussars and Pandours that attend their motions. These public reasons are fortified by some private motives, and to this delay I resign myself with a sigh for the present, and a hope for the future.

TAINT OF DEMOCRATICAL INFECTION.

What a strange wild World do we live in! You will allow me to be a tolerable historian, yet, on a fair review of ancient and modern times, I can find none that bear any affinity with the present. My knowledge of your discerning mind, and my recollection of your political principles, assure me, that you are no more a *Democrat* than myself. Had the French improved their glorious opportunity to erect a free constitutional Monarchy on the ruins of arbitrary power and the Bastile, I should applaud their generous effort; but this total subversion of all rank, order, and government, could be productive only of a popular monster, which after devouring every thing else, must finally devour itself. I was once apprehensive that this monster would propagate some imps in our happy island, but they seem to have been crushed in the cradle; and I acknowledge with pleasure and pride the good sense of the English nation, who seem truly conscious of the blessings which they enjoy: and I am happy to find that the most respectable part of opposition has cordially joyned in the support of "things as they are." Even this country has been somewhat tainted with the Democratical infection: the vigilance of Government has been exerted, the malecontents have been awed, the misguided have been undeceived, the feaver in the blood has gradually subsided, and I flatter myself that we have secured the tranquil enjoyment of obscure felicity, which we had been almost tempted to despise.

You have heard, most probably, from Mrs. Holroyd, of the long-expected though transient satisfaction which I received from the visit of the Sheffield family. He appeared highly satisfied with my arrangements here, my house, garden, and situation, at once in town and country, which are indeed singular in their kind, and which have often made me regret the impossibility of showing them to my dearest friend of the Belvidere. Lord S. is still, and will ever continue, the same active being, always employed for himself, his friends, and the public, and always persuading himself that he wishes for leisure and repose.* He has now a new care on his hands, the management and disposal of his eldest daughter, who is indeed a most extraordinary young woman. *There are various roads to happiness; but when I compare his situation with mine, I do not, upon the whole, repent that I have given the preference to a life of celibacy and retirement. Although I have been long a spectator of the great World, my unambitious temper has been content with the occupations and rewards of study; and although my library be still my favourite room, I am now no longer stimulated by the prosecution of any litterary work. The society of Lausanne is adapted to my taste; my house is open to many agreeable acquaintance, and some real friends; the uniformity of the natives is enlivened by travellers of all nations; and this summer I am happy in a familiar intercourse with Lady Spencer, the Dutchess of Devonshire, Lady Elizabeth Foster, and Lady Duncannon, who seems to be gradually recovering from her dreadful complaints. My health is remarkably good. I have now enjoyed a long interval from the gout; and I endeavour to use with moderation Dr. Cadogan's best remedies, temperance, exercise, and cheerfulness. Adieu, Dear Madam; may every blessing that Nature can allow be attendant on your latter season! Your age and my habits will not permit a very close correspondence; but I wish to hear, and I *presume* to ask, a speedy *direct* account of your own situation. May it be such as I shall hear with pleasure! Once more Adieu; I live in hopes of embracing you next summer at the Belvidere, but you may be assured that I bring over nothing for the press.*

593.

To Lord Sheffield.

Lausanne, August 23rd, 1792.

When I inform you that the design of my English expedition is at last postponed to another year, you will not be much surprized. The public obstacles, the danger of one road, and the difficulties of another, would alone be sufficient to arrest so unwieldy and inactive a Being; and these obstacles on the side of France, are growing every day more insuperable. On the other hand, the terrors, which might have driven me from hence, have in a great measure, subsided; our state prisoners are forgot; the country begins to recover its old good humour and unsuspecting confidence, and the last revolution of Paris appears to have convinced almost every body of the fatal consequences of Democratical principles, which lead by a path of flowers into the Abyss of Hell. I may therefore wait with patience and tranquillity till the Duke of Brunswick shall have opened the French road. But if I am not driven from Lausanne, you will ask, I hope with some indignation, whether I am not drawn to England, and more especially to Sheffield-place? The desire of embracing you and yours is now the strongest, and must gradually become the sole, inducement that can force me from my library and garden, over seas and mountains. The English World will forget and be forgotten, and every year will deprive me of some acquaintance, who by courtesy are styled friends: Lord Guilford and Sir Joshua Reynolds! two of the men, and two of the houses in London, on whom I the most relied for the comforts of society.

Even the satisfaction which I promised myself at Sheffield would at present be——

September 12th, 1792.

BRUNSWICK MARCHES ON PARIS.

*Thus far had I written in the full confidence of finishing and sending my letter the next post; but six post-days have unaccountably slipped away, and were you not accustomed to my silence, you would almost begin to think me on the road. How dreadfully, since my last date, has the French road been polluted with blood! and what horrid scenes may be acting at this moment, and may still be aggravated, till the Duke of Brunswick is master of Paris! On every rational principle of calculation he must succeed; yet sometimes, when my spirits are low, I dread the blind efforts of mad and desperate multitudes fighting on their own ground. A few days or weeks must decide the military operations of this year, and perhaps for ever; but on the fairest supposition, I cannot look forwards to any firm settlement, either of a legal or an absolute government. I cannot pretend to give you any Paris news. Should I inform you, as we believe, that *Lally is still among the cannibals*, you would possibly answer, that he is now sitting in the library at Sheffield. Madame de Stael, after miraculously escaping through pikes and poniards, has reached the castle of Copet, where I shall see her before the end of the week. If any thing can provoke the King of Sardinia and the Swiss, it must be the foul destruction of *his* cousin Madame de Lamballe, and of *their* regiment of guards. An extraordinary council is summoned at Berne, *but resentment may be checked by prudence*. In spite of Maria's laughter, I applaud your moderation, and sigh for a hearty union of all the sense and property of the country. The times require it; but your last political letter was a cordial to my spirits. The Duchess of D. rather dislikes a coalition: amiable creature! The Eliza (we call her Bess) is furious against you for not writing. We shall lose them in a few days; but the motions of Bess and the Duchess for Italy or England, are doubtful. Ladies Spencer and Duncannon certainly pass the Alps. I live with them.*

The interesting subjects of our late correspondence seem to have obliterated all memory of my private concerns, which have suffered as usual a rub when we thought them finally terminated. Although my ideas about money matters are grown somewhat confused, I do not believe there is much *caput mortuum* left, and have no doubt that the different channels of interest will be properly filled at Michaelmas, but I should be glad to see the greatest part of my decreasing short annuities well secured in a mortgage, and I flatter myself that yourself and agents are alive to that pursuit. But I must again put you in mind of two interesting queries to which I have not yet received any answer. 1. What is the nature of the three thousand pounds debentures which you purchased last Winter? Who is my debtor? and what and where is my security? Surely this is no idle curiosity on my side. 2. I wished to know in what hands the different deeds of my property are vested, and to possess something like a written attestation. The Buriton Mortgage and the aforesaid debentures are very properly, as I suppose, in Lord Sheffield's iron chest. *Fort bien.* My short annuities in their own books and in Mr. E. Darrel's—*pas mal*; my Sussex Navigation and India Bonds with Gosling, *passe encore*: but my claims on you, the Newhaven Mortgage and the Annuity are delivered—are they not, to Mr. Batt, an honourable but a sickly man? Should he fail, have we any to exhibit to his unknown heir? If delicacy, false delicacy, forbids your asking for a receipt, or taking them, which I should like better, into your own custody, I must seriously desire they may be sent over to me. Did I not express some anxiety on this head, you would have a right to call me a very careless fellow.

There are some minor matters which you may find in my long letter; such as a request to settle a shameful obsolete bill, my only one, at Wedgwood's, and to enquire whether Mr. John Nichols, bookseller in Red Lion Passage, Fleet Street, did not receive a letter from me last March which he has never answered. But I must insist on a hogshead of Madeira announced, shipped, and, I believe, paid six months ago, but which has never reached my lips or my cellar. This must be explored. *Adieu. Since I do not appear in person, I feel the absolute propriety of writing to my lady and Maria; but there is far from the knowledge to the performance of a duty.*

Ever yours,
E. G.

594.

To Mr. Cadell.

Lausanne, Sept. 28th, 1792.

DEAR SIR,

> EVERY DAY MORE SEDENTARY.

As you must have been informed by Lord Sheffield of my approaching arrival, I trust that you will feel some disappointment when you are told by myself that my journey to England is delayed to another year. The cause of this delay proceeds solely from the troubles of the continent. It would be madness to venture my life in the land of Cannibals, and the circuitous route by Germany would be attended with a large increase of trouble and expense. I grow every day more sedentary, and could I have the pleasure of shewing you my house, my library, and my garden, you would not be surprised that I should quit them with some reluctance. You may perhaps be likewise disappointed at hearing that I shall probably come empty-handed. A variety of untoward circumstances have contributed to encrease my indolence. I cannot please myself with the choice of a subject, and it may be prudent to enjoy rather than expose my historical fame.

Several months ago I wrote a very civil letter to *Mr. John. Nichols, Bookseller at Cicero's head, Red Lion Passage, Fleet Street*, which (had he received it) I can scarcely persuade myself he would have left without an answer. It related to a very curious paper about the Gibbon family inserted in the Gentleman's Magazine, August, 1788, p. 698, which had just fallen into my hands. I wished to know the author and by what means I could correspond with him on the subject. Perhaps you may be able, and I am sure you are willing, to clear up that point and put me in a proper channel by a personal application either to the aforesaid John Nichols or to some other person concerned in the Gentleman's Magazine.

Be so kind as to inform Elmsley of what he will hardly believe, that I am preparing materials for a letter to him, with a long list of commissions. Among these I wish you boldly to introduce the works of merit, history, travels, literature, philosophy, and even extraordinary novels which bear your authentic stamp.

My best compliments to Mr. Strahan.

595.

To Lord Sheffield.

Lausanne, October 5th, 1792.

FRENCH INVASION OF SAVOY.

---

*As our English newspapers must have informed you of the invasion of Savoy by the French, and as it is possible that you may have some trifling apprehensions of my being killed and eaten by those Cannibals, it has appeared to me that a short extraordinary dispatch might not be unacceptable on this occasion. It is indeed true, that about ten days ago the French army of the south, under the command of Mr. de Montesquiou, (if any French army can be said to be under any command,) has entered Savoy, and possessed themselves of Chamberry, Montmelian, & several other places. It has always been the practise of the King of Sardinia to abandon his transalpine dominions; but on this occasion the Court of Turin appears to have been surprized by the strange eccentric motions of a Democracy, which always acts from the passion of the moment; and their inferior troops have retreated, with some loss and disgrace, into the passes of the Alps. Mount Cenis is now impervious, and our English travellers who are bound for Italy, the Dutchesses of Devonshire, Ancaster, &c., will be forced to explore a long circuitous road through the Tirol. But the Chablais is yet intact, nor can our telescopes discover the tricolor banners on the other side of the lake. Our accounts of the French numbers seem to vary from fifteen to thirty thousand men; the regulars are few, but they are followed by a rabble rout, which must soon, however, melt away, as they will find no plunder, and scanty subsistence, in the poverty and barrenness of Savoy. N.B. I have just seen a letter from M. de M., who boasts that at his first entrance into Savoy he had only twelve battalions. Our intelligence is far from correct.

The Magistrates of Geneva were alarmed by this dangerous neighbourhood, and more especially by the well known animosity of an exiled citizen, Claviere, who is one of the six ministers of the French Republic. It was carried by a small Majority in the general council, to call in the succour of three thousand Swiss, which is stipulated by ancient treaty. The strongest reason or pretence of the minority, was founded on the danger of provoking the French, and they seem to have been justified by the event; since the complaint of the French resident amounts to a declaration of War. The fortifications of Geneva are not contemptible, especially on the side of Savoy; and it is much doubted whether M. de Montesquiou is prepared for a regular siege; but the malcontents are numerous within the walls, and I question whether the spirit of the citizens would hold out against a bombardment. In the meanwhile the diet has declared, that the first canon fired against Geneva will be considered as an act of hostility against the whole Helvetic body. Berne, as the nearest and most powerful Canton, has taken the lead with great vigour and vigilance; the road is filled with the perpetual succession of troops and artillery; and, if some disaffection lurks in the towns, the peasants, especially the Germans, are inflamed with a strong desire of encountering the murderers of their Countrymen. Mr. de Watteville, with whom you dined at my house last year, refused to accept the command of the Swiss succour of Geneva, till it was made his first instruction that he should never, in any case, surrender himself prisoner of War.

In this situation, you may suppose that we have some fears. I have great dependence, however, on the many chances in our favour, the valour of the Swiss, the return of the Piedmontese with their Austrian allies, 8 or 10 thousand men from the Milanese, a diversion from Spain, the great events (how slowly they proceed) on the side of Paris, the inconstancy and want of discipline of the French, and the near approach of the winter season. I am not nervous, but I will not be rash. It will be painful to abandon my house and library; but if the danger should approach, I will retreat before it, first to Bern, and gradually to the North. Should I even be forced to take refuge in England (a violent measure so late in the year) you would perhaps receive me as kindly as you do the French priests—a noble act of hospitality! Could I have foreseen this storm, I would have been there six months ago; but who can foresee the wild measures of the Savages of Gaul? We thought ourselves perfectly out of the Hurricane latitudes. Adieu. I am going to bed, and must rise early to visit the Neckers at Rolle, whither they have retired, from the frontier situation of Copet. Severy is on horseback, with his dragoons: his poor father is dangerously ill. It will be shocking if it should be found necessary to remove him. While we are in this very awkward crisis, I will write at least every week.

Ever yours,
E. G.

Write instantly, and remember all my commissions.

I will keep my promise of sending you a weekly journal of our troubles, that, when the piping times of peace are restored, I may sleep in long and irreproachable silence; but I shall use a smaller paper, as our military exploits will seldom be sufficient to fill the ample size of an English quarto.*

596.

To Lord Sheffield.

October 13th, 1792.

*Since my last of the 6th, our attack is not more imminent, and our defence is most assuredly stronger, two very important circumstances, at a time when every day is leading us, though not so fast as our impatience could wish, towards the unwarlike month of November; and we observe with pleasure that the troops of M. de Montesquiou, which are chiefly from the southern provinces, will not chearfully entertain the rigour of an Alpine Winter.

The 7th instant, M. de Chateauneuf, the French resident, took his leave with an haughty mandate, commanding the Genevois, as they valued their safety and the friendship of the Republic, to dismiss their Swiss allies, and to punish the Magistrates who had traiterously proposed the calling in these foreign troops. It is precisely the fable of the Wolves, who offered to make peace with the sheep, provided they would send away their dogs. You know what became of the sheep. This demand appears to have kindled a just and generous indignation, since it announced an Edict of proscription; and must lead to a Democratical revolution, which would probably renew the horrid scenes of Paris and Avignon. A General assembly of the Citizens was convened, the message was read, speeches were made, oaths were taken, and it was resolved, with only three dissentient votes, to live and dye in the defence of their country. The Genevois muster above three thousand well-armed citizens; and the Swiss, who may easily be encreased, in a few hours, to an equal number, add spirit to the timorous, and confidence to the well-affected: their arsenals are filled with arms, their magazines with ammunition, and their granaries with corn. But their fortifications are extensive and imperfect, they are commanded from two adjacent hills; a French faction lurks in the City; the character of the Genevois is rather commercial than military; and their behaviour, lofty promise, and base surrender, in the year 1782, is fresh in our memories. In the meanwhile, 4000 French at the most are arrived in the neighbouring camp, nor is there yet any appearance of mortars or heavy artillery. Perhaps a haughty menace may be repelled by a firm countenance.

If it were worth while talking of justice, what a shameful attack of a feeble unoffending state! On the news of their danger, all Switzerland, from Schaffouse to the Pays de Vaud, has risen in arms; and a French resident, who has passed through the country, in his way from Ratisbon, declares his intention of informing and admonishing the National convention. About eleven thousand Bernois are already posted in the neighbourhood of Copet and Nyon; and new reinforcements of men, artillery, &c., arrive every day. Another army is drawn together to oppose Mr. de Ferrieres, on the side of Bienne and the Bishoprick of Basle; and the Austrians in Swabia would be easily persuaded to cross the Rhine in our defence. But we are yet ignorant whether our sovereigns mean to wage offensive or defensive War. If the latter, which is more likely, will the French begin the attack? Should Geneva yield to fear or force, this country is open to an invasion; and though our men are brave, we want Generals; and I despise the French much less than I did two months ago. It should seem* from Trevor's letters, who is indeed low-spirited, *that our hopes from the King of Sardinia and the Austrians of Milan are faint and distant; Spain sleeps, and the Duke of Brunzwick (amazement!) seems to have failed in his great project. For my part, till Geneva falls, I do not think of a retreat; but, at all events, I am provided with two strong horses, and a hundred Louis in gold. Zurich would be probably my winter quarters, and the society of the Neckers would make any place agreable. Their situation is worse than mine: I have no daughter ready to lye in; nor do I fear the French aristocrates on the road.

Adieu. Keep my letters; excuse contradictions and repetitions. The Dutchess of Devonshire leaves us next week. Lady Elizabeth abhorrs you.*

Ever yours,
E. G.

597.

Lord Sheffield to Edward Gibbon.

Sheffield Place, 17th Oct., '92.

I have not patience to talk with you on the state of things, I am lamentably disappointed. De Custine's successful incursion into Germany, to which he seems to have been invited by the placing a large Magazine with a small guard in an unarmed town within a day's march of the large garrison of Landau. In short, that circumstance and the negociations at St. Menehould and the retreat of the combined armies have totally deranged all my notions of dignity, generalship, preponderance of military discipline, &c., &c., and all my speculations, moral, religious, political, and military, are sent into a troubled sea without rudder or compass. I had always some anxiety concerning the subsistence of a very large army from the Frontier to Paris, if the French should make up their mind to, and they could, lay waste the country, destroying forage, &c.; but I had never supposed the enterprise would end so abruptly in disgrace and calamity. I now see no prospect of any speedy settlement of French disturbances. The miscreants at Paris, encouraged by an appearance of success, will be active to extend their mischiefs, and my apprehensions are by no means quiet with respect to our own affairs.

Among the Dissenters it is thought there are a great many disposed to change. I am very far from satisfied with Charles Fox, much less with Gray, Lord Lauderdale, &c. Even in the trumpery town of Lewes there are some who hold meetings and correspond with certain Societies of the worst kind in the Borough, and of which you have probably heard; one of the creatures at Lewes said lately that, if the French business succeeded in any degree, it was perfectly sure that England would be in the same state as France is now in, before the end of ten years, and another declared that England would never do well until 5000 of the Nobility & Gentry were hung up.

DISCONTENT IN IRELAND.

Ireland is in no slight degree of alarm. The Roman Catholicks are much discontented. A ship-load of arms was lately landed for the discontented in the North. They have the impudence to exercise even in the neighbourhood of Drogheda. The natives return to their old tricks of shooting *Christians* in a most treacherous manner, and even in what is called the most civilized parts, and of houghing *Protestant cattle*. If the Government of Ireland continues to be feeble and not to act with firmness it may be difficult to say how matters will end—but there never was a time less favourable to the insurrection of Roman Catholicks, than the moment when it will not be possible for them to have assistance from foreign countries.

I am sorry the early meeting of Parliament which I announced to you, is not confirmed, yet I think it would have been a wise measure to have brought men together early, and not to have suffered the impressions made by the extravagance and cruelty of the Jacobins to wear out, or perhaps to receive a contrary direction. The worst cause when it seems fortunate will find defenders perhaps, but certainly will not want partisans.

Mrs. Moss has sent us a curious account of the dismay which took place in the Geneva State on the incursion into Savoy; but amidst all the calamities, we are glad to find from her, you are in good condition. I consider the French affairs so far out of the line of common Politicks, that I wish the whole world to declare against them, and run them down as pestiferous wolves, and therefore I wish all Switzerland to join against them; but I doubt whether it will be the policy of that country to engage in offensive war; and I suppose Geneva will not admit Swiss troops, if it will bring on a bombardment. I cannot conceive why some of the passes into Savoy were not defended. I long to hear that the retreat of the French is cut off. I am sorry I can see no prospect of the interference of this country. I think we might at least tell them, they must not fit out fleets against Nice or any place. Among many correspondents, and some of them the best informed, I find there is not the most distant guess of the intentions of Government. Perhaps they have no plan.

I believe my last mentioned that I have been much employed, by an attention to the poor refugees. Lally has been here and is gone, to return in a few days with the princess d'Henin and the Pauline. We have had the most curious details, and just now, from some respectable priests who were shut up with the Archbishop of Arles, &c., when the latter were massacred. Possibly you may not have so good an account at Lausanne, therefore I shall urge Maria to write it to you. The late massacres are infinitely more execrable than any French or English paper have stated.

We are exceedingly sorry to hear by Mrs. Moss, that M. de Severy is ill. You shall hear no more from hence untill you write to us.

598.

To Lord Sheffield.

October 20th, 1792.

Since my last, our affairs take a more pacific turn; but I will not venture to affirm that our peace will be either safe or honourable. Mr. de Montesquiou and three Commissioners of the Convention, who are at Carrouge, have had several conferences with the Magistrates of Geneva; several expresses have been dispatched to and from Paris, and every step of the negotiation is communicated to the deputies of Bern and Zurich. The French troops observe a very tolerable degree of order and discipline: and no act of hostility has yet been committed on the territory of Geneva.

599.

The Hon. Maria Holroyd to Edward Gibbon.

Oct. 24th, '92.

The amiable family at S. P. being infinitely delighted with your welcome dispatch, & still more so with the promise of writing *every week*, have had a dispute amongst themselves, who was to have the honor of answering you, & reminding you of that promise. I have gained permission to be the happy person, & happy I shall think myself, if you should direct *one* of the promised Letters to me. We talk and think of nothing but foreign news, & Mama is very abusive of the Jacobins. Massacres have sometimes enraged me a little, but I have borne every thing with tolerable patience, except that Wretches, who have no other idea of liberty, than the liberty of murdering defenceless prisoners, should dare to think of attacking a Nation, whose Ideas of freedom are not so *refined* as theirs, & whose valour is almost proverbial. Though I am perfectly satisfied that the tricolor Banner will never be erected in the town of Lausanne, yet I am very anxious to hear what becomes of the *Armée Montesquiou*. I am always wishing myself the guardian Angel of the Pais de Vaud. If I was, I am sure I should be inspired to do wonders. But, alas! I am a poor Mortal, & can only assist that Country by my best Wishes for its safety & prosperity.

How I wish you had let us remain & vegetate in our own little Island. I should have felt no other Interest in what is passing in your part of the World, than joy that you would be obliged to return to your native Country. You have likewise to answer for making me disatisfied with the famous Lakes & Rivers in the County of Sussex; & for shewing me a Country to which no other can compare, & which to see again I would give all my share of My lord's Sheep and Oxen, Ponds & Rivers. I do not know how to reconcile my wishes for the peace of Switzerland, with those for your return to England—as you seem resolved not to indulge us with your company, unless you are forced from your residence by a few thousand Marseillois. I cannot tell you how much I was disappointed when I was obliged to give up all expectation of seeing you this year. I wrote to Angletine a fortnight ago. I am very sorry indeed to hear her father is in a bad state of health. I hope you will be able to give a good Account of him, when you write next. Pray remember me to them very particularly, though I wish you had never made me acquainted with people I may probably never see again & yet cannot forget.

Papa is gone down the River Ouse, & ordered me to give you an account of the Emigrants; he would not think I had obeyed him very exactly, if he was to see my Letter—he would probably call it Stuff and Nonsense. I hope *you* will not, tho' I always feel myself so unworthy to write to you, that I generally suspect my poor Letters meet with a degree of criticism I am sure they cannot bear.

DISTRESS OF FRENCH REFUGEES.

Now for Papa's Emigrants. The Duc de Liancourt, who will have (when he can get it) the most considerable estate in France by the death of the Duc de Rochefoucauld, has been waiting for some weeks to come here, till Arthur Young should find it convenient to set off, as he had offered the Duke a seat in his Post chaise; he is in such distressed circumstances that his present plan is to go & settle in America. Mad^e. de Biron, who came over with so much difficulty and danger, that she lost her senses from fright and alarm, is returned to France to avoid the confiscation of her Estates. The same reason existing for her remaining there when she left the Country, it seems an extraordinary resolution to take, her returning, when she will be in as great danger as before. Mad^e. d'Henin is settled at Richmond, & Mad^lle. de Pully is arrived in England—we expect them here every day. Lally told us, when he was here, D. of Fitzjames was living in Germany upon *quinze sous par jour*, & saving out of that pittance to send something to her sons in the Army. A great number of french Priests have landed on our Coast. I suppose my lord informed you of the arrival of two here who had escaped from the Massacre at *les Carmes*—the detail of the death of the Archbishop of Arles is horrid, but too long for a Letter. The subscriptions in London are very great—one for the Clergy only, amounts to £12,000, & that for both Clergy and Laity to upwards of £4000. The latter has enabled some Swiss officers to reach their own Country, who intended to beg their way thro' Holland, & supports some french Ladies of fashion who had nothing but what they got by their needlework. Burke & Papa have had a vigorous correspondence on the subject—the former is very indignant that a case he had drawn up about Atheists calling themselves Philosophers in France was not received.

I do not dare *expect*, but I will *hope* to hear from you. Will you be so good as to remember me to M. & M^e. Levade? Do you know where the Legards and Grimstones are? Mama has some doubts, as to how she shall receive you; if you are obliged to fly to England, I shall be too well pleased with the effect to think of the cause.

Mama desires a great many pretty things to you. She is quite well & in good spirits; how unlucky we could not say the same last year. Louisa is still at Bath. I am in hopes of paying her a visit there next month. She *raves* about Switz. *almost* as much as me.

———————————

600.

To Lord Sheffield.

October 27.

*My usual temper very readily admitted the excuse, that it would be better to wait another week, till the final settlement of our affairs. The treaty is signed between France and Geneva; and the ratification of the Convention is looked upon as assured, if any thing can be assured in that wild Democracy. On condition that the Swiss Garrison, with the approbation of Berne and Zurich, be recalled before the first of December, it is stipulated that the independence of Geneva shall be preserved inviolate; that M. de Montesquiou shall immediately send away his heavy artillery; and that no French troops shall approach within ten leagues of the city. As the Swiss have acted only as auxiliaries, they have no occasion for a direct treaty; but they cannot prudently disarm, till they are satisfied of the pacific intentions of France; and no such satisfaction can be given till they have acknowledged the new Republic, which they will probably do in a few days, with a deep groan of indignation and sorrow; it has been cemented with the blood of their countrymen! But when the Emperor, the King of Prussia, the first General, and the first army in Europe have failed, less powerful states may acquiesce, without dishonour, in the determination of fortune. Do you understand this most unexpected failure? I will allow an ample share to the badness of the roads and the weather, to famine and disease, to the skill of Dumourier, a heaven-born General, and to the enthusiastic ardour of the new Romans; but still, still there must be some secret shameful cause at the bottom of this strange retreat.

A TUTORSHIP FOR SEVERY.

We are now delivered from the impending terrors of siege and invasion. The Geneva *Emigrés*, particularly the Neckers, are hastening to their homes; and I shall not be reduced to the hard necessity of seeking a winter azylum at Zurich or Constance: but I am not pleased with our future prospects. It is much to be feared that the present Government of Geneva will be soon modelled after the French fashion; the new Republic of Savoy is forming on the opposite bank of the lake; the Jacobin Missionaries are powerful and zealous; and the Malcontents of this country, who begin again to rear their heads, will be surrounded with temptations, and examples, and allies. I know not whether the pays de Vaud will long adhere to the dominion of

Berne; or whether I shall be permitted to end my days in this little paradise, which I have so happily suited to my taste and circumstances.

Last Monday only I received your letter, which had strangely loitered on the road since its date of the 29th of September. There must surely be some disorder in the posts, since the Eliza departed indignant at never having heard from you.*

I still am of opinion that it is both unseemly and unusual for *us* to propose any specific terms. You must hear the ideas of the parents or guardians. You must consider on the behalf of your client, how far a moderate interest may be enhanced by rank and character, how far a deficiency (less desirable) in those qualifications may be varnished with gold. If everything should unite, you may boldly accept; if you hesitate you must take the matter ad referendum, and they must expect our answer by the return of the post. You will say perhaps that the parties may be impatient, and that delay may be productive of danger. This I must acknowledge, nor is it only in this respect that I feel the disadvantage of his not being on the spot.—I much regret the M[arquis] of C[armarthen], his father the D[uke] of L[eeds] is a fair and honourable man. Your hint of General Bude (of whom I had never heard) shall not be neglected: when the Duchess of D. returns to England next year, I hope she will be able and willing to assist the young man, to whom she expressed much friendship, and whom she appointed her chevalier sans peur and sans reproche by the delivery of a feather and a cockade. He is now on service with his dragoons, but will probably be soon disbanded.

Without confessing that my fears and scruples were quite so *anile* as you are always disposed to think them, I am now in a great measure satisfied. I wish you may find a secure mortgage at four per cent.; but though I do not perfectly like the Debentures (which you never explained before), I cannot think they run much risk till our next meeting in England.

The case of my Wine I think peculiarly hard; to lose my Madeira, and to be scolded for losing it. Please to remember that the Wine Merchant never sent me any letter of advice, as he ought to have done, of the time and manner of its departure; and that when I first expressed my astonishment to you (in my great letter of at least four months ago) you were too much engrossed with a more interesting subject to return any answer. What could I do? my part was entirely passive, to expect its arrival, which I still expect. Yet I have now directed proper enquiries to be made at Basle and Ostend; the London Merchant must trace it forwards, and the last person in whose hands it has been must be responsible for the wine or its value. Whatsoever may be right, I have no intention of seeking a legal remedy; but on a similar occasion, I hope we shall never repeat the liberal confidence of such premature payment.

I am much indebted to Mr. Nichols for his Genealogical communications, which I am impatient to receive; but I do not understand why so civil a Gentleman could not favour me, in six months, with an answer by the post: since he entrusts me with these valuable papers, you have not, I presume, informed him of my negligence and awkwardness in regard to Manuscripts. Your reproach rather surprizes me, as I suppose I am much the same as I have been for these last twenty Years. Should you hold your resolution of writing only such things as may be published at Charing-cross, our future correspondence would not be very interesting. But I expect and require, at this important crisis, a full and confidential account of your views concerning England, Ireland, and France. You have a strong and clear eye; and your pen is, perhaps, the most useful quill that ever has been plucked from a goose. Your protection of the French refugees is highly applauded. Rosset and La Motte have escaped from Arbourg, perhaps with connivance to avoid disagreeable demands from the Republic. Adieu.

Ever yours,
E. G.

601.

Lord Sheffield to Edward Gibbon.

Bath, 5th Nov., 1792.

Among the whimsical events of the last three years, none is more extraordinary than an Hebdominal letter from you. Your character however is so bad on that head, that there is not much dependance on your perseverance, but it produces a desire and resolution in the Family to address you weekly as long as you give such encouragement.

THREE LATE FRENCH MINISTERS.

Here I am, not on account of my eyes (which continue very weak), but to attend the Mayor's Feast at Bristol this day. I arrived last night. I was but one night in London. I found the Hotel in Downing Street occupied by the Princess d'Henin, the Beautiful Comtesse Charles de Noailles, the Pauline, the Prince de Poix, Gouvernet, Lally, &c. I proceeded in the morning to Bulstrode to hold a conversation with the Duke, and from thence I moved to this place with the Maria, whom I shall leave with Aunt while I go through the necessary duties at Bristol, which will at least engage me till the 13th instant. Talking of Downing Street, I should mention the extraordinary *occurrence* in the dining-room there a few days since, of the three late French Ministers, St. Croix, Monciel, Bertrand and also Malouet, Gilliers, Gouvernet, Prince de Poix and Lally. They were in Committee on their deplorable affairs. For the sake of my eyes I shall give this to be finished by Maria. No man has a guess at the intentions of Gouvernment. There is not the slightest expectation that they will take the least part in the affairs of France. All those members of Opposition for whom you or others have respect are seriously well disposed to a junction of parties, and I am convinced, indeed I know, they would be very reasonable in their expectations. Pitt has said he could act in great confidence with Fox, notwithstanding sparrings which have taken place, and Charles Fox has said that a junction is so right a thing, that he cannot see otherwise than that it must take place. Yet there are great difficulties, and I am not sanguine. I shall have no opinion of Pitt's judgment or disposition if he does not remove them.

Poor Mrs. Gibbon was given over last week, a bilious attack. She has miraculously recovered, but the man who has bodily care of her, says she is so worn, she cannot pass the winter.

I should have added above that I fear Fox will be still *detestable* on the subject of French affairs. Pitt is suspected of Democracy, and it is said by some lately that he will himself move a Plan of Reform next Sessions.

JACOBIN SOCIETIES IN ENGLAND.

My Lord is gone to nurse his poor dear eyes, and leaves me to inform you of some of those extraordinary things to which I hardly expect you to give credit, but I shall name my authorities. Mr. Batt told us last Friday that the Attorney General had had information of the following event at Manchester, and that the said Attorney General had mentioned it to the *said* Mr. Batt. A person (we did not hear his name) at that place invited a number of people to dinner, among others the officers of the Scotch Greys, the day of the King's Accession, giving them notice there would be a *ceremony*. When the company was assembled there was an Ass brought into the room, dressed in a Blue Ribband, Crown and Sceptre, &c., which after many ridiculous formalities was killed, cut in pieces, and sent to different Societies in this Kingdom. I do not know if Lewes had a portion, but I know there is a Jacobin Society there. Burke called here yesterday evening to talk of a Plan for permanent relief of the poor priests, giving up all hopes of their returning to their native country. He proposed with the money in the hands of the Committee (£10,000) if Government would give any assistance towards settling them in the *Crimea*, Canada or Maryland, as the subscription cannot afford them subsistence in this country for three months longer.

Mrs. Moss is arrived in England. Have you received Lally's vessel which she sent you from Berne? How do the *Acacias*, &c., flourish upon the terrace?

602.

To Lord Sheffield.

November 10th, 1792.

*Received this day, November 9th, a most amiable dispatch from the too humble secretary of the family of Espee, dated October 24th, which I answer the same day. It will be acknowledged, that I have fulfilled my engagement with as much accuracy as our uncertain state and the fragility of human nature would allow.

I resume my narrative. At the time when we imagined that all was settled by an equal treaty between two such unequal powers, as the Geneva flea and the Leviathan France, we were thunderstruck with the intelligence that the Ministers of the Republic refused to ratify the conditions; and they were indignant, with some colour of reason, at the hard obligation of withdrawing their troops to the distance of ten leagues, and of consequently leaving the Pays de Gex naked, and exposed to the Swiss, who had assembled 15,000 men on the frontier, and with whom they had not made any agreement. The Messenger who was sent last Sunday from Geneva is not yet returned; and many persons are afraid of some design and danger in this delay. Montesquiou has acted with politeness, moderation, and apparent sincerity; but he may resign, he may be superseded, his place may be occupied by an *enragé*, by Servan, or prince Charles of Hesse, who would aspire to imitate the predatory fame of Custine in Germany.

In the mean while, the General holds a wolf by the ears; an officer who has seen his troops, about 18,000 men (with a tremendous train of artillery), represents them as a black, daring, desperate crew of buccaneers, rather shocking than contemptible; the officers (scarcely a Gentleman among them), without servants, or horses, or baggage, lying *higgledy piggledy* on the ground with the common men, yet maintaining a rough kind of discipline over them. They already begin to accuse and even to suspect their General, and call aloud for blood and plunder: could they have an opportunity of squeezing some of the rich Citizens, Geneva would cut up as fat as most towns in Europe. During this suspension of hostilities they are permitted to visit the City without arms, sometimes three or four hundred at a time; and the Magistrates, as well as the Swiss Commander, are by no means pleased with this dangerous intercourse, which they dare not prohibit. Such are our fears; yet it should seem on the other side, that the French affect a kind of magnanimous justice towards their little neighbour, and that they are not ambitious of an unprofitable contest with the poor and hardy Swiss. The

Swiss are not equal to a long and expensive War; and as most of our Militia have families and trades, the country already sighs for their return. Whatever can be yielded, without absolute danger or disgrace, will doubtless be granted; and the business will probably end in our owning the Sovereignty, and trusting to the good faith of the Republic of France: how that word would have sounded four years ago! The measure is humiliating; but after the retreat of the Duke of Brunswick, and the failure of the Austrians, the smaller powers may acquiesce without dishonour.

ENGLAND THE LAST REFUGE OF LIBERTY.

Every dog has his day; and these Gallic dogs have their day, at least, of most insolent prosperity. After forcing or tempting the Prussians to evacuate their country, they conquer Savoy, pillage Germany, threaten Spain: the Low Countries are ere now invaded; Rome and Italy tremble; they scour the Mediterranean, and talk of sending a squadron into the South Sea. The whole horizon is so black, that I begin to feel some anxiety for England, the last refuge of liberty and law; and the more so, as I perceive from Lord S.'s last epistle that his firm nerves are a little shaken; but of this more in my next, for I want to unburthen my conscience.

If England, with the experience of our happiness and French calamities, should now be seduced to eat the apple of false freedom, we should indeed deserve to be driven from the paradise which we enjoy. I turn aside from the horrid and improbable, (yet not impossible) supposition, that, in three or four years' time, myself and my best friends may be reduced to the deplorable state of the French emigrants: they thought it as impossible three or four years ago. Never did a revolution affect, to such a degree, the private existence of such numbers of the first people of a great Country: your examples of misery I could easily match with similar examples in this country and the neighbourhood; and our sympathy is the deeper, as we do not possess, like you, the means of alleviating, in some degree, the misfortunes of the fugitives. But I must have, from the very excellent pen of the Maria, the tragedy of the Archbishop of Arles; and the longer the better. Madame de Biron has probably been tempted by some faint and (I fear) fallacious promises of clemency to the Women, and which have likewise engaged Madame d'Aguesseau and her two daughters to revisit France. Madame de Bouillon stands her ground, and her situation as a foreign princess is less exposed. As Lord S. has assumed the glorious character of protector of the distressed, his name is pronounced with gratitude and respect. The D. of Richmond is praised, on Madame de Biron's account. To the Princess d'Henin, and Lally, I wish to be remembered.

The Neckers cannot venture into Geneva, and Madame de Stael will probably lye in at Rolle. He is printing a defence of the King, &c., against their Republican Judges; but the name of Necker is unpopular to all parties, and I much fear that the Guillotine will be more speedy than the press. It will, however, be an eloquent performance; and, if I find an opportunity, I am to send you one, to you, Lord S., by his particular desire: he wishes likewise to convey some copies with speed to our principal people, Pitt, Fox, Lord Stormont, &c. But such is the rapid succession of events, that it will appear, like the 'Pouvoir Executif,' his best Work, after the whole scene has been totally changed.*

Shall you never be able to place my £3000 on good Security? Was there ever before a two years' fruitless chace after a Mortgage? We are in hot pursuit from all quarters of my Madeira, and unless already drunk by the Hussars it must emerge.

Ever yours,
E. G.

P.S.—*The Revolution of France, and my triple dispatch by the same post to Sheffield-place, are, in my opinion, the two most singular events in the eighteenth Century. I found the task so easy and pleasant, that I had some thoughts of adding a letter to the gentle Louisa.* And a note to the most respectable Tuft. I should not have forgot Miss Firth, but I hear she is leaving you. Is she going to be married? *I am this moment informed, that our troops on the frontier are beginning to move, on their return home; yet we hear nothing of the treaty's being concluded.*

603.

To Lady Sheffield.

Lausanne, November 10, 1792.

NEITHER MONSTER NOR STATUE.

*I could never forgive myself, were I capable of writing by the same post, a political Epistle to the father, and a friendly letter to the daughter, without sending any token of remembrance to the respectable Matron, my dearest My lady, whom I have now loved as a sister for something better or worse than twenty years. No, indeed, the historian may be careless, he may be indolent, he may always intend and never execute, but he is neither a monster nor a statue; he has a memory, a conscience, a heart, and that heart is sincerely devoted to Lady S. He must even acknowledge the fallacy of a sophism which he has sometimes used, and she has always and most truly denied; that, where the persons of a family are strictly united, the writing to one is in fact writing to all; and that consequently all his numerous letters to the husband, may be considered as equally addressed to the wife. He feels, on the contrary, that separate minds have their distinct ideas and sentiments, and that each character, either in speaking or writing, has its peculiar tone of conversation. He agrees with the maxim of Rousseau, that three friends who wish to disclose a common secret, will impart it only *deux à deux*; and he is satisfied that, on the present memorable occasion, each of the persons of the Sheffield family will claim a peculiar share in this triple missive, which will communicate, however, a triple satisfaction. The experience of what may be effected by vigorous resolution, encourages the historian to hope that he shall cast the skin of the old serpent, and hereafter show himself as a new creature.*

And first let me congratulate yourself and your friends on the present happy state of your mental and corporeal faculties, of which I have gained the pleasing intelligence, not only from the hints in Lord S. and Maria's letters, but still more clearly from your own long and spirited Epistle to young Severy, which he received with gratitude and will answer with speed.

I lament, on all our accounts, that the last year's expedition to Lausanne did not take place in a golden period; the more familiar and cheerful intercourse with Madame de Severy would have opened your hearts to each other. I should have escaped many moments of painful though silent sympathy, and every object in Nature and society would have appeared to your eyes with a different aspect and colour. *But we must reflect, that human felicity is seldom without alloy; and if we cannot indulge the hope of your making a second visit to Lausanne, we must look forwards to my residence next summer at Sheffield-place, where I must find you in the full bloom of health, spirits, and beauty. I can perceive, by all public and private intelligence, that your house has been the open hospital Azylum of French fugitives; and it is a sufficient proof of the firmness of your nerves, that you have not been overwhelmed or agitated by such a concourse of strangers. Curiosity and compassion may, in some degree, have supported you. Every day has presented to your view some new scene of that strange tragical romance, which occupies all Europe so infinitely beyond any event that has happened in our time, and you have the satisfaction of not being a mere spectator of the distress of so many victims of false liberty. The benevolent fame of Lord S. is widely diffused.

From Angletine's last letter to Maria, you have already some idea of the melancholy state of her poor father. As long as Mr. de Severy allowed our hopes and fears to fluctuate with the changes of his disorder, I was unwilling to say anything on so painful a subject; and it is with the deepest concern that I now confess our absolute despair of his recovery. All his particular complaints are now lost in a general dissolution of the whole frame: every principle of life is exhausted, and as often as I am admitted to his bed-side, though he still looks and smiles with the patience of an Angel, I have the heartfelt grief of seeing him each day drawing nearer to the term of his existence. A few weeks, possibly a few days, will deprive me of a most excellent friend, and break for ever the most perfect system of domestic happiness, in which I had so large and intimate a share. Wilhelm (who has obtained leave of absence from his military duty) and his sister behave and feel like tender and dutiful children; but they have a long gay prospect of life, and new connexions, new families will make them forget, in due time, the common lot of mortality. But it is Madame de Severy whom I truly pity; I dread the effects of the first shock, and I dread still more the deep perpetual consuming affliction for a loss which can never be retrieved.

GIBBON'S ALTERED SITUATION.

You will not wonder that such reflections sadden my own mind, nor can I forget how much my situation is altered since I retired, nine years ago, to the banks of the Leman lake. The death of poor Deyverdun first deprived me of a domestic companion, who can never be supplied; and your visit has only served to remind me that man, however amused and occupied in his

Closet, was not made to live alone. Severy will soon be no more; his widow for a long time, perhaps for ever, will be lost to herself and her friends, the son will travel, and I shall be left a stranger in the insipid circle of mere common acquaintance. The Revolution of France, which first embittered and divided the Society of Lausanne, has opposed a barrier to my Sussex visit, and may finally expell me from the paradise which I inhabit. Even that paradise, the expensive and delightful establishment of my house, library, and garden, almost becomes an incumbrance, by rendering it more difficult for me to relinquish my hold, or to form a new system of life in my native Country, for which my income, though improved and improving, would be probably insufficient. But every complaint should be silenced by the contemplation of the French; compared with whose cruel fate, all misery is relative happiness. I perfectly concurr in your partiality for Lally; though Nature might forget some meaner ingredients, of prudence, economy, &c., she never formed a purer heart, or a brighter imagination. If he be with you, I beg my kindest salutations to him. I am every day more closely united with the Neckers. Should France break, and this country be over-run, they would be reduced, in very humble circumstances, to seek a refuge; and where but in England? Adieu, dear Madam: there is, indeed, much pleasure in discharging one's heart to a real friend.*

Ever yours,
E. G.

604.

To the Hon. Maria Holroyd.

Lausanne, Nov. 10, 1792.

In dispatching the weekly political journal to Lord Sheffield, my conscience (for I have some remains of conscience) most powerfully urges me to salute, with some lines of friendship and gratitude, the amiable secretary, who might save herself the trouble of a modest apology. I have not yet forgotten our different behaviour after the much lamented *separation* of October the 4th, 1791, your meritorious punctuality, and my unworthy silence. I have still before me that entertaining narrative, which would have interested me, not only in the progress of the *carissima famiglia*, but in the motions of a Tartar camp, or the march of a caravan of Arabs; the mixture of just observation and lively imagery, the strong sense of a man, expressed with the easy elegance of a female. I still recollect with pleasure the happy comparison of the Rhine, who had heard so much of liberty on both his banks, that he wandered with mischievous licentiousness over all the adjacent meadows. The inundation, alas! has now spread much wider; and it is sadly to be feared that the Elbe, the Po, and the Danube, may imitate the vile example of the Rhine: I shall be content, however, if our own Thames still preserves his fair character of

Strong without rage, without o'erflowing full.

These agreeable epistles of Maria produced only some dumb intentions, and some barren remorse; nor have I deigned, except by a brief missive from my chancellor, to express how much I loved the author, and how much I was pleased with the composition. That amiable author I have known and loved from the first dawning of her life and *coquetry*, to the present maturity of her talents; and as long as I remain on this planet, I shall pursue, with the same tender and even anxious concern, the future steps of her establishment and life. That establishment must be splendid; that life must be happy. She is endowed with every gift of nature and fortune; but the advantage which she will derive from them, depends almost entirely on herself. You must not, you shall not, think yourself unworthy to write to any man: there is none whom your correspondence would not amuse and satisfy.

I will not undertake a task, which my taste would adopt, and my indolence would too soon relinquish; but I am really curious, from the best motives, to have a particular account of your own studies and daily occupation.

What books do you read? and how do you employ your time and your pen? Except some professed scholars, I have often observed that women in general read much more than men; but, for want of a plan, a method, a fixed object, their reading is of little benefit to themselves, or others. If you will inform me of the species of reading to which you have the most propensity, I shall be happy to contribute my share of advice or assistance.

I lament that you have not left me some monument of your pencil. Lady Elizabeth Foster has executed a very pretty drawing, taken from the door of the green-house where we dined last summer, and including the poor Acacia, (now recovered from the cruel shears of the gardener,) the end of the terrace, the front of the Pavilion, and a distant view of the country, lake, and mountains. I am almost reconciled to d'Apples' house, which is nearly finished. Instead of the monsters which Lord Hercules Sheffield extirpated, the terrace is already shaded with the new acacias and plantanes; and although the uncertainty of possession restrains me from building, I myself have planted a bosquet at the bottom of the garden, with such admirable skill that it affords shade without intercepting prospect.

SOCIETY OF LADY E. FOSTER.

The society of the aforesaid Eliza, of the Duchess of Devonshire, &c. has been very interesting; but they are now flown beyond the Alps, and pass the winter at Pisa. The Legards, who have long since left this place, should be at present in Italy; but I believe Mrs. Grimstone and her daughter returned to England. The Levades are highly flattered by your remembrance. Since you still retain some attachment to this delightful country, and it is indeed delightful, why should you despair of seeing it once more? The happy peer or commoner, whose name you may assume, is still concealed in the book of fate; but, whosoever he may be, he will cheerfully obey your commands, of leading you from ——— Castle to Lausanne, and from Lausanne to Rome and Naples. Before that event takes place, I may possibly see you in Sussex; and, whether as a visitor or a fugitive, I hope to be welcomed with a friendly embrace. The delay of this year was truly painful, but it was inevitable; and individuals must submit to those storms which have overturned the thrones of the earth.

The tragic story of the Archbishop of Arles I have now somewhat a better right to require at your hands. I wish to have it in all its horrid details; and as you are now so much mingled with the French exiles, I am of opinion, that were you to keep a journal of all the authentic facts which they relate, it would be an agreeable exercise at present, and a future source of entertainment and instruction.

I should be obliged to you, if you would make, or find, some excuse for my not answering a letter from your aunt, which was presented to me by Mr. Fowler. I shewed him some civilities, but he is now a poor invalid, confined to his room. By her channel and yours I should be glad to have some information of the health, spirits, and situation of Mrs. Gibbon of Bath, whose alarms (if she has any) you may dispel. She is in my debt. Adieu; most truly yours.

605.

The Hon. Maria Holroyd to Edward Gibbon.

Sheffield Place, November, 1792.

Your three letters received yesterday caused the most sincere pleasure to each individual of this family so highly favoured by you—but to none more than myself. I flatter myself that I despise general compliments as they deserve, but praise (tho' I fear, beyond my deserts) from one whose opinion I so highly value, and whose esteem I so much wish to gain, is more pleasing than I can describe, & I really think, thus encouraged, & with your *example* before me, to shew *bad habits may* be conquered. I had not neglected to make the collection of facts which you recommend, and which the great variety of unfortunate persons whom we see, or with whom we correspond, enables me to make.

As to the other part of your letter about *my studies*, I can only say, the slightest hint on that subject will be always received with the greatest gratitude, and attended to with the utmost punctuality. French history I am most acquainted with—English, I am ashamed to say, I am much less versed in. I have read Hume, but not since I came to years of discretion, & what is read as a *task* seldom is well attended to. I am now reading a *certain* work, in 6 Vols. Quarto or 12 Duodecimo, which I was acquainted with before, only by reading it after supper, frequently with long interruptions caused by Company, &c., & which only raised my curiosity to give it more attention. It would be Impertinence or at best but a Drop in the Ocean to add my mite to the opinion of the generality of the World, & say how much the Subject interests or the Style delights me. When this work is read thro', I intend to proceed with English history. I again repeat, if you condescend to favour me with any directions on this subject, I shall follow them with the greatest pleasure; but if you should not, I am much flattered that you should desire to hear from me, & should have sent you the horrid account of the massacre aux Carmes before, if I had thought you would have been desirous of it. I have not seen the details in any newspaper, & one of the eight Priests, who dined here, & had escaped from the massacre, related the whole with such simplicity & feeling, as to leave no doubt of the truth of all he said.

MURDER OF THE ARCHBISHOP OF ARLES.

On the 2d of Sepber they went into the garden, as usual, to walk at five o'clock in the evening. They expressed their surprize at several large pits, which had been digging for two or three days past. They said to each other, "The day is almost spent, & yet Manuel told a person who interceded for us, last Thursday, that on the Sunday following not one should remain in captivity—we are still Prisoners." Soon after, they heard shouts, and some musquet shots were fired into the Garden. A number of National Guards, some Commissaires *de Sections*, & several Marseillois, rushed in. The unhappy victims who were dispersed about the Garden, assembled under the Walls of the Church, not daring to enter, least it should be polluted with blood. One, who was behind the rest, was shot dead. *Point de coups de fusil* said some of the Chiefs of the assassins, thinking this death too merciful. A number of them called for the Archbishop of Arles, & insisted that he should be given up to them, the Priests all crowded round him, & determined to defend him with their Lives. The Archbishop then said, "Let me pass; if we must all perish, it is of little consequence whether I die first or not, & if my death will appease them, is it not my duty to preserve your Lives at the expense of my own?" He asked the eldest of the Priests to give him Absolution—he knelt to receive it, & when he rose, advanced, with his arms crossed on his breast, towards the People. His appearance was so dignified & noble, that for ten minutes not one of these Wretches had courage to raise their hand against him. They reproached each other with cowardice & advanced—one look from the venerable Prelate struck them with involuntary awe, & they retired. At last, one of the assassins struck off his Cap with a Pike—their fury returned when they saw respect once violated, & another struck him on the head with a Sabre, & laid open his scalp. The Archbishop only said, "O mon Dieu!" & put up his right hand to his eyes. A second blow cut off this hand—he repeated his exclamation & raised the other. A third stroke left him sitting, & a fourth extended him lifeless, when all the Miscreants pressed forwards, to bury their Poniards in his bosom.

The Priests all agreed that the Archbishop of Arles was one of the most amiable men in France—his only *crime* was having parted with most of his private fortune to support the necessitous Clergy of his Diocese, since the beginning of the Revolution. When he was murdered, the National Guards made all the Priests go into the Church, telling them they should appear, one after another, before the *Commissaires du Section*, who would try them and determine their fate. They had hardly entered, before the People impatiently called for them to shew themselves—upon which, all kneeling before the Altar, they received Absolution from the Bp of Beauvais—& then, two by two, passed before one of the commissaires, who did not question, but only counted his victims. In this manner, perished 120 Priests, amongst whom were the Bishops of Beauvais and Xaintes, both of the Rochefoucauld family. *Our friends* escaped by getting over the Wall.

I am afraid I have tired your patience, & that you did not expect such a tedious history. Mad^e. d'Hénin & Pauline are at Boulogne; they have gained nothing by going there, & are afraid they may find it difficult returning to England. The seal of the Nation is put on all Mad^e. d'Hénin's effects; she is not able to keep a single servant—she says, Pauline & she must wait on each other. Papa, who is more alarmed than I ever saw him, will write to you soon, *politically*. Mama will likewise answer your letter, & in the mean time desires many thanks for it. Will you say everything affectionate to Angletine for her letter? I feel sincerely for the situation of that family, & if you can send any good news of M. de Severy's amendment, I trust you will write. It was particularly kind of Angletine to write when her mind must be so ill at ease—but it is not flung away upon me. I am anything but *une Ingrate*. Mrs. Moss is here, & speaks with delight of your house, your terrace, & of the great civility you showed her. Judge if Lausanne is ever the subject of our conversation.

We left Louisa & Aunt at Bath very well, they both desire to be remembered to you when we wrote. Mrs. Gibbon looks as well as ever, but is really very unwell.

———————————————

606.

Lord Sheffield to Edward Gibbon.

Bristol, 14th Nov., 1792.

I snatch an interval likely to be very short, to acknowledge you have some merit in a 14th day epistle, although you fasted as to your 7th day. I was glad to hear of the agreement on the subject of Geneva. As the French troops were immediately to return 10 leagues, and before the evacuation, I think it honourable, but my political barometer never was so low. During the last 35 years on no occasion it had materially sunk. It never experienced any great depression till the wonderful and in some degree inexplicable phenomena of the later part of last September. I had some hope that Europe would see the necessity of making a common cause against the Disturbers of the World. But I have not a ray of hope. The failure of the combined army has of course encouraged and increased a bad spirit in this country, but it has not as yet shewn itself except in some towns. And in such, mischief always begins. The respectable and considerable men of both parties among my constituents are right. Government had risked a foolish game in Ireland, playing Roman Catholics against Protestants, and openly supporting the former, granting too much, and giving further hopes, which has produced sedition and brought them to the brink of rebellion, but within a few weeks it has been determined to go no farther and to support the Protestant Ascendency—better late than never, but some knocks probably will ensue.

I believe I forgot to assure you in my last that Newspaper account of our friend Lord L. and his acceptance of Seals is premature, and that there is no prospect of such an event unless with the concurrence and accession of the Mass of the party. I rather suspect some of our friends have more of the shew than the reality, of wishing or expecting, or promoting healthy conjunction of parties—but they are few.

I scolded you about the Madeira because I thought it lost thro' your neglect of writing, but I have the pleasure of finding that it was only delayed, and is now on its road. So writes Muligan's correspondent in Holland. I shall send this to Maria to finish. My eyes are very weak.

I do not know what to add to Papa's *croaking* Epistle, except to ask if you will give us an Asylum at Lausanne when this country is in the state of France. If you should answer in the affirmative, I am afraid you would make me an enemy to my country and wish it very ill. *I* think Papa very *ungrateful* for your very great kindness and attention in writing so frequently—at a time so very interesting, but I believe he is afraid of praising you too much, least you should think you have done enough. If you were a witness of the pleasure your letters give all the family, I think you would not talk of sinking into a *long and irreproachable silence.* Mama assures me you will not write to me. Pray make her say the thing that is not, for once in her life. We leave Bath next Sunday, after having enjoyed the gaieties of the place a fortnight. Louisa is to remain here all the Winter. She desires to be particularly remembered to you. Switzerland is our daily subject of conversation and regret. Witness our hands this 15th day of November.

MARIA JOSEPHA HOLROYD,
LOUISA DOROTHEA HOLROYD.

607.

To Lord Sheffield.

*After the triple labour of my last dispatch, your experience of the creature might tempt you to suspect that it would again relapse into a long slumber. But, partly from the spirit of contradiction, (though I am not a lady) and partly from the ease and pleasure which I now find in the task, you see me again alive, awake, and almost faithful to my hebdomadal promise. The last week has not, however, afforded any events deserving the notice of an historian. Our affairs are still floating on the waves of the convention, and the ratification of a corrected treaty, which had been fixed for the 20th, is not yet arrived; but the report of the diplomatic committee has been favourable, and it is generally understood that the leaders of the French Republic do not wish to quarrel with the Swiss. We are gradually withdrawing and disbanding our militia. Geneva will be left to sink or swim, according to the humour of the people; and our last hope appears to be, that by submission and good behaviour we shall avert for some time the impending storm.

FLIGHT OF A FRENCH GENERAL.

A few days ago, an odd incident happened in the French army; the desertion of the general. As the Neckers were sitting, about eight o'clock in the evening, in their drawing-room at Rolle, the door flew open, and they were astounded by their servant's announcing *Monsieur le General de Montesquiou!* On the receipt of some secret intelligence of a *decrét d'accusation*, and an order to arrest him, he had only time to get on horseback, to gallop through Geneva, to take boat for Coppet, and to escape from his pursuers, who were ordered to seize him alive or dead. He left the Neckers after supper, passed through Lausanne in the night, and proceeded to Berne and Basle, whence he intended to wind his way through Germany, amidst enemies of every description, and to seek a refuge in England, America, or the moon. He told Necker, that the sole remnant of his fortune consisted in a wretched sum of twenty thousand livres; but the public report, or suspicion, bespeaks him in much better circumstances. Besides the reproach of acting with too much tameness and delay, he is accused of making very foul and exorbitant contracts: and it is certain that new Sparta is infected with this vice beyond the example of the most corrupt monarchy. Kellerman is arrived to take the command; and it is apprehended that on the first of December, after the departure of the Swiss, the French may *request* the permission of using Geneva, a friendly city, for their winter quarters. In that case, the democratical revolution, which we all foresee, will be very speedily effected.

I would ask you, whether you apprehend there was any treason in the Duke of Brunswick's retreat, and whether you have totally withdrawn your confidence and esteem from that once-famed general? Will it be possible for England to preserve her neutrality with any honour or safety? We are bound, as I understand, by treaty, to guarantee the dominions of the King of Sardinia and the Austrian provinces of the Netherlands. These countries are now invaded and over-run by the French. Can we refuse to fulfil our engagements, without exposing ourselves to all Europe as a perfidious or pusillanimous nation? Yet, on the other hand, can we assist those allies, without plunging headlong into an abyss, whose bottom no man can discover? But my chief anxiety is for our domestic tranquillity; for I must find a retreat in England, should I be driven from Lausanne. The idea of firm and honourable union of parties pleases me much; but you must frankly unfold what are the great difficulties that may impede so salutary a measure: you write to a man discreet in speech, and now careful of papers. Yet what can such a coalition avail if Fox be detestable and Pitt democratical? Where is the champion of the constitution? Alas, Lord Guildford! I am much pleased with the Manchester ass. The asses or wolves who sacrificed him have cast off the mask too soon; and such a nonsensical act must open the eyes of many simple patriots, who might have been led astray by the specious name of reform. It should be made as notorious as possible. Next winter may be the crisis of our fate, and if you begin to improve the constitution, you may be driven step by step from the disfranchisement of Old Sarum to the king in Newgate, the lords voted useless, the bishops abolished, and a house of commons without articles (*sans culottes*).

MADAME DE STAEL.

Necker has ordered you a copy of his royal defence, which has met with, and deserved, universal success. The pathetic and argumentative parts are, in my opinion, equally good, and his mild eloquence may persuade without irritating. I have applied to this gentler tone some verses of Ovid (Metamorph. 1. iii. 302, &c.) which you may read. Madame de Stael has produced a second son. She talks wildly enough of visiting England this winter.* Her friend the Vicomte de Narbonne is somewhere about

Dorking. If you could shew him any civilities she would thank us both. She is a pleasant little woman.

No news from Basil or Ostend of my Madeira. Pray contrive to get me a mortgage; there is nothing like land or landed security. Poor Mrs. G. in such a state! I can only wish her an easy dismission. I wish the same to poor Severy, whose *condition is hopeless. Should he drag through the winter, Madame de S. would scarcely survive him. She kills herself with grief and fatigue. What a difference in Lausanne! I hope triple answers are on the road. I must write soon; the *times* will not allow me to read or think. Ever yours.*

No. 6 (I believe). Send me a list of these letters, with their respective dates.

608.

To his Stepmother.

Lausanne, Nov. 25, 1792.

MY DEAREST MADAM,

My friend Lord Sheffield has just informed of your late illness and happy recovery, and though I will not oppress you by a long letter, I cannot refrain from writing six lines to express my concern for the one and my joy for the other. It is my intention (if any road be open) to reach England early next summer, when I shall hasten to Bath, and hope to find you perfectly revived in health and spirits. We have had some slight alarms in this country, but they are now past, and amidst the general hurricane we hope to sleep without any troublesome dreams. Adieu, my Dear Madam; if your hand be too feeble to write yourself, could you not employ that of a friend to send me a short and sincere account?

I am
Ever yours,
E. GIBBON.

609.

Lord Sheffield to Edward Gibbon.

Downing Street, 14 Dec., 1792.

Being harrassed in an extraordinary degree, I with ease persuaded myself that it should be better to delay my letter till this day, that I might say what passed in opening the Parliament yesterday. Your extraordinary effort to write so much would have immediately forced me to answer if I had not known that Maria had despatched a packet, and that My Lady threatened another. I must acknowledge that Maria pressed me every post to take up the political part of the correspondence. But you will be satisfied with my occupation lately.

THE CONSTITUTION IS THE FRENZY.

Government had information (I know it to be very serious, and not from them). The sudden withdrawing of the Troops from the coast to the City, the extraordinary assembling of Parliament, the calling out of a part of the Militia, of course caused great alarm, but the effect was good. The middle ranks in town proposed Associations. I believe we began in Sussex. I instantly took to it, gave a right direction, limited the business to support of Constitution as now established, and of exerting the Civil power which should be found necessary at this extraordinary crisis instead of patchwork and partial association by Towns. I have promoted one in each of the twelve Divisions of the County. My Division meets first. The Plan ran like wild-fire. The Constitution is the phrenzy more than Liberty, property and no excise, or coalition ever was. All the parishes in London are associating.

I had written the first page when the Princess d'Henin, who left Boulogne yesterday, entered my room, and the now immediate departure of post only allows me to say that Charles Fox on moving the amendment of the Address uttered the most mischievous doctrines, principles, &c., that could at this time be invented, declaring himself, however, a friend to the Constitution, yet admitting the necessity of some changes. We (Country Gentlemen) opposed him, 290 to 50. Lord Lansdown's men included in the latter. Most of the others were only with him because they thought it better not to throw him out of all chance of control. Just as I came into this house I met Lord Bute, who told me the Irish Catholicks were in arms. Whether we shall have war with France is far from settled.

I shall write by next post.

610.

Lord Sheffield to Edward Gibbon.

Sheffield Place, 20th Dec., '92.

JACOBINISM IN ENGLAND.

I wrote in much haste to you last Friday, and I know not at this time what I wrote. I suppose I mentioned to you that Fox had, contrary to the opinion of all the considerable and respectable men of the Party, uttered everything that his worst enemy could wish, and avowed everything which he seemed to keep back last Sessions. It is impossible to imagine anything more injudicious or more mischievous at this time. Every man in the street asked, "Is he mad?" On the report of the address he maintained still more extravagant language than the day before. The next day, Saturday, he moved an Address to the King to acknowledge and send an Embassy to the Republic, or to that effect. I had been considerably *elevated* by his speeches of the preceding day, and just before I came down to the House, I heard that Brissot had announced in his newspaper of the 10th, as a measure of Opposition, the acknowledgment of the Republic and an Embassy. I did not suppose that Fox had any communication with him, but it seemed that somebody who was in his councils had connection with Brissot. Thus figged, the moment Fox sat down, I burst, and expressed myself pretty vigorously, and I was not sorry for the opportunity, as I knew the country gentlemen were properly disposed, and I was glad to shew a *good example*. Some followed strongly against Fox's conduct. The speeches are wretchedly given in the common newspapers, but there is a good report of what I said in the Diary and Morning Chronicle, and if there should be room, Maria shall copy it at the end of this letter, as it is not long.

Your last letter of the 26th Nov. is not the 6th, but the 5th Bulletin of affairs in your neighbourhood. While you continue to write you shall have frequent accounts from hence.

I had not an opportunity of learning distinctly whether Pitt has at last positively declined the admission of Fox into Administration. I have heard it said that he had, and that he had not, both seemingly from good authority, but in truth I forgot to enquire from the only quarter that could inform. The Duke of Portland is greatly distressed by Fox's conduct—if he were to be desired, he might become more desperate.—Lord Loughborough is more vigorous in his opinion of the matter. There seems at present no probability of his accepting the Great Seal. It would be a situation of uncertainty, his acceptance would be reprobated, and he would involve himself in much more trouble and difficulty than at present; yet I do not see how Government can go on without a considerable addition of force. It seems to me, however, agreed among the better part of us in Opposition not to distress or obstruct Government by opposition at this time. The business is too serious. Jacobinism had lately slid rapidly through many parts of the country. Emissaries of all sorts and in great numbers have been very busy, and at a great expence.

I believe that I mentioned in a late letter that the Chief of the Propaganda was here.—Rotombeau, the most execrable of wretches, is here, and bragged that with his own hand he had murdered the Lamballe and 38 persons in one day. Many Frenchmen landed upon different parts of our coast with arms. Some imported them regularly and paid duty for them. Several men landed even near Ipswich with Fire-locks, Side-arms, and a dagger. The officer commanding took them from them, and the Mayor ordered them to be stored. The numbers in London were very great—a very considerable number of persons there, and especially in the Borough, were in concert with them. However wild it may appear, the Plan was to surprize the Tower and to deliver the hundred thousand muskets in the Armoury to the people, who they supposed would follow them. The number who have associated in the several clubs is said to consist of many thousands. Government had notice that an attack would be made on Sat. the 1st Decr. All the night of Friday Artillery and Artillery-men were marching to the Tower from Woolwich, and before day-break it was well-guarded. All this I know and not from friends of Government. The Tower has since been much strengthened; the gates fortified, the Ditch cleansed, and a considerable body of men is now there. All the Cavalry and Regulars within a hundred miles of London, were brought to its close neighbourhood.

FOX'S MISCHIEVOUS SPEECHES.

The country was of course alarmed, the shopkeepers at Lewes proposed Association in favour of the Constitution, the same disposition seems to have arisen at the same time in different parts of England. Finding it likely to run, I have been very active in giving it a direction. It appeared to me that nothing could be more advantageous than arranging the minds of the people under a good Principle, while they were in a ferment, and when once committed by their signature, it was likely they would be strenuous for measures which I endeavoured to make their own, as much as possible. Every division of this county is forming Associations to support the Civil

Power, and declaring in favour of a Government by King, Lords and Commons. The spirit is going through the whole kingdom. The Jacobins seem to be totally crushed and dismayed. Many French fled to the Ports to secure a passage. Whether C. Fox's speeches will revive them, I do not yet know, but they certainly will encourage many of the miscreants within the country. I do not know whether I mentioned to you the great facility with which several people, even in this county, talk of the foolish expence of maintaining a royal family. Association, giving an opportunity to such an immense proportion of the people to shew their attachment to the Constitution, has an excellent effect, and I have no doubt that the French Devils on the excellent appearance of things will give up their machinations. On the late explosion Rotombeau made an attempt to fly—he was told he would be safer in London. He is well *spied*—he sees four hundred persons in a day. I believe he is now gone.

I came here on Sunday to attend a great meeting of Associations (which I had promoted) on Monday. I intended to return, but on Tuesday I wrote to the D. of Portland & to Lord Loughborough, and told them I was so disgusted with Fox's conduct that I thought they would agree with me, that I had better remain at Sheffield Place till Parliament meets for business after Christmas. That I was sure a very small number of members indeed would follow him in his present career. That, as a well-wisher to the tranquility and safety of the country, I need not be apprehensive of any mischief, except what may arise from the language he holds, which cannot be prevented. That I do not like to seem separate from men with whom I have zealously acted ten out of the thirteen years of my political life.

(*Continued by the Hon. Maria Holroyd.*)

My Lord's Speech, taken from the Diary—he rose immediately after Mr. Fox's motion for an Embassy to France. "It is impossible to be silent. Are we then in that deplorable situation? Are we the vilest and most contemptible of nations? Are we to be the first to acknowledge, and cringe to these cut-throats and robbers, who have not the recommendation of being able to controul their own Banditti? Are we to league with them, to act in concert with them? How soon they may be invited here, he should not then attempt to guess—or to say how soon our gaols may be filled with the most respectable persons of the Nation, for the purpose of murdering them in cold blood without a trial—or how soon the most amiable of our women and of the highest ranks may lie on straw crowded in the most loathsome gaols, as in France, with the lowest dregs of the people, faultless however, except that their fathers, husbands, or sons may have ventured to maintain the constitution; he should leave to others more able than he was to detail the mischiefs of the monstrous proposition that had been made.

He was too much agitated to attempt it. He was almost ashamed of the enthusiasm he had hitherto felt in favour of the Right Honourable Mover. It is true he had made much enquiry, but he hoped other country gentlemen would communicate what they knew of the state of the country. In respect to war, he believed every man wished to avert it. That the surest means of avoiding it would be by vigorous preparation for it, and if it could not be avoided, that it would be better policy to meet it, than wait for it. That the Disturbers of the World when they had over-run other nations, envying and dreading our prosperity, would not fail with double force to visit us. His Lordship concluded with some observations on the late measures, and told the Ministers, that although he commended their promptness and vigour, yet he could not approve their unjustifiable interpretation of the word—Insurrection. They would have done much better if they had acknowledged that, in consequence of some uncommon danger which impended, they had for the public good laid themselves under the necessity of applying to the Legislature for indemnity, but that he had not objected to the Address or supported the Amendment, because he would not seem to countenance the many mischievous principles and suggestions which had been heard in that House the last two days from the Mover of the Amendment."

611.

To Lord Sheffield.

Lausanne, Dec. 14th, 1792.

*Our little storm has now completely subsided, and we are again spectators, though anxious spectators, of the general tempest that invades or threatens almost every country of Europe. Our troops are every day disbanding and returning home, and the greatest part of the French have evacuated the neighbourhood of Geneva. Monsieur Barthelemy, whom you have seen secretary in London, is most courteously entertained, as ambassador, by the Helvetic body. He is now at Berne, where a Diet will speedily be convened; the language on both sides is now pacific, and even friendly, and some hopes are given of a provision for the officers of the Swiss guards who have survived the Massacres of Paris.

January 1st, 1793.

REVOLUTION AT GENEVA.

With the return of peace I have relapsed into my former indolence; but now awakening, after a fortnight's slumber, I have little or nothing to add, with regard to the internal state of this country, only the revolution of Geneva has already taken place, as I announced, but sooner than I expected. The Swiss troops had no sooner evacuated the place, than the *Egaliseurs*, as they are called, assembled in arms; and as no resistance was made, no blood was shed on the occasion. They seized the gates, disarmed the garrison, imprisoned the magistrates, imparted the rights of citizens to all the rabble of the town and country, and proclaimed a *national* convention, which has not yet met. They are all for a pure and absolute Democracy; but wish to remain a small independent state, whilst others aspire to become a part of the republic of France; and as the latter, though less numerous, are more violent and absurd than their adversaries, it is highly probable that they will succeed. The Citizens of the best families and fortunes have retired from Geneva into the Pays de Vaud, but the French methods of recalling or proscribing emigrants will soon be adopted. You must have observed, that Savoy has now become *le Department du Mont Blanc.* I cannot satisfy myself whether the mass of the people is pleased or displeased with the change; but my noble scenery is clouded by the democratical aspect of twelve leagues of the opposite coast, which every morning obtrude themselves on my view. I here conclude the first part of the history of our Alpine troubles, and now consider myself as disengaged from all promises of periodical writing. Upon the whole, I kept it beyond our expectation; nor do I think that you have been sufficiently astonished by the wonderful effort of the triple dispatch.

You must now succeed to my task, and I shall expect, during the winter, a regular political journal of the events of your greater world. You are on the theatre, and may often be behind the scenes. You can always see, and may sometimes foresee. My own choice has indeed transported me into a foreign land; but I am truly attached, from interest and inclination, to my native country; and even as a Citizen of the World, I wish the stability and happiness of England, the sole great refuge of mankind against the opposite mischiefs of despotism and Democracy. I was indeed alarmed, and the more so, as I saw that you were not without apprehension; but I now glory in the triumph of reason and genuine patriotism, which seems to pervade the country; nor do I dislike some mixture of popular enthusiasm, which may be requisite to encounter our mad or wicked enemies with equal arms.

The behaviour of* Fox *rather afflicts than surprises me. You may remember what I told you last year at Lausanne, when you attempted his defence, that his inmost soul was deeply tinged with Democracy. Such wild opinions cannot easily be reconciled with his excellent understanding, but "tis true 'tis pity, and pity 'tis, 'tis true.' He will surely ruin himself in the opinion of the wise and good men of his party. You have now crushed the daring subverters of the Constitution, but I now fear the moderate well-meaners—reformers. Do not, I beseech you, tamper with Parliamentary representation. The present House of Commons forms in *practice* a body of Gentlemen who must always sympathize with the interest and opinions of the people, and the slightest innovation launches you without rudder or compass on a dark and dangerous ocean of Theoretical experiment. On this subject I am indeed serious.

Upon the whole, I like the beginning of '93 better than the end of '92. The illusion seems to break away throughout Europe. I think England and Switzerland are safe. Brabant adheres to the old constitution. The Germans are disgusted with the rapine and insolence of their deliverers. The Pope is resolved to head his armies, and the Lazzaroni of Naples have presented St. Januarius with a gold fuzee, to fire on the Brigands Français. So much for politics, which till now never had such possession of my mind. Next post I will write about myself and my own designs. Alas, your poor eyes! make the Maria write; I will speedily answer her. My Lady is still dumb. The German posts are now slow and irregular. You had better write by the way of

France, under cover, directed to *Le Citoyen Rebours, à Pontarlier, France.* Adieu.*

Ever yours,
G.

612.

To Lord Sheffield.

Lausanne, Jan. 6th, 1793.

*There was formerly a time when our correspondence was a painful discussion of my private affairs; a vexatious repetition of losses, of disappointments, of sales, &c. These affairs are now decently arranged: but public cares have now succeeded to private anxiety, and our whole attention is lately turned from Lenborough and Beriton, to the political state of France and of Europe. From these politics, however, one letter shall be free, while I talk of myself and of my own plans; a subject most interesting to a friend, and only to a friend.

I know not whether I am sorry or glad that my expedition has been postponed to the present year. It is true, that I now wish myself in England, and almost repent that I did not grasp the opportunity when the obstacles were comparatively smaller than they are now likely to prove. Yet had I reached you last summer before the month of August, a considerable portion of my time would be now elapsed, and I should already begin to think of my departure. If the Gout should spare me this winter, (and as yet I have not felt any symptom,) and if the spring should make a soft and early appearance, it is my intention to be with you in Downing-street before the end of April, and thus to enjoy six weeks or two months of the most agreeable season of London and the neighbourhood, after the hurry of parliament is subsided, and before the great rural dispersion. As the banks of the Rhine and the Belgic provinces are completely overspread with anarchy and war, I have made up my mind to pass through the territories of the French Republic. From the best and most recent information, I am satisfied that there is little or no real danger in the journey; and I must arm myself with patience to support the vexatious insolence of democratical tyranny. I have even a sort of curiosity to spend some days at Paris, to assist at the debates of the Pandæmonium, to seek an introduction to the principal Devils, and to contemplate a new form of public and private life, which never existed before, and which I devoutly hope will not long continue to exist. Should the obstacles of health or weather confine me at Lausanne till the month of May, I shall scarcely be able to resist the temptation of passing some part at least of the summer in my own little paradise.

But all these schemes must ultimately depend on the great question of peace and War, which will indeed be speedily determined. Should France become impervious to an English traveller, what must I do? I shall not easily resolve to explore my way through the unknown language and abominable roads of the interior parts of Germany, to embark in Holland, or perhaps at Hamburgh, and to be finally intercepted by a French privateer. My stay in England appears not less doubtful than the means of transporting myself. Should I arrive in the spring, it is possible, and barely possible, that I should return here in the autumn; it is much more probable that I shall pass the winter, and there may be even a chance of my giving my own country a longer tryal. In my letter to My Lady I fairly exposed the decline of Lausanne; but such an establishment as mine must not be lightly abandoned; nor can I discover what adequate mode of life my private circumstances, easy as they now are, could afford me in England. London and Bath have doubtless their respective merits, and I could wish to reside within a day's journey of Sheffield-place. But a state of perfect happiness is not to be found here below; and in the possession of my library, house, and garden, with the relicks of our society, and a frequent intercourse with the Neckers, I may still be tolerably content. Among the disastrous changes of Lausanne, I must principally reckon the approaching dissolution of poor Severy and his family. He is still alive, but in such hopeless and painful decay, that we no longer conceal our wishes for his speedy release. I never loved nor esteemed him so much as in this last mortal disease, which he supports with a degree of courage, patience, and even chearfulness, beyond all belief. His wife, whose whole time and soul are devoted to him, is almost sinking under her long anxiety. The children are most amiably assiduous to both their parents, and at all events, his filial duties and worldly cares must detain the son some time at home.

A LITERARY SECRET.

And now approach, and let me drop into your most private ear, a literary secret. Of the Memoirs little has been done, and with that little I am not satisfied. They must be postponed till a mature season; and I much doubt whether the book and the author can ever see the light at the same time. But I have long revolved in my mind another scheme of Biographical writing: the lives, or rather the characters, of the most eminent persons in arts and arms, in Church and State, who have flourished in Britain from the reign of Henry VIII. to the present age. This work, extensive as it may be, would be an amusement rather than a toil: the materials are accessible in our own language, and for the most part ready to my hands: but the subject, which would afford a rich display of human nature and domestic history, would powerfully address itself to the feelings of every Englishman. The taste or fashion of the times seems to delight in picturesque decorations; and this series of British portraits might aptly be accompanied by the respective heads, taken from originals, and engraved by the best masters. Alderman Boydell, and his son-in-law, Mr. George Nicol, bookseller in Pallmall, are the great undertakers in this line;* but your negociation with them will require the dexterity of an Auckland or a Malmsbury, as it is most essential that I be solicited, and do not solicit. In your walk through Pall Mall, you may call on the bookseller, who appeared to me an intelligent man, and after some general questions about his Edition of Shakespeare, &c., you may open the British portraits as an idea of your own to which I am perfectly a stranger. If he kindles at the thought, and eagerly claims my alliance, you will begin to hesitate. "I am afraid, Mr. Nichols, that we shall hardly persuade my friend to engage in so great a work. Gibbon is old, and rich, and lazy. However, you may make the tryal, and if you have a mind to write to Lausanne (as I do not know when he will be in England), I will send the application."

On the receipt of his proposal, the business will come properly before me, and it will then be in my power to deliberate, to demur, to state observations, and to prescribe terms. Should Nichols or Boydell be cool, you will be still colder; I shall hear from you the tone and motives of their refusal, and on my arrival in England I shall be free to consider, whether it may suit me to proceed in a mere literary work without any other decorations than those which it may derive from the pen of the author. *It is a serious truth, that I am no longer ambitious of fame or money; that my habits of industry are much impaired, and that I have reduced my studies to be the loose amusement of my morning hours, the repetition of which will insensibly lead me to the last term of existence. And for this very reason I shall not be sorry to bind myself by a liberal engagement, from which I may not with honour recede.

Before I conclude, we must say a word or two of Parliamentary and pecuniary concerns. 1. We all admire the generous spirit with which you damned the Assassins, but I hope that your abjuration of all future connection with Fox was not quite so peremptory as it is stated in the French papers. Let him do what he will, I must love the dog. The opinion of Parliament in favour of Louis XVI. was declared in a manner worthy of the representatives of a great and wise nation. It will certainly have a powerful effect; and if the poor King be not already murdered, I am satisfied that his life is in safety: but is such a life worth his care? Our debates will now become every day more interesting; and as I only expect from you opinions and anecdotes, I most earnestly conjure you to send me Woodfall's Register, with the margins cut close, as often (and that must be very often) as the occasion deserves it.* My direction, more distinctly than in my last letter, must be under cover to Le Citoyen le Rebours, Maitre de Poste a Pontarlier, dans le department du Doubs. *I now spare no expense for news.*

2. Will it never be possible to get me a good Mortgage for my £3000? I believe it may be advisable to change my stock from the Short Annuities, the value of which is wearing every day, to the 3 per Cents., which are now so low. Notwithstanding Sainsbury's death, I hope the Buriton interest is regularly paid; when there is a stoppage, the Goslings might give you or me notice that I may not be exposed to the danger of overdrawing. I want to have Caplin's direction, as I may have some orders that should be executed before my arrival. We have written twice to Ostend without obtaining an answer. Have you had no better success? I tremble for my Madeira.

I want some account of Mrs. G.'s health. Will my lady never write? How can people be so indolent! I suppose this will find you at Sheffield-place during the recess, and that the heavy baggage will not move until after the birthday. Shall I be with you by the first of May? The Gods only know. I almost wish that I had accompanied Madame de Staël.

Ever yours,
E. G.

613.

Lord Sheffield to Edward Gibbon.

Sheffield Place, Jan. 23rd, 1793.

Your silence, which seemed long after your extraordinary epistolary efforts, threw the family into a state of revolt; we abjured writing to you until we had further information of your state, &c. Your letters of the 1st & 6th (the latter rec^d. this day) promoted an immediate search for this large sheet of paper.

LORD SHEFFIELD ON SWISS POLITICS.

In respect to the French Revolution at Geneva, I consider it in a very serious light. I am perfectly satisfied that if a War with England does not take place, that the execrable french demons will produce the same Revolution in the Pays de Vaud. From what has passed lately, I have entirely changed my opinion of the Swiss character. I no longer expect that noble resistance which was supposed characteristic of them. This mortifies me, but I see a greater probability of your re-establishment in England than I had flattered myself with before. I acknowledge that no creature could leave your spot without deep regret. It is eminently beautiful and pleasant. Its convenience is of your own creation, your books are there—but tho' the translation of them to this island might cost you £400, it would not be impossible expence.

But war between this country and France is more certain than you seem to think it. You could not have read Lord Grenville's notice of Chauvelin's Paper. I like it much, it seemed to show that War is inevitable—indeed letters received this day mention it as certain, and Chauvelin's departure is immediately expected. The Devils seem damnably afraid of us, and I hope with reason. There can be little doubt that Spain and Holland will heartily join and compleat the Circle of Fire, except on the frontier of your poor Swiss. Surely it will be more politick and more economick for us to engage, when backed by all Europe, than to fight them single-handed hereafter. Our merchants however affect to be panic-struck on Acct. of our Turkey fleet, which they say is worth a million sterling. I should not forget a strange dilemma in which we find ourselves through a most extraordinary neglect of that essential naval store—cordage. All the Rope-yards in England will not in a considerable time be able to supply the quantity that is wanted. I have the pleasure however of observing that the War is not likely to be unpopular. Charles F. and they who bellowed most against it certainly most wish it, because it is the only thing that can eventually overturn the Administration. But you remark how few join in the cry against War. None of the innumerable declarations of Associations give the smallest hint of disapprobation.

FOX AND THE DUKE OF PORTLAND.

I believe I mentioned that I thought, if C. Fox should manage prudently, that the Party would not suffer essentially. But he seems totally to have discarded all attention to that respectable and most necessary though vulgar condescension. In the Debate, when Sir Gilbert Elliot stated that the Duke of Portland entirely differed from C. Fox, the latter distinctly said, that he had no reason to think so, but if that was the case, there was nothing left for him to do, but either to carry on the most fruitless opposition or to quit Parliament. It is said he went next morning to the Duke and repeated his threat to quit Parliament. The Duke was induced to send the Marquis of Titchfield to the House of Commons to contradict in a degree, or at least give a different colour to what Sir Gilbert had said, although the latter had taken down in writing the Duke's sentiments which he had delivered to the House. It is a most serious business to cast off or deny the Leader of the Party in the House of Commons, and such a man as Fox, with whom he has always acted. But it seems probable from the spirit of the times that the Duke will ruin himself with the Publick by adhering to him. It is probable that he will still remain enthralled with a connection which at this moment is neither consistent with his opinions, his interest, nor his estimation with those who have hitherto highly respected him; should that happen, it is impossible to unite two confidences so entirely opposite to each other, and no party can hold men together whose views for the Publick Interest are so totally different. The state of the times will accelerate decision. The ambiguous state in which things were left at the time of the Recess, must in some way be cleared up before our meeting, which is to take place a week hence.

Every appearance indicates War—a War for the very existence of the Constitution—half measures cannot be pursued with safety or honour. Charles seemed disposed to support the enemies of the country, against the country, as he and his Party did the last War. You will recollect how it used to affect my nerves, and how I used to execrate the conduct of Opposition. The second attempt at the same vile game revolts me in the highest degree, and I think it will be impossible for me ever to follow such a leader. I have kept out of the way, yet I find the Country Gentlemen and many others much disposed to follow the style I took up so vigorously on the proposition being made to acknowledge the Republick. What I then said is *vaunted* throughout Europe far beyond what it deserves. It has been nobly seconded by the Country Gentlemen. It certainly was not pronounced with indifference, but with the most hearty zeal. It was a natural effort, and probably the best of the kind I had ever made, and the friends of Government said it was the best and most useful speech that will probably be made this Sessions.

I hear since my absence that others and of high consequence are tired and disgusted with the uncertainty of the situation in which some of our friends have placed themselves, and with the multiplied intrigues that have been used to keep them in that state. In the country, by all accounts, and certainly in town, there has been a very general consent to the measures which have been taken to resist all that torrent of evil which was pouring in upon us from France; and it is truly mortifying, that those, who have done great good by their early favor to those measures, should suffer their conduct to be obscured and lose the credit of their good intentions. I believe I mentioned that I had reason to suppose L^d. L. would not accept the Seals, unless there should be something like a general coalition. But this was before the meeting of Parliament. Several of my correspondents say that he is certainly to have them immediately. The *disorganized* state of the Party and the wrong-headedness of a Chief among the Commons have perhaps promoted it.

In respect to your passage to this country. War renders it very difficult. After a declaration, you, especially a notorious aristocrate, will hardly venture it—a degree of acrimony is to be expected, and ought to be promoted by us between the two countries. The Rhine will not be a desireable route for such an unweildy personage, who could not easily shift as difficulties arose, but you might travel the road by which Mrs. Moss returned,—by Stutgard and Frankfort, without touching upon the Rhine till she came to Cologne. From Cologne or Dusseldörf you might find your way to the Hague, and there our friend Lord Auckland would contrive to amuse you till he could find a passage in a Frigate for you to England. I by no means intend to recommend this route to you early in the Spring, but in Summer, when the invading armies will probably have left the Rhine in their rear. But until they have left its neighbourhood—Frankfort, &c., I do not see a chance of even a more active person passing that way without disagrement. In short, I should think you rather wild if you attempted to go to Paris, even if there were not war; and if you were there, the uncivilized crowding at the Pandemonium would not delight you.

EXECUTION OF LOUIS XVI.

Since this was began a letter from the D. of Richmond announces the horrid account received yesterday from Paris, that, the King was condemned to death on Sunday, was to be executed on Monday, and that a general massacre of his friends was expected. I have not words to express myself. Life cannot be desireable to the unfortunate man—the abomination will in the end be useful—the execration of the World will be uniform and the extirpation of the miscreants surely must and will follow. The abhorrence of their principles will be compleat check to the further spreading of the greatest evils we have ever heard of, and on account of the odium which shall fall on their whole system. I rejoice that the worse than savage act should be done by the Assembly rather than by a tumultuous mob. I can hardly think on any other subject.

Another letter acquaints me that Parliament will meet for business sooner than I expected. Dundas has given notice of a message to come down on Monday the 31st, equivalent to a declaration of War.

I shall send the diary as you desire; I was astonished to receive your letters with the Pontarlier post-mark. You may know best; I should not have supposed France the surest way for them, as the War cannot last. I shall not think of selling your stock to lay it out on a Mortgage at present. I shall consult Darrell on the rational plan of exchanging the short annuities into 3 per Cents. I have told you more than once that I had information of your Madeira, and that it was moving towards you at last. Whether de Custine has since tasted it, I cannot say, but I shall enquire. I fear some letters must have miscarried. Mention dates.

I shall never consent to your dropping the Memoirs. Keep that work always going; but you should decide whether the book and the author are to see the light together, because it might be differently filled up according to that decision. A man may state many things in a posthumous work, that he might not in another; the latter often checks the introduction of many curious thoughts and facts. But I like your Biographical plan very much. It will give great satisfaction, and it may last as long as yourself. What think you of the manner of Plutarch? I shall mention the matter to Nicholls. Well-engraved portraits is a decoration that will be desired by all. We have a slight work by Birch which you know, and which accompanies some very good portraits.

We hear with most sincere concern of the state of that eminently honest *gentleman*, poor de Severy, and were highly concerned for the family. It must be obvious to you that a tolerable situation for the son, in the way you wish, becomes every day more unpromising. Nothing but the North and part of Germany is open, and the passage there during the war will not tempt our great people to send their sons, and I know and you may readily suppose that the market is overstocked in the greatest degree by the numberless Frenchmen of fashion who are soliciting for the office on any terms. So many solicit for them, Severy has scarce a chance during War.

I saw in a Newspaper some time ago a Paragraph which stated several circumstances concerning your present situation at Lausanne, and added that the account came from a noble Lord. I was a good deal annoyed, altho' the circumstance of great incorrectness proved that it did not come from me.

614.

Lord Sheffield to Edward Gibbon.

Downing Street, 29th Jan., '93.

Yesterday I dined with the Lord High Chancellor Loughborough and his Lady just as he had returned from the Queen's House with the Seals. I came from the country the day before to attend the King's message, which you will see in the papers. I am provoked to write to you a post sooner than I intended by letters from a miserable Frenchman in Switzerland, who signs himself Naijeiraud, chez Madame Lizardex, née Valtravers, au Bureau d'Avis, à Lausanne. He dates his letter from Payerne and Friburg. They contain expressions of the greatest distress. He supposes me the Director of all the hospitable measures in England. Enquire for him immediately, do something for him immediately, and learn whether he does not merit more. His letters are shocking to read. I shall not dislike to pay you; yet as you are a rich old fellow, I am of opinion you will take an opportunity of doing something yourself or of ordering some subscriptions in your name in this country.

FOX AND HIS FOLLOWERS.

I observe no others going into office with Lord Loughborough. The D. of Port. is enthralled by Charles Fox, notwithstanding he declares he thinks as we do on the present topics, who do not mean to follow Ch. Fox again. Many adhere to D. of Portland however, yet highly disapproving C. Fox's conduct. The latter, Erskine and Grey, &c., were daily and publickly with Chauvelin, &c., before his departure.

Maret is just come with credentials from the Republick, and it is said with *carte blanche,* and to enquire whether we will receive Dumouriez; offers to withdraw Troops from all the countries attacked, to do what we please in respect to Commercial Treaty, and to abide our arrangement of Peace with Europe. If this be true, it may embarras ministers here how to treat with Pache or men who may not exist two days. Would it not be infamous in respect to all Europe to treat with them at all?

615.

Lord Sheffield to Edward Gibbon.

D. S., 5th Feb., '93.

I obey your orders in sending the account of the last great debate, by the first post. Poor Woodfall is in a strait waistcoat, but the account is not badly given, & I have examined and find it the best. Charles F. told us distinctly that the Sovereignty was absolutely in the people, that the Monarchy was elective, otherwise the Dynasty of Brunswick had no right, and that the majority of the people, whenever they thought proper to change the form of Government, had a right to cashier the King. Perhaps the late conduct of the Prince of Wales (you know he has discarded Fox, Sheridan, Erskine, &c.) has promoted the utterance of these things. That which was called Opposition seems suspended in a comical state. The Duke of Portland adheres to Fox, and all the party disapprove Fox's conduct and almost all vote against him. I see no symptom as yet of anybody taking office with Lord Loughborough. I believe he is delicate in saying anything lest he should appear to use means to take from the Duke of P. The war is popular except among merchants, and those of London consider it as an unavoidable calamity. We are sending Artillery to the coasts of Sussex and Kent, and an Expedition to the West Indies. The beginning, particularly, of Pitt's speech was very fine. Fox's not so good as usual; and as to Windham, I should think he is become the best, at least the most sensible speaker of the whole.

616.

To Lord Sheffield.

Begun Feb. 9,—ended Feb. 18, 1793.

: DEATH OF M. DE SEVERY.
---

*The struggle is at length over, and poor de Severy is no more! He expired about ten days ago, after every vital principle had been exhausted by a perpetual complication of disorders, which had lasted above five months: and a mortification in one of his legs, that gradually rose to the more noble parts, was the immediate cause of his death. His patience and even chearfulness supported him to the fatal moment; and he enjoyed every comfort that could alleviate his situation, the skill of his physicians, the assiduous tenderness of his family, and the kind sympathy not only of his particular friends, but even of common acquaintance, and generally of the whole town. The stroke has been severely felt, yet I have the satisfaction to perceive that Madame de Severy's health is not affected; and we may hope that in time she will recover a tolerable share of composure and happiness. Her firmness has checked the violent sallies of grief; her gentleness has preserved her from the worst of symptoms, a dry, silent despair. She loves to talk of her irreparable loss, she descants with pleasure on his virtues; her words are interrupted with tears, but those tears are her best relief; and her tender feelings will insensibly subside into an affectionate remembrance. Wilhelm is much more deeply wounded than I could imagine, or than he expected himself: nor have I ever seen the affliction of a son and heir more lively and sincere. Severy was indeed a very valuable man: without any shining qualifications, he was endowed in a high degree with good sense, honour, and benevolence; and few men have filled with more propriety their circle in private life. For myself, I have had the misfortune of knowing him too late, and of losing him too soon. But enough of this melancholy subject.

The affairs of this theatre, which must always be minute, are now grown so tame and tranquil, that they no longer deserve the historian's pen. The new constitution of Geneva is slowly forming, without much noise or any bloodshed; and the patriots, who have staid in hopes of guiding and restraining the multitude, flatter themselves that they shall be able at least to prevent their mad countrymen from giving themselves to France, the only mischief that would be absolutely irretrievable. The Revolution of Geneva is of less consequence to *us*, however, than that of Savoy; but our fate will depend on the general event, rather than on these particular causes. In the meanwhile we hope to be quiet spectators of the struggle of this year; and we seem to have assurances that both the Emperor and the French will compound for the neutrality of the Swiss. The Helvetic body does not acknowledge the Republic of France; but Barthelemy, their Ambassador, resides at Baden, and steals, like Chauvelin, into a kind of extra official negociation. All spirit of opposition is quelled in the canton of Bern, and the perpetual banishment of the Van Berchem family has scarcely excited a murmur. It will probably be followed by that of Colonel Polier, &c.; the crime alledged in their sentence is the having assisted at the federation dinner at Rolle two years ago; and as they are absent, I could almost wish that they had been summoned to appear, and heard in their own defence. To the general supineness of the inhabitants of Lausanne I must ascribe, that the death of Louis XVI. has been received with less horror and indignation than I could have wished. I was much tempted to go into mourning, and probably should, had the Dutchess been still here; but as the only Englishman of any mark, I was afraid of being singular; more especially as our French emigrants, either from prudence or poverty, do not wear black, nor do even the Neckers. Have you read his discourse for the King? It might indeed supersede the necessity of mourning.

FRENZY-FEVER OF THE FRENCH.

I should judge from your last letter, and from the *Diary* (alas, poor Woodfall!), that the French declaration of war must have rather surprised you. I wish (though I know not how) it could have been avoided, that we might still have continued to enjoy our safe and prosperous neutrality. You will not doubt my best wishes for the destruction of the miscreants; but I love England still more than I hate France. All reasonable chances are in favour of a confederacy, such as was never opposed to the ambition of Louis XIV.; but, after the experience of last year, I distrust reason, and confess myself fearful for the event. The French are strong in numbers, activity, enthusiasm; they are rich in rapine; and although their strength may be only that of a frenzy-feaver, they may do infinite mischief to their neighbours before they can be reduced to a strait wastecoat. I dread the effects that may be produced on the minds of the people by the increase of debt and taxes, probable losses, and possible mismanagement. Our trade must suffer; and though projects of invasion have been always abortive, I cannot forget that the fleets and armies of Europe have failed before the towns in America, which have been taken and plundered by a handful of Buccaneers. I know nothing of Pitt as a War Minister; but it affords me much satisfaction that the intrepid wisdom of the new Chancellor is introduced into the Cabinet. I wish, not merely on your own account, that you were placed in an active, useful station in Government. I should not dislike you Secretary at War.

I have little more to say of myself, or of my journey to England: you know my intentions, and the great events of Europe must determine whether they can be carried into execution this summer. If * * * * * has warmly adopted *your* idea, I shall speedily hear from him; but, in truth, I know not what will be my answer: I see difficulties which at first did not occur: I doubt my own perseverance, and my fancy begins to wander into new paths. The amusement of reading and thinking may perhaps satisfy a man who has paid his debt to the public; and there is more pleasure in building castles in the air than on the ground. I shall contrive some small assistance for your correspondent, though I cannot learn any thing that distinguishes him from many of his countrymen. We have had our full share of poor emigrants; but if you wish that any thing extraordinary should be done for this man, you must send me a measure. Adieu. I embrace My lady and the Maria, as also Louisa. Perhaps I may soon write, without expecting an answer.*

Ever yours,
E. G.

617.

Edward Gibbon to Lord Chancellor Loughborough.

Rolle, February 23rd, 1793.

*My Lord,

I do not merely congratulate your lordship's promotion to the first civil office in the kingdom; an office which your abilities have long deserved, and which your temperate ambition, if I am not mistaken, had repeatedly declined. My satisfaction does not arise from an assurance of the wisdom and vigour which administration will derive from the support of so respectable an ally. But as a friend to government in general, I most sincerely rejoice that you are now armed in the common cause against the most dangerous fanatics that have ever invaded the peace of Europe; against the new barbarians, who labour to confound the order and happiness of society; and who, in the opinion of thinking men, are not less the enemies of subjects than of kings. The hopes of the wise and good are now fixed on the success of England; and I am persuaded that my personal attachment to your lordship will be amply gratified by the important share which your counsels will assume in that success. I could wish that some of your former associates possessed sufficient strength of mind to extricate themselves from the toils of prejudice and party. But I grieve that a man, whom it is impossible for me not to love and admire, should refuse to obey the voice of his country; and I begin to fear that the powerful genius of Mr. Fox, instead of being useful, will be adverse to the public service. At this momentous crisis we should inlist our whole force of virtue, ability, and spirit; and without any view to his private advantage, I could wish that our active friend, Lord Sheffield, might be properly stationed in some part of the line.

LORD CHANCELLOR LOUGHBOROUGH.

M. Necker, in whose house I am now residing on a visit of some days, wishes me to express the sentiments of esteem and consideration which he entertains for your Lordship's character. As a friend to the interest of mankind, he is warmly attached to the wellfare of Great Britain, which he has long revered as the first, and, perhaps, as the last azylum of genuine liberty. His late eloquent work, *du Pouvoir Executif,* which your lordship has assuredly read, is a valuable testimony of his esteem for our constitution; and the testimony of a sagacious and impartial stranger may have taught some of our countrymen to value the political blessings which they have been tempted to despise.

I cherish a lively hope of being in England, and of paying my respects to your lordship before the end of the summer: but the events of the year are so uncertain, and the sea and land are encompassed with so many difficulties and dangers, that I am doubtful whether it will be practicable for me to execute my purpose.

I am, my lord, most respectfully, and your lordship will permit me to add most affectionately, your most obedient and faithful humble servant.*

618.

Lord Sheffield to Edward Gibbon.

D. S., 15th March, '93.

We had intelligence of poor de Severy's death two or three weeks before the receipt of your letter. I had always thought of him as you describe him, "honourable, benevolent, and sensible." His family must lament him for ever, and I know none more likely to feel the loss.

As to the Pais de Vaud, the thorough diversion caused by the War with England will leave it in a sort of humiliated security, but I have little doubt, if that event had not taken place, that the revolutionary principle would have been insinuated thro' Geneva to the Pais de Vaud. The dereliction of character, to which the Swiss have thought it expedient to submit, subjects them to the whims of fortune and of nations. Perhaps, if the World should recover its senses, it may find itself nearly as it was, except what its dignity may have suffered; but you do not deserve to be a nation, wretches so compleatly in awe of the *sans cullotes*, that they did not dare even to wear mourning. As for you, you are a damned, unworthy, temporizing son of a bitch, and shall only be deemed a renegado Englishman in future. Never was a mourning so general in England. I did not (who seldom wore it in the morning before) quit it for a quarter of a moment. I was glad to see the lower ranks indignant, although to be sure Louis XVI.'s fort was being a martyr. It may be also added that a more innocent man was never more undeservedly put to death. I should have been indeed astonished that the Neckers did not wear mourning, if the panic meanness had not been so general in your parts. Although I may not flatter myself that *sans culotterie* will be suppressed in one campaign, yet I have few doubts in respect to the success of the Armies which attack France, especially after the experience of last campaign. It will not be necessary to take the beast by the horns and attack artillery in front, &c. In such a country as where war now flourishes, it will be easy to turn an enemy, and when an Army like that of France in such a case is obliged to make a movement, it is undone. As to the equipment of fleets, we seem to make a poor business of it. Lord Sandwich in a fortnight did much more than we have done in three months and an halfe; a timid style in respect to pressing produces the evil.

I manœuvred your business in respect to Nichols in my best possible manner. In return to my wishing he could tempt you and that I would second, he talked most feelingly that he and Boydell had £40,000—everything—involved in the Shakespear. He seemed to wish to talk over such a subject when you come to England. He thought such a work would be more than you could undertake, suggested the idea of your being the Chief—shewed me the Life of Milton by Hailey, prefixed to Mr. Cowper's edition, and said that kind of writing was his fort. Persevere; as you may be in England in a few months it is unnecessary to say more at present.

I have sent by Seigneux, Lally's defence of Louis XVI., and Le Songe d'un Anglois; you will be pleased with both. I sent 'Modern Gardening,' and the 'Standing Orders of my Regiment,' to Meluner, the Captain of Highlanders, with whom we were so much pleased. I sent in the same parcel a number of odd things relative to Establishments, Insurance, &c., which Commissioner Fischer might like, but I was obliged to reduce the parcel on account of its size, and I know not whether the remainder is worth sending to him—but you will judge.

MADAME DE STAEL IN ENGLAND.

Madame de Stael has lived in the neighbourhood of Dorking with Miss Burney, not forgetting M. de Narbonne. She is lately come to town; we endeavour to be civil. I am to conduct her to the Tower, &c., and she and some of her friends are to dine here. Small assistance will be sufficient for my correspondent, of whom I know nothing but his letter, and you say he has nothing to distinguish him. I have applied to those who were likely to be useful on the subject of what you mentioned for Wilhelm de S., but as yet without a glimpse of success. The market is over-stocked. The travelleable country is greatly circumscribed, and the measure of sending a leader is greatly exploded. I spoke to Lord Porchester, and he with great satisfaction asserted the excellence of the line he had pursued of sending his son with his schoolfellow. As speaking to people on these matters does not make so much impression as writing, I have applied to some by letter.

619.

Lord Sheffield to Edward Gibbon.

D. S., 26th March, '93.

My letter of last week did not enter on your affairs of money because Darell had not given me a final opinion; yesterday we had a full discourse thereon. The 3 per cents may sink more in proportion than the short annuities. The latter have fallen more than Mr. Darell expected, which he acknowledged when I remarked the opinion he had formerly given you. On the other hand, the 3 per cents are (for war-like times) surprisingly high. The constant regular purchase of one million of the stocks in the course of a year takes the whole of the floating stock; the great bankruptcies which have taken place, and the shyness of our monied men to discount Bills,—all these circumstances keep up the Funds. The extravagant extension of credit have produced the evil that was expected. It has been carried beyond anything that was ever known before. The War has helped to bring forward the crisis, but is not the cause of the mischief.

We seem to be *en train* to receive good tidings by every mail, but I cannot be content on the subject of our Fleet. The Publick begins to arraign the First Lord of Admiralty in respect to alertness and attention. It is extraordinary that John Bull bore so long the alarming state of the Mediterranean, 52 French ships of war of all sizes riding triumphant and insulting all nations in that sea—a superior French Fleet also in the West Indies. I flatter myself however we are going to do something there; nothing can prove the abject state of Holland more than the extreme joy on receiving the pitifull succour of 2000 English troops. The circumstance of sending the King's son had the greatest effect, and proved that England was in earnest.

Your late neglects have almost obliterated your famous three letters. You do not say whether you have received any letters from us; not the least notice is taken of Maria's or my letters. She wrote a good deal on our Politicks, she sent my *much admired* Foxippic copied from the Newspaper, also a detail of the massacre of the priests aux Carmes, and other matters. The Chancellor leaned from the Woolsack a few days ago, to tell me he had a letter from you, and asked where was Rolle. I am so abominably engaged that we seldom meet.

We had a very pleasant party here at dinner last Saturday to meet Madame de Stael, the Prince de Poix, Lally Tollendal, Princess d'Henin, Malouet,

Baron de Gillier. Narbonne was invited, but engaged. We all went in the evening to Lady Catherine Douglas, where Madame de Stael rather astonished the Chancellor. In conversation she disputed every principle of Government and Politicks—a kind of tête-à-tête. There is a great prejudice against her. She is supposed to be the most intriguing democrate likely to set the Thames on fire. I can hardly get people to agree that she is eminently lively, pleasant, endowed with extraordinary mental ability, though somewhat ridiculous. She goes out of Town Tuesday, and talks of going soon to Switzerland.

You do not mention whether you have rec^d. your Madeira. I have heard nothing lately of Mrs. Gibbon. I have hopes you will soon have a clear country to Frankfort, Cologne, and the Hague. My Lady and Maria contrive to go out daily. The latter not well.

620.

To Lord Sheffield.

Lausanne, April 27, 1793.

*My Dearest Friend, for such you most truly are, nor does there exist a person who obtains, or shall ever obtain, a superior place in my esteem and affection.

DEATH OF LADY SHEFFIELD.

After too long a silence I was sitting down to write, when, only yesterday morning (such is now the irregular slowness of the English post) I was suddenly struck, indeed struck to the heart, by the fatal intelligence from Sir Henry Clinton and M. de Lally. Alas! what is life, and what are our hopes and projects! When I embraced her at your departure from Lausanne, could I imagine that it was for the last time? When I postponed to another summer my journey to England, could I apprehend that I never, never should see her again? I have often deplored the nervous complaints which so deeply affected her happiness and spirits, but I always hoped that she would spin her feeble thread to a long duration, and that her delicate frame would survive (as is often the case) many constitutions of a stouter appearance. In four days! in your absence, in that of her children! But she is now at rest; and if there be a future state, her mild virtues have surely entitled her to the reward of pure and perfect felicity. It is for you that I feel; and I can judge of your sentiments by comparing them with my own. I have lost, it is true, an amiable and affectionate friend, whom I had known and loved above three and twenty years, and whom I often styled by the endearing name of sister. But you are deprived of the companion of your life, the wife of your choice, and the mother of your children—poor children! The energy of Maria, and the softness of Louisa, render them almost equally the objects of my tenderest compassion. I do not wish to aggravate your grief; but, in the sincerity of friendship, I cannot hold a different language. I know the impotence of reason, and I much fear that the strength of your character will serve to make a sharper and more lasting impression.

The only consolation in these melancholy tryals to which human life is exposed, the only one at least in which I have any confidence, is the presence of a real friend; and of that, as far as it depends on myself, you shall not be destitute. I regret the few days that must be lost in some necessary preparations; but I trust that to-morrow se'nnight (May the fifth) I shall be able to set forwards on my journey to England; and when this letter reaches you, I shall be considerably advanced on my way. As it is yet prudent to keep at a respectful distance from the banks of the French Rhine, I shall incline a little to the right, and proceed by Schaffhausen and Stutgard to Frankfort and Cologne: the Austrian Netherlands are now open and safe, and I am sure of being able at least to pass from Ostend to Dover; from whence, without passing through London, I shall pursue the direct road to Sheffield-place. Unless I should meet with some unforeseen accidents and delays, I hope, before the end of the month, to share your solitude, and sympathise with your grief. All the difficulties of the journey, which my indolence had probably magnified, have now disappeared before a stronger passion; and you will not be sorry to hear, that, as far as Frankfort to Cologne, I shall enjoy the advantage of the society, the conversation, the German language, and the active assistance of Severy. His attachment to me is the sole motive which prompts him to undertake this troublesome journey: and as soon as he has seen me over the roughest ground, he will immediately return to Lausanne. The poor young man loved Lady S. as a mother, and the whole family is deeply affected by an event which reminds them too painfully of their own. Adieu. I could write Volumes, and shall therefore break off abruptly. I shall write on the road, and hope to find a few lines à poste restante at Frankfort and Brussells. Adieu; ever yours.*

621.

To Lord Sheffield.

Lausanne, May, 1793.

*My dear Friend,

: ADVICE FOR FRIENDS IN GRIEF.

I must write a few lines before my departure, though indeed I scarcely know what to say. Nearly a fortnight has now elapsed since the first melancholy tidings, without my having received the slightest subsequent accounts of your health and situation. Your own silence announces too forcibly how much you are involved in your own feelings; and I can but too easily conceive that a letter to me would be more painful than to an indifferent person. But that amiable man, Count Lally, might surely have written a second time; but your sister, who is probably with you; but Maria, alas! poor Maria! I am left in a state of darkness to the workings of my own fancy, which imagines every thing that is sad and shocking. What can I think of for your relief and comfort? I will not expatiate on those common-place topics, which have never dryed a single tear; but let me advise, let me urge, you to force yourself into business, as I would try to force myself into study. The mind must not be idle; if it be not exercised on external objects, it will prey on its own vitals.

A thousand little arrangements, which must precede a long Journey, have postponed my departure three or four days beyond the term which I had first appointed; but all is now in order, and I set off to-morrow, the ninth instant, with my Valet de Chambre, a courier on horseback, and Severy, with his servant, as far as Frankfort. I calculate my arrival at Sheffield-place (how I dread and desire to see that mansion!) for the first week in June, soon after this letter; but I will try to send you some later intelligence. I never found myself stronger, or in better health. The German road is now cleared, both of enemies and allies, and though I must expect fatigue, I have not any apprehensions of danger. It is scarcely possible that you should meet me at Frankfort, but I shall be much disappointed at not finding a line at Brussels or Ostend. Adieu. If there be any invisible guardians, may they watch over you and yours! Adieu.*

621*.

To Lady Elisabeth Foster.

Lausanne, May the 4th, 1793.

I know not whether you are already informed of the sudden death of poor Lady Sheffield after four days' illness; but I am sure that your feeling affectionate mind will not be surprized to hear that I set out for England next week, and that in a journey undertaken at the call of friendship all the dragons of the way have already vanished. I go by Basle, Frankfort, Cologne, Brussels, and Ostend, and I flatter myself that the success of our allied arms will contribute every week to open my passage; it is even possible, though scarcely probable, that I may embark from the English town of Calais. Your answer to my last letter is doubtless on the road and will follow me: but you must write immediately to Sheffield place, and I promise you a speedy and sincere account of our afflicted friend. I wish to hear of your motions and projects; I now sigh for your return to England, and shall be most bitterly disappointed if I have not the pleasure of seeing you in that happy island, yourself and the most amiable of Dutchesses before the end of the autumn: I cannot look with confidence beyond that period.

My friend and your Chevalier will guard me as far as Cologne or Frankfort; his tender attachment to his mother who is still very melancholy will recall him from thence to Lausanne; but in the course of next winter he has thoughts of visiting England. The circumstances of the times which impoverish every one, have persuaded him to listen to my advice of conducting on his travels some English pupill of fashion and fortune. Such a pupill will be fortunate in finding a real Gentleman, and I trust that the Dutchess and yourself will exert your omnipotence in providing some connection equally honourable and advantageous for my friend, and your sincere Votary. Adieu. Excuse brevity and address a Classic prayer in my behalf before some statue of Mercury the God of travellers.

622.

To his Stepmother.

Lausanne, May the 8th (my fifty-seventh birthday), 1793.

DEAR MADAM,

JOURNEY TO ENGLAND.

I have the pleasure of acquainting you that to-morrow, the 9th instant, I set forwards for England, but the pleasure of revisiting my friends and my native country is deeply embittered by the melancholy tidings from Downing Street, which have fixed and hastened my Journey. I travel by the way of Frankfort and Brussells, and your tenderness should not feel the slightest apprehension for my safety. Every enquiry is made, every convenience is provided, every precaution is taken, and though there will undoubtedly be some fatigue, I can assure you with truth, that there does not remain the shadow of a danger. I may expect to reach Sheffield-place the first week in June, from whence I will immediately give you a line. My first cares must be devoted to poor Lord S., whose grief I feel and even fear, but I shall be impatient to see the Belvidere and the maternal countenance of my most faithful friend. May the progress of fine weather confirm your health and spirits. My own are perfectly good, and I never, in my whole life, found myself better qualified for a long Journey.

I am, Dear Madam,
Ever most affectionately yours,
E. GIBBON.

623.

Lord Sheffield to Edward Gibbon.

Mercer's Hall, 14th May, 1793.

We shall ever acknowledge that you are a right good friend. I was hardly able to read your letter. This is the first foreign post since its arrival. I had hopes you would come forthwith, but hardly expected such an effort as your speedy departure required. Maria & Louisa rejoice at your approach, Sarah is with us. Your apartment will be prepared; your letter arrived too late for me to write to you at Francfort. I shall address this to Brussels. All Friends wish me to involve myself as much as possible in business; I am so with a vengeance in a commission (at the Head of which I am) for the Issue of 5 millions of Exchequer Bills for the relief of Commercial Credit—a matter very interesting indeed, & which I flatter myself will be of great service. I pass the day at Mercer's Hall with my fellow Commissioners—16 of the chief men of the City, excellent men, and four others.

Yours ever,
S.

624.

To Lord Sheffield.

Frankfort, May 19th, 1793.

FRENCH COURAGE DESERVES BETTER CAUSE.

*And here I am, in good health and spirits, after one of the easiest, safest, and pleasantest journies which I ever performed in my whole life; not the appearance of an enemy, and hardly the appearance of a War. Yet I hear, as I am writing, the canon of the siege of Mayence, at the distance of twenty miles; and long, very long, will it be heard. It is confessed on all sides, that the French fight with a courage worthy of a better cause: the town of Mayence is strong, their artillery admirable; they are already reduced to horse-flesh, but they have still the resource of eating the inhabitants, and at last of eating one another; and, if that repast could be extended to Paris and the whole country, it might essentially contribute to the relief of mankind. Our operations are carried on with more than German slowness, and when the besieged are quiet, the besiegers are perfectly satisfied with their progress. A spirit of division undoubtedly prevails; and the character of the Prussians for courage and discipline is sunk lower then you can possibly imagine. Their glory has expired with Frederic. I am sorry to have missed Lord Elgin, who is beyond the Rhine with the King of Prussia. As I am impatient, I propose setting forwards to-morrow afternoon, and shall reach Ostend in less than eight days. The passage must depend on winds and packets; and I hope to find at Brussels or Dover a letter which will direct me to S. P. or Downing-street. Severy goes back from hence. Adieu: I embrace the dear Girls.

Ever yours,
E. G.*

625.

To Lord Sheffield.

Brussels, May 27, 1793.

*This day, between two and three o'Clock in the afternoon, I am arrived at this place in excellent preservation. My expedition, which is now drawing to a close, has been a journey of perseverance rather than speed, of some labour since Frankfort, but without the smallest degree of difficulty or danger. As I have every morning been seated in the Chaise soon after sunrise, I propose indulging to-morrow till eleven o'Clock, and going that day no farther than Ghent: on Wednesday the 29th instant I shall reach Ostend in good time, just eight days, according to my former reckoning, from Frankfort. Beyond that I can say nothing positive; but should the winds be propitious, it is possible that I may appear next Saturday, June 1st, in Downing Street. After that *earliest* date, you will expect me day by day till I arrive. Adieu. I embrace the dear Girls, and salute Mrs. Holroyd. I rejoyce that you have anticipated my advice of plunging into business; but I should now be sorry if that business, however important, detained us long in town. I do not wish to make a public exhibition, and only sigh to enjoy you and the precious remnant in the solitude of Sheffield-place.

Ever yours,
E. G.

If I am successful I may outstrip or accompany this letter. Yours and Maria's waited for me here, and overpaid the Journey.*

626.

To his Stepmother.

Downing Street, June 13th, 1793.

DEAR MADAM,

As you know that I am now safe, well and happy at my friend Lord Sheffield, you will easily excuse a delay of some days in my promised letter.

As long as I was on the road, and it was a long time, your apprehensions, I am much afraid, were awakened not so much in proportion to the real magnitude of the danger, as to the exquisite sensibility of your own feelings. For my own part, though the scene was nearer and more familiar to me, I must fairly own, that I saw through a magnifyer, and that my resolution to visit Lord Sheffield in his state of affliction was an effort of some courage. But I was most agreably surprized to find the Lyons whom I had seen at a distance become little gentle lap-dogs on a nearer approach. I wheeled round behind the armies by the way of Basel, Frankfort, Cologne, Brussells, and Ostend, without meeting with any hostile impediment, and indeed without seeing the face of a Soldier. My passage from Ostend was short and prosperous, and I reached Downing Street not in the least affected by the fatigue of a rough and tedious journey. I found Lord S. much better and even more chearful than I could have expected: he feels his loss, but the new scenes of public business in which he verily wisely engaged have alleviated his grief by occupying his mind. The Ladies are gone into the Country, and he proposes to follow them next week. I could much have wished to visit Bath without delay: but Lord S. will not hear of so early a separation, and as he is the immediate object of my journey, I must submit, unless you particularly desire to see me very soon. Adieu.

Dear Madam,
I am ever yours,
E. GIBBON.

627.

Mrs. Gibbon to Edward Gibbon.

Thursday Noon.

MY DEAREST SIR,

MRS. GIBBON'S JOY.

I truely rejoice, & congratulate you on your being once more safely arrived in your native Country; may health & happiness attend you in it. I am so happy that you have escaped all the evils I foresaw & dreaded, that I find myself better then I have been this year, & this letter is a proof of it; my last but one was to you, as a complaint in my head frighted me from attempting to use a pen, & I hope the forbearance has cured it. I wish'd to tell you so yesterday, but the joy your letter gave would not suffer my hand to be steady enough to write. I thank you most sincerely for writing so soon, & shall impatiently expect the letter you promise me. I am glad you are with Lord Sheffield. When you write tell me how he does; & the young ladies are. I shall soon acknowledge Mrs. Holroyd's kindness in writing to me; make best & kindest Compliments for me, & believe me,

My Dear Sir,
Most affectionately yours,
D. GIBBON.

628.

Mrs. Gibbon to Edward Gibbon.

Belvedere, Bath, August 29, '93.

My Dear Sir,

I have but one excuse for not answering your last letter, to wit, not being able, as I could not hold a pen steady enough to write; yet I never felt myself happier, because I never was so miserable, as from the time those vile miscreants the french Democrats was within forty miles of Lausanne, till you arrived safe in England. Many has been the disappointments I have borne with fortitude, but the fear of having my last & only friend torn from me, was very near overseting my reason: my aggitation prevented my feeling my excessive weakness, till after I had answered your letter, which gave me a joy I shall never again experience, at least I hope not, as I trust you will not be any more expos'd to such eminent danger.

If I have the satisfaction of seeing you next month, I shall be more able to enjoy your Conversation, as my health & strength are wonderfully improv'd within this fortnight; but as much as I long to see you, I would not be the cause of bringing you from agreeable partys & places you like, till it is convenient to you to come. I have not been out this twelve month, dare not encounter the heat, & have little company at home. Your friend Mrs. Gould is as agreeable as ever, Mrs. R. grows old, Mrs. Shelly just as usual. Madame Ely & Mrs. Bonfoy are here. Mrs. Holroyd has probably told you that Miss Gould is now Mrs. Horneck. I wish she had been Mrs. Gibbon.

I am very sorry to hear Miss Louisa Holroyd's health is so indifferent, she is a charming girle, & her sister a very fine one, pray say every thing that is kind to both the Ladies for me; make my best compliments to Lord Sheffield, I make my own to Mrs. Holroyd; let me know when I may hope to see you, and believe me to be,

My Dear Sir,
Your most affectionate
D. Gibbon.

629.

To his Stepmother.

Sheffield Place, Sept. 3, 1793.

DEAR MADAM,

Many days have passed away, since I have received any letter so truly, so dearly acceptable as your last. I had no occasion indeed for any fresh assurances of that regard and tenderness which I have invariably known and felt during the space of thirty-five years: but I was delighted at seeing under your own hand, and again confirmed by your letter of the same date to Mrs. Holroyd, the clearest evidence of your health, spirits, and strength, and I am still more persuaded that some minds will rise superior to the infirmities which Nature has attached to the advanced period of human life.

ANXIETY TO SEE MRS. GIBBON.

My own inclinations would immediately have carried me to the Belvidere from Dover or London; but reason compelled me to acknowledge that, as Lord Sheffield's unexpected misfortune had prompted me to undertake a Journey more hazardous in appearance than in reality, my first attention was due to him, and that it was incumbent on me to try how far the society of a friend might contribute to his relief and amusement. In the three months which we have now spent together I have had the satisfaction of finding that my labours have not been unsuccessful. Our domestic society, which is much improved by the presence of Mrs. Holroyd, some chosen company in the house, the seasonable diversion of Camps and visits, and above all, the very important business of the Exchequer bills which frequently calls him to Mercer's hall, have seconded my endeavours, and I shall leave him in a placid and even chearful temper of mind. As I now find myself of less use, I had fixed my departure about the 15th or 20th instant, but he absolutely insists on keeping me here till the end of the month; and as we expect a very agreable friend, Mr. Douglas, who married Lady Catherine North, I am almost inclined to yield to his importunity. At all events, as I shall only pass three or four days in town, you may depend on seeing me at Bath in the first week of October. I remember that your elegant little mansion will not admit of an additional inhabitant, though I may be perfectly accommodated as heretofore either in your court or over the way. But I am likewise ignorant whether our dining together, at my Lausanne hours of two or three o'Clock, may not be too great an exertion for your returning strength. Should you content yourself with receiving my morning and afternoon visits (and perhaps such an arrangement would be the most prudent), I might be tempted to prefer the Hotel, from whence a chair would convey me in a few minutes to the Belvidere. I shall expect on that subject a line from yourself or our old friend Mrs. Gould. Lord S., who is gone to town this morning, and the young Ladies beg to be kindly remembered to you. Mrs. H. will soon answer your obliging letter. I have a thousand things to say, but they will be best deferred for our interview, which I impatiently desire.

I am, Dear Madam,
Ever yours,
E. GIBBON.

630.

To Lord Sheffield.

October 2nd, 1793.

The Cork Street hotel has answered its recommendation; it is clean, convenient, and quiet, but the expence for a Winter residence, five guineas per week for two small rooms and closet, would much surpass that of a similar lodging without affording any superior advantages. *My first evening was passed at home in a very agreeable *tête-à-tête* with my friend Elmsley. Yesterday I dined at Craufurd's with an excellent set, in which were Pelham and Lord Egremont. I dine to-day with my Portuguese woman at Grenier's, most probably with the well-washed feet of Lady W[ebster], whom I met last night at Devonshire-house; a constant, though late, resort of society. The Duchess is as good, and Lady Elizabeth as seducing, as ever. No news whatsoever. You will see in the papers Lord Hervey's Memorial. I love vigour, but it is surely a strong measure to tell a gentleman you have *resolved* to pass the winter in his house. London is not disagreeable; yet I shall probably leave it Saturday. If any thing should occur, I will write.* Douglas with the Doctor, &c., called on me this morning. *Adieu; I embrace dear little Aunt and la Marmaille. Ever yours.*

P.S.—I have not had your letter, and if you could impart particulars, they should be entrusted only to Vulcan.

631.

To his Stepmother.

Cork Street Hotel, Friday, October 4th, 1793.

DEAR MADAM,

FROM LONDON TO BATH.

I propose to reach Bath next Monday for a *very* late dinner at York-house, where my old friend Will Budd will be so good as to secure me a bed-chamber and dining-room on the same floor with accommodations for two servants. I am very impatient to embrace you, but must postpone that pleasure till the *usual* time of your rising next day: for not the minutest circumstance of your life must be disarranged on my account, as I mean to leave you in every point of health and spirits at least as well as I find you.

I am
Ever yours,
E. G.

632.

To Lord Sheffield.

York-house, Bath, October 9th, 1793.

*Sunday afternoon I left London, and lay at Reading, and Monday in very good time I reached this place after a very pleasant airing; and am always so much delighted, and improved, with this union of ease and motion, that, were not the expence enormous, I would travel every year some hundred miles, more especially in England. I passed the day with Mrs. G. yesterday. In mind and conversation she is just the same as twenty years ago. She has spirits, appetite, legs, and eyes, and talks of living till ninety. I can say from my heart, Amen. We dine at two, and remain together till nine; but, although we have much to say, I am not sorry that she talks of introducing a third or fourth actor. Lord Spenser expects me about the 20th; but if I can do it without offence, I shall steal away two or three days sooner, and you shall have advice of my motions.

The troubles of Bristol have been serious and bloody. I know not who was in fault; but I do not like appeasing the mob by the extinction of the toll, and the removal of the Hereford militia, who had done their duty. Adieu. The Girls must dance at Tunbridge. What would dear little Aunt say if I was to answer her letter? Drop in my ear something of your secret conversations.

Ever yours, &c.,
E. G.

I still follow the old style, though the Convention has abolished the Christian Era, with months, weeks, days, &c.*

633.

To Lord Sheffield.

York-house, Bath, October 13th, 1793.

*I am as ignorant of Bath in general as if I were still at Sheffield. My impatience to get away makes me think it better to devote my whole time to Mrs. G.; and dear little aunt, whom I tenderly salute, will excuse me to her two friends, Mrs. Hartley and Preston, if I make little or no use of her kind introduction. A *tête-à-tête* of eight or nine hours every day is rather difficult to support; yet I do assure you, that our conversation flows with more ease and spirit when we are alone, than when any auxiliaries are summoned to our aid. She is indeed a wonderful woman, and I think all her faculties of the mind stronger and more active than I have ever known them. I have settled, that ten full days may be sufficient for all the purposes of our interview. I should therefore depart next Friday, the 18th instant, and am indeed expected at Althorp on the 20th; but I may possibly reckon without my host, as I have not yet apprized Mrs. G. of the term of my visit; and will certainly not quarrel with her for a short delay. Adieu. I must have some political speculations. The Campaign, at least on our side, seems to be at an end. Ever yours.*

634.

To his Stepmother.

Star Inn, Oxford, Friday evening, Oct. 18, 1793.

DEAR MADAM,

If true friendship were not always a coward, it would be almost useless to say that after a very pleasant airing I am arrived here without accident or fatigue. By the first post you shall hear of me from Althorp.

I am
Ever yours,
E. G.

635.

To his Stepmother.

Althorp, Oct. 20th, 1793.

DEAR MADAM,

The remainder of my Journey has been as easy and prosperous as the beginning, and I am now most agreably settled for a fortnight at this place. The society of a very pleasing and friendly family does not however make me forget the Belvidere, and I wish that I could have given myself a larger scope for my visit to Bath. Yet I have the satisfaction of thinking, that of the narrow span I did not lose any part, and as you were my sole object, I never deviated into any other company or amusement. As we were almost always alone, we enjoyed perhaps as much of each other's society in ten days, as we should have had with the common dissipations of the World in ten weeks. I had the satisfaction of finding and leaving you in a state of health, spirits, and even *mental* youth, which you have the fairest prospect of preserving to a very late period of life, and what more can either yourself or your friends desire? My best compliments to Mrs. Gould.

I am, Dear Madam,
Ever yours,
E. G.

636.

To Lord Sheffield.

Althorpe library, Tuesday, four o'clock, Nov., '93.

We have so completely exhausted this morning among the first editions of Cicero, that I can only mention my departure hence to-morrow, the sixth instant. I lye quietly at Woburn, and reach London in good time Thursday. By the following post I write somewhat more largely. My stay in London will depend, partly on my amusement, and your being fixed at Sheffield-place; unless you think I can be comfortably arranged for a week or two with you at Brighton. An insignificant Minister is often soothed by sops and jobbs. *The military remarks seem good; but now to what purpose! Adieu. I embrace and much rejoyce in Louisa's improvement. Lord Ossory was from home at Farning Woods.*

637.

To Lord Sheffield.

London, Friday, Nov. 8th, four o'clock.

Walpole has just delivered yours, and I hasten the direction, that you may not be at a loss. I will write to-morrow, but I am now fatigued, and rather unwell. Adieu. I have not seen a soul except Elmsley.

638.

To Lord Sheffield.

St. James's Street, Nov. 9th, 1793.

*As I dropt yesterday the word *unwell*, I flatter myself that the family would have been a little alarmed by my silence to-day. I am still awkward, though without any suspicions of gout, and have some idea of having recourse to medical advice. Yet I creep out to-day in a chair, to dine with Lord Lucan. But as it will be literally my first going down stairs, and as scarcely any one is apprized of my arrival, I know nothing, I have heard nothing, I have nothing to say. My present lodging, a house of Elmsley's, is chearful, convenient, somewhat dear, but not so much as a Hotel: a species of habitation for which I have not conceived any great affection. Had you been stationary at Sheffield, you would have seen me before the twentieth; for I am tired of rambling, and pant for my home, that is to say, for your house. But whether I shall have courage to brave *P. of W.* and a bleak down, time only can discover. Adieu. I wish you back to S.-pl. The health of dear Louisa is doubtless the first object; but I did not expect Brighton after Tunbridge. Whenever dear little aunt is separate from you, I shall certainly write to her; but at present how is it possible?*

Ever yours,
E. G.

639.

To Lord Sheffield.

[Most private.]

St. James's Street, Nov. 11th, 1793.

*I must at length withdraw the veil before my state of health, though the naked truth may alarm you more than a fit of the gout. Have you never observed, through my *inexpressibles*, a large prominency *circa genitalia*, which, as it was not at all painful, and very little troublesome, I had strangely neglected for many years? But since my departure from Sheffield-place it has increased, most stupendously, is increasing, and ought to be diminished. Yesterday I sent for Farquhar, who is allowed to be a very skilful surgeon. After viewing and palping, he very seriously desired to call in assistance, and has examined it again to-day with Mr. Cline, a surgeon, as he says, of the first eminence. They both pronounce it a *hydrocele* (a collection of water), which must be let out by the operation of tapping; but from its magnitude and long neglect, they think it a most extraordinary case, and wish to have another surgeon, Dr. Bayley, present. If the business should go off smoothly, I shall be delivered from my burthen, (it is almost as big as a small child), and walk about in four or five days with a truss. But the medical gentlemen, who never speak quite plain, insinuate to me the *possibility* of an inflammation, of fever, etc. I am not appalled at the thoughts of the operation, which is fixed for Wednesday next, twelve o'clock; but it has occurred to me that you might wish to be present, before and afterwards, till the crisis was past; and to give you that opportunity, I shall solicit a delay till Thursday, or even Friday. In the mean while, I crawl about with some labour, and much indecency, to Devonshire-house, where I left all the fine ladies making flannel waistcoats; Lady Lucan's, &c. Adieu. Varnish the business for the ladies; yet I am afraid it will be public;—the advantage of being notorious. Ever yours.*

640.

To his Stepmother.

MY DEAR MADAM,

My friend Lord S. having left me to return into Sussex, I thought you would not be sorry to receive a short assurance of my health under my own hand. You may justly reproach me with the long neglect of a growing complaint, but I am now in the hands of the most skillful physicians and surgeons, who have given me immediate relief, and promise me a safe and radical cure. With their approbation I live as usual, and dine abroad every day, and in a fortnight, when my friends return from Brighton, I shall meet them at S. P. and remain there till after Christmas.

I am
Ever yours,
E. G.

641.

To Lord Sheffield.

St. James's, Nov. 25, '93.

A SECOND OPERATION NEEDED.

*Though Farquahar has promised to write you a line, I conceive you may not be sorry to hear directly from me. The operation of yesterday was much longer, more searching and more painful than the former, but it has eased and lightened me to a much greater degree: no inflammation, no feaver, a delicious night, leave to go abroad to-morrow and to go out of town when I please *en attendant* the future measures of a radical cure. If you hold your intention of returning next Saturday to S. P., I shall probably join you about the Thursday following, after lying two nights at Beckenham. The Devons are going to Bath, and the hospitable Craufurd follows them. Yet I do not want dinners. I passed a delightful day with Burke; an odd one with Monsignor Erskine, the Pope's Nuncio.—Of public news, you and the papers know much more than I do. We seem to have strong sea and land hopes; nor do I dislike the Royalists having beaten the *Sans-Culottes* and taken Dol. How many minutes will it take to guillotine the seventy-three new members of the Convention who are now arrested? Adieu. I embrace the Ladies.*

Ever yours,
E. G.

642.

Lord Sheffield to Edward Gibbon.

Brighton, Tuesday, Nov. 26, 1793.

We are very much content with the account of you, especially Mr. Farquar's. His is really excellent. As this air does not particularly suit Louisa, & as I brought a bowel complaint with me from London and cannot bathe, the Ladies will settle at Sheffield Place to-morrow & I shall settle there on Thursday. We shall expect you on the Thursday following, at furthest, perhaps sooner. I suppose you write to Mrs. Gibbon, but I do not know why I suppose it. There is little or no Society here. I have had one pleasant dinner with Gerrard Hamilton, who is tolerably well, and am to dine with him to-morrow.

I have seen an officer just come from Portsmouth, who says that the Fleet, with Sir Charles Grey, dropped down to St. Helens yesterday, & that Lord Moira has ordered all his officers to be on board to-morrow. I understand that Lord Moira will have from ten to fifteen thousand troops. They are to rendezvous at Jersey, & afterwards, if circumstances are favourable, their destination is somewhere about Cancale. There are good accounts of the encreasing scarcity of provisions among the Infidels & murderers. The garrison at Fort Louis have judiciously preferred the surrendering prisoners of War to the deadly privilege of going home.

A letter from Lord Auckland talks of going for three or four days to Lambeth soon. I have mentioned in a letter that you proposed to pass two nights with him. I shall be sorry if you should not see him.

Ever yours,
SHEFFIELD.

Aunt shall be much obliged if Mr. G. can obtain for her Louisa *Les pensees de Paschal* in one Vol. to bring down with him.

643.

To Lord Sheffield.

St. James's Street, Nov. 30, '93.

*It will not be in my power to reach S. P. quite so soon as I wished and expected. Lord Auckland informs me that he shall be at Lambeth next week Tuesday, Wednesday, and Thursday: I have therefore agreed to dine at Beckenham on Friday. Saturday will be spent there, and, unless some extraordinary temptation should detain me another day, you will see me by four o'clock Sunday the ninth of December. My conversation with the Ambassador in what relates to you shall be *proper*: but a Swiss Philosopher is not a match for his Excellency. I dine to-morrow with the Chancellor at Hampstead, and what I do not like at this time of the year, without a proposal to stay all night. Yet I would not refuse, more especially as I had denied him on a former day.—My health is good but I shall have a final interview with Farquhar before I leave town.—We are still in darkness about Lord Howe and the French ships: but hope seems to preponderate.—Adieu, nothing that relates to Louisa can be forgot.*

Ever Yours,
E. G.

644.

To Lord Sheffield.

St. James's Street, Dec. 6th, 1793.
16 du mois Frimaire.

The man tempted me and I did eat—and that man is no less than the Chancellor, whose frigid reserve has thawed into sudden kindness and civility. I dine and lye to-day, as I intended, at Beckenham: but he recalls me (the third time this week) by a dinner to-morrow (Saturday) with Burke and Windham, which I do not possess sufficient fortitude to resist. Sunday he dismisses me again to the aforesaid Beckenham, but insists on finding me there Monday, which he will probably do supposing there should be room and wellcome at the Ambassador's. I shall not therefore arrive at Sheffield till Tuesday the 10th instant, and though you may perceive that I do not want society or amusement, I sincerely repine at the delay. You will likewise derive some comfort from hearing of the spirit and activity of my motions. Farquhar is satisfied, allows me to go, and does not think I shall be obliged to precipitate my return. Shall we never have anything more than hopes and rumours from Lord Howe? Pray embrace the Ladies for me, and assure Mr. Greg. Way of my concern that our different arrangements have not permitted us to meet at Sheffield.

Ever yours,
E. G.

645.

To his Stepmother.

Sheffield-place, Dec. 12, 1793.

MY DEAR MADAM,

I should have continued to write from London, if the state of my health, or rather my particular complaint, on the subject of which it is not easy to be explicit, had afforded any events. But you may rest assured that I am now in the best hands, and that my occasional relief will be concluded in due time by a safe and radical cure. I have not been advised to make any change in my way of life, and after enjoying as usual the best Society in London, my physician has allowed me to visit Sheffield-place. I arrived here yesterday, and shall remain in this quiet retirement till the middle of January. Lord Sheffield is nervous and rather low-spirited, complains of his eyes and bowels, and appears to me more affected with his loss than he was some months ago. The three Ladies pass the winter in the Country, but he will frequently visit town and the house of Commons. They all wish to be remembered to you, and Mrs. H. has enclosed a letter for her maid. Adieu, my Dear Madam, believe me with the warmest feelings of affection and gratitude,

Ever Yours,
E. GIBBON.

646.

Mrs. Gibbon to Edward Gibbon.

A thousand thanks to you, my Dear Sir, for your very kind letter; none ever gave me so much joy. I truly congratulate you on your recovery, and sincerely hope it will improve every day to good & lasting health, yet I fear you will make too free with the liberty you have obtain'd, & therefore beg you to remember it is the middle of winter; I am too happy at present to reproach you, & too much rejoiced to express myself as I wish. I love L^d. Sheffield dearly, indeed I cannot say how much, & shall be glad to hear you are at S. P.

I cannot help thinking you have had some share in certain appearances at Court. Has L^d. S. refused the Irish vice royalty? Next to you, I think of my Country. Ah, what a falling off from Roman Fortitude. I shall add no more, but that I hardly know myself how much I am interested in your health & happiness; may both attend you, & alway think of me as

Your most affectionate
D. GIBBON.

647.

To Lord Sheffield.

St. James's Street, four o'clock, Tuesday, Jan. 7, 1794.

This date says every thing. I was almost killed between Sheffield-place and East Grinsted, by hard, frozen, long, and cross ruts, that would disgrace the approach of an Indian wigwam. The rest was something less painful; and I reached this place half dead, but not seriously feverish, or ill. I found a dinner invitation from Lord Lucan; but what are dinners to me? I wish they did not know of my departure. I catch the flying post. What an effort! Adieu, till Thursday or Friday.

Gibbon died at 76, St. James's Street, on January 16, 1794. He was buried in Lord Sheffield's family burial-place in Fletching, Sussex.

LAST MOMENTS OF GIBBON.

The following account of his last moments is given by Lord Sheffield in his edition of Gibbon's *Miscellaneous Works* (1814), vol. i. pp. 422-425:—

"After I left him on Tuesday afternoon, the fourteenth, he saw some company, Lady Lucan and Lady Spencer, and thought himself well enough at night to omit the opium draught, which he had been used to take for some time. He slept very indifferently; before nine the next morning he rose, but could not eat his breakfast. However, he appeared tolerably well, yet complained at times of a pain in his stomach. At one o'clock he received a visit of an hour from Madame de Sylva, and at three, his friend, Mr. Craufurd, of Auchinames, (for whom he had a particular regard,) called, and stayed with him till past five o'clock. They talked, as usual, on various subjects; and twenty hours before his death, Mr. Gibbon happened to fall into a conversation, not uncommon with him, on the probable duration of his life. He said, that he thought himself a good life for ten, twelve, or perhaps twenty years. About six, he ate the wing of a chicken, and drank three glasses of Madeira. After dinner he became very uneasy and impatient; complained a good deal, and appeared so weak, that his servant was alarmed. Mr. Gibbon had sent to his friend and relation, Mr.

Robert Darell, whose house was not far distant, desiring to see him, and adding, that he had something particular to say. But, unfortunately, this desired interview never took place.

"During the evening he complained much of his stomach, and of a disposition to vomit. Soon after nine, he took his opium draught, and went to bed. About ten, he complained of much pain, and desired that warm napkins might be applied to his stomach. He almost incessantly expressed a sense of pain till about four o'clock in the morning, when he said he found his stomach much easier. About seven, the servant asked, whether he should send for Mr. Farquhar? he answered, no; that he was as well as he had been the day before. At about half past eight, he got out of bed, and said he was '*plus adroit*' than he had been for three months past, and got into bed again, without assistance, better than usual. About nine, he said that he would rise. The servant, however, persuaded him to remain in bed till Mr. Farquhar, who was expected at eleven, should come. Till about that hour he spoke with great facility. Mr. Farquhar came at the time appointed, and he was then visibly dying. When the *valet de chambre* returned, after attending Mr. Farquhar out of the room, Mr. Gibbon said, '*Pourquoi est-ce que vous me quittez?*' This was about half past eleven. At twelve, he drank some brandy and water from a tea-pot, and desired his favourite servant to stay with him. These were the last words he pronounced articulately. To the last he preserved his senses; and when he could no longer speak, his servant having asked a question, he made a sign, to shew that he understood him. He was quite tranquil, and did not stir; his eyes half-shut. About a quarter before one, he ceased to breathe.

"The *valet de chambre* observed, that Mr. Gibbon did not, at any time, shew the least sign of alarm or apprehension of death; and it does not appear that he ever thought himself in danger, unless his desire to speak to Mr. Darell may be considered in that light."

FOOTNOTES:

[1] Anna, Lady Miller (1741-1781), author of *Letters from Italy, by an Englishwoman* (1776), a verse-writer and a well-known character at Bath, held a literary salon at her villa at Batheaston. She held, writes Walpole, January 15, 1775, "a Parnassus-fair every Thursday, gives out rhymes and themes, and all the flux of quality at Bath contend for the prizes." An antique vase, purchased in Italy, was placed on a modern altar decorated with laurel, and each guest was invited to place in the urn an original composition in verse. The author of the one declared to be the best was crowned by Lady Miller with a wreath of myrtle. Selections from these compositions were published at intervals. "Nothing here," said Miss Burney in 1780, "is more tonish than to visit Lady Miller." Lady Miller died suddenly at Bristol Hot Wells on June 24, 1781. Her husband, Sir John Riggs Miller, died in 1798.

[2] Probably C. Jenkinson, M.P. for Saltash and Secretary at War; afterwards Earl of Liverpool.

[3] Lord North resided at Bushy, Lady North having been appointed in July, 1771, Keeper and Ranger of Bushy Park.

[4] Probably C. J. Fox.

[5] Fanny Barton, Mrs. Abington, first appeared on the stage at the Haymarket in 1755. Her great success was, however, gained at Drury Lane, after her return from Dublin, from 1764 onwards. She was the first Lady Teazle, and acted Ophelia to Garrick's Hamlet. She died in 1815.

[6] Sir Roger Hill was a Baron of the Court of Exchequer at the time of the Commonwealth, and therefore, it is suggested, would have shrunk from contact with a player. He was an ancestor of Lady Sheffield.

[7] Wills Hill, second Viscount Hillsborough, in 1789 created first Marquis of Downshire (1718-1793). In November, 1779, he succeeded Lord Weymouth as Secretary of State for the northern department, and held that office till the resignation of the Government in March, 1782. Walpole, writing on September 11, says the combined French and Spanish fleets were at the entrance of the Channel, "where they certainly will not venture to stay long."

[8] The Hon. William Conway, afterwards Lord Sheffield's colleague in the representation of Coventry.

[9] Parliament met November 27, 1781, and sat till December 20.

[10] Lord North, while his own house was under repair, occupied Lord Sheffield's house in Downing Street.

[11] Parliament met January 21, 1782.

[12] Lord North resigned on March 20, and the new ministry, with the Marquis of Rockingham as first Lord of the Treasury, was finally settled on Sunday, March 24.

The new Cabinet consisted of the following ministers:—

Marquis of Rockingham	First Lord of the Treasury.
Lord Thurlow, to continue Lord Chancellor.	
Earl of Shelburne }	Principal Secretaries of State.
Charles James Fox }	
Lord J. Cavendish	Chancellor of the Exchequer.
Admiral Lord Keppel	First Lord of the Admiralty.
Duke of Grafton	Lord Privy Seal.
Lord Camden	President of the Council.
Duke of Richmond	Master-General of the Ordnance.
General Conway	Commander-in-Chief.
John Dunning (Lord Ashburton)	Chancellor of the Duchy of Lancaster.

[13] Lady Elizabeth Hervey, daughter of Frederick, Earl of Bristol, and Bishop of Derry, married, in 1776, John Thomas Foster. Her father, says Walpole to Mann in December, 1783, though a rich man, allowed her to be governess to a natural daughter of the Duke of Devonshire. Lady Elizabeth Foster, writes Miss Burney (*Diary and Letters of Madame d'Arblay*, vol. v. p. 225), "has the character of being so alluring, that Mrs. Holroyd told me it was the opinion of Mr. Gibbon no man could withstand her, and that, if she chose to beckon the Lord Chancellor from his woolsack, in full sight of the world, he could not resist obedience." Lady Elizabeth, who, in October,

1809, married as her second husband William, fifth Duke of Devonshire, died March 30, 1824.

[14] On April 12, 1782, Admiral Sir George Rodney "broke the line," and defeated the French under the Comte de Grasse in the West Indies, the French Admiral and his flagship the *Ville de Paris*, the largest ship afloat and the present of the city of Paris to Louis XVI., being taken. "The late Ministry are thus robbed of a victory that ought to have been theirs; but the mob do not look into the almanac" (Walpole to Sir H. Mann, May 18, 1782).

[15] Rodney was superseded by Admiral Pigot, who was one of the Lords of the Admiralty in the new administration.

[16] The Marquis of Rockingham died July 2, 1782, aged fifty-two.

[17] The poem to which Gibbon alludes is the *Essay on Epic Poetry in five Epistles to the Rev. Mr. Mason* (London, 1782). Hayley's mother was Mary Yates (1718-1775), who married Thomas Hayley in 1740, and died in 1775. The lines to which Gibbon alludes occur in the fourth epistle (ll. 439 to end).

"Nature, who deck'd thy form with Beauty's flowers,

Exhausted on thy soul her finer powers;

Taught it with all her energy to feel

Love's melting softness, Friendship's fervid zeal,

The generous purpose, and the active thought,

With Charity's diffusive spirit fraught;

There all the best of mental gifts she plac'd,

Vigor of judgment, purity of Taste,

Superior parts, without their spleenful leaven,

Kindness to Earth, and confidence in Heaven."

[18] On the death of Lord Rockingham, Fox endeavoured to force on the King, as the new Premier, the Duke of Portland, "a dull man, but a convenient block to hang Whigs on." Failing in his attempt, he resigned.

[19] Lord John Cavendish and Lord Althorpe, two of the Lords of the Treasury, Burke, Paymaster-General, Lord Duncannon and the Hon. John Townshend, Lords of the Admiralty, retired with Fox. Lord Keppel and General Conway continued in office; also the Duke of Richmond, Fox's uncle.

[20] Parliament was prorogued on July 11 till December 5, 1782. Gibbon's list of the new Ministry is accurate, except that the Lord Advocate, the Hon. Henry Dundas (afterwards Lord Melville), became Treasurer of the Navy, *vice* Colonel Isaac Barré, who became Paymaster of the Forces. "Places are cheaper than mackerel," writes Lord Loughborough to his cousin William Eden, July 4, 1782 (*Lord Auckland's Journal and Correspondence*, vol. i. p. 2).

[21] Gibbon probably refers to the defeat of Colonel Brathwaite in the Tanjore district (February, 1782), by Tippoo, Hyder's son, and M. Lally.

[22] The combined French and Spanish fleets were collected in the Channel, intending to prevent the relief of Gibraltar and effect a junction with the Dutch. Lord Howe had already driven the Dutch into the Texel, and he now sailed to protect the Jamaica convoy, and watch the enemy, single ships being sent to reinforce him as they could be made ready. On September 11, Lord Howe sailed with a powerful fleet for the relief of Gibraltar, and landed his troops and stores October 13-18.

[23] General Sir William Draper is best known from the attack upon him by Junius, his share in the defence of Fort St. Philip in Minorca (1781-2), and his subsequent charges against the Governor. He was twice married, but, after the death of his second wife in 1778, remained a widower. He died at Bath in 1787.

[24] Edward James Eliot married, in September, 1785, Lady Harriet Pitt, second daughter of the first Earl of Chatham. She died September 25, 1786, leaving a daughter, born September 20, 1786. Edward Eliot died in 1797, predeceasing his father.

[25] Gilbert Stuart (1742-1786) published in 1780 his *History of the Establishment of Religion in Scotland*, 1517-1561; and in 1782 the *History of Scotland from the Reformation till the Death of Queen Mary*. His best-known work was his *View of Society in Europe* (1778). The story of his attack on Robert Henry, and his attempt to ruin him, are related in Disraeli's *Calamities of Authors*. If Gibbon alludes to Stuart, Mrs. Gibbon seems to have been justified in her prejudice.

[26] Lord North was Warden of the Cinque Ports.

[27] Lord Loughborough married as his second wife, on September 12, 1782, the Hon. Charlotte Courtenay, daughter of the first Viscount Courtenay.

[28] Lord Howe arrived at Gibraltar early in October. On September 13 the final effort of the French and Spaniards to capture the Rock had been

repulsed by Sir George Eliott, who destroyed their floating batteries. Lord Howe returned to Portsmouth November 15, 1782.

[29] Probably William Eden, who had been secretary to the Earl of Carlisle during his Lord-Lieutenancy of Ireland. But he married Eleanor, daughter of Sir Gilbert Elliot, and sister of the first Earl of Minto. Eden, who was created Lord Auckland in the Irish peerage in 1789, was advanced to an English peerage in 1793, and died in 1814.

[30] The reference probably is to the letter which Fox, before his resignation, wrote to the American agents in Paris, offering *"to recognize the independence of the United States in the first instance, and not to reserve it as a condition of peace."* Fox interpreted this as an absolute recognition of American independence; Lord Shelburne and his colleagues held that it was a conditional recognition dependent on peace being concluded.

[31] In September, 1780, Hyder Ali invaded the Madras district; Warren Hastings at once negotiated peace with the Mahrattas in order that he might send all available troops to Madras. Sir Eyre Coote defeated Hyder at Porto Novo (July 1, 1781) and at Pollilore (August 27). The full Treasury was the result of the recent overthrow of Cheyte Singh, Rajah of Benares, and the spoliation of the Begums of Oude. In the summer of 1782 the House of Commons resolved that it was the duty of the Court of Directors to recall Hastings. In compliance with this resolution the directors voted an order of recall, but afterwards rescinded it and maintained the Governor-General at his post. See note to Letter 487, on page 85 of this volume.

[32] Sir George Augustus Eliott, created Lord Heathfield for his defence of Gibraltar.

[33] Parliament, which had been prorogued to November 26, was further prorogued to December 5, in order that the negotiations for peace might be completed. Peace was provisionally signed with the United States at Paris on November 30, 1782.

[34] Pitt's first meeting with Gibbon is thus described by Sir James Bland Burges, Bart. (*Letters and Correspondence*, pp. 59-61). The dinner was given in Lincoln's Inn to the officers of the Northumberland Militia, who were quartered in the Inn during the Gordon Riots.

"I invited the four military gentlemen, our committee, and six other persons the best qualified I could meet with, among whom were my father, Lord Carmarthen, and Mr. Gibbon, the historian, who was then at the zenith of his fame, and who certainly was not at all backward in availing himself of the deference universally shown to him, by taking both the lead, and a very ample share of the conversation, in whatever company he might honour with his presence. His conversation was not, indeed, what Dr.

Johnson would have called *talk*. There was no interchange of ideas, for no one had a chance of replying, so fugitive, so variable, was his mode of discoursing, which consisted of points, anecdotes, and epigrammatic thrusts, all more or less to the purpose, and all pleasantly said with a French air and manner which gave them great piquancy, but which were withal so desultory and unconnected that, though each separately was extremely amusing, the attention of his auditors sometimes flagged before his own resources were exhausted.... He had just concluded, however, one of his best foreign anecdotes, in which he had introduced some of the fashionable levities of political doctrine then prevalent, and, with his customary tap on the lid of his snuff-box, was looking round to receive our tribute of applause, when a deep-toned but clear voice was heard from the bottom of the table, very calmly and civilly impugning the correctness of the narrative, and the propriety of the doctrines of which it had been made the vehicle. The historian, turning a disdainful glance towards the quarter whence the voice proceeded, saw, for the first time, a tall, thin, and rather ungainly-looking young man, who now sat quietly and silently eating some fruit. There was nothing very prepossessing or very formidable in his exterior, but, as the few words he had uttered appeared to have made a considerable impression on the company, Mr. Gibbon, I suppose, thought himself bound to maintain his honour by suppressing such an attempt to dispute his supremacy. He accordingly undertook the defence of the propositions in question, and a very animated debate took place between him and his youthful antagonist, Mr. Pitt, and for some time was conducted with great talent and brilliancy on both sides. At length the genius of the young man prevailed over that of his senior, who, finding himself driven into a corner from which there was no escape, made some excuse for rising from the table and walked out of the room. I followed him, and, finding that he was looking for his hat, I tried to persuade him to return to his seat. 'By no means,' said he. 'That young gentleman is, I have no doubt, extremely ingenious and agreeable, but I must acknowledge that his style of conversation is not exactly what I am accustomed to, so you must positively excuse me.' And away he went in high dudgeon, notwithstanding that his friend [Lord Sheffield] had come to my assistance."

[35] Mrs. Siddons first appeared on the London stage in December, 1775, when she acted Portia at Drury Lane. She gained no great success, and in June, 1776, received her dismissal from the managers. In the provincial theatres, and especially at the Bath Theatre, then managed by Palmer, she became famous. At Bath, in 1780, she had twice acted the part of Lady Townly in Vanbrugh's and Cibber's play of *The Provoked Husband*. In 1782 she reappeared in London (October 10) at Drury Lane, in the part of Isabella in Southerne's tragedy of *The Fatal Marriage*. On October 30 she took the part of Euphrasia in Murphy's *Grecian Daughter*. On November 8

she played Jane Shore in Rowe's tragedy of that name. W. Hamilton's picture of Mrs. Siddons as Isabella belongs to the nation.

[36] The "Hertford family" included Francis, first Earl and Marquis of Hertford; his brother, General Conway; his eldest son, Lord Beauchamp, M.P. for Orford; and his youngest son, William Conway, who was at this time standing at a by-election for Coventry.

[37] The preliminaries of peace were signed at Versailles with France and Spain, January 20, 1783, and Parliament met, after the Christmas recess, January 21.

[38] On Monday, February 17, 1783, an address of thanks to his Majesty for the peace was moved by Thomas Pitt, M.P. for Old Sarum, and William Wilberforce, M.P. for Kingston-upon-Hull. Amendments were moved by Lord J. Cavendish and Lord North, which were carried at 8 a.m. on Tuesday, February 18, by 224 to 208. On February 21, a resolution, proposed by Lord J. Cavendish, that the concessions made to the United States were excessive, was carried by 207 to 190.

[39] On February 24, 1783, Lord Shelburne resigned office in consequence of the vote of February 21; and Pitt, as Chancellor of the Exchequer, publicly stated that he only retained his post till his successor was appointed. On March 24, Mr. Coke, M.P. for Norfolk, moved and carried an address to the king, asking for the appointment of a new administration.

[40] Pitt, on March 31, resigned the office of Chancellor of the Exchequer. On April 2 the new administration was formed; the principal members were—

The Duke of Portland	First Lord of the Treasury.
Lord North}	Secretaries of State.
Mr. Fox }	
Lord J. Cavendish	Chancellor of the Exchequer.
Lord Keppel	First Commissioner of the Admiralty.
Lord Stormont	President of the Council.
Lord Carlisle	Lord Privy Seal.

Lord Townshend	Master of the Ordnance.
Mr. Burke	Paymaster-General.
Lord Northington	Lord Lieutenant of Ireland.

The Great Seal was put in commission. The first seven formed the Cabinet.

Lord Townshend said "he had always foreseen the Coalition Ministry could not last, for he was at Court when Mr. Fox kissed hands, and he observed George III. turn back his eyes and ears just like the horse at Astley's, when the tailor he had determined to throw was getting on him" (*Correspondence of C. J. Fox*, vol. ii. p. 28).

[41] The session closed July 16, 1783.

[42] "Gibbon and I," writes Lord Sheffield to William Eden (*Lord Auckland's Journal and Correspondence*, vol. i. p. 53), "have been walking about the room and cannot find any employment we should like in the intended establishment. He agrees with me that the place of dancing-master might be one of the most eligible for him, but he rather inclines to be painter, in hopes of succeeding Ramsay."

[43] Part of the grounds of M. Deyverdun's house at Lausanne, in which Gibbon lived from 1783 to 1793, is now occupied by the Hôtel Gibbon. Henry Mathews (*Diary of an Invalid*, p. 317) speaks of a visit to the house paid in June, 1818. "Paid a visit to the house in which Gibbon resided. Paced his terrace, and explored the summer-house, of which he speaks in relating, with so much interesting detail, the conclusion of his historical labours."

[44] *Poésies Helvétiennes*. Par M. B * * * * * (*i.e.* J. P. L. Bridel). Lausanne. 1782. 8°. Épître au Jardinier de la Grotte, pp. 66-72.

"Que j'ai passé de charmantes veillées,

Dessous ce chaume au fond de ton verger!

Loin du fracas d'un monde mensonger,

Par le plaisir elles etaient filées.

* * * * * * * *

Tantôt quittant ce chaume solitaire,

Asyle heureux qu'un palais ne vaut pas,

Sur ta terrasse accompagnant tes pas,

Nous contemplions les jeux de la lumière;

L'astre des nuits à nos yeux se levant

Se dégageait lentement des montagnes,

Poursuivait l'ombre au travers des campagnes;

Et scintillait dans les eaux du Léman."

[45] Cagliostro, whose real name is said to have been Giuseppe Balsamo, came to Strasbourg in 1780. Jean Benjamin de la Borde, in his *Lettres sur la Suisse* (published 1783), expresses enthusiastic admiration for his skill and character. For his share in the Necklace Scandal at Paris in 1785-6, Cagliostro was banished from France. He left the country, saying that he should not return till the Bastille was *une promenade publique*. At Rome he was condemned in the Papal Court to perpetual imprisonment, and died, it is said, in 1795.

[46] Lord Sheffield, however, was convinced of the wisdom of Gibbon's plan. "Gibbon," he writes to Mr. Eden, August 7, 1783, "has baffled all arrangements; possibly you may have heard at Bushy or Bedford Square, of a continental scheme. It has annoyed me much, and of all circumstances the most provoking is, that he is right; a most pleasant opportunity offered. His seat in Parliament is left in my hands. He is here [Sheffield Place]. In short, his plan is such, that it was impossible to urge anything against it" (*Lord Auckland's Journal and Correspondence*, vol. i. p. 56.)

[47] Peter Elmsley (1736-1802) succeeded Paul Vaillant as a bookseller opposite Southampton Street, in the Strand. His special department was the importation of foreign books. He was a man of great general knowledge, and possessed a remarkable knowledge of the French literature and language. Gibbon died at his house, 76, St. James's Street, at the corner of Little St. James's Street.

[48] Thomas Pelham, M.P. for Sussex (afterwards second Earl of Chichester) (1756-1826), served as Irish Secretary under Lord Northington in the Coalition Government from 1783 to 1784.

[49] William Windham (1750-1810), M.P. for Norwich, resigned the Irish Secretaryship in 1783. He was Secretary at War from 1794 to 1801, and War and Colonial Secretary 1806-7. He was a powerful speaker, a brilliant talker, a patron of pugilism, and, from his irresolution and love of paradox, nicknamed "Weather-cock."

[50] Meaning Lady Sheffield.

[51] *I.e.*, probably, before applying direct to Lord North (Bushey), wait to see what Lord Loughborough may do.

[52] Gregory Lewis Way, son of Lewis Way by his second wife, was half-brother to Lady Sheffield.

[53] Sir John Russell, Bart., died on his way to Sheffield Place, August 8, 1783.

[54] Mr. Silas Deane.

[55] Probably "Fish" Crauford, a friend of C. J. Fox, and distinguished by his Eton nickname, given him for his curiosity, from his brother "Flesh" Crauford.

[56] The treaties of peace with the United States, France, Spain, and Holland were signed at Versailles, September 2, 1783.

[57] Gibbon hoped that he might be appointed either a Commissioner of Excise, or secretary to the British Legation at Paris, where the Duke of Manchester was at this time ambassador. The latter post was given to Anthony Morris Storer, M.P. for Morpeth, one of the Admirable Crichtons of the day, celebrated as a dancer, skater, gymnast, musician, and writer of Latin verse. His magnificent library he left to Eton College at his death in 1799. Fox, no doubt, used his influence on this occasion against Gibbon. His lines have been already quoted. Another illustration of his impression that Gibbon was bought by a place is afforded by the following extract from Walpole's *Journal of the Reign of King George III. from the Year 1771 to 1783*, vol. ii. p. 464. "June 28, 1781: Last week was sold by auction the very valuable library of an honourable representative" (C. J. Fox) "of Westminster, and which had been taken, with all his effects, in execution. Amongst the books there was Mr. Gibbon's first volume of the *Roman History*, and which appeared by the title-page to have been given by the author to his honourable friend, who thought proper to subscribe the following anecdote:—'The author at Brookes's said, there was no salvation for this country until six heads of the principal persons in Administration were laid on the table. Eleven days after, this same gentleman accepted a place of Lord of Trade under those very Ministers, and has acted with them ever since.' Such was the avidity of bidders for the smallest production of so wonderful a genius, that by the addition of this little record the book sold for three guineas."

[58] By Article IV. of the Treaty with the United Provinces.

[59] The policy of Great Britain towards America in matters of trade, on which Lord Sheffield had spoken in April, 1783, and, later in the same year, published a pamphlet.

[60] Sir Henry Clinton succeeded Sir William Howe as commander-in-chief in America in 1778. He was severely blamed for leaving Cornwallis

unsupported in the Southern Colonies, and for the disaster at York Town in 1781. He died in 1795, as governor of Gibraltar. His son, General Sir William Clinton, who served with distinction in the Peninsular War, married Lord Sheffield's second daughter, Lady Louisa Holroyd.

[61] Mr. Oliver Cromwell, a solicitor with whom Gibbon and Lord Sheffield had business transactions. The Protector's son, Henry Cromwell, married Lady Elizabeth Russell, and had, among other children, a son, Henry, who was born in 1658. This son, afterwards Major Henry Cromwell, married Mary Hewling. Their grandson was this Mr. Oliver Cromwell of Cheshunt (1742-1821), the great-great-grandson of the Protector.

[62] Henry Laurens had been detained as a prisoner in the Tower since his capture in 1779.

[63] Sir Benjamin Thompson, Count of Rumford (1753-1814), was born in Massachusetts. He was Secretary to the Province of Georgia, and afterwards Under Secretary of State under Lord G. Germain. He fought on the Loyalist side as a Colonel of Dragoons, and also served as a volunteer on board H.M.S. *Victory*, under Sir C. Hardy. His *Essays, Political, Economical, and Philosophical*, were published at London in 1796-1802. He was knighted by George III. in 1784, and became a Count of the Holy Roman Empire in 1791.

[64] *Observations on the Commerce of the American States*. The pamphlet was written by Lord Sheffield, but published anonymously (London, 1783, 8vo). It reached a sixth edition in 1784, and was translated into both French and German. In it Lord Sheffield opposed Pitt's plan of relaxing the navigation laws in favour of America.

[65] Gibbon's dog.

[66] The Abbé Raynal (1713-1796) published in 1770 his *Histoire philosophique des établissements et du commerce des Européens dans les deux Indes*. The work was put on the Index for its anti-religious tendency. His book, says Michelet, was for twenty years the Bible of two worlds. Toussaint l'Ouverture learned passages from it by heart; Bernardin de St. Pierre was inspired by it; to its author Napoleon Bonaparte dedicated in 1787 his manuscript *Essai sur l'histoire de la Corse*. Dr. Johnson, according to Hannah More, refused to shake hands with the Abbé. "Sir," he said to a friend, "I will not shake hands with an infidel!" Raynal published a new edition in 1780, which was still more outspoken in its religious and political views. In consequence he was obliged to leave France, and settled in Switzerland. In 1788 he returned to France, and died in 1796.

[67] Simon André Tissot (1728-1797) was one of the most skilful physicians of the day, excelling, says Madame de Genlis, alike in the theory and

practice of his art. Among his voluminous works in Latin and French were *Avis au peuple sur sa santé* (1761), and *De valetudine litteratorum* (1766), which he translated into French under the title of *De la santé des gens de lettre* (1769).

[68] Baron Sheffield of Dunamore (1781) was, in September, 1783, created Baron Sheffield of Roscommon, with remainder to his daughters severally. His heir was at this time his daughter, the Hon. Maria Holroyd, afterwards Lady Stanley of Alderley.

[69] The north-east wind.

[70] Lady Elizabeth Foster.

[71] Sir Andrew Snape Hamond, R.N., created a baronet in December, 1783, for his services in the American War, was apparently treating for the seat of Lymington.

[72] Lord Sheffield's *Observations*. See note to Letter 481.

[73] Sébastien Mercier (1740-1814) was the author, among other works, of *L'An 2440*, a dream of the future (1771), and of the *Tableau de Paris* (1781), in which he advocated many useful reforms. For this latter work he was prosecuted, and took refuge in Switzerland.

[74] The Prince de Ligne (1735-1814) served with distinction as a general of the Austrian troops in the Seven Years' War and the War of Bavarian Succession. He was noted for his wit, and was a voluminous author both in prose and verse. He died at Vienna during the Congress in 1814.

[75] Sir H. Burrard, Bart., the proprietor of the preponderating interest in borough of Lymington.

[76] Lord Sheffield was sitting on a Select Committee appointed to inquire into frauds committed on the revenue.

[77] Early in 1781 two committees of the House of Commons were appointed to inquire into the affairs of India. One, a Select Committee, considered the best means of governing the British possessions in the East Indies; the other, a Secret Committee, inquired into the causes of the war in the Carnatic, and the condition of the British possessions in those parts. On April 9, 1782, the Lord Advocate, Henry Dundas, the chairman of the Secret Committee, moved that the reports of that committee be referred to a committee of the whole House. On April 25 he laid three sets of resolutions on the table. The first set, which were postponed, related to the general misconduct of the Company; the second set, condemning the administration of the Presidency of Madras, was voted; the third, containing criminal charges against Sir Thomas Rumbold, the President of the Madras Council, was also voted. On these two sets of resolutions was

founded a Bill of pains and penalties (April 29) against Rumbold; but on July 1, 1783, a motion was carried to adjourn the further consideration of the Bill till October 1. The proceedings, therefore, fell to the ground and were not resumed.

Meanwhile, the resolutions as to the general misconduct of the Company were severally agreed to by the House on May 28, 1782. On them was founded a resolution, calling on the directors to remove Warren Hastings, Governor-General of India, and William Hornsby, President of the Council of Bombay. This resolution being carried, the directors passed an Order of Recall; but the order was rescinded on October 31 by the General Court of Proprietors.

Side by side with these proceedings, the reports of the Select Committee were also considered. On April 24, 1782, their chairman, General Smith, presented a series of resolutions which were carried, and on them an address was presented to the king to recall Sir Elijah Impey, Chief Justice of the Supreme Court of Bengal.

On November 20 and 26, 1783, Fox brought in two India Bills: (1) vesting the affairs of the Company in the bands of seven commissioners; (2) providing for the better government of the territorial possessions of the Company. The first Bill passed the House of Commons on a division of 208 to 102, after long debates, in which the House frequently sat till 5 a.m., on December 8, 1783, and was carried up to the House of Lords on December 9. The first reading took place on December 9, and the second reading on December 15. A motion for adjournment was carried against the ministers by 87 to 79, and on December 17 the Bill was rejected by 95 to 76.

On the following day the king called upon the Secretaries of State to resign their seals; and on the 19th the rest of the Cabinet were dismissed.

The new Ministry was thus composed:—

William Pitt First Lord of the Treasury and Chancellor of the Exchequer.
Earl Gower President of the Council.
Lord Thurlow Lord Chancellor.
Lord Sydney } Secretaries of State.
Marquis of Carmarthen }
The Duke of Rutland Lord Privy Seal.
Lord Howe First Lord of the Admiralty.
Duke of Richmond Master of the Ordnance.
Henry Dundas Treasurer of the Navy.

The first seven on the list formed the Cabinet.

The Duke of Dorset replaced the Duke of Manchester as Ambassador at Paris, and Daniel Hailes succeeded Anthony Storer as Secretary to the Legation.

Lord Temple, the "stormy petrel" of politics, accepted office as Secretary for the Foreign Department on December 19, but resigned on December 22.

[78] The Hon. George Augustus North (afterwards Lord Guilford) and Lord Lewisham were two of the seven commissioners named in Fox's India Bill.

[79] This letter, as printed here, was written by Edward Gibbon to his stepmother; a similar letter, in which some of the same phrases are repeated, is printed in Lord Sheffield's edition of Gibbon's *Miscellaneous Writings* (vol. ii. pp. 340-344), addressed to his aunt, Miss Catherine Porten.

[80] His aunt, Miss Porten, and his stepmother.

[81] His aunt, Miss Hester Gibbon.

[82] William Woodfall, formerly assistant editor of the *Public Advertiser*, was at this time editor of the *Morning Chronicle*. He was called "Memory Woodfall" from his accuracy in remembering the speeches in Parliament, of which no notes were then allowed to be taken. He was, it is said (*Auckland Correspondence*, vol. iii. p. 165), for many years paid £400 a year, "for giving the speeches of Mr. Fox and Mr. Sheridan much more at length and better than he did those of Mr. Pitt and Mr. Dundas." He was afterwards editor of a paper called *The Diary*, which failed. He died in 1803. His brother, Henry Woodfall, published the *Letters of Junius*.

[83] The fall of the Coalition. See note to Letter 487.

[84] The long delay in accepting the Coalition Cabinet. See note to Letter 487.

[85] The House of Commons, after deferring the third reading of the land-tax Bill, and addressing the king against dissolving Parliament, adjourned from December 26 to January 12, 1784.

[86] As soon as Parliament reassembled after the Christmas recess (January 12, 1784), the House of Commons resolved itself into a committee on the state of the nation in order to prevent an immediate dissolution. Two resolutions were carried: (1) that to pay out public money before the same was appropriated by Act of Parliament was a high crime and misdemeanour; (2) that the Mutiny Bill be postponed till February 23. It was further resolved, that an Administration, which commanded the confidence of the House, was peculiarly necessary in the present situation

of the kingdom, and that the late ministerial changes had been preceded and accompanied by reports and circumstances which alienated the confidence of the House. On January 14, Pitt proposed his India Bill, which was rejected (January 23) by 222 to 214. On January 16 a resolution was carried, by 205 to 184, that the continuance of the present ministers in office was "contrary to constitutional principles and injurious to the interests of his Majesty and his people."

[87] Dunning's motion, here referred to, was proposed April 24, 1780, and rejected by 254 to 203.

[88] On December 22, 1783, Mr. Bankes, M.P. for Corfe Castle, an intimate friend of William Pitt, assured the House that the Government did not intend to advise the king to dissolve or prorogue Parliament, and that the Chancellor of the Exchequer, if such advice were offered, would oppose it, and, if it were accepted, would resign.

[89] On January 16, 1784, Mr. Powys, M.P. for Northamptonshire, proposed a compromise by a coalition between the contending parties. Fox, however, declared that no compromise was possible till Pitt had resigned. The idea of a compromise was taken up on the 20th by the "country gentlemen." Stormy scenes took place on January 23, when Pitt declined to make any statement as to the advice which he might offer the king. But on Saturday, January 24, he stated that, while refusing to pledge himself further, the House should not be dissolved till it had met on Monday, the 26th. Advantage was taken of this statement to call a meeting, attended by seventy members of the "country gentlemen" party, at the St. Alban's Tavern, to consider the possibility of compromise on the basis of a "Broad Bottom administration." The plan proved futile, and was abandoned February 18. The proceedings closed with a dinner given to the seventy members at Carlton House by the Prince of Wales on March 10, 1784.

[90] An address to his Majesty was presented on February 25, 1784, asking the king to take measures for the formation of such an united administration as the House of Commons had declared to be necessary. The king replied (February 27) that he did not think the dismissal of his present ministers would promote such union. A second address, asking the removal of the present ministers, was carried (March 1) by a majority of twelve, and presented March 4. The king's answer was practically a repetition of his former reply. A representation on the affairs of the nation, addressed to the king, was carried by 191 to 190 on March 8, and, with this last effort, the opposition subsided. The Mutiny Bill passed without a division on March 10, and on March 25 Parliament was dissolved.

[91] Upwards of one hundred and sixty members lost their seats, and of these almost all had supported the Coalition of Fox and North. Among "Fox's Martyrs" was Lord Sheffield. Sir Sampson Gideon, afterwards Lord Eardley, and Mr. John Wilmot were elected for Coventry, the seat previously held by Lord Sheffield and Mr. Conway.

[92] Teague is the Irish servant of Hermes Wouldbe in Farquhar's play of *The Twin Rivals*.

[93] Lady Charlotte Herbert, daughter of Lady Pembroke (formerly Lady Elizabeth Spencer), was born July, 1773, and died in April, 1784.

[94] Prince Henry of Prussia, brother of Frederick the Great, was one of the most brilliant soldiers of the day. His relief of Breslau (1760) and victory at Freyberg (1762) were turning-points in the Seven Years' War. In the War of Bavarian Succession he maintained his position in Bohemia against the Austrian troops (1778-9). He was offered the crown of Poland in 1764, and in 1784 had been envoy at the court of Louis XVI. He died in 1802.

[95] His picture by Sir Joshua Reynolds.

[96] The Constitution of 1782 had not satisfied Ireland. The cry was raised for parliamentary reform, and for the extension of the franchise to Roman Catholics. Napper Tandy and his friends held meetings with French emissaries; and an attempt was made to convene a Congress of three hundred representatives at Dublin in October, 1784, backed by the volunteers. The Lord Lieutenant, the Duke of Rutland, acted with vigour, and the proposed Congress collapsed. Lord Sheffield had taken part in the proceedings against the magistrates of Roscommon and Leitrim, who had called the meetings of representatives and signed the resolutions in favour of parliamentary reform during the summer of 1784.

[97] Jacques Necker (1734-1804), appointed Director-General of Finance in 1777, published, in 1781, his *Compte Rendu*. In the same year he was compelled to resign his office. In 1784 he published his *Administration des Finances*. He was recalled to office as Director of Finances in August, 1788, was dismissed July 11, 1789, recalled July 16 in the same year, and finally retired in September, 1790. "M. Necker est parti. Il a eu une si belle peur de la menace d'être pendu, qu'il n'a pu résister à la tendresse de sa vertueuse épouse qui le pressoit d'aller aux eaux." Madame Elisabeth à Madame de Bombelles, Sept. 6, 1790 (Feuillet de Conches, vol. i. p. 348). Necker's work, *Sur l'Administration de M. Necker, par lui-même*, was published in 1791. His daughter mentioned here was afterwards Madame de Staël.

[98] Lord Sheffield published, in 1785, his *Observations on the Manufactures, Trade, and Present State of Ireland*.

[99] Sir Willoughby Aston, the last baronet, married, in 1772, Lady Jane Henley, sister of Lord Northington, and died in 1815, without children.

[100] The Hon. John Hampden Trevor, second son of Lord Hampden, was British Envoy at the Court of Turin, 1783-99. He married, in 1773, Harriot, only daughter of the Rev. Daniel Barton, Canon of Christ Church.

[101] Lady Clarges (*née* Skrine) was the widow of Sir Thomas Clarges, third baronet, M.P. for Lincoln, who died in 1783.

[102] Second Lord Northington, formerly M.P. for Hampshire.

[103] Lord Spencer, who succeeded his father as second Earl Spencer in 1783, married Lady Lavinia Bingham, eldest daughter of the first Earl of Lucan.

[104] The Right Hon. John Foster, Lord Oriel (1740-1828), Chancellor of the Exchequer in Ireland (1784), Speaker of the Irish House of Commons (1785-1800), was the author of the Irish Corn Law of 1784, the founder of the National Bank, and closely connected with Lord Sheffield by their common interests in commercial and financial questions. He was elected Speaker August 15, 1785.

[105] Commissioners had been appointed to draw up a scheme for regulating the commercial intercourse of Great Britain and Ireland. Pitt's eleven propositions for the development of Irish Trade, in their original form, were practically rejected by the Irish Parliament in February, 1785. Remodelled, and increased to twenty, they were laid before the English House of Commons in May, 1785, and a Bill based on them was read the first time in July. This Bill was then introduced into the Irish House on August 12; but it was carried by so small a majority (127 to 108) that it was abandoned.

[106] The Emperor Joseph II., "à qui jamais rien n'a réussi," reigned 1780-1790. His attempted reforms in the Low Countries created a revolution against Austria; the two insurgent parties of the *Statistes* and *Vonckistes*,— the one conservative and aristocratic, the other commercial and resembling in their views the French Constitutionalists,—made common cause and expelled the Austrian governor, the Duke of Saxe-Teschen. "Vôtre pays," said Joseph, a few days before his death, to the Prince de Ligne, "m'a tué. La prise de Gand a été mon agonie; l'abandon de Bruxelles, ma mort."

[107] Frederick II. of Prussia died August 17, 1786. He had recently endeavoured to mediate between the Republican party in Holland and the Stadtholder, who was, in 1786, deprived of the government of the Hague and of his military powers as captain-general. He had also, in 1778 and 1785, interfered to prevent Austria's designs upon Bavaria.

[108] Lord Sheffield did not *publish* his *Observations on the French Treaty and Commerce.* [S.]

[109] On August 18, 1787, the Right Hon. W. Eden (afterwards Lord Auckland) was appointed Ambassador Extraordinary and Plenipotentiary to the King of Spain; but he was at this time in Paris, assisting the Duke of Dorset in negotiating a Treaty of Commerce with France. His conduct in accepting from Pitt the mission to France was severely condemned by the old followers of Lord North. Among the numerous squibs which his action provoked, the following may be quoted:—

"A mere affair of trade t' embrace,

Wines, brandies, gloves, fans, cambrics, lace;

For this on me my Sovereign laid

His high commands, and I obey'd—

Nor think, my Lord, this conduct base.

"Party were guilt in such a case,

When thus my country, for a space,

Calls my poor skill to Dorset's aid,

A mere affair of trade!

"Thus Eden, with unblushing face,

To North would palliate his disgrace:

When North, with smiles, this answer made:

'You might have spar'd what you have said—

I thought the business of your place

A mere affair of trade!'"

[110] In 1787 the Prince of Wales, after authorizing Fox to make a public denial of his rumoured marriage with Mrs. Fitzherbert, received an additional £10,000 a year, £161,000 to pay his debts, and £20,000 for the repair of Carlton House.

[111] A Treaty of Commerce and Navigation between Great Britain and France was signed at Versailles on September 26, 1786, and a Supplementary Convention was signed between the same powers on January 15, 1787. Both treaties were signed on behalf of Great Britain by William Eden.

[112] Jeanne Pauline Polier de Bottens, afterwards successively Madame de Crousaz, and Madame de Montolieu, was the daughter of the Pastor at Lausanne, and was descended from an ancient family in Languedoc which had emigrated at the time of the Reformation. She was a voluminous writer. One of her best-known works is a continuation of the *Swiss Family Robinson*. Madame de Genlis, who claims to have been the *éditeur* of *Caroline de Lichtfield*, tells the following story of Gibbon falling on his knees and proposing to Madame de Crousaz, afterwards Madame de Montolieu. She refused him. "M. Gibbon prit un air consterné, et cependant il restait à genoux, malgré l'invitation réitérée de se remettre sur sa chaise; il était immobile et gardait le silence. 'Mais, monsieur,' répéta Madame de Crouzas, 'relevez-vous donc.'—'Hélas! madame,' répondit enfin ce malheureux amant, '*Je ne peux pas.*' En effet, la grosseur de sa taille ne lui permettait pas de se relever sans aide. Madame de Crouzas sonna, et dit au domestique qui survint: '*Relevez M. Gibbon*'" (*Souvenirs de Félicie*, p. 279). Madame de Montolieu, it should be added, stated that the anecdote was entirely without foundation (Rossel, *Histoire Littéraire de la Suisse*, vol. ii. p. 275).

The same story is told in verse by George Colman the younger in "The Luminous Historian; or, Learning in Love" (*Eccentricities for Edinburgh*, pp. 67-91).

Caroline, par Madame de * * *, was published at Lausanne in 1786. At Paris, in the same year, a new edition appeared, under the title of *Caroline de Lichtfield, avec des corrections considérables.* It was translated into English by Thomas Holcroft, and published by the Minerva Press. The Lausanne edition has on the title-page the following lines, which may allude to Gibbon:—

"Idole d'un cœur juste et passion du sage,

Amitié que ton nom soutienne cet ouvrage;

Regne dans mes écrits, ainsi que dans mon cœur,

Tu m'appris à connaître, à sentir le bonheur."

(Voltaire, *Mélanges de Poésies.*)

[113] Lord Sheffield had let his house in Downing Street to the Duchess of Gordon. "The Duchess of Gordon will dance my house in Downing Street down" (Lord Sheffield to William Eden, February 27, 1787: *Auckland Correspondence*, vol. i. p. 405).

[114] "I went to London," writes Lord Sheffield to William Eden from Sheffield Place, on August 22, 1787, "for a few days to conduct the Gibbon to this place. The Gibbon is settled here till winter; he will reside with us in Downing Street in winter and spring. The three quartos will appear in the

spring, but as to remaining in this country, he has not the slightest notion of it. I have not yet succeeded in infusing a proper political zeal into him" (*Lord Auckland's Journal and Correspondence*, vol. i. pp. 435, 436).

[115] Charles Alexandre de Calonne (1734-1802) was Director-General of Finances from 1783 to 1787. By his advice the Assembly of Notables was convened on February 22, 1787. He laid before it the financial condition of the kingdom, and proposed, among other measures, a land tax, the taxation of the lands of the clergy, and, generally, the equalization of public burdens. So great was the clamour against him, that in April he resigned and took refuge in England. "I am entertained," writes Lord Sheffield to William Eden, November 2, 1787, "with the reception Calonne meets with in London. Lately he was the most terrible peculator" (*Auckland Correspondence*, vol. i. p. 444). He was succeeded by Cardinal de Brienne, Archbishop of Toulouse, afterwards Archbishop of Sens.

[116] Wilhelm de Severy, the son of Gibbon's friends at Lausanne, had, at his suggestion, paid a visit to England.

[117] John Gibbon, the herald, was Bluemantle Pursuivant at Arms, 1671-1718. He died August 2, 1718.

[118] M. Wilhelm de Severy.

[119] Vols. iv., v., and vi. of the *Decline and Fall* were published in April, 1788.

[120] The preface to the last three volumes of the *Decline and Fall of the Roman Empire* contained the following eulogium on Lord North: "Were I ambitious of any other Patron than the public, I would inscribe this work to a Statesman, who, in a long, a stormy, and at length an unfortunate administration, had many political opponents, almost without a personal enemy; who has retained, in his fall from power, many faithful and disinterested friends; and who, under the pressure of severe infirmity, enjoys the lively vigour of his mind, and the felicity of his incomparable temper. Lord North will permit me to express the feelings of friendship in the language of truth; but even truth and friendship should be silent, if he still dispensed the favours of the Crown."

[121] Lady Sheffield's lapdog.

[122] "We were kept in London about twelve days by Mr. Sheridan's speeches. One day would have sufficed me, who have heard many long speeches: but the ladies rebelled, the Gibbon supported them, and thus we were detained till towards the middle of June" (Lord Sheffield to William Eden, July 29, 1788: *Lord Auckland's Journal and Correspondence*, vol. ii. p. 219).

[123] The trial of Warren Hastings began in Westminster Hall on February 13, 1788. Sheridan's speech on the Begums of Oudh was delivered on June 3, 6, 10, and 13. The trial was adjourned on June 14 till the following session. "Mr. Sheridan," writes Horace Walpole, June 5, 1788, "I hear, did not quite satisfy the passionate expectation that had been raised; but it was impossible he could, when people had worked themselves into an enthusiasm of offering fifty—ay, *fifty* guineas for a ticket to hear him." Macaulay's account of Sheridan's knowledge of stage-effect, and of his sinking back, "as if exhausted, into the arms of Burke," is based on this letter of Gibbon. Sir Gilbert Elliot, however (*Life and Letters*, vol. i. pp. 206-219), gives a different account. "Burke caught him in his arms as he sat down, which was not the least affecting part of the day to my feelings, and could not be the least grateful testimony of his merit received by Sheridan. I have myself enjoyed that embrace on such an occasion, and know its value." In his speech, as reported in the *Morning Chronicle* for June 14, 1788, Sheridan said that "nothing equal in criminality was to be traced either in ancient or modern history, in the correct periods of Tacitus or the luminous page of Gibbon." The story, told by Moore in his *Memoirs* of Sheridan, that the orator really used the word "voluminous," is repudiated by Mr. Fraser Rae (*Sheridan*, vol. ii. p. 69).

[124] C. J. Fox.

[125] In 1788, on a by-election caused by Lord Hood's acceptance of office as one of the Commissioners of the Admiralty, Lord John Townshend won the seat against Hood. In Bond Street there was a battle between Lord Hood's sailors and the Irish chairmen and butcher-boys. Several were killed and wounded.

[126] Charles James Fox married Elizabeth Bridget Cane, otherwise Mrs. Armitstead, at Wyton, Huntingdonshire, on September 28, 1795. She survived her husband. In 1799, on his fiftieth birthday (January 24), Fox addressed to her the following lines:—

"Of years I have now half a century past,

And none of the fifty so blessed as the last.

How it happens my troubles thus daily should cease,

And my happiness thus with my years should increase,

This defiance of nature's more general laws

You alone can explain, who alone are the cause."

[127] Sylvester Douglas, afterwards Lord Glenbervie (1743-1823), who married, in September, 1789, Catherine, eldest daughter of Lord North. He

was educated at Leyden as a doctor, a circumstance to which Sheridan alludes in the lines—

"Glenbervie, Glenbervie,

What's good for the scurvey?

For ne'er be your old trade forgot."

He became a barrister, reported in the King's Bench, and was made a K.C. After his marriage he left the Bar for a political career, and held several minor appointments.

[128] Brienne retired to Italy in August, 1788, and Necker was recalled in the same month. He at once took steps for summoning the States-General which met at Versailles, May 4, 1789.

[129] In the summer of 1788 George III. showed symptoms of mental derangement; but he had signed a warrant for the further prorogation of Parliament from September 25 to November 20. In that interval he grew rapidly worse, and was placed under restraint. The evidence of the king's physicians was laid before the Privy Council and Parliament, and a motion was made in the Lower House for a committee to search for precedents of proceedings in the case of the interruption or suspension of the royal authority. Pitt, on December 16, 1788, moved three resolutions: (1) that the personal exercise of the royal authority was interrupted; (2) that the two Houses have the right to supply this defect of the royal authority; (3) that it was necessary to determine the means by which, during the continuance of the king's incapacity, the royal assent should be given to bills passed by the two Houses. The resolutions were carried in both Houses. The plan of a regency was then submitted to the Prince of Wales, and five resolutions embodying the scheme were proposed and carried in January, 1789. On February 5, 1789, the Regency Bill was introduced in the House of Commons, carried, and sent up to the Lords. It was still under discussion when, on February 19, the Lord Chancellor announced the king's convalescence, and further proceedings were suspended.

[130] James, first Earl of Malmesbury, the distinguished diplomatist, married Harriet Mary, daughter of Sir G. Amyand, Bart.

[131] George Ellis (1753-1815) is best known for his *Specimens of the Early English Poets* (1790) and his *Specimens of Early English Romances in Metre* (1805). He was, wrote Sir Walter Scott, "the first converser I ever saw. His patience and good breeding made me often ashamed of myself, going off at score upon some favourite topic." To him Scott addresses the lines in the fifth canto of *Marmion*, beginning—

"Thou who canst give to lightest lay

An unpedantic moral gay," etc.

He had been employed in diplomatic work by Lord Malmesbury at the Hague in 1784, and accompanied him for the same purpose to the Lille Conference in 1797. He was at this time travelling on the Continent with Lord and Lady Malmesbury. The lines on Pitt in Number ii. of the *Rolliad* are attributed to him—

"Pert without fire, without experience sage,

Young, with more art than Shelburne glean'd from age,

Too proud from pilfer'd greatness to descend,

Too humble not to call Dundas his friend,

In solemn dignity and sullen state,

This new Octavius rises to debate!" etc., etc.

[132] *De la monarchie Prussienne sous Frédéric le Grand* (1788, 4°); and *Histoire Secrète de la Cour de Berlin, ou Correspondance d'un voyageur Français* (1789, 8°). Both books were by Honoré Gabriel Riquetti, Comte de Mirabeau.

[133] His stepmother, Mrs. Gibbon.

[134] His aunt, Miss Hester Gibbon.

[135] It may be mentioned that Lord Sheffield married, in January, 1798, as his third wife, Lady Anne North, daughter of the Earl of Guilford, and sister of Lady Catherine Douglas.

[136] Alluding to Sheffield Place.

[137] Sir S. Porten died June 7, 1789.

[138] The Comte d'Artois (1757-1836), brother of Louis XVI., and afterwards Charles X., was one of the earliest *émigrés*.

[139] Yolande Martine Gabrielle de Polastron, Duchesse de Polignac (1749-1793), was the most intimate friend of Marie Antoinette. To her and her royal mistress public opinion attributed many of the worst evils of the monarchy. When the daughter of the duchess married the Duc de Guiche (afterwards Duc de Grammont), the king gave the bride a dower of 800,000 *livres*. "Mille écus," said Mirabeau, "à la famille d'Assas pour avoir sauvé l'État, un million à la famille de Polignac pour l'avoir perdu." (The Chevalier d'Assas lost his life in an heroic action at Klostercamp, October 15-16, 1760. The Government of Louis XV. allowed him to go unrewarded. Louis XVI., at the instigation of Marie Antoinette, conferred on his family a perpetual pension of 1000 *livres*.) The duchess emigrated with her husband shortly after the taking of the Bastille. She died at Vienna

in December, 1793, her death being, it is said, hastened by the murder of Marie Antoinette. Her second son, afterwards Prince de Polignac, was the favourite minister of Charles X.

[140] Necker was dismissed July 11, 1789, and ordered to quit the kingdom.

[141] Richard Price, D.D. (1723-1791), the celebrated mathematician and economic writer (*Observations on Reversionary Payments, Annuities*, etc., 1769; *Appeal on the Subject of the National Debt*, 1772), the opponent of Dr. Priestley (*A Free Discussion of the Doctrine of Materialism and Philosophical Necessity*, 1778), was also a voluminous political writer, a champion of the cause of American Independence, and an advocate of principles then regarded as revolutionary. His *Observations on the Nature of Civil Liberty* (1776) procured him an invitation from Congress to come and reside in America. In 1789 he published his *Discourse on the Love of our Country*, severely criticized by Burke in his *Reflections on the Revolution in France*. His last work, *Britain's Happiness*, was published in 1791, the year of his death.

[142] The Marquis de Castries (1727-1801), Marshal of France (1783), had served in the Seven Years' War, was Ministre de la Marine 1780-87, and in 1792 held a command in the Prussian army of invasion. He died at Wolfenbuttel in 1801.

[143] Adrien Louis de Bonnières, Comte, afterwards Duc, de Guines (1735-1806), had been ambassador in England, 1770-76. As ambassador at Berlin he had been a favourite with Frederick the Great, with whom he played the flute. He emigrated at the beginning of the Revolution.

[144] J. Joseph Mounier (1758-1806), the author of *Considérations sur le gouvernement qui convient à la France* (1789), was a prominent champion of constitutional liberty in the States-General and the National Assembly. He emigrated at the end of 1789.

[145] Gérard, Marquis de Lally-Tollendal (1751-1830), the son of the unfortunate governor of the French possessions in India, emigrated after the events of October 5-6, 1789. Returning to France in 1792, he was arrested after August 10, and imprisoned in the Abbaye; he escaped and took refuge in England.

[146] Étiennette de Montconseil, daughter of the Marquis de Montconseil, married, in 1766, Charles Alexandre Marc Marcellin d'Alsace-Hénin-Liétard, Prince d'Hénin, brother of the Prince de Chimay and Madame de Cambis, and nephew of the Maréchale de Mirepoix and the Prince de Beauvau. The princess was appointed in 1778 *dame du palais* in the household of Marie Antoinette. Her intimate relations with Lally-Tollendal were well known. Madame D'Arblay, who knew her well, says of her, twenty years later, that "Lally was her admiring and truly devoted friend,

and by many believed to be privately married to her. I am myself of that opinion" (*Diary and Letters*, vii. 89). The Prince d'Hénin was captain of the body-guard of the Comte d'Artois. He played a conspicuous part in the *chronique scandaleuse* of the day. His affection for Sophie Arnould gave rise to the following verses of the Marquis de Louvois:—

"Chez la doyenne des catins

Ta place est des plus minces.

Tu n'es plus le prince d'Hénin,

Mais bien le nain des princes."

[147] Probably Lord Sheffield's portrait, painted by Sir Joshua Reynolds in March, 1788.

[148] Major James Rennell (1742-1832) had already published his Maps of Bengal and of the Mogul Empire. His geographical work on Africa and map appeared in 1790.

[149] His portrait.

[150] At the general election for 1790, Lord Eardley and John Wilmot were returned for Coventry, and the Marquis of Worcester and Lord Sheffield for Bristol. Lord Sheffield sat for Bristol from 1790 to 1802, when he was summoned to the British House of Peers.

[151] Lord Sheffield's pamphlet, *Observations on the Project for Abolishing the Slave Trade*, was published anonymously in 1790. The second edition (1791) bore the author's name.

[152] Sir Joseph Banks (1743-1820) sailed with Captain Cook in the *Endeavour* in 1768. He was President of the Royal Society from 1778 to 1820.

[153] In May, 1790, a message from the king was delivered to the House of Commons by Pitt, informing them that two British ships had been seized in Nootka Sound off the coast of California by two Spanish men-of-war, that satisfaction had been demanded, that Spain claimed exclusive rights in those waters, and was making active preparations for war. Spain, relying on the family compact, asked aid from France, and Louis XVI. communicated the demand to the National Assembly, asking that a fleet should be equipped to send assistance. Preparations were made at Brest to send assistance; but the mutinous conduct of the French sailors apparently alarmed the Spanish Government, which withdrew its claims, restored the property seized, and offered compensation. The Convention between England and Spain was signed October 28, 1790. "The first and great news is the pacification with Spain. The courier arrived on Thursday morning

with a most acquiescent answer to our ultimatum" (Walpole to the Miss Berrys, November 8, 1790).

[154] James Bruce of Kinnaird, F.R.S., published in 1790 his *Travels to discover the Sources of the Nile*, in five quarto volumes.

[155] *Origines Guelficæ, quibus potentissimæ gentis primordia, magnitudo, variaque fortuna exhibentur.* Opus præeunte G. G. Leibnitii stilo J. G. Eccardi literis consignatum, postea a J. D. Grubero novis probationibus instructum. (Ad finem perduxit atque edidit C. L. Scheidius. Accedit duplex index, etc., curante J. H. Jungio.) Hanoveræ, 1750-80, fol.

[156] *Decline and Fall of the Roman Empire* (edition of 1862), vol. vii. p. 119.

[157] "Mr. Gibbon writes that he has seen Necker, and found him still devoured by ambition, and I should think by mortification at the foolish figure he has made" (Walpole to the Miss Berrys, February 28, 1791).

[158] Louis Joseph, Prince de Condé (1736-1818), was the son of the Duc de Bourbon who was minister to Louis XV. He had served in the Seven Years' War, and commanded the *émigrés* on the banks of the Rhine, who were known as the *armée de Condé*. Both his son and grandson died by violence. His son, the Duc de Bourbon (1756-1830), was found hanged in his room. Suspicion, probably without reason, fell on his mistress, Madame de Feuchéres. With him was extinguished the family of Condé, for the grandson here mentioned was the Duc d'Enghien (1772-1804) who was shot at Vincennes in 1804.

[159] Burke's *Reflections on the Revolution in France* were published in October, 1790. "Gibbon admires Burke to the skies, and even the religious parts, he says" (Walpole to the Miss Berrys, February 28, 1791).

[160] The Earl of Guilford (1704-1790) died August 4, 1790, and was succeeded by his eldest son Frederick, better known as Lord North.

[161] Lord Sheffield's *Observations on the Corn Bill now depending in Parliament* was published in 1791. The Corn Regulation Bill was introduced early in that year. The House went into committee on the Bill on February 22, 1791, Lord Sheffield protesting against its principle, but not dividing the House. Lord Sheffield twice beat Pitt (March 11 and April 11) on the question of warehousing foreign corn. He also argued for 52*s.* instead of 48*s.* as the lowest price at which, in the interest of farmers, it was possible to admit foreign corn (April 4).

[162] Lord Sheffield opposed Wilberforce's motion (April 18, 1791) for the Abolition of the Slave Trade on the ground that the West Indian Assemblies alone could deal with the question fairly in all its bearings.

[163] This was probably the debate of May 6, 1791, when Burke declared that, even if loss of friends were the consequence, he would still, with his latest breath, exclaim, "Fly from the French Constitution!" "There is no loss of friends," said Fox. "Yes, there is," retorted Burke. "I know the price of my conduct! I have indeed made a great sacrifice: I have done my duty, though I have lost my friend." Burke's speech was made on the Quebec Bill, and Lord Sheffield moved, and was supported by Fox, that dissertations on the French Constitution were not pertinent to the question before the House. Fox's panegyric on the French Revolution, to which Burke's speech was a reply, was delivered on the treaty between Russia and the Porte.

[164] In the spring of 1791 war with Russia seemed probable. Catharine had in the preceding year concluded peace with Sweden, and the winter campaign of 1790-91 placed the Ottoman Porte at her mercy. Great Britain endeavoured to secure favourable terms for Turkey, and made active preparations to enforce her efforts. The king's message to the House of Commons (March 28, 1791) asked for an increase to the navy in order to bring pressure to bear on Russia. But Great Britain was without allies. Prussia was irresolute, Sweden exhausted, Denmark unwilling to quarrel with Russia, Austria intent on recovering the Austrian Netherlands. Her protest was, however, not without effect. Catharine refused to recognize Great Britain as a mediator or to recede from her demands. But she made peace with Turkey at Galacz in August, 1791, restoring all her conquests except Otchakov and the surrounding territory between the Bug and the Dniester. The strong opposition to war with Russia doubtless influenced Pitt. But it is said that the opinion of the Dutch Admiral, Kingsbergen, that Sebastopol, not Otchakov, was the real danger to Turkey, finally changed his view. The Duke of Leeds resigned the Secretaryship of State on the question, and was succeeded by H. Dundas.

[165] Probably his treatise *De l'administration de M. Necker, par lui-même.*

[166] The words in the original letter are torn out by the seal.

[167] Jacques Marie de Cazalès (1752-1805), whom Madame Roland called, for his ability, the "astonishing" Cazalès, was an eloquent defender of the Monarchy. Suspected of conniving at the king's escape from Paris in June, 1791, he was arrested, and was possibly in prison at the time when Gibbon's letter reached Lord Sheffield. After the capture of Louis XVI. at Varennes, he left France, and, as an *émigré*, took part in the campaign of 1792.

[168] The Abbé Maury (1746-1817), one of the supporters of the Church and the Monarchy in the States-General, left France in September, 1791, after the dissolution of the Constituent Assembly. Made by Napoleon

Archbishop of Paris (1810-14), he was deprived of episcopal authority by the Pope, who had previously given him a cardinal's hat. At the fall of the Empire he was summoned to Rome, and confined for some months in the Castle of St. Angelo.

[169] On Saturday, June 25, news reached London that Louis XVI., his wife and children, had on the previous Tuesday escaped from Paris. They travelled with a passport made out for the Baroness de Korff, obtained at the request of M. Simolin, the Russian Ambassador, who was ignorant of the use to which it was to be put. The king intended to reach Montmédy, and there place himself under the protection of the Marquis de Bouillé, who commanded the army of the Meuse and Moselle. At Ste. Menehould the fugitives were recognized by the Postmaster Drouet, arrested at Varennes, and brought back to Paris.

[170] The ambassador at Paris.

[171] On June 26, 1791, a plan was presented to the National Assembly for the prosecution of the king and of those who assisted him in his escape. After a warm debate, commissioners were nominated to inquire into the events of June 20-21, and three commissioners were separately appointed to take the signed declarations of the king and queen. The proposal to distinguish the case of the king and queen from that of inferior persons was unsuccessfully opposed by Robespierre.

[172] The three Gardes du Corps, brought back on the top of the royal carriage, bound with ropes, were MM. de Valery, de Moustier, and de Malden. The two former published accounts of the flight to Varennes.

[173] François Claude Aymour, Marquis de Bouillé (1739-1800), born at the Château de Cluzel in Auvergne, died at London in 1800. He had distinguished himself both in the Seven Years' War and in the American War of Independence. In 1790 he became governor of the provinces of les Trois Évêchés, Alsace, Lorraine, and Franche Comté, and commander-in-chief of the army of the Meuse, Sarre-et-Moselle, with his head-quarters at Metz. His letter to the National Assembly was written, as he states, to divert the wrath of the Assembly from the king to himself. In it he assumed the whole responsibility for the affair. His letter, says M. Feuillet de Conches (*Louis XVI., Marie Antoinette et Madame Elisabeth*, vol. iv. pp. 469-471), produced a deep impression throughout Europe. Three autograph letters, addressed by Louis XVI., and the Kings of Sweden and Prussia, to the marquis, are there quoted. After the arrest of Louis XVI. at Varennes he fled to Coblentz, summoning officers and men to join him. He served in the army of the Prince of Condé in 1791, and in that of the Duke of York in 1793. He afterwards retired to England, where his *Mémoires sur la Révolution* were published in 1797.

[174] Elizabeth Vassall, a West Indian heiress, married, May 27, 1786, Sir Godfrey Webster, Bart., of Battle Abbey, Sussex. She was divorced from her husband on July 3, 1797, and, three days afterwards, married the third Lord Holland.

[175] François Choderlos de Laclos (1741-1803), novelist, poet, and soldier, was at this time editor of the *Journal des amis de la Constitution*. He helped Brissot to draw up the petition for the deposition of Louis XVI., July 17, 1791.

[176] Voltaire died at Paris in May, 1778. His body, lest burial should be refused, was carried to the Abbey of Scellières. Thence the remains were brought, Sunday, July 10, 1791, to the ruins of the Bastille, and placed the next day in the Pantheon.

[177] On Wednesday, July 13, 1791, the report of the seven committees on the affairs of the king was read before the National Assembly, detailing the circumstances of the king's escape, and stating the manner in which, by the laws of the Constitution, the Assembly should conduct itself towards the king. Practically, the report was in favour of the inviolability of the king's person. In this sense it was adopted on July 15, 1791, and against it was held the meeting of the Champs de Mars on July 17.

[178] J. Pierre Brissot (*de Warville*) (1754-93) was at this time a supporter of the Duc d'Orléans. He afterwards led the *Brissotins* against the *Montagnards*, and was guillotined with the Girondists in October, 1793.

[179] On the Island of St. Pierre, in the Lake of Bienne, J. J. Rousseau lived in 1765.

[180] After the meeting of the Emperor of Austria and the King of Prussia at Pilnitz, Coblentz became the rallying-point of the *émigrés*—"a small extra-national Versailles: a Versailles *in partibus*."

[181] The family of Guiche were descended from *la belle Corisande*, who, left a widow at twenty-six by the death of her husband, the Comte de Guiche, became the mistress of Henry IV., then only King of Navarre. The Duc de Guiche (afterwards Duc de Grammont) married, in 1779, a daughter of the Duchesse de Polignac, and to her interest he owed his place as captain of the Villeroy Company of the Gardes du Corps. He was also colonel of the *Dragons de la Reine*. The duke is a "good-natured young man" (*Lord Auckland's Journal and Correspondence*, vol. i. p. 412).

[182] Charles Theodore, Elector of Bavaria and of the Palatinate.

[183] Monsieur, the title given to the eldest brother of the reigning King of France, was the Comte de Provence, afterwards Louis XVIII. (1755-1824). Madame, his wife, was Maria Josephine Louisa, daughter of Victor

Amadeus III. of Sardinia. They escaped from Paris on the same night as Louis XVI.

[184] The Prince of Nassau-Siegen sailed round the world with Bougainville (1766-69), served in the Spanish army at the siege of Gibraltar, then entered the service of the Empress Catharine, and, as an admiral, commanded the Russian fleet against Turkey and afterwards against Sweden.

[185] Count Nicholas Romanzov, son of the distinguished Russian general.

[186] Marc Hilaire de Conzie (1732-1805), Bishop of St. Omer, became, in 1769, Bishop of Arras. With his brother, who succeeded him as Bishop of St. Omer, he administered the province of Artois. He followed the Comte d'Artois in his flight to Italy, and at London was afterwards his chief political adviser. He was a friend of Madame du Deffand, who writes of him enthusiastically. The Duc de Lévis (*Souvenirs et portraits*) speaks of him less favourably: "Il ne fit que du mal à son parti."

[187] The Baron de Luckner (1722-1794), a Bavarian, entered the French service after the Seven Years' War, was made a marshal in 1791, and guillotined in 1794.

[188] The Duc de Broglie (1718-1804), one of the most distinguished of the French generals during the Seven Years' War, was made a marshal in 1759. Louis XVI. appointed him in 1789 Minister of War; but he was among the earliest of the *émigrés*. He entered the Russian service in 1794.

[189] In August, 1790, the Swiss Regiment of Château-Vieux mutinied at Metz, demanding arrears of pay. They fired upon the National Guard, seized the regimental treasury, and killed Desilles. The outbreak was quelled by Bouillé. Of the survivors of the Regiment of Château-Vieux, twenty-three were hanged, and forty-one sent to the galleys. These galley-slaves were subsequently released; a *fête* in their honour was decreed by the Assembly; their chains hung up as trophies in the Jacobin Club at Brest, and the men carried through Paris in triumph on April 15, 1792.

[190] The meeting of the King Frederick William of Prussia and the Emperor Leopold of Austria at Pilnitz in 1791, excited the greatest interest in Europe. It was supposed at the time that the second partition of Poland was there concerted. But no definite declaration in common seems to have been signed at that time by the two sovereigns, except an engagement to make certain representations to the French Government as to Louis XVI., the Monarchy, and the restoration of property to the *émigrés*, and to invite an European concert for the purpose of enforcing these representations.

[191] In his *Letter to a Member of the National Assembly*, dated January 19, 1791 (*Works* (1855), vol. ii. pp. 546, 547), Burke spoke severely of Mounier and

Lally. He took up the position of a French aristocrat, and treated the English Constitution as unsuited to France. Lally replied to him in his *Lettre au très hon. Edm. Burke, membre du parlement d'Angleterre* (June 20, 1791), and in his *Seconde lettre* in 1792. In these letters he defended the aims of the constitutional reformers in France.

[192] On October 1, 1791, the Duke of York was married at Berlin to the Princess Frederica of Prussia. On November 23 they were remarried, at seven o'clock in the evening, at "the Queen's house" in London.

[193] In India against Tippoo. See note at the end of the letter.

[194] Between 9 and 12 a.m. on December 21, 1791, the Duke of Richmond's house in Privy Gardens, now called Whitehall Gardens, was almost completely destroyed by fire.

[195] Henrietta, daughter of John, second Earl of Buckinghamshire (born 1762), married, in 1780, Armar Corry, Earl of Belmore, from whom she was divorced in 1792. She afterwards, April 16, 1793, married William, Earl of Ancram.

[196] The Countess of Tyrconnel, the second wife of the Earl of Tyrconnel, was the youngest daughter of Lord Delaval, and therefore a niece of the notorious Sir Francis Delaval. Rumour had coupled her name with that of the Duke of York (Wraxall's *Posthumous Memoirs*, vol. iii. p. 192).

[197] John Boydell, in 1786, began to prepare his illustrated edition of Shakespeare, and built a gallery in Pall Mall for the exhibition of the pictures painted for the work. The work was published in eighteen parts, of which the first appeared in 1791, and the whole was completed in 1802.

[198] The third Mysore war began with the invasion of the protected district of Travancore in 1789 by Tippoo, who laid waste the Carnatic almost to the gates of Madras. The war lasted for three years. Lord Cornwallis, in April and May, 1791, advanced from Bangalore to Seringapatam, and drove Tippoo's army before him into the capital (May 15). General Abercromby, advancing towards the same point from the west, reached Periapatnam. But, owing to the difficulty of crossing the swollen Cavery, the two forces could not unite. A few days later, the heavy rains and want of provisions compelled Cornwallis (May 26) to retire, leaving the greater part of his heavy artillery. At the same time Abercromby retreated to Tellicherry on the east coast. Near Bangalore, Cornwallis unexpectedly encountered the Mahratta horse advancing to his assistance. In the autumn and winter months many hill-forts were reduced on the road to Seringapatam, and on February 5, 1792, Cornwallis once more arrived before its walls. Tippoo, on March 18, 1792, signed a peace by which he

surrendered half his territories, paid a war indemnity, and gave up two of his sons as hostages for the due performance of the treaty.

[199] The States-General met May 5, 1789. On June 17, 1789, the Third Estate formed itself into a National Assembly, which was dissolved September 30, 1791. The Legislative Assembly, also constituted a National Assembly, sate from October 1, 1791, to September 21, 1792. In December, 1791, Louis XVI. threatened that, if the Electors of Trèves and Mayence did not prevent the assembly of troops in their territories, he would declare war. On March 1, 1792, the Emperor Leopold II. died, and was succeeded, as King of Hungary and Bohemia, by his son Francis Joseph. Against him France declared war, April 20, 1792.

[200] Gustavus III., King of Sweden (1746-1792), was assassinated by Anckarström in March, 1792. He had offered his services against France as generalissimo of the forces of the Allied Powers.

[201] Russia, after withdrawing her ambassador from Paris, ordered the French minister to leave St. Petersburg in August, 1792.

[202] The negroes in the French or western part of the Island of St. Domingo rose against the whites in August, 1791. In September the General Assembly of the island appealed to the National Assembly at Paris for aid, by a letter detailing the horrors of the insurrection, and later (November 30) by sending a deputy, who was heard in the National Assembly. The insurrection was the first step in the independence of Hayti, which was recognized by the French in 1825. A Comte d'Argout succeeded the Comte d'Ennery as governor of the colony in 1777.

[203] A commission presided over by M. Fischer, supported by two or three thousand militia of the Canton of Berne, was sent to inquire into the attempts to introduce the principles of the French Revolution into the Pays de Vaud. Several persons were arrested, and secretly examined. MM. Rosset and La Motte were confined in the Castle of Chillon, and being afterwards condemned to a long period of imprisonment for correspondence with the French, were transferred to the Castle of Arbourg, whence they escaped.

[204] Lally's tragedy of *Strafford*, in five acts and verse, was printed at London in 1795. His *Essai sur la vie de Thomas Wentworth, Comte de Strafford*, was published at London in the same year. Madame d'Arblay, in February, 1792, speaks of Miss Fanshawe having heard "the famous M. Lally Tolendahl read a French tragedy upon an English subject written by himself! The subject was the death of Strafford." Lally was probably attracted to the subject by the circumstances of his own father's execution.

[205] Marie Antoinette was born November 2, 1755.

[206] Bouillé, warned by a messenger from Choiseul that the king was detained at Varennes, rode from Dun-sur-Meuse, about twenty-two miles from Montmédy, to within sight of the village, but could not cross the Aire; thousands of the National Guard had mustered, and the king was already on his return journey to Paris.

[207] The Comte de Damas, who was stationed on the Ste. Menehould side of Varennes, joined the king at Clermont-en-Argonne, where the road westward from Ste. Menehould strikes to the north to Varennes and Montmédy. The Duc de Choiseul and his hussars, who had been posted on the Montmédy side of Varennes, also joined the king at Varennes. But their troops refused to act against the National Guard. The relays were stationed at the further side of the bridge over the Aire, which had been blocked by Postmaster Drouet.

[208] In Westmoreland County, Jamaica, "particularly in the parish of St. Elizabeth, there have been nightly meetings of the Negroes, where they have not hesitated to call Wilberforce their King, by the name (in their way) of *King Wilberforce*." (Extract from a letter quoted in the *Gentleman's Magazine* for February, 1792, vol. 62, p. 174.)

[209] Amélie de Boufflers, only daughter of the Duc de Boufflers, was born in 1751. J. J. Rousseau speaks enthusiastically of her, when he saw her as a girl at the house of her grandmother, the Maréchale de Luxembourg. She married, in 1766, Armand Louis de Gontaut, Duc de Lauzun, who succeeded his uncle as Duc de Biron. Dissolute and a spendthrift, the duke hated the king and queen because he had not been appointed to succeed his uncle as Colonel of the Guards (*Souvenirs et Portraits*, par le Duc de Lévis, pp. 191-201). He joined the extreme revolutionary party. His wife, who had lived apart from him for many years, in 1791-2 passed some months at Lausanne. She returned to France from England in November, 1792, was arrested and released at the intercession of her husband, whom she had not seen for fifteen years. In England she lived with the Princesse d'Hénin till October, 1793, when she again returned to France. She was arrested and guillotined in 1794. The Duc was executed in December, 1793.

[210] Louis Necker (1730-1801), elder brother of Jacques Necker the statesman, assumed the name of de Germanie on succeeding to an estate of that name which he inherited from his father. He had made a fortune as a banker at Marseilles.

[211] The Baron de Staël-Holstein was Swedish Ambassador at Paris from 1783 to 1792.

[212] M. de Narbonne-Lara was Minister of War from December, 1791, to March, 1792. Born in 1755, he is said to have been the son of Madame

Adelaide and the Comte de Narbonne, her chamberlain. He was one of the few persons who, according to Talleyrand, were completely in the confidence of Mirabeau. "Le Comte Louis de Narbonne est enfin ministre de la guerre, d'hier," wrote Marie Antoinette to Count Fersen. "Quelle gloire pour Mme de Stael, et quel plaisir pour elle d'avoir toute l'armée ... à elle!" (Klinckowström, *Le Comte de Fersen et la Cour de France*, i. 269). After the insurrection of August 10, 1792, Narbonne was saved by Madame de Staël and M. Bollmann, and took refuge in England.

[213] Antoine de Lessart, Minister of the Interior and of Foreign Affairs (1791-2), was accused of corresponding with the *émigrés* and the emperor, tried before the High Court of Orleans for treason, and murdered in the September massacres of 1792.

[214] The Emperor Leopold II. died March 1, 1792, and was succeeded by his son Francis Joseph, who, pending his election as emperor, took the title of King of Bohemia and Hungary.

[215] Taine traces to the action of Marseilles in the autumn of 1791 the first crop of the "arbre révolutionnaire" (*La Révolution*, vol. ii. c. vi.). Marseilles, in fact, became a Republic which undertook the conquest of southern provinces. In February, 1792, four thousand Marseillais marched upon Aix, and disarmed and pillaged the Swiss Regiment of Ernest. In the following March, they made themselves masters of Arles. Their troops, "vraie Sodome errante," pillaged the country, and plundered, outraged, or massacred peaceful inhabitants. Avignon, which with the Comtat Venaissin was united to France in September, 1791, was the next object of their attack. It had been, in October, 1791, the scene of the horrible massacres of La Glacière perpetrated by Jourdan *Coupe-Tête* and the "Brigands of Avignon." Jourdan's cruelties had produced a reaction. But in April, 1792, he was carried in triumph by the Marseillais through the streets of the city, and restored to his usurped position as governor and commander-in-chief. Jourdan, it may be added, was guillotined in May, 1794.

[216] In April, 1792, Wilberforce brought forward his annual motion for the abolition of the slave trade. Pitt made one of his most eloquent speeches in its support. Dundas moved as an amendment a gradual measure of abolition. His amendment, though opposed by Fox, was carried (April 2) by 193 to 125. He subsequently (April 23) moved a series of resolutions to effect a gradual abolition. These were taken up by Pitt, and, with some amendments, carried. In the Lords a proposal to receive evidence on the subject was carried (May 8), and there for the time proceedings stopped. The Bill for the general abolition of the slave trade received the royal assent in March, 1807.

[217] On June 7, 1792, Captain John Kimber was tried at the Old Bailey for the murder of a negro girl on board the *Recovery*. He was acquitted, and two of the witnesses for the prosecution were committed for trial for perjury. On February 19, 1793, Surgeon Dowling, the principal witness against Kimber, was convicted of perjury. The charge against Kimber was urged by Wilberforce in his speech of April 2, 1792.

[218] *The Jockey Club; or, A Sketch of the Manners of the Age* (Parts i., ii., iii.), by Charles Pigott, is an attack on monarchy and aristocracy, a defence of the French Revolution, and an appeal to Fox to use his influence in favour of France in a war which is "the general cause of all human nature. It is the cause of sovereigns and certain individuals enjoying exclusive privileges to the injury of the rest, against the combined immortal cause of the whole world."

[219] On April 30, 1792, Mr. Grey, in consequence of a resolution adopted by the "Friends of the People," gave notice of his intention to move for an inquiry into the representative system. On this notice a debate followed. Grey was supported by Fox. Pitt, on the other hand, declared that if ever there was a time when such a question should not be raised, the present was that time. Burke spoke in the same sense, attacking Paine's *Rights of Man*, and all clubs and societies which recommended the principles of that work. On May 6, 1792, Grey presented a petition from the "Friends of the People," in which the abuses of the electoral system were exposed, and moved that it be referred to a committee. After a debate of two nights, he found only forty-one supporters.

[220] Gibbon probably refers to the "Friends of the People," an association for the reform of the representative system, to which Lord Lauderdale, Grey, Sheridan, Erskine, and twenty-five other members of Parliament belonged.

[221] Berne.

[222] Dumouriez, in April, 1792, despatched three armies to invade Belgium. The column directed against Tournay dispersed, and murdered Dillon, their commander. That which marched against Mons fled as soon as they came in sight of the Austrians near Jemappes.

[223] Name erased.

[224] "Cet audacieux et rusé Harris" is the phrase used by Mirabeau of Lord Malmesbury (*Cour de Berlin, Lettre* xxxvii., vol. ii. p. 13).

[225] Gibbon's library at Lausanne was bought, in 1796, from Lord Sheffield by Beckford for £950. Beckford shut himself up in it "for six weeks, from early in the morning until night, only now and then taking a

ride," and read himself "nearly blind" (Cyrus Redding's "Recollections of the Author of Vathek," *New Monthly Magazine*, vol. lxxi. p. 307). Growing tired of it, he gave it to Dr. Scholl, a physician at Lausanne. Miss Berry, who visited the library in July, 1803 (*Journals and Letters*, vol. ii. p. 260), says, "It is, of all the libraries I ever saw, that of which I should most covet the possession—that which seems exactly everything that any gentleman or gentlewoman fond of letters could wish." "Gibbon's library," says Henry Mathews in 1818 (*Diary of an Invalid*, p. 318), "still remains, but it is buried and lost to the world. It is the property of Mr. Beckford, and lies locked up in an uninhabited house at Lausanne." In 1830 the library was divided into two parts. Half was sold for £500 to an English gentleman; the other half went at the same price to a bookseller at Geneva. The half which was sold to an English purchaser was, in 1876 (*Notes and Queries*, 5th series, vol. v. p. 425), still kept together in the possession of a Swiss gentleman near Geneva.

[226] John Nichols, F.S.A. (1745-1826), the author of numerous works of great literary and historical value, and from 1778 to 1826 printer, proprietor, and, from 1792, sole manager of the *Gentleman's Magazine*, to which he constantly contributed.

[227] The letter is published in the *Gentleman's Magazine* for January, 1794.

[228] The letter referred to in the *Gentleman's Magazine* is signed "N. S." It gives the Gibbon pedigree from 1596 down to the historian. It no doubt at first attracted Gibbon's attention from the circumstance of its immediately preceding a communication entitled "Strictures on Some Passages in Mr. Gibbon's History." The article in the *Gentleman's Magazine* was by Sir Egerton Brydges, whose grandmother was a Gibbon, the heiress of Edward Gibbon of West Cliff, and first cousin to the South Sea director who was the historian's grandfather. Gibbon's letter on the subject to Sir Egerton Brydges is quoted by the latter in his *Autobiography* (vol. i. pp. 225-227).

[229] Probably General Budé, who is mentioned by Madame d'Arblay as holding an appointment about the court at Windsor (*Diary and Letters*, iii. 40).

[230] A large number of troops were assembled at Bagshot Camp on July 23, and were reviewed by the king on July 26, and engaged in sham-fights on July 27, 30, 31.

[231] On May 21, 1792, the king issued a proclamation against tumultuous meetings and seditious writings. Both Houses concurred in an address of thanks to the king for the proclamation (June 1). The question divided the Whig party, the majority of which from this time supported Pitt. Fox for the next few years scarcely mustered fifty followers.

[232] Lord Sheffield expressed an opinion which at the time was common. The sympathy which was avowed by leading Nonconformists with some of the objects of the Revolution was not unnaturally misinterpreted at a period of public excitement. Dr. Price was chairman of the Revolution Society, which corresponded with various societies in France. Their correspondence with French clubs was published in 1792; but it is significant that the letters on the king's escape and subsequent arrest, sent to the Jacobin Club in 1791, the existence of which was revealed by the answer of the Jacobins, were omitted from the publication. Dr. Priestley, subsequently elected to the National Convention, presided at the meeting of the Unitarian Society at the King's Head Tavern, in February, 1791, when, among other toasts, "Thomas Paine and the Rights of Man," and "The National Assembly of France, and may every tyrannical government undergo a similar revolution," were drunk with enthusiasm. Such distinguished Nonconformists as Dr. Kippis, Dr. Rees, and Dr. Towers were also prominent members of these or similar societies. The Society of Constitutional Whigs, who addressed the National Assembly in the autumn of 1792, declaring that, if any attempt were made to enslave the French people, they would die in their defence, also appealed to Dissenters. In *A Few Queries to the Methodists in General* occurs the following:—"*Query*: Does not both reason and revelation teach us, that in order to lay the axe at the root of the tree of wickedness, we must begin with kings and princes, and bishops and priests?"

[233] Lord Chancellor Thurlow, whose influence with the king was immense, and whose intrigues with Fox at the time of the Regency Bill were well known, opposed Pitt's Sinking Fund and the Bill for the encouragement of the growth of timber in the New Forest, and denounced his colleagues as traitors to the interest of their sovereign. He was dismissed from the Lord Chancellorship in June, 1792.

[234] The actual fusion of parties did not take place till July, 1794, when Lord Camden had died and Lord Stafford retired, and Dundas, retaining the Colonies, resigned the Secretaryship at War to Windham. It was delayed by the indecision of the Duke of Portland, of whom Lady Malmesbury said, "The Duke of Portland is our Duke of Brunswick—no party will be led to victory by either" (*Life and Letters of Sir G. Elliot*, vol. ii. p. 72).

[235] Lord Loughborough, Lord Malmesbury, the Duke of Portland, and Dundas attempted to effect a coalition between Pitt and Fox in the summer and autumn of 1792. The negotiations failed. "Fox," says Lord Malmesbury (July 30, 1792), "made Pitt's quitting the Treasury a *sine quâ non*, and was so opinionate and fixed about it, that it was impossible even to reason with him on the subject." "You see how it is," said Burke; "Mr. Fox's coach stops the way."

[236] Lord Guilford, better known as Lord North, died August 5, 1792.

[237] Sir Joshua Reynolds died February 23, 1792.

[238] The Duke of Brunswick, as commander-in-chief of the combined armies of Austria and Prussia, issued his manifesto on July 25, 1792, before crossing the French frontier and directing his march on Paris.

[239] Lally left France for Switzerland after October, 1789, and thence passed to England. Realizing the dangerous position of the king and royal family, he returned to Paris in May, 1792, and with Bertrand-Molleville, Malouet, La Fayette, and others, endeavoured to effect the escape of the king and queen. On August 10, 1792, he was arrested and imprisoned in the Abbaye. On August 22, 1792, ten days before the September massacres, the French Minister of Foreign Affairs informed the National Assembly that Lally Tollendal demanded a passport for England, of which country he had become a naturalized subject. He also produced a letter from Lord Gower claiming Lally as a British subject. According to Madame de Staël he owed his escape to Condorcet.

[240] Madame de Staël, in her *Considérations sur la Révolution Française* (ed. 1818, tom. ii. ch. x.), describes her appearance before Robespierre at the Hôtel de Ville in the Place de Grève, and attributes her escape, on September 2-3, 1792, to Manuel.

[241] Marie Thérèse de Savoie-Carignan married, in 1767, Louis de Bourbon-Penthièvre, Prince de Lamballe. She was murdered at La Force in the September massacres of 1792, and her head, raised on a pike, was paraded before the windows of the Temple where the queen was confined. The Swiss Guard, nearly eight hundred in number, were massacred in the attack upon the Tuileries on August 10, 1792. Of the few who escaped, fifty-four were murdered in the Abbaye at the September massacres. Their death is commemorated by Thorwaldsen's lion at Lucerne.

[242] See letter of May 30, 1792.

[243] On September 21, 1792, without any declaration of war, Montesquieu entered Savoy, seized Montmélian and Chambéry, and in a few days overran the whole duchy. In Piedmont the French troops under General Anselme, supported by Admiral Truguet and the Toulon fleet, captured Nice and Villa Franca. The Duchy of Savoy was incorporated with France in November, 1792, as the Department of Mont-Blanc, and the Comté of Nice as the Department of the Maritime Alps.

[244] Etienne Clavière (1735-1793), formerly a banker in Geneva, had been banished in 1784 for his writings. As a member of the Executive Council, he urged upon his colleagues the attack upon Geneva, and orders to that

effect were given to Montesquieu by Servan, the Minister of War. Geneva appealed for aid to Zurich and Berne under a treaty of 1584, and prepared for defence. A treaty was signed, October 22, 1792, between Montesquieu and the Republic of Geneva, slightly modified by a fresh treaty signed on November 2. By its terms the French troops were to withdraw, and the Swiss troops, sent by the cantons of Zurich and Berne, were to evacuate Geneva by December 1, 1792. Clavière committed suicide in 1793.

[245] At Geneva.

[246] At Geneva the Government was vested in the two hundred and fifty citizens who composed the *Petit Conseil* and the *Conseil des Deux-Cents*. Against this hereditary oligarchy Rousseau gave the signal of revolt by his *Lettres de la Montagne* (1764). Two parties were formed: one, the *Représentants*, demanding a revision of the constitution; the other, *Négatifs*, opposing it. In 1781 the popular party gained the upper hand. The aristocratic party, appealing to the treaty of 1738, which only allowed constitutional changes to be made with the sanction of France and Sardinia, demanded the help of those two powers. A combined Swiss, French, and Sardinian force was sent, and in July, 1782, the popular party, who had promised to emulate the citizens of Saguntum, surrendered the city without a struggle, and the aristocratic constitution was restored. Brissot de Warville, as *le Philadelphien à Genève*, and Mallet du Pan were both eye-witnesses of the events of the revolution.

[247] Albert, the second son of Madame de Staël, was born at this time.

[248] Adam de Custine (1740-1794), a veteran of the Seven Years' and American Wars, commanded part of the French army of the Rhine. He made himself master of Spire, Worms, Mayence, and Frankfort; but was afterwards driven out of the two latter places by the Prussians. He was executed at Paris January 3, 1794.

[249] The Prussian army, entangled in the wood of Argonne between the Meuse and the Marne, were outgeneralled by Dumouriez and Kellerman. The Duke of Brunswick, after the battle of Valmy (September 20), opened negotiations with Dumouriez (September 22-28) at Ste. Menehould, and then (October 1) retreated across the French frontier. The Austrians failed to take Lille, and, at the approach of Dumouriez, retired into the Low Countries (October 8). Dumouriez, following them, won the battle of Jemappes (November 6), and overran Belgium. At the same time the French troops were masters of Savoy and Nice, and of the country between the Rhine and the Maine. Fox rejoiced at the flight of the invaders. "No public event, not excepting Saratoga and York Town, ever happened that gave me so much delight" (C. J. F. to Lord Holland, October 12, 1792).

[250] The French Revolution had stirred the political spirit of the Irish nation as, ten years before, it had been aroused by the American War. It appealed most strongly to the people by the abolition of tithes and all religious disqualifications. The Presbyterians of the North were Republican in their sympathies, and ready to make common cause with the Roman Catholics for the repeal of all penal laws and the extension of the franchise. The United Irishmen were the growth of this approximation of parties. Among the Roman Catholics also there was a rapid spread of the democratic spirit. The English Government was ready to grant a liberal measure of Catholic relief and to extend the suffrage to the Roman Catholics. At first the Irish Government strongly opposed any change which threatened the maintenance of Protestant ascendency. But the danger of union between the Protestant Republicans and the Catholic democrats became apparent, when the Catholic Convention met at Dublin in December, 1792, and a Relief Bill, repealing many oppressive enactments and conceding the franchise, was carried, almost without opposition, in the beginning of 1793. The Roman Catholics, it may be added, were excluded from the Irish Parliament in the reign of William III. (3 W. & M. c. 2) and deprived of the franchise in that of George II. (1 Geo. II. c. 9). Lord Sheffield, as a later letter shows, agreed with the Lord Lieutenant, Lord Westmorland, in advocating resistance to the Catholics "*in limine* and *in toto*," and in thinking that the suspicion, that the "British Government means to take up the Catholics, and to play what is called a Catholic game," would disastrously weaken the hold of the Government upon the country. Burke (*Correspondence*, vol. iv. p. 32) seems to suggest that Lord Sheffield was prejudiced by the possession of Irish property in the county of Louth.

[251] Miss C. Moss, a frequent visitor at Sheffield Place.

[252] Mdlle. Pauline de Pully.

[253] The massacres of September, 1792.

[254] The Duc de Liancourt (1747-1827) took the title of Rochefoucault-Liancourt on succeeding to his cousin, the Duc de la Rochefoucault who was murdered at Gisors in September, 1792. He had been a distinguished member of the Feuillants, or constitutional reformers. He escaped to England and thence to the United States. On his return to France he occupied himself with philanthropic works and the management of his estates. Both he and his cousin were generous patrons of Arthur Young during his travels in France (1787-89), and promoted that revival of agriculture at the close of the eighteenth century which corresponded with the similar movement in England.

[255] The Princesse d'Hénin was rescued from Paris by Madame de Staël (Forneron, *Hist. des Emigrés*, vol. i. p. 244). It was at her house that Malouet,

La Fayette, and the Constitutionnels had planned an escape for Louis XVI. in May, 1792.

[256] The Duchess of Fitzjames was the daughter of the Comte de Thiars, and *dame de palais* in the household of Marie Antoinette. Charles, her eldest son, died with the army of the princes. Edward, her second son, who succeeded to the title, distinguished himself by his oratorical powers in the Chamber of Peers at the Restoration, and in that of the Deputies under Louis Philippe.

[257] On September 17, 1792, seventy-six French priests, and among them the Bishop of Avranches, landed at Hastings.

[258] The report of the French Diplomatic Committee upon the two treaties of October 22 and November 2 was delivered by Brissot on November 21. It neither ratified nor rejected the treaties, reserving the question whether a free people could bind itself by treaties. At the same time the Convention ordered the French troops to respect the neutrality of Geneva, if the Swiss troops evacuated the city by December 1, 1792.

[259] The Duke of Brunswick was charged with being bribed to retire. No ground for the accusation has ever been alleged, except that, on the duke's return, he paid off heavy debts. The charge was made by Talleyrand in 1802. It is repeated by both Lacretelle and Thiers in their histories. It is omitted by Michaud in his article on Brunswick, which appeared in the *Biographie Universelle* in 1812; but it is given in the articles which the same writer contributed on Dumouriez and Drouet to the supplementary volume (1837). It is also made by the Comte d'Allonville in his *Mémoires Secrets* (vol. iii. pp. 94-97).

[260] The Comtesse Charles de Noailles, *née* Nathalie de Laborde, the daughter of the banker of that name, married in 1790 Charles de Noailles, son of the Prince de Poix.

[261] Louis Philippe Antoine de Noailles, Prince de Poix, eldest son of the Maréchal and Maréchale de Mouchy, who were guillotined on July 22, 1794. He commanded the Noailles Company of the Royal Body-guard. He was arrested in August, 1792, but escaped on his way to the Abbaye. He married Anne de Beauvau, who died in 1834.

[262] The Comte de la Tour-du-Pin Gouvernet had been aide-de-camp to Bouillé at the repression of the mutiny at Nancy. He was entrusted with the task of opening the plan, formed for the rescue of the king and royal family in the early summer of 1792, to Marie Antoinette. Her distrust of La Fayette caused its failure. "Plutôt périr qu'être sauvé par La Fayette et les Constitutionnels!" was her well-known exclamation. Gouvernet subsequently went to America, and died at Lausanne in 1837.

[263] The seat of the Duke of Portland.

[264] Bigot de Sainte Croix, Minister for Foreign Affairs, was one of the agents in the schemes for the rescue of Louis XVI.

[265] Terrier de Monciel, a member of the Constitutional party, Minister of the Interior from June 18 to July 9, 1792, endeavoured to organize a military force for the protection of the king which should be disassociated from the foreign allies of the *émigrés*. It was the discovery of this and other schemes for the king's rescue, in which Bertrand, Malouet, Mallet du Pan, and Clermont-Tonnerre were the leaders, that led to the disbanding of the Constitutional Guard, and the insurrections of June 20 and August 10, 1792. Monciel died in 1831.

[266] The Marquis de Bertrand-Molleville (1744-1818) was *Ministre de la Marine* in 1791. He took refuge in England in 1792, and there wrote his *Mémoires* and his *Histoire de la Révolution de France*.

[267] Victor Malouet (1740-1814), distinguished by his explorations and his services in the French colonies (see his *Collection des Mémoires sur l'administration des colonies*, Paris, 1802, 5 vols.), was a bold and skilful supporter of Louis XVI. in the Constituent Assembly. He returned to France in 1801, and was employed by Napoleon in the administration of the navy. He was appointed Ministre de la Marine by Louis XVIII. in 1814.

[268] Probably the Baron de Gilliers, whose estates were near Romans in Dauphiné, and of whom Rivarol tells a story to illustrate the suspicion with which every aristocrat was regarded. Suspected of a royalist plot, the baron was charged with manufacturing cannon when he was only making drain-pipes; his house was occupied by hundreds of armed men, and his family narrowly escaped with their lives. He was gentleman-in-waiting to Madame Elizabeth.

[269] Burke's plan for the settlement of the refugees in Maryland is discussed by him in a letter to his son, dated November 2, 1792 (*Correspondence*, vol. iv. pp. 25, 26).

[270] Miss Holroyd.

[271] Sheffield Place.

[272] Joseph Servan (1741-1808), author of the *Soldat Citoyen* (1780), Minister of War in the Girondin administration (March to June, 1792). Dismissed by Louis XVI., he was restored to his office after August 10, 1792. He resigned his post in October, 1792, and afterwards commanded the troops which opposed the march of the Spaniards upon Bayonne in April, 1793.

[273] Prince Charles of Hesse-Rheinfels-Rothenburg (1752-1821) entered the French service as a young man. He was made a lieutenant-general in 1792, and took up the command at Besançon, where he was received with enthusiasm as the *citoyen-général-philosophe*. He accompanied his words with gestures which were almost convulsive in their violence, and closed his sentences by grinding his teeth, "un tigre doué de la parole." As a journalist (1795-99) he came into collision with the Government, and was imprisoned for several years in the island of Rhé. He died at Frankfort in 1821.

[274] Henriette d'Aguessau, who married the Duc d'Ayen, was, like Madame de Biron, guillotined.

[275] Marie, Princess of Hesse-Rheinfelz, married the Duc de Bouillon, the head, and last direct representative, of the family of La Tour d'Auvergne. She was by her marriage connected with the Princesse de Poix, and her cousin, the Princesse d'Hénin. The three ladies were known as *les trois princesses combinées*. Madame de Bouillon and her husband both died in exile.

[276] Necker's *Réflexions offertes à la nation française* appeared in November, 1792.

[277] Louis Pierre Manuel (1751-1793) was one of the leaders in the insurrections of June 20 and August 10, 1792. He was at this time *procureur* of the Commune of Paris. At the king's trial he defended Louis XVI., and, accused of being a counter-revolutionist, was guillotined in November, 1793.

[278] Jean Marie François Dulau.

[279] They were brothers, and belonged to the family of Rochefoucauld-Bayers.

[280] Lord Loughborough accepted the Great Seal as Lord Chancellor in January, 1793.

[281] *I.e.* the treaty of November 2.

[282] The report of the Diplomatic Committee (November 21) on the treaties which Montesquieu had signed with Geneva, speaks of him as a man who "had put his name to many fraudulent and usurious proceedings, and who appeared to regard the Revolution as a speculation and a new kind of stock-jobbing."

[283] François Christophe de Kellerman (1735-1820) was the hero of the battle of Valmy. In 1804 he was created Duc de Valmy by Napoleon.

[284] Gibbon's surmise proved correct. On December 3, and again on December 27, the *Représentants* rose in arms, threatened to call in the aid of the French army if they were opposed, and replaced the Petit Conseil and

the Conseil des Deux-Cents by two committees, organized on a popular basis, who exercised all the powers which were previously in the hands of the aristocracy.

[285]

Quà tamen usque potest, vires sibi demere tentat.

Nec, quo centimanum dejecerat igne Typhœa,

Nunc armatur eo: nimiùm feritatis in illo.

Est aliud levius fulmen; cui dextra Cyclopum

Sævitiæ, flammæque minus, minus addidit iræ:

Tela secunda vocant Superi.

[286] On December 1 an Order in Council was passed, calling out part of the militia. Another portion was called out on the western and southern coasts by a second Order of December 5. Parliament met on December 13 to ratify the step taken by the Government, within the fourteen days required by statute.

[287] An association was formed, in November, 1792, at the St. Alban's Tavern, of members of Parliament and other persons of influence, including Lord Sheffield. A declaration was issued, stating that, in the opinion of those who signed it, it was in the present moment incumbent upon us "to give to the executive government a vigorous and effectual support, in counteracting the numerous efforts of sedition, in detecting and bringing to legal punishment the persons concerned therein, and in suppressing in their beginnings all tumults or riots, on whatever pretence they may be excited." Another association at the Crown and Anchor, presided over by Mr. Reeves, a barrister, and containing in the list of signatures the name of J. T. Batt, Lord Sheffield's friend, issued a similar declaration. Other associations were formed with the same object by the merchants and bankers of London, by the merchants, etc., at Lloyd's, by the general body of Protestant Dissenters in London and Westminster, by many of the Livery Companies, and by the Corporation of the City of London. The declaration to be signed in the county of Sussex is quoted in full at the beginning of the *Gentleman's Magazine* for July to December, 1792. The following note is added: "Association, on the best principle, is taking place throughout England, and nowhere in a better form than in Sussex, under the auspices of Lord Sheffield."

[288] Fox, on December 13, declared the calling out of the militia to be a "ministerial manœuvre," and moved as an amendment to the address, "That his Majesty's faithful Commons, assembled in a manner new and alarming

to the country, think it their first duty, and will make it their first business, to inform themselves of the causes of this measure, being equally zealous to enforce a due obedience to the laws on the one hand, and a faithful execution of them on the other."

[289] Lord Malmesbury thus analyzes the minority: "21 were reformers, 4 Lord Lansdowne's members, and the rest people personally attached to Fox, and who, from this feeling, and *against their sentiments*, voted with him. Such were Crewe, Lord Edward Bentinck, Lord George Cavendish, Lord Milton, Lionel Damer, and others" (*Diaries and Correspondence*, vol. ii. p. 476).

[290] On Saturday, December 15, Fox moved that an address be presented to his Majesty, "that a minister may be sent to Paris to treat with those persons who exercise provisionally the functions of executive government in France." The motion was negatived without a division.

[291] "Some of the very worst of the French murderers on the 10th of August and beginning of September have been here, particularly one *Rotundo*, who was a principal performer in the massacres of the prisoners on the 2nd and 3rd of September. He was one of the executioners of Madame de Lamballe, of which I understand he boasted when in England, for I hear he is gone back" (*Life and Letters of Sir Gilbert Elliot*, vol. ii. p. 91). It is difficult to trace the foundation for the statement. One Petit Mamin was accused of having boasted that he had killed the princess; but he denied having made the boast, and proved, to the satisfaction of the jury, that he was not in Paris at the time (Mortimer-Ternaux, *Histoire de la Terreur*, 1792-94, vol. iii. pp. 632, 633). In Lescure's *Vie de la Princesse de Lamballe* (pp. 426-428) the names of the murderers are given as Charlat and Grison. M. Feuillet de Conches (*Louis XVI., Marie Antoinette, et Madame Elisabeth*, vol. vi. p. 316) says that Gonchon was the name of the man who first struck down the princess.

[292] François, Marquis de Barthélemy (1750-1830), concluded three treaties at Basle in 1795—with Prussia, the United Provinces, and Spain. He was a member of the Directory; but, suspected for his moderation, was sent, first to Cayenne, then to Sinnamari. Thence he escaped to England. He assisted in drawing up the charter at the restoration of Louis XVIII.

[293] Boydell was Lord Mayor in 1790-91.

[294] On December 21, 1792, a copy was read to the House of Commons of the instructions sent to Earl Gower, the British Ambassador at Paris, signifying his recall in August on the ground that, as the executive power was withdrawn from Louis XVI., the credentials under which the ambassador acted were no longer available. In the instructions, the king, while "adhering to the principles of neutrality in respect to the settlement

of the internal government of France," considered it "no deviation from those principles to manifest, by all the means in his power, his solicitude for the personal situation of their most Christian majesties, and their royal family; and he earnestly and anxiously hopes that they will, at least, be secure from any acts of violence, which cannot fail to produce one universal sentiment of indignation through every country of Europe." It was unanimously resolved that the paper should remain on the table of the House. The king was sentenced to death by the Convention, January 17, 1793. His appeal to the nation was rejected, January 19-20, and the final sentence announced to him on Sunday, January 20. He was executed the following day.

[295] Chauvelin had been accredited by Louis XVI. in May, 1792. But he now (December 27) addressed a note to Lord Grenville, as agent of the Executive Council of the French Republic, asking whether Great Britain was to be considered as a belligerent or as a neutral power. Lord Grenville declined (December 31) to acknowledge his official position, but explained the policy of the British Government. On January 18, 1793, Lord Grenville replied to M. Chauvelin that the British Government would continue its preparations to protect the country and its allies, and to oppose a barrier to French views of aggrandizement and the propagation of destructive principles. On January 24, M. Chauvelin was ordered to leave the kingdom within eight days. He left on January 25. The Convention declared war against England and Holland, February 8, 1793, and against Spain, March 7.

[296] Lord Sheffield alludes to the debate on the second reading of the Alien Bill (December 28, 1792). Fox opposed the Bill; Sir Gilbert Elliot spoke for it, and stated that the Duke of Portland was in its favour, and that the majority of the Opposition, of which the duke was the leader, intended to support the Government. After the debate, Elliot, Wyndham, and Fox met at the Duke of Portland's, when the duke stated that Sir Gilbert had correctly expressed his views. Fox, however, recovered his ascendency over the Duke of Portland, who authorized the Marquis of Titchfield (December 31), his eldest son, M.P. for Buckinghamshire, to confine the support of the Opposition to this particular measure. The marquis ended his speech with an attack upon the individual ministers, a passage added, it is said, by Fox, which neutralized the effect of his support (*Diaries and Correspondence of Lord Malmesbury*, vol. ii. pp. 494, 495).

[297] The Parliamentary recess lasted from January 4 to January 28, 1793.

[298] Louis XVI. was executed in the Place de la Révolution at 10.22 in the morning of Monday, January 21, 1793.

[299] The message was delivered on January 28, laying before the House the correspondence between Lord Grenville and M. Chauvelin, and asking for an augmentation of the forces by sea and land.

[300] *The Heads of Illustrious Persons of Great Britain, with their Lives and Characters*, 2 vols. fol., 1743-52, by the Rev. Thomas Birch, D.D. The engravings are by Houbraken, Gravelot, and Vertue.

[301] Hugues Bernard Maret, afterwards Duc de Bassano (1763-1839), was editor of the *Bulletin* in which were reported the debates of the National Assembly. He had served in Belgium in concert with Dumouriez. He had already been sent to England by the Convention. He now returned with fuller powers. He remained in London till February after the dismissal of Chauvelin, and only left when the war was declared. He was a favourite of Napoleon, and Minister of the Interior under Louis Philippe.

[302] Jean Nicolas Pache (1740-1823) replaced Servan as Minister of War in October, 1792. In February, 1793, he became Mayor of Paris, and was responsible for many of the worst horrors of that year.

[303] The debate on the king's message for the augmentation of the forces took place on February 1. Fox spoke against the increase. It may be added that Mr. Whitbread, speaking on the same side, and alluding to the Duke of Brunswick's manifestos, said that they breathed the spirit of Attila, "who, in the emphatical words recorded by Mr. Gibbon, had said, 'Where Attila's horse sets his foot, the grass never grows.'"

[304] Probably Mr. George Nicol. See p. 359.

[305] This letter is printed in Lord Campbell's life of Lord Chancellor Loughborough as from the Rosslyn Manuscripts, and Lord Campbell remarks in a note that in 1796, when about to publish the first edition of Gibbon's miscellaneous works, Lord Sheffield applied to Lord Loughborough for permission to include this letter, but was refused. He made a second application, offering to erase his name and the name of his office (which in effect was done), but "Lord Loughborough was sensitive upon the subject of his coalition with Mr. Pitt, and he remained inflexible." However, the letter *does* appear in the first edition, a fact which must have escaped Lord Campbell's attention.

[306] "All ranks of people have put on mourning for the unfortunate king." Lady Malmesbury to Lady Elliot, January 28, 1793 (*Life and Letters of Sir G. Elliot*, vol. ii. p. 110).

[307] Throughout 1793, and especially in September, Lord Chatham as First Lord of the Admiralty was in dispute with the Master of the Ordnance, the Duke of Richmond. One alleged that the fleet was ready but

that the guns were not; the other stated that the ships were not ready to take the guns. Lord Sandwich was Lord of the Admiralty during the American War.

[308] The *Songe d'un Anglois* and the *Plaidoyer pour Louis XVI.*, both by Lally Tollendal, are printed in the second volume (pp. 251-286 and 357-388) of the "Collection des meilleurs ouvrages qui ont été publiés pour la Défense de Louis XVI.," par A. J. du Gour: Paris, 1796. From an autograph letter in George III.'s copy of *Strafford*, it appears that Lally, through Lady Sheffield, presented a copy of the *Plaidoyer* to the king.

[309] Probably Horace Walpole's *Essay on Modern Gardening*, which was written in 1770, and printed at the Strawberry Hill Press in 1785 (4to), with a French translation on opposite pages by the Duc de Nivernois.

[310] "Madame de Staël, daughter of M. Necker, is now at the head of the colony of French noblesse, established near Mickleham. She is one of the first women I have ever met with for abilities and extraordinary intellect." Miss Burney to Dr. Burney, February 4, 1793 (*Diary and Letters*, vol. v. p. 394).

[311] Lord Porchester, son of Gen. the Hon. W. Herbert, fifth son of the Earl of Pembroke, was created Earl of Carnarvon in July, 1793.

[312] The Duke of York.

[313] Lady Sheffield died April 3, 1793. Her death is said to have been occasioned by her attendance upon the sick *émigrés* at Guy's hospital (*Gentleman's Magazine* for 1793, part i. p. 379).

[314] Wilhelm de Severy.

[315] A select committee appointed (April 25, 1793) to consider the state of commercial credit reported (April 29), recommending, *inter alia*, that five millions should be issued in Exchequer Bills for the relief of credit. The report was considered on April 30; a resolution, and subsequently a Bill, were carried for the issue of the Bills. A commission was appointed (May 3), with Lord Sheffield at the head of it, to effect the necessary arrangements.

[316] Mayence was invested by the Prussian and Austrian forces early in April, 1793. It was surrendered July 22, 1793.

[317] Thomas, Lord Elgin, was appointed in August, 1792, Envoy Extraordinary at Brussels. Subsequently appointed Ambassador at Constantinople in 1799, he collected the Elgin marbles.

[318] Madame de Sylva.

[319] John Augustus, Lord Hervey, a captain in the Royal Navy, second son of the Bishop of Derry, and brother to Lady Elisabeth Foster, was ambassador at Florence from 1787 to 1794. In 1793 he insisted in a violent note on the dismissal of the French Minister, La Flotte, from the court of the Grand Duke of Tuscany. "It was generally supposed," writes Lord Holland, (*Memoirs of the Whig Party*, p. 56), "in the *maldicente* city of Florence, that resentment at the French Minister for having supplanted him in the good graces of a lady quickened his hatred of the French Republick, or at least gave it the turn of insisting on the dismissal of his rival." Lord Hervey, in consequence of the affair, was recalled from Florence in 1794.

[320] New toll-gates had been placed on the bridge at Bristol; but they were burnt by a mob which, from September 30 to October 3, attacked the toll-houses, and broke the windows of the Guildhall and Council-house. The Herefordshire Militia were twice called out and ordered to fire on the mob; eleven rioters were killed and forty-five wounded. The attempt to raise a toll was abandoned.

[321] 76, St. James's Street.

[322] Gibbon had, in 1761, consulted Mr. (afterwards Sir Cæsar) Hawkins, the surgeon, who wished to see him again. But he never returned, or consulted any other medical man till November, 1793.

[323] Sir Walter Farquhar, Bart. (cr. 1796), was originally an army doctor. He died in 1819.

[324] Henry Cline (1750-1827) was a pupil of Hunter, and at this time surgeon of St. Thomas's Hospital.

[325] For the soldiers serving in Flanders under the Duke of York.

[326] At Lord Auckland's, at Eden Farm.

[327] Sir Charles Grey, afterwards first Earl Grey (1729-1807), sailed November 23, in joint command with Jervis, afterwards Earl St. Vincent, on an expedition against the French West Indian Islands.

[328] Francis Rawdon Hastings, second Earl of Moira and first Marquis of Hastings (1754-1826), had served with distinction in the American War. The expedition here alluded to was that which sailed in December, 1793, to aid the French royalists in Brittany. The expedition returned without effecting anything.

[329] Fort Louis, part of the position held by the French army in Alsace, was besieged by the Austrians, November 10, 1792. It surrendered on November 14, and the four thousand French troops who formed its garrison became prisoners of war.

[330] Gibbon was a diligent student of Pascal, and his irony was cultivated by constant reading of his works. One curious parallel may be noted in their writings. "Abu Rafe," writes Gibbon (*Decline and Fall*, ed. 1862, vol. vii. p. 252), "was an eye-witness, but who will be witness for Abu Rafe?" Similarly Pascal, in the *Lettres Provinciales: neuvième lettre*, p. 154 (ed. Firmin Didot, 1853), writes, "'Mais, mon père, qui nous a assuré que la Vierge en répond?' 'Le père Barry,' dit-il, 'en répond pour elle.' 'Mais, mon père, qui répondra pour le père Barry?'"

[331] Dr. John Moore (1730-1805), Archbishop of Canterbury (1783-1805), was, by his marriage to Catherine Eden, daughter of Sir Robert Eden, connected with Lord Auckland.

[332] Lord Loughborough.

[333] Richard, Earl Howe (1726-1799), had sailed (November 9) in search of the French; but he was compelled to return to Spithead (November 29) without bringing them to action. "We continue in the same eternal state of anxious expectation of news from Lord Howe. Nothing is yet heard" (Lord Auckland to Lord H. Spencer, December 3, 1793: *Correspondence*, iii. 151). Gibbon did not live to hear of the victory of June 1, 1794.

[334] Gibbon met Pitt at Eden Farm. "He was much pleased," writes Lord Sheffield, December 17, 1793, of this stay at Beckenham, "with his visit there, and his occurrence with the minister, in a family way, was a great satisfaction to him" (*Auckland Correspondence*, iii. 158).

[335] "The Gibbon is better, but I am by no means without inquietude on his account. It is thought necessary that he should go to London on Tuesday; probably I shall follow him shortly for two days, for I shall be impatient to see how he goes on" (Lord Sheffield to Lord Auckland, January 5, 1794: *Auckland Correspondence*, iii. 168).